Virginia Woolf

and the Languages of Patriarchy

Virginia Woolf

and the Languages of Patriarchy

Jane Marcus

INDIANA UNIVERSITY PRESS
Bloomington & Indianapolis

Manufactured in the United States of America

Library of Congress Cataloging-in-Publication Data

Marcus, Jane.
  Virginia Woolf and the languages of patriarchy.

  Includes index.
    1. Woolf, Virginia, 1882-1941—Criticism and
interpretation.   2. Patriarchy in literature.
3. Women in literature. I. Title.
PR6045.072Z8147 1987   823'.912   86-45470
ISBN 0-253-36259-8
ISBN 0-253-20410-0 (pbk.)

1 2   3   4   5 91 90 89 88 87

for Michael

... we, I mean all human beings—are connected with this; that the whole world is a
work of art; that we are parts of the work of
art. *Hamlet* or a Beethoven quartet is the
truth about this vast mass that we call the
world. But there is no Shakespeare; there is
no Beethoven; certainly and emphatically
there is no God; we are the words; we are
the music; we are the thing itself. ...

—Virginia Woolf, *Moments of Being*

Why, why did my father teach me to read?

—Virginia Woolf, "A Society"

... she had a message to deliver, a call to
sound. She was a champion of human liberty, of the right of individual men and
women to serve truth in freedom.

—Editorial on the death of Virginia Woolf,
Time and Tide, April 12, 1941

Can one admit the rhapsodies?

—Virginia Woolf,
Notebook for *Mrs. Dalloway*

The words we seek hang close to the tree.
We come at dawn and find them sweet
beneath the leaf.

—Virginia Woolf, *Jacob's Room*

CONTENTS

PREFACE

For the past decade I, like most American feminist critics, have been thinking and writing about Virginia Woolf. Seeing her as our role model in *A Room of One's Own, Three Guineas*, and the volumes of critical essays, we first sought to revive her reputation as a political thinker, then to understand the fiction in feminist terms and to re-think the official biography. These tasks were accomplished, here in the United States, if not in England, I like to think, largely because of the collective nature of our scholarly research and writing. Derision labelled us the "lupine critics"; a sense of common struggle led us to adopt the label as our own.

This is an interesting chapter in American literary history and in the development of feminist criticism and theory over the same decade, for Virginia Woolf was often at the center of the most spirited critical debates. Our quarrels with Quentin Bell and the Literary Estate may be seen as a test case for feminist scholarship, a kind of custody battle over her reputation. For an overview of the history of feminist Woolf criticism in the United States, I refer the reader to my "Storming the Toolshed," in *SIGNS* 7, no. 3 (1982): 622–40. It is also reprinted in *Feminist Theory: A Critique of Ideology*, ed. N. Keohane, M. S. Rosaldo, and B. Gelpi, University of Chicago Press, 1982, as well as "Tintinnabulations" in *Marxist Perspectives* 2, no. 1 (Spring 1979): 144–67. Further debate is continued in "Quentin's Bogey," *Critical Inquiry* 2, no. 3 (Spring 1985): 486–97 as well as in the last decade's *Virginia Woolf Miscellany*.

The arrangement of the essays in this book, for essays they are, rather than chapters in a clear coherent view of Woolf and her works, has caused me to look at my own growth as a reader over this decade. Consequently the order of the essays represents the order of my writing, not the order in which Virginia Woolf wrote her novels. The oddities of this ordering remind me of the oddities of my origins as a critic and so this preface is in a sense a conversation with myself on the occasion of the somewhat painful separation of some of these essays from the sister essays that surrounded them when they were first published. I was trained in both intellectual history and formalist new criticism, twice, as women scholars of my generation often were, once in seventeenth-century religious writing at Brandeis, again in modern British literature at Northwestern, and my interests were in the history of English feminism, particularly women's suffrage and research in Victorian and Edwardian documents regarding women's rights and women writers' interpretations of feminism in their writing. Admiring the social history of the E. P. Thompson school, I wanted to combine a close reading of women's texts with a pragmatic historical reading of their personal lives and political movements. I thought of this activity as Marxist until Marxist criticism in England and on the continent grew more sexist and formal-

ist. This puzzled me. Why should Marxists do idealist formalist readings of
over-canonized texts when to do (or re-do) biography in political and historical
settings seems much more material and pragmatist a practice? Marxist critics
seemed to privilege only one historical moment in the production of a text, its
publication. But in the case of Virginia Woolf, very often the drafts and unpublished versions seemed "truer" texts—spectacularly truer in the case of *The
Years*. Perhaps it would be true of all women writers. Perhaps it would be true of
all oppressed peoples' writings, of blacks and lesbians, that the published text is
not the most interesting text. The censorship of editors, publishers, husbands,
as well as the enormous pressure of self-censorship on a woman writer, makes
the reader mistrust the published text and makes the critic mistrust any
methodology that accepts without question the privilege of the printed text.
While it seemed to me an inherently materialistic activity to grub around in
libraries reading drafts of novels, letters, and diaries, proceedings of political
meetings, and newspapers, Marxism was moving in quite other directions. I
shifted my ground. I called myself a socialist feminist critic, hoping that the
word socialist would carry the freight of a materialist enterprise that did not
despise biography and history as old-fashioned and hopelessly outmoded tech-
niques for literary criticism. It does seem to be a political move on the part of
much contemporary theory to pitch out these practical tools just when women,
blacks, and other oppressed groups are busily building their own cultural history and need more than ever to develop a sophisticated practice in the contruc-
tion and reconstruction of our pasts.

Analyzing Woolf's intriguing political stance in *A Room of One's Own* and
Three Guineas, her socialist feminist pacifism, in "No More Horses: Virginia
Woolf on Art and Propaganda" in Madeline Moore's special issue of *Women's
Studies* (vol. 4, nos. 2 & 3, 1977), I argued that one was the "propaganda of hope"
and the second the "propaganda of despair." The canonization of these texts, in
feminist circles at least, has led to many fascinating new readings. In the present
book the new essays, "Taking the Bull by the Udders" and "Sapphistry: Narration as Lesbian Seduction in *A Room of One's Own*," use contemporary theory
to study the rhetorical structure of the text, concentrating, as I did in "Thinking Back Through Our Mothers" in *New Feminist Essays on Virginia Woolf*
(Nebraska, 1981), on the woman writer's special relationship with her woman
reader. This bridging of the gap between reader and writer in a gigantic "we" I
called "the collective sublime" in Woolf's work. My students have pointed out
to me that this relationship has been theorized by reader-response critics, Wolf-
gang Iser in particular. But in the interest of literary history I want to make clear
that this work came directly out of close reading of the texts, not from the imposition of theory on Woolf's writing. I am not arguing that the relative worth of
this work is better or worse because the theory came out of the reading rather
than the other way around, but simply stating it as a fact in the often maligned
American pragmatic tradition. Similarly, an anthropologist colleague pointed
out to me that Erving Goffman had written an essay on the form of the lecture
that is like my analysis of Woolf's deconstruction of the lecture form in "Taking

the Bull by the Udders" and "Sapphistry." Again, it was the structure of the text that engaged me and led to these conclusions, and the conviction that gender determined Woolf's relationship to language and form.

My first essay on Virginia Woolf, however, was "Enchanted Organ, Magic Bells: *Night and Day* as a Comic Opera." I came to Woolf through her least valued novel, seeing it in its social context in the genre of suffrage novels of the period, and then was entranced by its daring reversal of Mozart's *The Magic Flute*. Published by Ralph Freedman in *Virginia Woolf: Revaluation and Continuity* (Berkeley, 1979), the essay was written four years earlier and rejected by many academic journals. For years I kept tacked above my desk a torn slip of yellow lined paper on which was scrawled "Another piece of feminist trash," which served as a rejection letter from a prestigious journal. Reading the essay after a decade, I would make only one major change, and that is due to Gilbert and Gubar's powerful arguments for subversive subtexts in Victorian women's novels. The subtext is lesbian and the attraction between Mary and Katherine ("Mary fingered the fur of the skirt of the old dress") is what is buried beneath the marriage text. I have also added footnotes to Naomi Black's splendid subsequent work on Woolf's relationship to the women's suffrage movement.

The two essays on *The Years*, included here as chapters 2 and 3, were originally one. Their origin is in Virginia Woolf Society seminars at the MLA and David Erdman's invitation to serve as guest editor of *The Bulletin of the New York Public Library* (Winter 1977). The essay was, as usual, too long, and spilled over into the next issue. The most important work published in this issue was Grace Radin's edition of "Two Enormous Chunks" of "The Pargiters," as *The Years* was called, and subsequently her book-length study of the manuscripts has appeared (University of Tennessee Press, 1981). Also out of this project came the New York Public Library's edition of *The Pargiters* (1977, now in paperback, Harcourt Brace Jovanovich), which contains the original long version of Woolf's often quoted "Professions for Women." The chapters of "The Pargiters" when read alternately with *The Years* and Grace Radin's edition of other deleted chapters, as well as the original speech version of "Professions for Women," together make a splendid addition to our knowledge of the political and feminist Virginia Woolf.

Chapter 4, "Liberty, Sorority, Misogyny" was delivered in a session on revolution organized in honor of David Erdman at the 1981 English Institute and published in *The Representation of Women in Fiction*, edited by Margaret Higgonnet and Carolyn Heilbrun (Johns Hopkins, 1982). The subject of an upper-class English homosexual misogyny and hegemony over culture is still a controversial one. While Eve Sedgwick dismisses as homophobic this analysis of the Cambridge Apostles and the brilliant work of Maria-Antonietta Macciocchi on brotherhood on which it was based (in *Between Men: English Literature and Male Homosocial Desire*, Columbia University Press, 1985), the liberal wish not to offend homosexuals leads to avoidance of the issues of the relation of powerful male homosexuals to women within the English class system as well as class exploitation. For a further discussion of this issue, see my essay on Oscar

Browning in *Victorian Studies* (Spring 1985, 556-58). In this essay I first explored the uses of the Procne and Philomel myth for a theory of sisterhood in *Between the Acts*, which led directly to "Still Practice A/Wrested Alphabet: Towards a Feminist Aesthetic," an argument for an aesthetic of process and community in women's culture. This essay appears in the feminist theory issue of *Tulsa Studies in Women's Literature*, 1984 and will appear in *Feminist Issues in Literary Scholarship*, edited by Shari Benstock (Indiana University Press, 1987).

Much of "Liberty, Sorority, Misogyny" concerns itself with the languages of patriarchy spoken by Woolf's powerful predecessors in the Stephen family, both male and female, from her great-grandfather's anti-slavery bill pushed through reluctantly by her grandfather, "Mr. Mother-Country Stephen," and his brilliant exploitation of the maternal metaphor for an ideology of colonial exploitation, to the codification of English law done by her uncle Fitzjames Stephen and the production of English history as the lives of heroic men accomplished by her father, Leslie Stephen, in his monumental *Dictionary of National Biography*. In "The Niece of a Nun: Virginia Woolf, Caroline Stephen, and the Cloistered Imagination," first published in *Virginia Woolf: A Feminist Slant* (Nebraska University Press, 1983) and appearing here as chapter 6, I concentrated on the influence of Woolf's Quaker aunt on her writing and thinking. Indirectly but importantly, the impulse to this research into English sisterhoods and the role of women in Quaker communities came from Martha Vicinus's exciting and thorough research on communities of women in England. For a different version of Caroline Emelia Stephen's experience, her writing of a history of sisterhoods, and her conversion to the Quakers as well as her reinvigorating of the Quaker community, see the chapter on sisterhoods in Martha Vicinus's *Independent Women* (University of Chicago Press, 1985).

Chapter 5, "Virginia Woolf and Her Violin: Mothering, Madness, and Music," was written for delivery at several Woolf centenary celebrations in 1982 and published in briefer form in Elaine Ginsberg and Laura Gottlieb's *Virginia Woolf: Centennial Essays* (Whitston Press, 1983) and Ruth Perry and Martine Brownley's *Mothering the Mind* (Holmes and Meier, 1984). Its purpose was to offer a reading of Woolf's life in relation to a community of women rather than Bloomsbury, as well as to counter the deplorable method of Woolf's official biographer and the editors of her letters and diaries in which her biography is constructed backwards from her suicide and her "madness" is the determining factor in all judgments, leading to the projection of a weak apolitical figure. In addition I included here my earlier research on her doctor, George Savage.

Chapter 7 appears in abbreviated form in *Virginia Woolf and Bloomsbury: A Centenary Celebration* (Indiana University Press, 1986) delayed in publication because of problems with permissions. However, along with chapter 8, also on *A Room of One's Own*, it has been given as a lecture at meetings of the National Women's Studies Association, the Conference on British Studies, and the Berkshire Women's History meeting, benefitting from critiques of the participants and the audience, particularly Louise De Salvo, Martha Vicinus, Cora Kaplan,

Judith Walkowitz and Angela Ingram. However, I still disagree with Kaplan's reading of the passage on Charlotte Brontë in *A Room of One's Own* in her "Pandora's box: subjectivity, class and sexuality in socialist feminist criticism" in *Making a Difference: Feminist Literary Criticism,* ed. Gayle Greene and Coppélia Kahn (Methuen, 1985). The argument is in yet another essay on Woolf, "Art and Anger," *Feminist Studies* 4, no. 1 (1978): 68–98.

"A Rose for Him to Rifle," the introductory chapter, is also new and deals with the drafts of *To the Lighthouse,* arguing that the influence of Colette makes it a "French" novel. In addition I have used, for the purpose of socialist feminist criticism, the radical French feminist critic Kristeva's work on the semiotic and symbolic in language, in ways Lacanians would not approve, to argue that the recurring figure of the charwoman in Woolf's work, as the origin and fount of language, is her most powerful strategy in subverting the languages of patriarchy, and that this romantic displacement of the mother with a working-class female figure is what makes Woolf's novels powerful socialist as well as feminist readings of our culture. The tension between those mythologized women and the evidence in her diaries and letters of her daily struggles with what her relationship should be to her own maids and cooks is instructive for modern feminists, showing us how much one is of one's culture while struggling against it. The dialectic between the romanticization of the working-class woman as the mother of language and Woolf's personal inability to communicate across class lines to the women who cleaned her house reinforces one's admiration for her proto-socialist feminist position and cautions the critic about her own attitudes toward race and class.

The essays in *Virginia Woolf and the Languages of Patriarchy* are offered here in the hope that, even out of the communal setting of feminist criticism and Woolf scholarship in which many of them were first conceived, they will be read in that spirit as part of the history of our work in the seventies and eighties in the United States. I would also hope that in establishing the consistent current in Woolf's work of socialist, pacifist, feminist, and anti-fascist politics, this book will contribute to the wider redefinition of modernism currently being explored by feminist critics.

ACKNOWLEDGMENTS

My thanks to the editors of journals and books in which some of these essays first appeared:

Carolyn Heilbrun and Margaret Higonnet for "Liberty, Sorority, Misogyny," which, as a paper delivered at the English Institute, appeared in *The Representation of Women in Fiction*, Johns Hopkins University Press;

David Erdman, editor of the now defunct *Bulletin of the New York Public Library*, where my chapters on *The Years* first appeared;

Ralph Freedman, editor of *Virginia Woolf: Revaluation and Continuity*, University of California Press, Berkeley, where the essay on *Night and Day* first appeared;

Willis G. Regier of the University of Nebraska Press for "The Niece of a Nun" which appeared in *Virginia Woolf: A Feminist Slant*;

T. M. Farmiloe of Macmillan, London, who published my two collections of feminist essays on Virginia Woolf ("Taking the Bull by the Udders" in an earlier draft appears in *Virginia Woolf and Bloomsbury: A Centenary Celebration*);

and Ruth Perry, editor of *Mothering the Mind* and Elaine Ginsberg and Laura Gottlieb, editors of *Virginia Woolf: Centennial Essays*, where other versions of "Virginia Woolf and Her Violin" appeared.

Thanks are also due to the Virginia Woolf Estate, for permission to quote from her published and unpublished work, and to the libraries and librarians who have supported this work of literary history, Lola Szladits of the Berg Collection, New York Public Library, Ellen Dunlap and Cathy Henderson of the Humanities Research Center, University of Texas, the helpful staffs of Sussex University Library, the Newberry Library, Washington State University at Pullman, and Northwestern University Library. My deepest debt is to the community of Woolf scholars and in particular to my friend and colleague, Louise De Salvo, who demanded that this work be done. I am also very grateful to Carolyn Heilbrun for her continuing encouragement of my work. My thanks also to the following people for their help: Elizabeth Abel, Richard Bauman, Theodora Calvert, Margaret Comstock, Blanche Cook, Alice Fox, Angela Ingram, Madeline Moore, Grace Radin, Brenda Silver, Susan Squier, Robert Tod, Martha Vicinus, and Judith Walkowitz. Thanks also to the University of

Texas Research Institute and Dean William Livingston for grants for the typing of the manuscript, and to Susanne Fawcett for translating my outmoded long-hand and long yellow sheets into the machine age. The final work on the manuscript was done on a grant from the University of Texas Research Institute, Fall 1985.

Virginia Woolf

and the
Languages of
Patriarchy

INTRODUCTION

A Rose for Him to Rifle

> She gave my father a look of loving suspi-
> cion. And after all, you, what have you to do
> with me? You aren't even a relation.
>
> —Colette, *My Mother's House*

> . . . for the transaction between a writer and
> the spirit of the age is one of infinite deli-
> cacy, and upon a nice arrangement between
> the two the whole fortune of his works
> depends. Orlando had so ordered it that she
> was in an extremely happy position; she
> need neither fight her age, nor submit to it;
> she was it, yet remained herself. Now, there-
> fore, she could write, and write she did. She
> wrote. She wrote. She wrote.
>
> —*Orlando*

An Introduction

Appropriately enough for this introduction, it is in a story called "The Introduction" that we find Virginia Woolf speculating on the role of feminist criticism. A drama is enacted at Mrs. Dalloway's party, which may serve as a psychic
representation of the struggle of my generation of feminist critics to come into
being. Lily Everit is introduced, socially and intellectually, to the patriarchy.
The structure of its initiation rites is relentless and cruel. The "coming out" of
the young scholar is a tribal ritual in Edwardian London, a tribal ritual of intellectual clitoridectomy, of sexual lobotomy. The thinking woman's sexuality as
well as the feeling woman's critical thought are ravaged and plundered in public. And yet, the story is an allegory for survival. Just as the critical introduction
precedes the book and the social introduction precedes the marriage, the public
rites of initiation, which Lily experiences as rape, precede her rebirth as a
woman and a feminist critic. She is scarred by the experience, marked for life,
but she emerges triumphantly to insist that "this civilisation depends on me."[1]
As a performative allegory of the birth of a feminist critic, "The Introduction"
is more melodramatic than most of Woolf's fiction, and it is easier for us to read

1

there the story of our own initiation rites than in the more complex portrait of Lily Briscoe in *To the Lighthouse*. In the social sea of her first party, Lily Everit hugs to herself "as a drowning man might hug a spar in the sea" the thought of her essay on the character of Dean Swift, which only that morning had been handed back by her professor "with three red stars: First rate." His praise is the "cordial" she drinks at this party, as we feminist critics uncomfortably savored the praise of our male professors. She divides life into fact and fiction, rock and wave, and "essays were the facts of life." But public exposure of herself in a party frock (like public exposure of feminist critics as women) robs her of her intellectual confidence, and the thought of her essay wobbles and wilts, turns "into a mist of alarm, apprehension and defence," and she stands "at bay." She is described as a frail butterfly just out of her chrysalis, "a flower which had opened in ten minutes." The stars from her professor fade as she realizes that "it was not hers to dominate, or to assert; rather to air and embellish this orderly life where all was done already." "What had she to oppose to this massive masculine achievement? An essay on the character of Dean Swift!"

Lily recognizes the patriarchy in Bob Brinsley, his ownership of culture, his "direct descent from Shakespeare"; he is the creator of parliaments and churches and telephone wires. At the "supreme trial" of her introduction to him, she despairs: "what could she do but lay her essay, oh and the whole of her being, on the floor as a cloak for him to trample on, as a rose for him to rifle." His chivalry arouses her gallantry and obeisance as she plays Walter Raleigh to his Queen Elizabeth. Her work is a cloak she flings down so his feet won't touch the mud, a flower to be stripped and plundered by him.

The reversal of gender here, where the woman plays Walter Raleigh and the male Queen Elizabeth, is interesting. For Woolf was haunted by a story about Walter Pater and the head of an Oxford women's college at a "Gaudy," which she used in *The Pargiters* (125–26). In Thomas Wright's 1907 biography of Pater, which she quotes, the story is told that the woman scholar dropped her glove and Pater thought she did it on purpose, and so stepped on it. He told his companion, "If I had not remembered how, in spite of the honours heaped upon him by Queen Elizabeth, Sir Walter Raleigh was in the end led out to execution, perhaps I, too, might have made a fool of myself. Believe me, my dear sir, it was an insinuation of the devil that caused this woman to drop her glove" (TP, 126). The biographer then goes on to compare Pater's contempt for women's wit with Swift's. The allusion then to Lily's essay, significantly on Swift's character, not his writing, is to the male scholar's fear of women's intellectual power, and the pervasive misogyny of English men, which links Bob Brinsley to Pater. Lily fears that her writing means death from the patriarchy. This fear, however unfounded or even as pathological as Pater's "Believe me, my dear sir, it was an insinuation of the devil that caused this woman to drop her glove," is real to Lily and to the woman reader, especially when we recall that Leslie Stephen wrote a biography of Swift and that Perry Meisel has convincingly argued for Woolf's conscious imitation of Pater's style.

Further on in the fifth essay of *The Pargiters*, Woolf discusses Joseph Wright and her belief that working-class men have more respect for women than professors have. "He did not pick up her handkerchief or tread upon it. He never pinched her knee. He talked to her as frankly as he talked to a man. . . . Was it true that some men really admired women? not as old Chuffy and old Lathom (professors) admired them; that they did not tread on their handkerchiefs or pick them up? That one could therefore respect a man? and find him interesting to talk to?" (TP, 127-28). In "The Introduction," there is no mediating working-class male voice and Lily overcomes her fear alone. The cloak or the handkerchief (now significantly changed from a glove) flung beneath the feet of a male is the woman's text and the woman's body. Her textuality and her sexuality are inseparable. The pages of her essay, like Desdemona's handkerchief in *Othello*, represent her woman's "honor"; both are blood-stained, like bridal sheets. They expose chivalry and misogyny as two sides of the same patriarchal coin.

"Rifle" is an interesting word for Woolf to use. It uncannily suggests rape in its Old French origin. In fact, Shakespeare uses it this way ("Pure chastity is rifled of her store"). But my own feeling is that Woolf found it in Una Troubridge's translation of Colette's *My Mother's House and Sido* (1922). Colette is remembering her sister's wedding, and her mother's pained insistence on calling the situation, however properly performed by a priest, an abduction. The child is fascinated by the word and goes to stare at an old print in the hall called "The Abduction." She sees the ruffled petticoats of the girl in the picture as a rifled rose. Given her mother's role as guardian of flowers, "rifle" means not only rape, but robbery from the mother, an aspect of the Demeter/Persephone myth that clearly moved both ambivalent writers about their mothers.

What Colette recalls in *My Mother's House*, aside from a "young man dressed in taffeta and a young woman whose ruffled skirts suggest the rifled petals of a rose," is the importance of the missing figure in the engraving, the absence of the mother. When her sister married, Colette moved into her room. She tells of being carried back in the middle of the night to her old nursery adjoining her mother's room, waking in the morning to cry to her "abductor," "Mother! Come quick! I've been abducted!" A rape or abduction is always a triangle. Some lover, husband, or father is implicated as well as the victim and the rapist. Colette's wish/fear of being "abducted" by her mother articulates a taboo as resonant for her as it was for Virginia Woolf. The most important absent figure in the rape triangle for many women is the mother. In "The Introduction," Lily is literally handed over to Bob Brinsley by Mrs. Dalloway, her surrogate mother. Seeing Lily and Bob react as "the concussion of steel upon flint" at her matchmaking, Mrs. Dalloway feels moved by "the loveliest and most ancient of all fires." The mother abandons the daughter, as Helen abandons Rachel in *The Voyage Out*, but, while Rachel succumbs, Lily survives.

The rifled rose and the trampled cloak suggest male violence and rape of woman's textuality and sexuality. They are as resonant as the swallow and the nightingale figures in *Between the Acts*, of patriarchal rape of women's tongues (see chapter 4). Woolf's answer is sketched out in her notes for "Professions for Women":

> A set of values was ready-made. And these values were always half an inch to the right or left of my own. To say what one thought—that was my little problem— against the prodigious Current; *to find a sentence that could hold its own against the male flood* [emphasis added] . . . But I think you will find it extremely difficult to say what you think—and make money. For instance, about the war. If I were reviewing books now, I would say this was a stupid and violent and hateful and idiotic and trifling and ignoble and mean display. I would say I am bored to death by war books. I detest the masculine point of view. I am bored by his heroism, virtue and honour. I think the best these men can do is not to talk about themselves any more. [*The Pargiters*, 164]

In Woolf's "The Introduction," Brinsley patronizes Lily, asks if she likes reading, and assumes that she writes poetry. As he "insolently" and "arrogantly" talks about himself, Lily sees him tearing the wings off a fly and protects herself, tries to "crouch and cower and fold the wings down flat on her back." This allusion echoes Shakespeare, Hardy's *Tess*, and Katherine Mansfield's "The New Dress" and reinforces the sense of female victimization in the text. As he talks, her essay on Swift becomes "obtrusive," burning "with a terrible lustre, no longer clear and brilliant, but troubled and bloodstained" from her unspoken battle with Brinsley and patriarchal civilization. Though he shrivels her wings and charges "her light being with cloud," she emerges from battle shouldering her feminist responsibilities: "this civilization . . . depends on me." So Woolf herself emerged from battles with Bloomsbury men, and feminist critics from battles with the academy. Like Lily's, our shoulders are bent with this burden, and our writing loses clarity and brilliance, becomes streaked with blood and cloudy with struggle.

Perhaps these remarks are an apology for my own prose in this book, for the bloody streaks and cloudy passages of "assertion" and "domination" which come from opposing and fighting a tradition rather than accepting it, unable to find Orlando's middle way. The patriarchal fire, so lovely and bright to Mrs. Dalloway, seems menacing and dangerous to us. What Lily Everit had to say about Swift's character did not, perhaps, accord with the views of Sir Leslie Stephen. What I have to say about Virginia Woolf in this book does not accord with the views of her biographer of the editors of her letters and diaries. Woolf anticipated that a new generation of women writers would not have "the shoddy fetters of class on their feet," and that men would eventually learn to "tolerate free speech in women." This burden of battle with patriarchal hegemony over culture is very bad for one's writing. It preaches and prods, gets on its high horse, exhorts and tries to convert. But I am confident that this work is transitional, that even now, Lily Everit's granddaughters are writing feminist criticism that is neither caked with blood nor cloudy with anger.

My basic assumption in this book is that all of Virginia Woolf's work is an attack on the patriarchal family, from the early essay, "A Society," to *Three*

Guineas, where she makes her radical claim that the origin of fascism is in the patriarchal family. It therefore seemed natural to study her grandfather Mr. Mother-Country Stephen, her uncle James Fitzjames Stephen, her cousin J. K. Stephen, her aunt Caroline, the Quaker mystic. It also seemed sensible to study those novels where fact and fiction, Lily's rock and wave, mix—*Night and Day* and *The Years*. My celebration of these "factual" novels may seem eccentric, but I find there explicit evidence, less buried than in her other novels, of her battle with the tyranny of the patriarchal family. But, of course, the Woolf book that means most to feminist critics of my generation is *A Room of One's Own*. As our literary feminist bible, it is the one most subject to critical exegesis, most quoted and argued over in feminist critical work of the last decade. I do not claim that in these chapters I have exhausted its meaning. But the experience of teaching it has made me realize that American students miss so many of its references and jokes, so many of the historical references to its age, that an attempt to place it in context was essential.

This book is a literary history about a writer whose first impulse was to be a historian, a work of socialist feminist criticism about a writer who was one of the first socialist feminist critics. Like Lily Everit, Woolf shouldered the social responsibility of expressing her differences with the patriarchy, her passionate hatred for the Victorian patriarchal family, her utopian vision of social equality for women and working-class men. Like Lily, she said "there are no sanctuaries, or butterflies." It is this Virginia Woolf I hope to have captured here. There are many portraits of Virginia, the butterfly, in the ivory tower of class and social privilege; this is a portrait of Woolf, the rebel, a study of those sentences which hold their own against the male flood.

A Mother's Alphabet:
To the Lighthouse as a French Novel

Woolf scholars have recently debated the anomalous fact that Woolf published a French version of the "Time Passes" section of *To the Lighthouse* in a translation made by Charles Mauron in the Princess di Bassiano's journal *Commerce* in the Winter 1926 issue. James Haule has discovered the typescript, which differs considerably from the holographs as well as the two published versions, and discussed the accepted reading of the many revisions as a response to Roger Fry's critique.[2] Why did Woolf publish part of an unfinished novel in France, something she had never done before and would never do again? It is my opinion that the gesture was an attempt to gain the attention of French women writers and readers, to place her novel about her mother in sisterhood with Colette's *Sido* and *My Mother's House*, and to place herself as a writer in relation to the powerful community of women artists in Paris in the twenties where, as I argue in "Liberty, Sorority, Misogyny," women recreated Sappho's island community. "The Window" is like the window passage in *Sido* where Colette watches her mother suffer her sister's birth pangs vicariously.

And it is interesting that in creating her own "mother's house" Woolf chooses to create St. Ives rather than Hyde Park Gate, associating the mother with nature as Colette does.

If the woman writer was reaching out to a female community in which the mother's relation to writing was a natural topic, why didn't Woolf publish a section where Mrs. Ramsay figures more importantly? My answer is that "Time Passes" in all its several versions is a lament for the dead mother. The figure of the empty house, the questioning of the meaning of life, the horror and chaos of the universe, devastation and meaninglessness, is a portrait of the dead mother's body and the daughter's appalling sense of loss. For women *are* their houses. While critics like Gayatri Spivak read this section as a recreation of the experience of madness, it seems to me that these early versions make clear that the void in the house expresses the death of the mother. Woolf drew *To the Lighthouse* as two blocks connected by a tunnel. In the tunnel, time is fluid and personality is stable, while in the flanking blocks, personality is fluid and time is stable. Time is experienced according to the mother's presence or absence.

Colette's relation to the father-writer was the opposite of Woolf's. A spiritualist saw " . . . behind you the "spirit" of an old man is sitting. . . . You are exactly what he longed to be. But he himself was never able" (*MMH*, 194). She recalls his "works," "a row of volumes bound in boards with black linen spines." The titles grace "hundreds and hundreds of blank pages. Imaginary works, the mirage of a writer's career":

> There were so many of these virgin pages, spared through timidity or listlessness, that we never saw the end of them. My brother wrote his prescriptions on them, my mother covered her pots of jam with them, her granddaughters tore out the leaves for scribbling, but we never exhausted those cream-laid notebooks, his invisible "works." All the same my mother exerted herself to that end with a sort of fever of destruction: "You don't mean to say there are still some left? I must have some for cutlet frills. I must have some to line my little drawers with . . ." And this not in mockery but out of piercing regret and the painful desire to blot out this proof of incapacity. At this time when I was beginning to write, I too drew on this spiritual legacy. Was that where I got my extravagant taste for writing on smooth sheets of fine paper, without the least regard for economy? I dared to cover with my large round handwriting the invisible cursive script, perceptible to only one person in the world like a shining tracery which carried to a triumphant conclusion the single page lovingly completed and signed, the page that bore the dedication (to Sido). [*MMH*, 196–97]

The daughter's legitimate task is to take the father's place as writer in courting the mother. Colette's father's unwritten works fall into the male "symbolic" mode, to use Kristeva's term, while her mother's last letter ends the book in the realm of the female "semiotic," a non-rational "feminine" discourse that became Colette's trademark.[3] Her father's titles were mathematical and military, but Colette's *entitlement* as a writer came from her mother. In a later portrait of her mother (*Break of Day*, 1961) she describes her mother's last letter:

> Two pencilled sheets have on them nothing more than apparently joyful signs, arrows emerging from an embryo word, little rays, "yes, yes" together, and a single "she danced," very clear. Lower down she had written "my treasure" . . . I feel a scruple in claiming for myself so burning a word. It has a place among strokes, swallow-like interweavings, plant-like convolutions—all messages from a hand that was trying to transmit to me a *new alphabet* . . . So that instead of a confused delirium, I see in the letter one of those haunted landscapes where, to puzzle you, a face lies hidden among the leaves, an arm in the fork of a tree, a body under a cluster of rock. [*BD*, 142]

Though "the little rays" are much like Katharine Hilbery's algebraic marks in *Night and Day*, her "pages all speckled with dots and dashes and twisted bars," Woolf's entitlement to the mother's alphabet was less clear. By publishing in Paris I suggest she sought sisterly courage to write the loss of the mother's body, the mother's house, and began a dialectic of identification with the woman reader. But she extends her project from the purely female desire to rejoin the mother at Kristeva's "semiotic," or preoedipal, level of language acquisition, to make a "genotext" of class as well as gender. Kristeva cites the *chora*, rhythmic sounds, laughter, music, all excluded from Plato's conception of "symbolic," or phallogocentric, art, as inaccessible to women. *To the Lighthouse* proves her wrong. Mrs. McNab is the voice of the semiotic. Her lurching and rolling rhythms of working are the origins of language. Thus Woolf can turn the personal mourning of daughter for mother into a more universal choral dirge by and for the human repetitions of daily life in the charwoman. Mrs. McNab's *jouissance* is a politics and poetics of life over death.

In *A Room of One's Own*, Virginia Woolf articulates her notion of writing as a historical process, that "if we are women writers, we think back through our mothers." Women writers are influenced by their predecessors and so are feminist critics. I suggest that this passage is an intellectual statement of another graphic and sensual passage in *My Mother's House*. Colette describes "my mother, the garden and the circle of animals," "the great basket overflowing with indistinguishable cats":

> Bijou, four times a mother in three years, from whose teats hung a chaplet of newborn offspring, was herself engaged in noisily sucking, with an overlarge tongue and a purring not unlike the roar of a log fire, the milk of the aged Nonoche, who lay inert with comfort, one paw across her eyes. Bending nearer, I listened to the double purring, treble and bass, that is the mysterious prerogative of the feline race; a rumbling as of a distant factory, a whirring as of a captive moth, a frail mill whose profound slumber stops its grinding. I was not surprised at the chain of mutually sucking cats. [*MMH*, 50]

It is perfectly obvious that the author of *To the Lighthouse* is indebted to the author of *My Mother's House* and *Sido*. But it also seems to me that Woolf translates Colette's physical and sensual description of a natural linked chain of nurturance into a political statement of the dependence of women writers and critics upon their foremothers. My students have been more shocked by this passage in Colette than by any other writing we read by women. They seem to need to see mothers as independent sources of nurturance, never needy themselves, merely as the great givers of life and sustenance, bottomless bowls of warm and nurturing soup. *The* dangerous subject has been touched upon here—that mothers too need nurturance, and that there is an electric current of sexuality, of desire and pleasure, in the act of sucking, for both mothers and their offspring. In the relationship between Lily Briscoe and Mrs. Ramsay, some of this desire is expressed in Lily's wish to merge with her adopted mother, like "waters poured into one jar." What remains unexpressed, except in Mrs. Ramsay's orgasmic relation with the lighthouse beam, is the sexuality and need of the mother. Yet Woolf was able to make the image of a linked chain of mutual nurturance into a clear, rational statement about writing. Colette herself took her father's name and, as a writer, filled the blank books that he left behind him when he died. As the writing daughter, she played the father's role of suitor and lover to the mother. While as a socialist feminist I harbor a deep suspicion of claims to universal experience in psychological development, one can claim that this pattern is similar in Colette and Woolf. That Colette's father's books were absolutely blank gave her a freedom that Woolf could not share, bowed down as she was, like Lily Everit, by the weight of the Stephen family's writing past as the makers of English civilization, as the writers and speakers of all the languages of the patriarchy. Lily Everit feels that "the yoke that had fallen from the skies onto her neck crushed her," and the guests notice that she bears this burden like all the members of her family "as if she had the weight of the world upon her shoulders." Woolf, as the writing daughter, is also playing the role of lover and suitor to the lost mother. But in her case, there were volumes and volumes of the father's text and the family's text to write *against*, the many *languages of the patriarchy*.

If writing is for some women, then, the assumption of the father's role, in order to court the mother, the empty white sheets Colette filled did not fight with her female experience. She did not have to eat her father's words before forming her own. In her essay in *Mothering the Mind*, Jane Lilienfeld describes the scene in which Willy locked Colette in her room to write, as a version of Rumpelstiltskin ordering his prisoner to spin straw into gold. In some ways, this was an easier task than Woolf's swallowing her father's words and spitting them out again before creating her own style. She was oppressed, she told Ethel Smyth, by "those 68 black books" of her father's *Dictionary of National Biography*. The heritage of blank pages seems more appealing than a heritage of indigestible black books. Woolf had to write between the lines of thousands of words penned by her family; Colette wrote hymns and love letters to her mother to fill the empty spaces. If the father's text is either an empty white book or an over-full black one, the daughters' texts have replaced and erased them with a series of slim volumes stained with the green of the natural world of the mother's garden, the deep red of the walls of the mother's house.

In a review of novels by Dorothy Richardson and Romer Wilson, Woolf describes the prose of women writers: "There are no mouse-coloured virtues; no gradual transitions; all is genius, violence and rhapsody, and her thick crowded utterance, often eloquent and sometimes exquisite, recalls the stammer of a bird enraptured with life in June" (*CW*, 123). She describes Richardson's "psychological sentence of the feminine gender" as "of a more elastic fibre than the old, capable of stretching to the extreme, of suspending the frailest particles, of enveloping the vaguest shapes." We find this elastic sentence, the prose umbilical cord to the mother voice, stretching itself over the territory of Woolf's novels and Colette's. But Colette does not attack her French matriarchal family, for her mother was the dominant element in it. Woolf blames the patriarchal family for the loss of her mother, and extends that personal loss into a lifelong political campaign against this common enemy of the freedom of women. In a 1918 review of a novel by Hugh Walpole, *The Green Mirror* (*CW*, 71, 72), we see how this overriding passion makes her exult when her cause is shared by another rebel:

> If the family theme has taken the place of the love theme with our more thoughtful writers, that goes to prove that for this generation it is the more fertile of the two. . . .you may destroy the family and salute the dawn by any means at your disposal, passion, satire or humour, provided that you are in love with your cause. . . . The hammer is thrown and the mirror comes down with a crash. Upstairs a very old Mr. Trenchard falls back dead; and out we pour into the street looking askance at the passers-by as though we ought to tell them too that another English family has been smashed to splinters and freedom is stealing over the roof-tops.

The most obvious example of destroying the family and saluting the dawn is in *The Years*, though it is a major theme in all Woolf's fiction, as well as *A Room of One's Own* and *Three Guineas*. Aside from her well-documented intellectual and political commitment to a socialist feminist attack on the family, Woolf was unquestionably "in love with her cause," because it was, emotionally, part of the project of the daughter's recovery of the mother.

Before we leave Colette's *My Mother's House* I want to suggest one other way in which Woolf's work engages with it as part of that writing "chain of mutually sucking cats," of women writers, the sound of which is a "double purring, treble and bass." Colette's "Epitaphs" may be seen to express in concrete graphic terms a patriarchal model against which Woolf shaped the effort of her fiction to resurrect her own dead, so that, struggling for a word to replace "novel," she chose "elegy."[4] Colette describes her brother's habit of creating a world of imaginary dead people, making a miniature cemetery of tombstones and mausoleums, writing eloquent epitaphs to perpetuate "the sorrow of the surviving and the virtues of the supposed deceased." Aside from being a devastatingly ironic description of male history and literature, it obviously influenced Virginia Woolf: "Here lies Astoniphronque Bonscap, who departed this life 22 June 1874;

aged fifty-seven. A good husband and a good father, heaven awaits him and the earth deplores his loss. Passer-by, give him your prayers!" To Colette's inquiry about the life of his imaginary corpse, he replies, "He drank and used to beat his wife." "Then why have you put 'a good husband and a good father' on his epitaph?" "Because that's what you always put when people are married." (*MMH*, 54) Besides being a paradigm of male elegiac writing, Colette's brother's mausoleum-making is also a male cover-up or "pargetting," whitewash of the faults of men, a lie. It is Kristeva's "symbolic" male discourse. He also sentimentalizes dead mothers:

> "O thou model of Christian spouses! Reft from us at the age of eighteen, already four times a mother! The lamentations of thy weeping children have not availed to keep thee with them! Thy business is in jeopardy and thy husband vainly seeks oblivion!"

Sido is outraged at this city of the dead in her garden of life, and stomps it out as "delirium, sadism, vampirism, sacrilege." The Stephen children called Leslie's memoir of Julia Stephen and other family members "the Mausoleum book." It suffers from the same vices as Colette's brother's lugubrious prose. Woolf tried, with Colette's example before her, to bring her dead to life in fiction, to exorcise the maudlin and the sentimental from her portraits, to tell the truth, ambivalent as it was, about how we love and hate at the same time, and in the name of Orlando's lover, Marmaduke Bonthrop Shelmerdine, she acknowledges the creator of Astoniphronque Bonscap. Orlando finds "something romantic and chivalrous, passionate, melancholy, yet determined about him which went with the wild, dark-plumed name—a name which has in her mind the steel blue gleam of rooks' wings, the hoarse laughter of their caws, the snake-twisting descent of their feathers in a silver pool . . . "(*O*, 163). *Orlando*, you may say, belies my thesis. It cannot deal with the politics of the family because Orlando has no family, unless you count the portraits of ancestors hanging upon the walls of Vita Sackville-West's beloved Knole. Precisely. In fact, *Orlando* may be Woolf's strongest blow against the patriarchal family because it is clear that his/her freedom depends on the absence of family to curb his growth or cramp her style.

Moaning and Crooning: The Charwoman's Song

Some contemporary critical theorists describe women as outside of language. Virginia Woolf's whole *oeuvre* disproves this claim. *Orlando* itself is a brilliant mockery of the history of English patriarchal literature. One must first master the form in order to deconstruct it. Despite sex changes and the passage of centuries, Orlando is the female erotic, an eternal language of desire and creativity that remains stable as patriarchal language changes with the times.

The old bumboat woman frozen under the ice in *Orlando* is only one of many old working women who suggest death and resurrection, like the tube station muse in *Mrs. Dalloway*. Her appearance (*O*, 36–37) and reappearance (*O*, 151, 274) suggests in her frozen blue lips, the unsung song of the female Orpheus, the semiotic burble of the origins of art *in women's work*. Woolf thaws those blue lips in the voice of the charwoman in all her novels.

My methodology in the following chapters casts the socialist feminist critic in the role of reader of culture as well as texts, of biography and history as well as structures and discourses. This materialist critical practice pays attention to the drafts of novels, to diaries and letters and to the work of other women novelists and to Woolf's family. I have felt it necessary to research the work of her psychiatrist, George Savage, as well as to study the function of repetition in *The Years*. What holds this reading practice together as a socialist feminist poetics is Woolf's own example in her critical essays. Even more insistent is her voice, its feminist passion to lick the *logos* into shape for women's use, as a mother cat washes a kitten. If the reader feels confronted by a basketful of cats rather than a book, may I respectfully ask that reader to listen for the double purring, however faint its rumble, which links the woman reader to the woman writer.

In much of my work on Virginia Woolf, in journals ranging from *Women's Studies* to *Marxist Perspectives*, from *SIGNS* to *Critical Inquiry*, I have argued that Virginia Woolf's socialist politics are inseparable from her feminist writing practice. As we listen to her feminist voice, let us not isolate the treble from the bass. Let us remember that she never privileged the oppression of women over the oppression of the working class, that her radical project of overthrowing the form of the novel and the essay derives from a radical politics. The letters of the mother's alphabet and the rumbling and whirring of Colette's cats are matched in Woolf by the voices of the charwomen, the cooks and maids, the violet sellers and the caretaker's children in *The Years*, who act as chorus in all her novels. We hear it in the "ee um fah um so/foo swee too eem oo" of the tube station ancient singer in *Mrs. Dalloway* to the pidgin Greek of the janitor's children in *The Years*: "Etho passo tanno hai,/Fai donk to tu do,/Mai to, kai to, lai to see/To dom to tuh do-." If women's language, then lesbian language, is being made out of "words that are hardly syllabled yet," every Woolf text suggests that other oppressed voices of race and class, of difference and colonial subjectivity, are beginning to syllable themselves, like the Kreemo, Glaxo, Toffee or KEY spelled by the mysterious sky-writing airplane in *Mrs. Dalloway* or Septimus's pictographs that may save the world, "little faces laughing out of what might perhaps be waves, the map of the world."

In "Thinking Back Through Our Mothers" (in *New Feminist Essays on Virginia Woolf*) I argued that Virginia Woolf's position in her culture as a woman writer was analogous to that of Walter Benjamin's as a Jew in Weimar Germany. Like Orlando, both outsiders had one foot in and one foot out of the discourse of power. Both were, as critics, administering a culture for those who denied their right to do so. Terry Eagleton, writing of blacks, puts the case well:

> Oppressed peoples are natural hermeneuticists, skilled by hard schooling in the necessity of interpreting their oppressors' language. They are spontaneous semioticians, forced for sheer survival to decipher the sign systems of the enemy and adept at deploying their own opaque idioms against them.[5]

Virginia Woolf's language challenges phallogocentricism both from her marginal position as a woman within her culture, contradicting the fact of her class position as inheritor of its language, and from without, by a conscious alliance with the working class, as in *Three Guineas*. The gender gap between Woolf and her enemies and the class gap between Woolf and her allies is most often expressed not in words, but in their absences, in ellipses, so that the dot dot dot of unfinished sentences and uncompleted thoughts, which increases dramatically throughout her writing career, is an exact representation in the novels, of her own position in relation to her culture. We know from Carol MacKay's work on Annie Thackeray that Woolf's ellipses and exclamation points come directly from her aunt's prose. Woolf's representation of the charwoman as the unacknowledged bearer of culture in her fiction solves aesthetically the problem she wrestled with and could not solve in daily life. It reflects the ideology of the suffrage movement of her youth, whose propaganda always posed the struggle as led by an alliance of ladies and their maids against middle-class couples and the family itself.

We know from Susan Dick's edition of the holographs of *To the Lighthouse* (Toronto/Hogarth, 1983) that Woolf's first plan was to narrate the "Time Passes" section through Mrs. McNab, and that Cam's project as a budding woman artist was to translate the language of the kitchen as well as the patriarchal language of her father's study. In the draft Woolf records Mrs. McNab's "moments of illumination" at the washtub, and places the charwoman's words at the origins of women's acquisition of language: "the broken syllables of a revelation more . . . confused, but more profound" (than rational) (Dick, 216). The narrator asks "why, with no gift to bestow + no gift to take, did she yet desire life + sing as she dusted and leered"? (215). Mrs. McNab's "rolling and lurching" gait has a rhythm related to her song, which "rolled out like the . . . voice of witlessness + endurance . . . the voice of the ~~indomitable~~ principle of life." (211, 212) Woolf is defining a socialist feminist aesthetic in "her old amble + hobble dusting, singing" (212), "this incongruous song of the twisted + crazed + thwarted" reflecting the "dumb persistency of the fountain of life." (213) In her song "it seemed as if *a channel were tunnelled in the heart of obscurity*" (215, emphasis added). Mrs. McNab has a vision of the void, "something altogether alien to the process of domestic life," but she and Mrs. Bast conquer it with their voices and their work: "There was a force: (they came with their brooms + their pails they moaned: they crooned—they got to work.) There was a force perhaps in their craziness . . . which slowly and painfully stayed the corruption + the rot . . ."(229).

What Woolf sees in the charwomen's rhythms and words, tunnelling a channel into the obscure origins of language, is the place where art and work meet, where language follows the rhythms of the body. She is searching for the female *logos* at the meeting place of art and labor, tunnelling back to the obscure origins of a female aesthetic, trying to record its language. "They moaned: they crooned—they got to work." It is clear that whether one reads the moaning and crooning as pure examples of Kristeva's definitions of the *semiotic* as opposed to the patriarchal *symbolic* or as examples of Cixous's "writing the female body," Woolf's feminist project is also deeply concerned with class. She writes the female body engaged in domestic work. She records the semiotic laughter and songs and cries of old women on streetcorners, marks the silence of women absent from the lectures that make up *A Room of One's Own* because they are washing up the dishes, as translations of a temporary antiphallogocentric discourse, awaiting the time when the charwoman herself will write fiction.

Unlike Colette, who is content to write the mother's body, the arrows, rays, "yes yeses," strokes, and "plant-like convolutions" in her new female alphabet, Woolf goes deeper into the semiotic realm to write the crippled and twisted body of the working-class woman. She syllables not only gender but class and age.

In the "French" text of "Time Passes" Woolf develops an extraordinary dialectic between the visionary and mystical woman artist standing on the beach trying to make intellectual order out of the nothingness and cruel indifference of the universe, and Mrs. McNab's ancient song of life. Mrs. McNab's "message" is given in "the broken syllables of a revelation more confused but more profound (could one have read it) than any accorded to solitary watchers, pacing the beach at midnight" (*TCL*, 285). Woolf definitely privileges the charwoman over women mystics like herself who "heard an absolute answer . . . the truth had been made known to them. But Mrs. McNab was none of these. She was no skeleton lover, who voluntarily surrenders and makes abstract and reduces the multiplicity of the world to unity and its volume and anguish to one voice piping clear and sweet an unmistakable message" (*TCL*, 284). Here is the clash of the semiotic and the symbolic within women's words and visions and Woolf resists the pull of the patriarchal symbolic, siding with the old woman's more material, disorderly voice. Mrs. McNab forgives life for its mistreatment of her. "For what reason did there twine about her dirge this incorrigible hope?" (*TCL*, 284).

Unlike many feminist writers Woolf does not privilege gender over class and recognizes that once the woman writer's voice finds its tongue and speaks and writes it own language, other oppressed voices will find their tongues and write the languages of class and race. Mrs. McNab's song is the ancient noise of life itself:

> a sound issued from her lips—something that had been gay twenty years before on the stage perhaps, had been hummed and danced to, but now coming from the toothless, bonneted, care-taking woman was robbed of meaning, was like the voice of witlessness, humour, persistency itself trodden down but springing up

again, so that as she lurched dusting, wiping, she seemed to say how it was one long sorrow and trouble, how it was getting up and going to bed again, and bringing things out and putting them away again.[TCL, 284]

I have argued that repetition and dailiness are the principles of a female aesthetic which is based on process, rather than finished works of art.[6] Here Woolf has expressed it as well. Helping Mrs. McNab in her eternal rounds of housekeeping are the airs, "ghostly confidantes," animal-like and related to the "spies," ancient guardian figures who protect human life. They appear often in her work, notably in "The Narrow Bridge of Art." They are Jane Harrison's *keres*, unquenchable spirits. Harrison describes a particular tribe of ancient *keres*, the *kerykes* (*Prolegomena*, 212). Their function in the ancient world was to clean up pollution. They were the charwomen of the spiritual world, the Mrs. McNabs of the universe. In "Time Passes," then, Virginia Woolf has written a socialist feminist dialectic on life and death, a world view that includes the mystical and the material, an aesthetic that relates the poet's "single voice piping clear and sweet" to the moan of a charwoman's music-hall song. Woolf's poetics of gender and class is also very seriously a home economics that studies the patriarchal family and its kitchen muse, translating for her readers all the languages opposed to the patriarchy which are within her experience.[7]

In "Thinking Back Through Our Mothers," I argued that Woolf's project was "untying the Mother Tongue," in her search to free language from patriarchal patterns, to write the "feminine sentence." In several recent essays Sandra Gilbert and Susan Gubar have argued that this is a "fantasy," not a successful strategy for writing as a woman, an argument that echoes Elaine Showalter's earlier negative reading of *A Room of One's Own* as a "tomb" in *A Literature of Their Own*.[8] I remain convinced that Woolf's strategy works, agreeing with Rachel Du Plessis in her brilliant *Writing beyond the Ending*.[9] The missing element in these readings is class. The "rude mouth" of the battered old woman by the tube singing Strauss's "Last Songs" for the resurrection of the dead on All Saints' Day in *Mrs. Dalloway* is the origin of art:

> As the ancient song bubbled up opposite Regent's Park Tube Station, still the earth seemed green and flowery: still though it issued from so rude a mouth, a mere hole in the earth, muddy too, matted with root fibers and tangled grasses, still the old bubbling burbling song, soaking through the knotted roots of infinite ages, and skeletons and treasure, streamed away in rivulets . . . fertilizing, leaving a damp stain. [*MD* 91]

Very early in her career Woolf sought to solve the problem of how the middle-class writer could capture the speech of working-class women. Reviewing *The Village Wife's Lament* by Maurice Hewlett in 1918, she wrote:

> Nowadays many whose minds have not been used to turn that way must stop and ponder what thoughts the country people carry with them to their work in the

fields, or cogitate as they scrub the cottage floor. It is a matter for speculation and shyness since the gulf between the articulate and the inarticulate is not to be crossed by facile questioning, and silence may seem after all the best we can offer by way of sympathy to people whose lives seem so mysteriously and for such ages steeped in silence. [*Contemporary Writers,* 87]

Admiring Hewlett for basing "her life deep down among the roots of the earth," as she was later to do with all her charwoman characters, Woolf nevertheless found him too genteel:

> Perhaps it is coarseness—the quality that is the most difficult of all for the edu-cated to come by—that is lacking. By coarseness we mean something as far removed from vulgarity as can be. We mean something vehement, full-throated, carrying down in its rush sticks and stones and fragments of human nature pell-mell. [*CW,* 89]

This "coarseness" is in all Woolf's charwomen, like the "old blind woman" in *Jacob's Room* "singing out loud . . . from the depths of her gay, wild heart" to Mrs. Dempster in *Mrs. Dalloway* crying "pity for the loss of roses" after a life-time of house-cleaning. The "wonderful words," "words of one syllable" which Miss LaTrobe drags out of the mud come from the same source. The puzzling "Rattigan Glumphoboo" which sums up Orlando's career is a similar encoding of a female alphabet in a coarse "full-throated rush."

Colette in *My Mother's House* recalled the pleasures of reading in a book-lined womb/room and her childhood creation of "an invisible and magic word," "*Aphbicécladggalkymariodphorebstevanzy.*" Making up words recalls the deepest chord of the mother-child bond. Made-up words are indelible. They cannot be erased. When the woman writer's private language becomes public in a gesture to the woman reader, the mother tongue is untied in the "rude mouth" of the outsider woman, the crone, the charwoman, or the lesbian, and female free speech is assured. Virginia Woolf's last ancient murmuring crone, guardian of the fountain of life and speech, is the ladies' lavatory attendant in "The Watering Place," the last finished story, created and then excised in the typescript. Like the deep cavern of the tube station that yields up song to the guardian crone in *Mrs. Dalloway* or the primeval mud that spurts up words for Miss LaTrobe's play in *Between the Acts,* it is the maternal sea in this last story that washes and flushes out the words of "womanliness bred by manliness," those women like Isa, imprisoned in the patriarchal system during wartime and unable to speak as women. The memoirs of the cleaner of the public lavatory, says the narrator, "have never been written." "When, in old age, they look back through the corridors of memory, their past must be different from any other. It must be cut up: disconnected. The door must be always opening and shutting. They can have no settled relations with their kind."[10] Woolf's last effort was to connect with the voice of the most distant and debased of her heroic charwomen, to find again the voice whose "coarseness" she had sought in 1918, singing "something vehement, full-throated, carrying down in its rush sticks and stones and fragments of human nature pell-mell."

Was the mother tongue as she set it speaking in these "rude mouths" strong enough to drown out the patriarchal voices plaguing her as King Edward shouting obscenities and the birds speaking Greek, the language of male hegemony? The "corrupt murmurs with their clink of the baser sort" surfaced again in a draft of *Between the Acts:* "these voices merely stir the long hairs that grow in the conch of the ear and make strange music, mad music, jangled and broken sounds . . ."[11] Like Colette, by writing as a woman, Virginia Woolf traced a "haunted landscape" in her "new alphabet." Placing words together on a page she set free the fertile and promiscuous Mother Tongue. As I have argued in "Thinking Back Through Our Mothers,"[12] Woolf's belief in the power of language to change history was profound. "Words are dangerous things let us remember. A republic might be brought into being by a poem."

As I have re-read this book I am surprised to find that, like a work of fiction, the text I have made of Woolf's work and life has a villain, her uncle James Fitzjames Stephen. His name recurs as the signature of the language of the patriarchy, the inventor of modern legal discourse, to whom generations of law students turned for definitions of crime and punishment, the harsh discourse of discipline, the voice of an Old Testament judge. But this text also has a heroine, the classical anthropologist Jane Ellen Harrison, whose cross-disciplinary and specifically *anti-textual* work on the origins of Greek art in ancient ritual laid the basis for Lévi-Strauss and modern structuralism. Under her influence Woolf continually reached back deep in the subconscious to the primeval mud of "semiotic" origins in art, pre-symbolic discourse, the Mother Tongue. Differentiating between "eikonism" and "aneikonism" or sign and symbol-making, Harrison first of all anticipates most modern *theorists* of language and culture. In *Alpha and Omega* (Sidgwick and Jackson, 1915) she describes a priest consecrating Westminster Cathedral by tracing Greek and Latin letters in ashes on the floor:

> The rite is a piece of primitive magic. The alphabet is made up of elements, out of which the whole human speech is compounded. These elements (*stoicheia*) stand for the elements out of which the universe is compounded; and their order, the row (*stoichos*) in which they stand, is the world order. By the might of the elements you have the power to control the universe. [*Alpha and Omega,* 182]

Francis Cornford wrote that Jane Harrison worked as if she had the key to all languages. Virginia Woolf spent her life trying to write "the feminine sentence" in a similar magic ritual, trying to write in the rhythms of gender, imagining, like Colette in making up "*Aphbicécladggalhymariodphorebstevanzy*" from the letters on the backs of an encyclopedia, the patriarchy's book of knowledge, that she could "control the universe" in answer to her own father's compendium of knowledge, the "68 black books" of the *Dictionary of National Biography*. Her millions of words, in novels, essay, diaries, and letters, extend a legacy to women readers of a female alphabet with which to counteract the spell of the languages of the patriarchy.

Virginia Woolf's vatic charwomen and ancient crones embody Jane Harrison's concept of *Themis*:[13] "Themis is in a sense prophecy incarnate, but it is only in the old sense of prophecy, utterance, ordinance, not in the later sense of forecast of the future." Harrison describes *themis* as " the force that convenes," thus binding Woolf's prophetic outsider figures with Mrs. Hilbery of *Night and Day* and Eleanor Pargiter of *The Years*, with the Mrs. Ramsay who gives a dinner party, visits the poor, and worries about the milk, and with Mrs. Dalloway, whose party is what makes social and community life possible. Harrison claims of *themis* that "she is the force that brings and binds men together, she is the 'herd instinct'; the collective conscience." Together Woolf's women are themis incarnate, the voice of civilization. Let us remember that Woolf's work is not simply a feminist valorization of women but that it is always marked with a socialist or class analysis. What she called in "On Being Ill" "the beggar's hieroglyphic" of human misery marks all her writing.

ᴄ⤳ 1 ᴄ⤳

Enchanted Organ, Magic Bells:
Night and Day *as a Comic Opera*

It's a wise tune that knows its own mother.
—(with apologies to Samuel Butler)

Where a book ends and the reader begins is as difficult to determine as any other objective and subjective problem.

—Anne Thackeray Ritchie

By nature, both Vanessa and I were explorers, revolutionists, reformers.

—*Moments of Being*, 126

The Divine Rage to Be Didactic

Critics have not been kind to *Night and Day*. Even female critics, who might perhaps be expected to respond approvingly to the feminist content of the novel, have found it unsatisfactory. "A lie in the soul," said Katherine Mansfield. "An academic exercise," said Virginia Woolf herself. When a work by a major artist is so generally deplored, and when it is formally unlike those works that are admired, then one is surely justified in asking whether indeed the hostile critics have looked for the right things.

I think that *Night and Day* is an extraordinarily interesting novel. It is a natural daughter of the Meredith novel, a minor masterpiece, a pleasure to read. The disappointment of contemporary readers—like E. M. Forster, Clive Bell, or Katherine Mansfield—was, I think largely due to outrage felt at the audacity of using the comic form in a novel written during the war and published in 1919. But the search for order that impelled Eliot and Joyce to shape their feelings of despair in ancient mythological structures was the same impulse that drove Virginia Woolf to shape *Night and Day* around the initiation, quest, and journey myths of *The Magic Flute*.[1]

I suspect that those who reject the novel do so from two different points of view. Some, with Forster, Bell, and Mansfield, find the comic mode impertinent in wartime and Woolf out of character stylistically and temperamentally.[2] Modern critics do not hear the "authentic" voice of Woolf in this novel and find it mannered. But *Night and Day* can be read as the Dreadnought Hoaxer's Merry Pranks. Woolf described this adventure in "A Society" as part of the effort of a group of young women to discover why men could not achieve "the objects of life," namely, "to produce good people and good books"—one of the themes of *Night and Day*.[3] The female hoaxer (Rose, who later turns up in *The Years*), dresses up as the Prince of Abyssinia (with no apologies to the author of *Rasselas*) and violates *The Dreadnought*, a secret man-of-war. The masquerade managed to attack the British patriarchy at its most vulnerable point effectively and Sylvia Pankhurst chose this motif as a rallying title, first for her socialist feminist newspaper *The Women's Dreadnought*, then, at the founding of the British Communist party, *The Workers' Dreadnought*.[4]

Allusively, then, Woolf is engaged in serious play with the history and ideology of her culture, with biography, autobiography, and with the way in which literature shapes our expectations of life as individuals, couples, families, and generations. The tone of serious playfulness, the structure of the book as lively/deadly game, links *Night and Day* with *Orlando* and *Flush*, the least admired of her books. They are certainly as experimental in form as her major works. As satirical comedies, they all challenge the fundamental myths of patriarchal society. They are melodramatic, operatic, and flamboyantly visual. They "strike the eye," as she said, and as such they annoy some literary purists. Looking back from the thirties Woolf told composer Ethel Smyth that *Night and Day* might well be her best book and that the vision that accompanied its composition was the key to her creative life.

Night and Day depends structurally on Mozart, stylistically on Jane Austen, and thematically on Ibsen. *The Magic Flute*, *Pride and Prejudice*, and *The Master Builder* may seem to be an odd combination of sources for a twentieth-century novelist. But all three had a special appeal for the consciously feminist and consciously female writer's imagination. The novel's structural relation to Mozart is what concerns me here.

Actual "evidence" that my reading of the novel is not completely in the realm of fantasy may be grounded for some readers in the fact that Virginia Woolf saw a great deal of Goldsworthy Lowes Dickinson during the composition of *Night and Day* (1917-1920). Quentin Bell has pointed out to me that Dickinson was writing *The Magic Flute: A Fantasia* at the time. Whether she saw the manuscript or not, Woolf must have heard some discussion of the subject, which in Dickinson's version, far more than in Mozart's, was bound to raise the eyebrows of any female, feminist or not. While it took courage, Rebecca West has said, for Virginia Woolf to affront natural male vanity in her novels, she was only "chastised with whips";[5] the homosexual intellectuals of Woolf's set "chastised her with scorpions." Dickinson's *Fantasia* is a rather puerile "Greek" vision of patriarchy, the quest, and Sarastro's band of pure men. I find it comic but am sure it was not meant to be. He makes Tamino not Oriental but English, fair and original Angle/Angel; the magic flute is not the gift of the Queen of the Night (in Mozart she is Muse and Mother, of his music and his masculinity), but comes from one of his ancestors (from an old English house, no doubt) who had gotten it from Sarastro. The Queen of the Night is robbed of her stars and her crown: she is Chaos incarnate,

> Death in life, and life in death,
> Passion's most authentic voice,
> Foes of reason and of choice,
> Secret urge behind the will,
> Now to gender, now to kill![6]

Dennis Proctor read the *Fantasia* as an antiwar pamphlet; Forster concentrated on its exaltation of reason and mysticism and the introduction of Jesus and Buddha, who are not in Mozart's libretto. Since an earlier *Fantasia* was performed in Roger Fry's Omega Workshops, this one was undoubtedly familiar to the same circle of friends.

E. M. Forster praised the *Fantasia* as being beyond Mozart: "[the] slight pantomime of Tamino and Pamina is exalted into a mythology of Wagnerian scope"; the fire is the war, the water twentieth-century doubt, the castle of Sarastro the modern mind.[7] He found it a "lovely book"; modern readers would perhaps find it as priggish and smug as the institutionalized genteel homosexuality it represents and be glad that it inspired in Virginia Woolf not anger but the warm, light-hearted, realistic response to life and work she made of *Night and Day*.

The Covent Garden Liar

"I went to *Tristan* the other night," Woolf wrote to Barbara Bagenal in 1923, "but the love making bored me. When I was your age I thought it the most beautiful thing in the world—or was it only in deference to Saxon? I told many lies in Covent Garden opera house. My youth was largely spent there. And we used to write the names of operas in books."[8]

But the same audience who recognized the antiwar theme in Lowes Dickinson would have recognized it in Woolf. The brilliant Cambridge Dent/Clive Carey revival of *The Magic Flute* in 1911 appealed to the imagination of the Apostles. There were Masons among the founders of the secret society and traces of Masonic ritual, especially the ark, in its ceremonies. Parsons and Spater have pointed out that Leonard Woolf was especially intrigued by these rites. This led to a London production during the war, greeted by a full-page leader in the *Times Literary Supplement* praising the opera as pacifist; and young men wrote from the front saying that they did indeed feel like Sarastro's band of pure young men and that the Prussians were Monostatos and his followers, representing chaos and militarism.

Arthur Clutton Brock's review (*TLS*, June 29, 1916, of the Aldwych production) saw Mozart's opera as religious and magical: "So, we feel if we had the music, we could make the Prussians march their goose-step back to Potsdam, so we could play all solemn perversity off the stage of life." He compared it to a great cathedral with High Mass being celebrated while children play hide-and-seek behind the pillars. He wished that Mozart were alive to tame the Germans with his music as the "naughty" Queen of the Night, "the ugly negro and all his goose-stepping attendants," are tamed at the end. These male mysteries were very confusing to women.

Virginia Woolf recorded in her dairy the feeling that Lowes Dickinson and his young friend, who were sitting in the same row with her, at the 1919 production, had an instinctive ease with the opera, which escaped her. Her novel, then, is a feminist pacifist's answer to masculinist pacifism. Oliver Schreiner, who shared her views, was a great admirer of *Night and Day*. That the first principle of Bloomsbury-Cambridge pacifism was hatred of women did not escape Woolf.

The Magic Flute is patriarchy's most glorious myth of itself as civilization. It tells the story of the transition from matriarchy to patriarchy, the maintenance of the male moral order by forcing the daughter to reject her mother. Anthropologically accurate, it stresses the key role of the uncle in maintaining the incest taboo and structuring the patriarchal family by seeing that the daughter marries a foreigner or stranger.

The 1911 Cambridge *Magic Flute* was a direct response to the political upsurge of militant feminism. *Night and Day* is an antiwar novel: it is against the "sex war," the most important political issue in Edwardian England, and it is against the misogyny of Cambridge-Bloomsbury culture, which appropriated the classics and music as male property.

In "A Society" Woolf had appropriated for women the symbols of the elite Cambridge Apostles, as she does in *Night and Day*, for feminist purposes. If her male compatriots appropriated *The Magic Flute* as an assertion of English cultural and military superiority to the Germans in war time, she would use it to explore male/female relations in the "sex war." The classics are continually being reinterpreted according to the ideological needs of the age. The 1911, 1916, and 1919 Cambridge and London performances of *The Magic Flute* emphasized, as Dent himself claimed, manliness and male friendship, secret mystic rites of brotherhood, and the subordination of women (Dent, 336). This explains homosexual devotion to this opera as well as Wagner's *Parsifal* in the celebration of male chastity and brotherhood and the equation of women with evil in the figures of Kundry and the Queen of the Night. Ingmar Bergman's recent film of *The Magic Flute* is also close to *Parsifal* and provides a more modern misogyny for contemporary audiences by actually distorting the libretto to make Sarastro Pamina's father, not her uncle, and inventing a scene in which the Queen of the Night demands that Pamina kill her "father." In case this merry misogyny is not clear enough, Bergman's camera continually moves from the opera's action to the lollipop lips of a little girl in the audience, reportedly his own daughter, repeating the message that mothers are murderesses and daddys are rational and kind.

Some interesting notes by Woolf on the opera (1906) in the Monks House Papers, Sussex, suggest a debate within herself over the question of a state opera house. Unlike Shaw, she feared cultural controls but liked the idea of the military protecting the opera house. Covent Garden appealed to her because of the conjunction of cabbages and kings, squalor and splendor, though her 1909 essay on Bayreuth suggests a conversion due to the marriage of nature and art achieved in Wagner's opera house.

Woolf has written the names of operas in her book and even composed *Night and Day* as a modern *Magic Flute*. But more to the point is the confession that she lied in Covent Garden opera house. Mansfield said that *Night and Day* was a lie and I think other critics feel this as well: They see "the truth" in the tragic visionary novels, *To the Lighthouse, The Waves, Between the Acts*. But comedy does not always lie, as Meredith tells us; it is most hampered from telling the truth when relations between men and women are unequal. Perhaps this is the source of the strain in *Night and Day*. Perhaps, like Tolstoy, Woolf only told the truth about men in *Three Guineas*, when she had one foot in her watery grave. Nevertheless, since all fiction lies in order to tell the truth (though we may at times prefer the tragic lie to the comic lie), let us look at Virginia Woolf in her costume as Covent Garden liar. One of *The Magic Flute's* finest themes is lying, comically repeated in *Night and Day*.

Woolf's achievement in *Night and Day* was formal. Actually to write of such high, moral, and serious subjects with such abandoned and yet controlled gaiety was a demanding task she set for herself. But to write so comically (the scene in the zoo, the engagement ring between owners rolling to "father's" feet) seemed almost sacrilegious while Western culture was destroying itself on the battlefield.

To imitate Mozart, to mock Shakespeare and Henry James, to poke fun at her own passionate commitment to the feminist movement, to turn Ibsen's tragedies upside down, was daring enough for a woman. But it is the tone that shocks. The utter self-confidence of the impersonal female narrator of the story makes us as secure as children in our mother's arms. God and the narrator, as in Jane Austen, may be as distant as the stars that demand Katharine's gaze, but they have an order of their own. We are sure she knows what she is doing.

The tragic icons, Lily Briscoe's triangle and Bernard's "fin in a waste of waters," have often seemed more significant than the comic harmony of the circle that shapes *Night and Day* as an eighteenth-century opera. One is disconcerted to find women's suffrage exposed by such a comic touch—especially that a novel that manages to curtsey so gracefully to the past can manage a stiff little nod in the direction of Ibsen and the future.

Its thirty-three chapters circle the subject of initiation into society, courtship, and marriage. The characters are engaged in an elaborate ritual, like an eighteenth-century dance. Mozart's *Magic Flute* is invoked as William

Rodney's model for a new poetic drama. And Cassandra plays Mozart throughout the second part of the novel while the music both kindles and calms the emotions of the characters. But *The Magic Flute* was based on the symbolism of Masonry; it is about initiation into patriarchal society, the preservation of which demands the quelling of the forces of evil represented by the Queen of Night. Woolf reverses the terms and demands no ritual patricide. Night and Day are more in harmony than in opposition. The upset to the patriarchal order takes place at twilight and on the thresholds of lighted rooms and dark streets. The twilight of the old gods is extinguished not by Brünnhilde's torch but by the light in Mary Datchet's room, which represents "something impersonal and serene in the spirit of the woman within, working out her plans far into the night—her plans for the good of a world that none of them were ever to know" (ND, 506).

Brigid Brophy said that Virginia Woolf brought to English prose an ear that was "quite outstandingly defective."[9] Obviously, she had never read *Night and Day*. For *Night and Day* is the perfect libretto for a classical opera in the comic but melancholy mode of Mozart, with some appropriately modern stylistic dissonances. One wishes that Virginia Woolf's friend Ethel Smyth had composed a score for it. Their shared feminism, love of England, and respect for the formal and classical harmonies was combined with an outrageous sense of humor and a modern visionary sense that alienation could be both expressed and controlled by artistic experimentation.

The magical bells of *The Magic Flute* ring out in the novel in praise of the marriage of those magical Bells, Vanessa and Clive. But the joyful peals of its praise have an undertone of irony. For when Virginia Woolf wrote *Night and Day* the marriage of the Bells had expanded to include other members, most notably Duncan Grant. And Virginia Woolf's admiration for their domestic bliss was aroused by awe at the sheer number of works of art it produced.[10] One also has the odd feeling that the only really satisfactory ending to the novel would be in Katharine Hilbery's marriage, not to Ralph but to Mary Datchet. Desire is present in the novel's one erotic moment when Mary touches Katharine's skirt.

That primitive instrument the glockenspiel, which is so effective in the opera in summoning love and controlling rebellion, is in Woolf's hands a magic wand. It is a kind of blessed baton (in the opera it was a parting gift from the King of Day to the Queen of Night) which creates splendid music on an eternal theme.[11] Woolf makes her "Four Passionate Snails" dance to the tune of "an enchanted organ" (her phrase for the prose style of her aunt, Lady Ritchie, who was the prototype of Mrs. Hilbery).[12] Lady Ritchie records thinking of "literature as music," of hearing the music of literature (*Letters*, 256). But as they conclude the figures of this ancient courtship dance, the happy couple realize that their happiness is made possible by those who are excluded from the dance. Mary Datchet, Sally Seale, and "old Joan up at Highgate" have worked and will work so that Katharine and Ralph can love one another.[13] The spirit of Virginia Woolf's feminism was as strongly, although perhaps unconsciously, at work in *Night and Day* as the "masculinism" of Masonry was in Mozart's *Magic Flute*.

No reader of the first volume of Virginia Woolf's letters can fail to realize that she educated herself in Covent Garden and that her primarily visual imagination found much stimulation there. As Robert Moberly explains it, the staging of the second act of *The Magic Flute* reflects a Masonic structure that is visually apparent. Pyramids of nines are placed on eighteen seats with a great black horn encrusted with gold. Behind them are palm trees. Sarastro and his priests march in carrying palm branches.[14] In Woolf's version it is Mrs. Hilbery who carries armfuls of palm, since it is she and the female tradition that inform the novel.

The point I would like to make is that there is a connection between Mozart's and Woolf's uses of these Masonic structures. She was inspired by his music and the visual representation of it in Covent Garden Opera house in the same way that Mozart was inspired by the mysteries and harmonies of Masonry. When Rhoda fantasizes in *The Waves* that "the players take the square and place it upon the oblong. They place it very accurately; they make a perfect dwelling-place" (W, 163), she is visualizing a moral and social structure formed by the patterns of the music, but she is also saying that the greatest art makes the reader or listener feels she has come home. Katharine's "square boxes halved and quartered by straight lines" (ND, 306) are part of the same imaginative process and quite different from Ralph's vision of "a little dot with flames around it," which is the emblem the Sun-King gave to Sarastro in *The Magic Flute*. Katharine says she shares this vision but knows it has nothing to do with her.

Virginia Woolf's description in "The String Quartet" invokes this patriarchal scene from *The Magic Flute*, where the pillars of Sarastro's castle are plainly antifemale:

> As the horns are joined by trumpets and supported by clarions there rise white arches firmly planted on marble pillars . . . Tramp and trumpeting. Clang and clangour. Firm establishment. Fast foundations. March of myriads. Confusion and chaos trod to earth. But this city to which we travel has neither stone nor marble; hangs enduringly; stands unshakeable; nor does a face, nor does a flag greet or welcome. Leave then to perish your hope; droop in the desert my joy; naked advance. Bare are the pillars; auspicious to none; casting no shade; resplendent, severe. Back then I fall, eager no more, desiring only to go—[HH, 26–27][15]

The most serious connection between *Night and Day* and *The Magic Flute*, however, is structural, not thematic. *Night and Day* takes from Mozart's opera the Triple Accord (which Mozart took from Masonry and mythology). Among them we note those three knocks on the door repeated as Ralph's *leitmotif* throughout the novel. We also discover myriad repetitions, those manifestations Woolf calls, in *Between the Acts*, the "triple ply" and "the threefold melody." All of them, we may assume can be found in the indelible impression made on Woolf's ear by the "magic number three" in Mozart's music. In Covent Garden, Woolf's ear was educated to an eternal classical rhythm that she never forgot. Her obsessive trinities were used to form character, as Mozart had done, to suggest dialectical action, and eventually, in *Three Guineas*, to suggest the boring but compelling repetitions of human action in history. While most critics do not credit Woolf's educated ear but recognize the painterly qualities of her eye, I think that she made triangles and squares on oblongs out of the desire to make visual what her inner ear heard, as she has shown in "The String Quartet." I also believe that in *Night and Day* Mozart was a stronger influence than Roger Fry.[16]

"Stone-breaking," as we shall see, was Virginia Woolf's term for this classical kind of composition. An appropriately pre-Masonic process, it suggests breaking down the old structures and building new ones, both literally and morally. The archetype of her architecture is different from Mozart's Masonic temple to the sun. The Queen of Night's temple to Isis is not a fit house, either, for her modern hero and heroine. When night and day are at peace with one another, at dusk, their vision is of a cottage in the country.

The dream house can only be attained, however, by getting Katharine out of that Chelsea monument to the Victorian family, the Cheyne Walk temple-within-a-temple to great men. But all the other dwellings figure importantly in the novel as well—Rodney's eighteenth-century rooms, Ralph's tower with its rook in Highgate, Mary's Bloomsbury office, her room of her own in the City, her family's ancient parsonage in Lincoln, and the Otways' Stogdon House, a "portly three-decker" nineteenth-century sailing ship. It is Mrs. Hilbery, "the magician" as Katharine calls her, who embraces all the structures in her abundant arms. As the female artist and her father's daughter, she comes back from Shakespeare's tomb refreshed and makes order out of chaos. She encircles London in her carriage and abducts the young men from those buildings that are exclusively male, those seats of patriarchal power. She brings Ralph from Lincoln's Inn and Rodney from Whitehall, passes St. Paul's, and conjures up a fantasy of her daughter's wedding in Westminster Abbey. In the temple of art she blesses the two couples and sends them out. She has been as effective in liberating the young men as the young women. For the economic facts are such that the women will provide the money to buy Ralph's pastoral peace in a country cottage and Rodney's Chelsea town house, in which he can find the intellectual stimulation he needs to write.

"'There's always work,' she said, a little aggressively"

Night and Day celebrates, as classically as its title suggests, the union of the eternal opposites, night and day, nature and reason, duty and freedom, man and woman. A sweet and comic Epithalamion, the marriage song is also ironic and melancholy.[17] The ill-matched couples are sorted out and mated, blessed, initiated, and brought into society as in Mozart, the classical master of the celebratory humanistic values to which the novel constantly refers. In the academic year from fall to spring that fixes the story in time, William Rodney, the rather pedantic poet, moves from studying the score of *Don Giovanni* to *The Magic Flute*.

The connections are concretely made. It is that modern Sarastro, Mr. Hilbery, who demands that Cassandra play Mozart. Like Pamina's uncle in *The Magic Flute* he is also, despite his wisdom, rather careless about his niece's male associates. Katharine's presence is "like a strain of music" to Ralph, though neither listens to Mozart—he is the means of pacifying the family so that they may meet and talk. They "felt an enormous sense of relief at the license which the music gave them to loosen their hold upon the mechanism of behaviour." Even Mrs. Hilbery "charmed herself into good spirits again by remembering the existence of Mozart." "The melody of Mozart seemed to express the easy and exquisite love of the two upstairs" (ND, 384, 416, 424).[18]

The thirty-three chapters circle through Katharine's purgatorial sufferings as Angel in the House and Ralph's as Breadwinner, to the infernal betrayals and insecurities of all the characters, to a resolution as a purely human comedy. The descents and ascents suggest the joys and sorrows of love, the hope for Mozart's heaven here on earth. Ralph and Katharine, like Pamina and Tamino, endure both the trial by fire and the trial by water in the last chapter of the novel. In fact, Pamina's "mad scene" is imitated in Katharine's "mad scene" when she fears she has lost Ralph.[19] None of the characters have faith in Isis and Osiris, but rather in the one legacy they can accept from the Victorians, the desire for hard work.

The pastoral idyll, which her sister Vanessa seemed to be living in the country with Duncan Grant, was Woolf's inspiration for the novel. What most impressed her was that their domestic arrangements allowed them the freedom to work. It was a scene of great creative outpouring. The perceptive novelist shows in *Night and Day* a brilliantly accurate historical portrait of the differences in attitudes toward work of middle-class Edwardian men and women. William Rodney begrudges every minute of drudgery in his government office that keeps him from his poetic drama. Ralph Denham chafes at the bonds of domestic responsibility that keep him in his law office. To the women it is another matter altogether. Katharine daydreams about marriage (first to William and then to Ralph), with no thought of sex but with a deep longing for the opportunity to work: "she had come in from a lecture, and she held a pile of books in her hand, scientific books, and books about mathematics and astronomy which she had mastered," and later "fancy the evenings of married life spent thus . . . or with a book, perhaps, for then she would have time to read her books, and to grasp firmly with every muscle of her unused mind what she longed to know" (ND, 138, 282).

And Mary, with her discipline and decision, goes from that time-honored condition of women, volunteer work (even though the cause is women's suffrage), to become the salaried secretary of a movement for greater social change. Margaret Llewelyn-Davies, of the Working Women's Cooperative Guild, called "Mary Datchet" in Woolf's letters to her, devoted her life to the cause of social justice, and she appears again as Eleanor in *The Years*. She suppresses her personal relationships as well as her writing in a conscious effort to find salvation in work.

When Ralph complains to Mary about loneliness and his sufferings in love, she utters my favorite line: "'There's always work,' she said, a little aggressively." Ralph thinks that Mary wants him to leave, but she is thinking about Katharine: "She doesn't know what work is . . . But it's the thing that saves one—I'm sure of that . . . Where should I be now if I hadn't got to go to my office every day? Thousands of people would tell you the same thing—thousands of women. I tell you, work is the only thing that saved me, Ralph" (ND, 391–92).

This is one of Woolf's amazing political perceptions: that the ideal of the female utopia was to be in paradise alone, to work. (Work elevated to the status of the highest Christian virtues was what made Masonry appealing to Mozart.) And surely "opera" as "works" tells us of Woolf's own industrious approach to art. For the middle-class heroines of this novel both marriage and the rejection of marriage are the means to an end, domestic peace and freedom to work. Even the blithe Cassandra views marriage to Ralph as an opportunity to be educated. We expect these marriages to produce not babies, but books.[20] Just as the woman writer, in Woolf's terms, was struggling from the personal to the impersonal, on a different time scale from the male writer, so the aspiring young woman needed work and discipline when her male counterpart was rejecting those Victorian values.

As we move from October to June, we realize that it is not only the year which is academic. (But this "male" academic year is paralleled by a "female" matriarchal year, deriving from Jane Harrison's studies of preclassical Greece and structuring the time sequence of all the novels.) The novel ends with Ralph and Katharine at the half-open door, on the threshold of a new life. They are about to try a new experiment with an old institution, a marriage that will provide peace and respect, a mutual silence so that both can work. Their gentle "good night" suggests that most of their passion has been spent opening and closing the doors and windows that have architecturally and symbolically shaped the book into a comedy as surely as they shaped *The Master Builder* into a tragedy. *The Magic Flute* gives us Sarastro's castle in real as well as Masonic terms; unlike Ibsen's dream "castles in the air," it is the model of the patriarchal home.

The score of *Don Giovanni* lies open on William Rodney's piano, dominating the tone of the first half of the novel. His playing Don Juan is amusingly depicted: Katharine calls him "half poet and half old maid," and Ralph thinks, "that little pink-cheeked dancing-master to marry Katharine? that gibbering ass with the face of a monkey on an organ? that posing, vain, fantastical fop? with his tragedies and his comedies, his innumerable spites and prides and pettinesses?" (ND, 68, 303).

By chapter 22 the music master has brought in a new score, *The Magic Flute*. Katharine has become a cold, stargazing sorceress, the Queen of the Night, and Rodney finds himself a more feminine friend in Cassandra. Her "melodious and whimsical temperament" appeals to him. She even plays the flute: "He recalled with pleasure the amusing way in which her nose, long like all the Otway noses, seemed to extend itself into the flute, as if she were some inimitably graceful species of musical mole" (ND, 280). Significantly, Cassandra was the name of Jane Austen's sister, who, by burning her letters, saw to it that she would be "impersonal" forever. It was also the name Florence Nightingale took in her autobiographical fragment railing at the indiscriminate education of girls like Cassandra—which Virginia Woolf's friend Ray Strachey printed in her history of women's suffrage, *The Cause*, and which Woolf recommends to readers of *A Room of One's Own*.[21] Cassandra and Mary, natural woman and rational woman, then, are in possession of those magic instruments that the King of Day has left to his "star-flaming queen" in Mozart's opera. They are given to the questing males, Tamino and Papageno, and are used both to win and to make joyful the angry rebellious slaves in *The Magic Flute*.

Masonic misogyny and the ancient rituals of patriarchal culture form the structure of the opera, but Woolf's novel has made the energy of culture a female force embodied in the figure of the abundant Mrs. Hilbery. And it is Mr. Hilbery as Sarastro, formidable and rational benevolent despot, who is driven from the temple, "the extravagant, inconsiderate, uncivilized male, outraged somehow and gone bellowing to his lair with a roar which still sometimes reverberates in the most polished of drawing rooms" (ND, 500). At the same time, Ralph Denham makes a wonderfully serious recreation of Papageno, bird-catcher and liar.[22] He keeps a "decrepit rook" in his room, watches birds instead of shooting them with Mary's brothers in Lincoln, feeds the sparrows in the park as he lies to Mary and confesses he is a liar. He sees Katharine as "a bright-plumed bird poised easily before further flight." It is Ralph, the natural man, not William the artist, who is Woolf's visionary character:

> an odd image came to his mind of a lighthouse besieged by the flying bodies of lost birds, who were dashed senseless, by the gale, against the glass. He had a strange sensation that he was both lighthouse and bird; he was steadfast and brilliant; and at the same time he was whirled, with all other things, senseless against the glass. (ND, 394)

These are the only lines in the novel which seem to speak in Woolf's "authentic" voice. Her truth-teller is a liar.

George Bernard Shaw once said that *The Magic Flute* was the music of his humanist and rationalist religion, an allegory of the human struggle for personal goodness and order.[23] It does seem at times like *Pilgrim's Progress* with comic relief.[24] But in *Night and Day* Woolf took up this age-old story and told it from the female point of view. Tamino's question at the end of act I, "O endless night! hast thou no breaking? When dawns the day mine eyes are seeking?" is universal. Woolf, like Mozart, preferred to place her high moral seriousness in a comic setting.

The same, of course, had been done by Shakespeare, and consequently he, too, is one of the heroes of the novel.[25] But even Shakespeare is treated comically. Mrs. Hilbery misquotes and mumbles; one of the aunts carries him in her pocket; Katharine refuses to read him; Rodney impersonates him; tea and dinner conversation are full of him. But the best joke of all is Mrs. Hilbery's pilgrimage to Stratford with her theory that Anne Hathaway wrote the sonnets. She "knows" that this theory implies a "menace to the safety of the heart of civilization itself" (ND, 427-28). According to Quentin Bell this incident is based on an actual one, as Mrs. Hilbery is based on Virginia Woolf's aunt.[26] She said to Samuel Butler while he was working on his own theories of the *Odyssey's* female author, "Oh, Mr. Butler do you know my theory about the Sonnets—that they were written by Anne Hathaway?" but he didn't know she was joking.[27]

A musical inspiration may have also come from another direction. Lady Ritchie was Thackeray's daughter and the sister of Leslie Stephen's first wife. Virginia Woolf reviewed her letters in an essay called, oddly enough, "The Enchanted Organ." She describes her aunt's style as musical—"so merry and so plaintive." "The guns are firing," Woolf wrote "and there she sits scribbling brilliant nonsense in her diary about 'matches and fairy tales.'" "To embrace oddities and produce a charming, laughing harmony from incongruities was her genius" might be a description of *Night and Day*. Woolf's tribute to her aunt reads: "And the music to which she dances, frail and fantastic, but true and distinct, will sound on outside our formidable residences when all the brass bands of literature have (let us hope) blared themselves to perdition."[28]

The character of Mrs. Hilbery and the novel itself are Woolf's tribute to that music created by the females in her family, truly an "enchanted organ," a hymn to the feminine search for freedom and order as *The Magic Flute* was a hymn to the masculine quest.

For Woolf it is the patriarchs who represent the forces of darkness, while the matriarchs are as sunny as Mrs. Hilbery with her arms full of flowers from Shakespeare's tomb. The vision is one of future creative flowering for women, built on the strength of the women who have gone before. Katharine is blessed and helped by her mother, "that ancient voyager." She has appropriated to herself the study of Greek, mathematics, and astronomy, stormed the bastion of patriarchal culture by demanding discipline in those closed spheres of learning by which our culture defines its highest values. Ralph, less classbound than William Rodney, has no stake in preserving patriarchy. He is not threatened by her love of the abstract. He hates great men as much as she hates great books. The natural lower-in-class-than-she man meant freedom for the upper-middle-class woman. In *The Magic Flute* that odd duet praising married love as heaven here on earth is sung by Papageno and Pamina.

Men may be mocked in *Night and Day* but they are not murdered. In *The Magic Flute* the male moral order is preserved only when the princess rejects her mother. The patriarchal blessing is bestowed only after the Queen of Night and the slaves have been banished forever. Woolf is not so severe in her reversal. Mrs. Hilbery's blessing is not contingent on Katharine's rebellion against her father. Mrs. Hilbery, the rather muddled matriarch, will mend that breach too.

Woolf had a kind of fondness for Victorian fathers not shared by Samuel Butler and Lytton Strachey in their attacks.[29] If one takes the tragic view of the "flower beneath the foot" in relations between women and men or children and fathers, the result is sheer suicidal anger. Sylvia Plath's Nazi boot in "Daddy" may be an apt metaphor for her sense of oppression, but the writer who plays victim loses the reader, as Virginia Woolf well knew.

The monstrous slippers of the great Victorian poet in *Night and Day* make us laugh. Yet they symbolize effectively his domestic tyranny. Enshrined as they are, and lovingly fingered by his admirers, they expand in the reader's mind. They have that formidable fatherly bulk of the statue in *Don Giovanni*. We wonder, if the poet's biography were ever written, if it would expose the idol's clay feet. We think of the slippers in *Hedda Gabler*; Hedda rejects the role of domestic slavery when she refuses to accept her husband's slippers, piously proffered by his devoted aunt. Surely we are meant to make these connections. But it is only possible to do so because the scene is described with comic irony. Those Victorian slippers clearly will not fit, and Katharine, with Ralph's help, will not put them on.

Woolf attacks the fathers, as Mozart attacks the mothers. Her weapons are different from Ibsen's but they do the job. She has exorcised Victorian family ghosts without once mentioning syphilis. Her lack of sexual frankness seems to have disturbed some of her critics. But killing the Angel in the House was a revolution in itself; she left some work for the women who would come after her.

Night and Day does not even pay its debt to the author of *The Master Builder* with quotation marks.[30] But Woolf has invented no Hilda Wangel. The terms of the novel are female and the liberating spirit is male and inhabits the person of Ralph Denham, who arrives in the Hilberys' drawing room like a breath of fresh air. He insists on class distinctions and needs no alpenstock and hobnailed boots. It is the "alps of his mind" which are impressive. Mary Datchet's walking stick entwined with ivy may resemble the glockenspiel only visually, but still it is appropriately symbolic of the lonely role of peacemaker she has assumed between the factions of the radical causes she believes will change the world. Like Hilda's alpenstock in *The Master Builder*, it also heralds the arrival of "the younger generation knocking at the door." The magic bell is Ralph Denham on the telephone.

Ibsen's name is invoked, along with Samuel Butler's, as a saint in the litany of free love which Katharine supports in her cousin's life, but eventually rejects for her own, softened by her mother's definition of love without marriage as "ugly." Significantly, the grounds for rejection are artistic, not moral.

In conscious imitation of Jane Austen, the opening of *Night and Day* reads: "It was a Sunday evening in October and in common with many other young ladies of her class, Katharine Hilbery was pouring out tea" (ND, 9). Irony, wit, and social criticism dissect love and marriage in the English middle classes in the Austen manner. The weapons of the novelist are small and sharp and brightly polished; most of the action takes place in that twilit hour between night and day, when social conventions are alternately preserved and strained over the teacups. Henry James's *Portrait of a Lady* is also recalled here for a portrait of what the feminist Vera Brittain called the making of a "lady into woman." Katharine Hilbery Denham also recalls Katharine Dereham, the heroine of *A Dark Lantern*, reviewed by Woolf in 1905, in which the feminist novelist Elizabeth Robins allows her sensitive female artist to be liberated from a nervous breakdown by a lower-class man.

Ibsen's theme in *The Master Builder* of "the younger generation knocking at the door" is repeated as a theme in a Mozart opera, where the structure demands that there be a happy ending. The eighteenth century is constantly invoked; its literary and political values are a kind of order Woolf wants to impose on the chaos of the contradictions and conflicts between the Victorians and the Edwardians.

All of Ibsen's revolutionary heroines are their fathers' daughters.[31] They slam the doors and break all the windows in the house of the patriarchal family. With no opportunity for education or self-expression they force men to build "castles in the air" for them, as Hilda does in *The Master Builder*. The play is a warning to society about giving women the opportunity to do useful work so their dreams of power do not destroy men. Ibsen saw that it was the male artist who was destroyed by the frustrated woman, in his desire, like the master builder Solness, to build spires to her aspirations.

Katharine confides to Mary her own desire "to beat people down." "I want to assert myself," she exclaims. "Ah, but I want to trample upon their prostrate bodies!" (ND, 58-59). So she would, we feel, if she married William Rodney. But tragedy is avoided when Woolf provides her with a suitable lower-in-class man, a comrade who is convinced (with some effort on Katharine's part) that she will neither be exploited nor worshiped. If left alone, she will have no need to live vicariously through him. Like Tamino, Ralph is an exotic "foreigner" and seeks knowledge, not power.

The self-proclaimed fathers' daughters in *Night and Day* are Sally Seale and Mrs. Hilbery. It makes them both romantic and visionary—they seem stuck in the nineteenth century, at odds with Katharine's eighteenth-century rationality and Mary's twentieth-century courage. But as Mrs. Hilbery shakes off her girlish role and pays her debts to the fathers at Stratford, at St. Paul's, and at Westminster Abbey, she seems to realize that she is much more interested in maternal than paternal family history. The reason that the biography of her father never gets written is that Mrs. Hilbery is really much more interested in her mother. It is not revelations about her father's sex life that distress her, but those about her mother's. It is when Mrs. Hilbery and her daughter abandon their roles as priestesses in the temple and speak woman to woman about their ancestress that real communication begins. Her theory about Anne Hathaway writing the sonnets perhaps expresses her own suspicions about the source of her father's poetry. Mrs. Hilbery leaves her father's house at rather a late age for finding her own identity, but Woolf was aware that society makes things more difficult for women. She returns dreaming of her daughter's wedding in the place of her father's funeral.

Hilda Wangel had of course insisted on a complete break with the past; Solness must not only build her a new church but overcome his fear of heights by crowning the spire with a wreath. The act combines sex and death when the view of woman's desire for power is based on fear. He plunges to his death. Ralph, described as one of Woolf's male mountaineers, does not see marriage as a battle of the sexes, a competition with winners and losers. We expect Katharine and Ralph to transform the old institution together, as Virginia Woolf felt she and Leonard and Vanessa and Clive Bell would.

The building metaphors of *Night and Day* reflect Ibsen's concern with social questions and the role of the artist who distinguishes between being an architect and being a skilled laborer ("stone-breaking" and "flying" were Woolf's terms) and Mozart's Masonic metaphors about building a moral character. The vision is remarkably like Rhoda's in *The Waves:*

> "There is a square; there is an oblong. The players take the square and place it upon the oblong. They place it very accurately; they make a perfect dwelling place. Very little is left outside. The structure is now visible; what is inchoate is here stated; we are not so various or so mean; we have made oblongs and stood them upon squares. This is our triumph; this is our consolation.
>
> The sweetness of this content overflowing runs down the walls of my mind, and liberates understanding. Wander no more, I say; this is the end." [W, 163]

Even Katharine, secret geometrix, would draw "square boxes halved and quartered by straight lines" (ND, 306).

Unlike Ibsen or Mozart, Woolf does not demand that the old cities and temples be razed so the "younger generation" can inhabit them. Let the temples to dead men be opened to living women, she cries. And not only to heroic women alone, but to women and men. Let them record not only the history of male achievements, male work, but women's work as well.

It was a rather optimistic view, surely, and one she had changed by the time she wrote *Three Guineas.* For those buildings were not so elastic as she imagined, and the cottage in the country did not satisfy all her desires. But *Night and Day* is as bent on blessing as is *The Master Builder* on hurling a curse at the old order. Mozart is clearly the stronger influence.

The characters of *Night and Day* agree in their rejection of the tragic drama of Ibsen and Wagner. William Rodney, as the new Shakespeare, chose his models in Shakespeare's comedies and Mozart's *Don Giovanni* and *The Magic Flute.* William attempts the role of Byron's *Don Juan* (Woolf had "fallen in love" with Byron while writing *Night and Day*) but his paper is about Shakespeare. His poetic drama, experimental in form, will be more like *All's Well That Ends Well* than *Don Juan.*

But the plot of his life seems arranged by the author of *Man and Superman*, for Woolf recognized as Shaw did that Mozart's comic treatment of the theme had been far more difficult to execute than Wagner's tragedy. In fact, Shaw felt that Wagner's concept of love-death was a more dangerous and revolutionary idea than anything in Marx. Woolf followed Shaw's lead in rejecting a romantic nineteenth-century tragic view of love and marriage.

Virginia Woolf made the same assertation critically when she compared Austen to the Greeks:

> In Jane Austen, too, we have the same sense, though the ligatures are much less tight, that her figures are bound and restricted to a few definite movements. She too, in her modest, everyday prose, chose the dangerous art where one slip meant death.[32]

That is rather strong language. But it is almost the same language in which Shaw asserts the superiority of the moral allegory of Mozart over Wagner. (Did she find the lovemaking in *Tristan* boring because it was romantically tragic?)

When William Rodney instructed Cassandra "to read Pope in preference to Dostoevsky until her feeling for form was more highly developed" (ND, 280), he was describing what the novelist tried to do in *Night and Day*. The clashes between the old and young, male and female, the workers for and the observers of humanity, are deliberately shaped and orchestrated to produce harmony.

Woolf pounces on Rodney's male vanity and his pedantry to reveal not only the folly of being masculine, but how unmasculine it is to be foolish. Rodney with his mirror, his male props about him (the faded red dressing gown, slippers, pipes, books, photographs of Greek statues) is less a man than someone playing the role of a man. His "rather prominent eyes and the impulsive stammering manner," as well as his angularity, suggest Lytton Strachey. (He did of course admire Pope.) He is not an appropriately androgynous artist. Not Don Juanish, he is merely donnish.

His fussiness about dress and propriety first amuses Katharine, then depresses her. He recommends marriage for her and all women: "Why, you're nothing at all without it; you're only half alive" (ND, 66). In a misogynist mood he boasts to Denham that Katharine is "spoilt" and leads "an odious, self-centered life." Chapter 11 is a farcical representation of the clash between the masculine and feminine, as Katharine cries "My oysters!" and William reads aloud his play. Demonstrating his theory that "every mood has its meter," he asks for her criticism, not of his skill but of his rendering of passion: "I trust you where feeling is concerned" (ND, 140). But Katharine is bored. "Still, she reflected, these sorts of skill are almost exclusively masculine; women neither practice them nor know how to value them; and one's husband's proficiency in this direction might legitimately increase one's respect for him, since mystification is no bad basis for respect" (ND, 140).

William criticizes her coldness, silence, inattention to dress, and lack of respect for her elders and betters; his praise is for her beauty and her French accent. When he criticizes her again at the Otways', she rebuffs him, and her cousin thinks that "women have a peculiar blindness to the feelings of men." Woolf describes Rodney's response in her most Austenish tone:

> Perhaps, for he was a very vain man, he was more hurt that Henry had seen him rebuffed than by the rebuff itself. He was in love with Katharine, and vanity is not decreased but increased by love, especially, one may hazard, in the presence of one's own sex. But Rodney enjoyed the courage which springs from that laughable and lovable defect, and when he had mastered his first impulse, in some way to make a fool of himself, he drew inspiration from the perfect fit of his evening dress. He chose a cigarette, tapped it on the back of his hand, displayed his exquisite pumps on the edge of the fender, and summoned his self-respect. [ND, 203]

His man-to-man talk with Henry repeats the earlier scene with Ralph, where Rodney's man-of-the-world advice about women is a result of a rebuff from Katharine:

> You talk to them about their children, if they have any, or their accomplishments—painting, gardening, poetry—they're so delightfully sympathetic. Seriously, you know I think a woman's opinion of one's poetry is always worth having. Don't ask them for their reasons. Just ask them for their feelings. [ND, 205]

Tamino says the same thing in *The Magic Flute*.

Rodney, as Don Juan, attempts to win Katharine with a patter song enumerating her faults: "Katharine doesn't like Titian. She doesn't like apricots, she doesn't like peaches, she doesn't like green peas. She likes the Elgin marbles and gray days without any sun. She's a typical example of the cold northern nature" (ND, 173). All he does is make herself clearer to herself and, as she gains in self-definition, realizing that her rebellions and dreams have a pattern, she moves further away from him.

When Don Juan suffers hell in this infernal comedy, he deserves it. After telling Mary and Katharine that he has acquired his knowledge of art from men— "it's a way men have"—he mocks Katharine in his proprietary way:

> "She pretends that she's never read Shakespeare." And why should she read Shakespeare, since she is Shakespeare—Rosalind, you know," and he gave his queer little chuckle. Somehow this compliment appeared very old-fashioned and almost in bad taste. Mary actually felt herself blush, as if he had said "the sex" or "the ladies"... "She knows enough—enough for all decent purposes. What do you women want with learning, when you have so much else—everything. I should say—everything. Leave us something, eh, Katharine?" [ND, 175–176]

Four Passionate Snails

Sex and the eighteenth century, Virginia Woolf might well agree with Brigid Brophy, are perennially interesting subjects. While the brilliant, impersonal, socially ironic style of *Night and Day* may inspire the reader to congratulate this twentieth-century writer for the sheer audacity of her tribute to Jane Austen, Woolf confided to her diary that she would rather be known as the author of *Four Passionate Snails* than as the new Jane Austen. It was Katherine Mansfield who saw the source in Austen, but missed it in Mozart: Pamina in *The Magic Flute* wishes she were a snail to hide from Sarastro.

But Woolf had more in common with "the most perfect artist among women" than comic wit; for *Night and Day* is as "biting of tongue but tender of heart" as her model's, as "impersonal" and "inscrutable." The novelist "wishes neither to reform nor to annihilate; she is silent," said Virginia Woolf in praise of Jane Austen, describing Austen as she herself might be described: "charming but perpendicular, loved at home but feared by strangers."[33] The critics berated them both for not writing of war. The little scenes they describe, like *The Magic Flute*, may be pastoral, even utopian in their expression of the dream of human goodness, of the possibility of happiness. But the struggle against the fear of death, which is the drama of the conflicts of the approach to marriage and the initiation into society, both saw as eternal. Perhaps *Night and Day* is a comic lie, but it is also as brave and affirmative an act as marriage itself was in Virginia Woolf's eyes.

As Woolf's memoirs of a dutiful daughter, *Night and Day* is remarkably free of resentment. The novel is an act of filial piety and rebellion at the same time. A gift from sister to sister, it celebrates sisterhood. It bows, awkwardly and comically, perhaps, to the women of Woolf's own family through the generous and saintly, funny and eccentric character of Mrs. Hilbery. It enshrines mothers who bless their daughters, who open the doors to love and freedom, preparing and making easier "the way of all flesh." And, most important, it buries the signature of female desire and lesbianism, Mary fingering the fur of Katharine's dress, as successfully as Mozart buried the theme of male homosexual desire in brotherhood in *The Magic Flute*. Marriage in both Woolf and Mozart is a sublimation of homosocial desire.

❦ 2 ❦

The Years *as Götterdämmerung,*
Greek Play, and Domestic Novel

It is from them that we must escape; the
hours; the works, the divisions, rigid and
straight, of the old British week.[1]

If the House be ruinous . . . all the external
Painting and Pargetting imaginable . . . can
neither secure the Inhabitants from its Fall.[2]

The ruinous house in Virginia Woolf's *The Years*[3] is inhabited by the Pargiter
family, three branches in three generations, and the novel portrays their
decline and fall with the realism of a family chronicle. At the same time, because
The Years is as daring in the use of mythical motifs and as radical in form as
Ulysses and *The Waste Land*, it attains the power of a threnody for the dying
Victorian patriarchal family. Drawing for themes and structure on both
Sophocles' *Antigone* and Wagner's *Ring of the Nibelung*,[4] the novel—entitled
"The Pargiters" in its manuscript version—is a kind of Greek opera, simultaneously a dirge and a dithyramb celebrating the death and rebirth of the Spirit
of the Year.[5] Even as a family chronicle its angle of vision is radical, for the relationships it dwells upon are those of daughter/father, sister/brother, of female
cousins, of maiden aunt with niece or nephew. The London the characters live
in is very real and very wet, at once a city of incest like Sophocles' Thebes and
yet ablaze like Wagner's Valhalla. The rose and gold light that suffuses the work
shines into some very musty corners of British family life. The fathers are
wounded from their wars; they have renounced love for money; and the
daughters are buried alive.

The Myths of Matriarchal Origins

The "modern" is as indebted to anthropology as the Victorian is to history.
When Joyce wrote *Ulysses* he could expect that educated readers (with a little

academic guidance) could at once read his book as a modern Odyssey, and readers of Eliot's *The Waste Land* hardly needed his footnotes to recognize its sources in *The Golden Bough* and *From Ritual to Romance*. But the matriarchal mythology employed in *The Years* was largely unknown to readers educated in a patriarchal culture. Although both *The Golden Bough* and *From Ritual to Romance* reflect an urge in late Victorian anthropology to get back to the mother of us all—consider Schliemann's seeking the bottom layer of Troy or the positing by Bebel and Bachhofen and Engels and certain utopian socialists of a peaceful prehistory, a warm woman-world, which would serve as an ideal to work toward—Frazer in reaction concentrated almost exclusively upon rituals of the death and rebirth of the male/son while scarcely noting that such rituals were once part of the worship of the Great Mother. Freud himself described the unconscious as one of the bottom layers of Troy. Victorian readers knew the ancient goddesses only through what Jane Harrison calls the corruption of their original positive force, through the retelling of their stories in classical Greece and Rome. T. S. Eliot's mythic passages express pity for the suffering male; in *The Waste Land* he appears to attribute loss of spirituality, order, communal purity, and joy to the influence of women, the masses, and Jews—precisely those outsiders to patriarchal culture whose spirituality and vision Woolf celebrates in *The Years*.[6]

Joyce seemed to Woolf childish and "egotistical." Her objection to Joyce was, in the first place, to his giving prominence to individual heroes, whose monologues or dialogues she considered of less interest than the voice and spirit of a people, especially as uttered in "the chorus" of working men and women of all classes, once the serious "song" of drama.[7] But egotism she always associated with men. She abhorred the confessional and personal style of self-pity in art, wishing instead to raise the level of seriousness in the novel, the woman's form, to that of Greek drama, and of Wagnerian opera as she heard it performed at Bayreuth. (The same impulse to dignify and historicize lesbianism is behind Natalie Barney and Renee Vivien's use of archaic rather than modern French for their Sapphic poems.)

Preclassical Greece, in Jane Harrison's recreation of it, shows woman as a splendid spiritual source of society's rituals of breaking apart and coming together, of "natural" time and the death and rebirth of the Year-Spirit. Rich in imaginative resourcefulness and eloquent in style, Harrison's work aroused Woolf's own quest for a female past. When Harrison demonstrated that only the worship of the Mother Goddess had produced works of art representing "dualities" and "trinities," the duo of mother and maiden or the trio of three women, and claimed that even the concept of a triune god, three persons in one, was exclusively traceable to worship of the goddess, Woolf felt armed for that aesthetically most insistent and exciting aspect of her art, the rhythmic, repetitive "three." That plaintive motif, sometimes a dialectic, sometimes a dirge, is repeated like a witch's spell or a child's nursery rhyme, "remember, remember, remember," and readers are tempted to ask: Is this then the final form of the "female sentence" that Woolf had sought since *A Room of One's Own?* In a sense *The Years* is *about* repetition as well as repetitive in style. Structurally the obsessive repeating seems circular; it seems to mimic the spiraling movement of the novel downward to Dante's Inferno, to Wagner's underground caves of the dwarfs, to Antigone's brick burial-mound; we seem to hear a wailing aloud like Demeter's after her daughter Persephone, calling her up from the underworld, that the old year may give birth to the new, the younger generation repeat the old patterns but "live better." A lullaby and a lament, the music of the novel is also lyrical, full of songs like Sara's for singing oneself to sleep or like the care-taker's children's, for waking up the world. *The Years* offers a ritual purification and purgation of the whole community such as the Eleusinian mysteries pro-vided and such as Wagner had aspired to in his building at Bayreuth and with his essays on music-drama.[8] Elevating the role of the chorus in the modern novel to its position in Greek drama as Virginia Woolf did was the aesthetic equivalent of a revolutionary political act, a socialist's demonstration of faith in the people. I hear the song of the children as the vatic voice of the Delphic oracle.[9] (Woolf said the novel had been boiling within her since her visit to Delphi.) It is a riddle that the poet-priest must answer—but the potential priest, North, is nowhere to be seen when it is uttered. Maggie and Eleanor, mother and maid, are the attendant priestesses. They do not translate, they accept. "And now?" the novel asks. And now it is for North to interpret the lives of the stevedores and seamstresses to his own class, and for Peggy to heal their wounded in the forthcoming battles. The song of the children and the inability of anyone but Eleanor to understand it represents British imperialism come home to roost, the Indian and African languages of the children of the colonies that displace the mother tongue in polyglot London. But Woolf's deliberate use of nonsensical Greek sounds recalls Aristophanes' *The Birds* and its sounds without meaning, as well as the scene in Peacock's *Crotchet Castle* that mocks reformers' speeches as Aristophanes' babbling bird-speak in Cloud Cuckoo Land or "Nephelococcygia." All during the writing of *The Years*, as her diary testifies so powerfully, Woolf was worried that her socialist-feminist reforming zeal would spoil the novel. But the song has a deeper resonance when we recall that Woolf heard the birds speaking in Greek during her "madness." Greek was the language of patriarchal power, the symbol of English male control over cul-ture. Her attempts to master the language and to find Sappho paralleled that of other women modernists like Barney and Vivien. Many heroes of folktale and legend gain their power from understanding the birds, Siegfried and Papageno among them. This linguistic power of mystical translation is an analogue to the polyglossia, or "speaking in tongues," which the children, like religious figures, do in their song. As part of her feminist project to create "a little language un-known to men," this scene, where a woman instinctively understands speech unintelligible to others, reflects a mystical communion between women and children like mothers' understanding of baby talk, on one level, and on another the social worker's solidarity with immigrants. It is significant that the house where the party is held is recognized by the women as the scene of their former efforts at reform, Delia for her Irish cause, and Rose for her suffrage meeting. It resembles the house in Gerrard Street where the leftist 1917 Club used to meet (including Jane Harrison) and Woolf's diary in the years following the Russian Revolution reveals how important it was to both her and Leonard. While the last scene is a "family reunion," the family whose life is celebrated is the *political* family of antifascists, the left's ideal replacement of the moribund patriarchal family. One reason for the phenomenal success of *The Years* as a best seller in this bleak decade may have been its vision of working-class children and middle-class reformers greeting the rosy dawn.

Stucco and Gold

An example of the novel's complexity and beauty may be found in Woolf's variations upon the meanings of the word "Pargiter" itself, the family's and at first the novel's name. It is defined in the *English Dialect Dictionary* of Joseph Wright, an Oxford professor of working-class origins who bore witness to the richness of the English speech of ordinary people. I first looked into the *Dictionary*—and read, absorbed the *Life of Joseph Wright* by his wife Elizabeth—in response to Woolf's note in *Three Guineas* that recommends these along with Margaret Llewelyn-Davies's *Life as We Have Known It, by Cooperative Working Women*.[10] A philological prodigy, Wright compiled many dictionaries and grammars and was an "idle" man (as he claimed) only in the sense that he came from a township of that name.[11] Virginia Woolf admired the work of a man who gave her more tools for her trade, for work was one Victorian value that she accepted.

"Pargetter" means plasterer. Any reader of *A Writer's Diary* can imagine the pleasure Woolf had in finding that word and using it. For she always used images of building to convey what heavy work writing was: "stone-breaking," "bricklaying." Eleanor is the pargetter in *The Years*. She spends her life literally plastering the ceilings of the slums, fixing leaky roofs, and cleaning smelly drains. The word bears also the meaning of lying or covering up in the sense of "whitewash," but that is the province of the men in the novel (Abel Pargiter's affair, Morris in the law courts, Martin in the chop house, Edward's translating from the Greek). Abel Pargiter could have consulted his daughter about the leak in his mistress's roof. But the positive meaning is to "patch up," as Eleanor does. As guardian of the hearth she keeps the family together by mending the chimney. (A literary example of the destruction of the family through neglect of the crack in the chimney is Ibsen's *The Master Builder*.) The traditional materials for pargetting were lime and cow dung; Sara calls their houses "caves of mud and dung." The cave and the grave are female symbols, with ambiguities Woolf was aware of, male symbols of structure are the chimney and the tower. In "The Leaning Tower," a lecture in which she criticizes certain male poets of the thirties, Woolf calls their middle-class birth a "tower of stucco" and their expensive education a "tower of gold."[12] In her eyes their poetry was only a parget on a ruinous house.

The house, then, is both a grave and a tower. And the shape of *The Years* is a cone or helix—for every one of Woolf's novels has a geometrical structure, from the tunnel of *The Voyage Out* to the circle of *Night and Day* and the triangle of *To the Lighthouse*. Its base is the burning circle of London. Seen in small, it is a red pillar-box laden with explosives; in large, a golden Tower of Babel tottering like the patriarchal family and capitalist culture, from internal rot and external warfare.

The Years moves in elemental reality from the cesspool to the fountain, the rubbish heap to the pure flame, the "cave of mud and dung" to Kitty's fruitful Northern land, the polluted city air with its babble of voices to the fleecy clouds and golden sky full of birds. Earth, air, fire, and water are the ancient forms of life; they change and yet remain the same, an affirmation of Bergsonian durée, Woolf's own personal quest for spiritual permanence, and the years themselves, the heroines of this novel.

Pargetting as painting to hide ugliness is used in Ben Jonson's *Silent Woman*: "She's above fiftie too, and pargets." Peggy is well under fifty and she pargets; Eleanor says that lipstick would make her feel "bedizened." The American professor's wife pargets in the Oxford section, and Sara in an extraordinary metaphor tells North how angry the sight of a wealthy woman painting her mouth made her: "polishing that spade, her mouth." Like the artist, the pargetter is both a liar and a builder; she embellishes the old house of fiction, and she secures the foundation of the new.

Dictionaries delighted Virginia Woolf; they provided her with her tools, words:

> the wildest, freest, most irresponsible, most unteachable of all things. Of course, you can catch them and sort them and place them in alphabetical order in dictionaries. But words do not live in dictionaries; they live in the mind—they are much less bound by ceremony and convention than we are. Royal words mate with commoners. English words marry French words, German words, Indian words, Negro words, if they have a fancy. Indeed, the less we enquire into the past of our dear Mother English the better it will be for that lady's reputation. For she has gone-a-roving, a-roving . . .

Words need privacy, she says; "Our unconsciousness is their privacy; our darkness is their light."[13]

In that vivid darkness of her dictionary wanderings and her wanderings in the lore of Jane Harrison, Virginia Woolf would have discovered that "Eleanor" is "Helen," from Helios, the sun; she puts the sunflower symbol on the houses she builds, later remembering the crack in the *terra cotta*. A "helyer" is one who lays tiles on a roof, covers up or buries. "Hel" is the underworld. The Pargiter house is in Abercorn Terrace, not to be found on London street maps. But "abier" is to be found in Wright, meaning dead but unburied. With "corn" and "terrace" it suggests the ritual of the death and rebirth of the Year-Spirit and Antigone's burial of her brother. The dictionary further reveals the irony that "Abel" denotes a man who lives in continence after marriage; "Edward" means guardian of property; "Eugénie," like Virginia Woolf's first name "Adeline," means wellborn.[14] Mother English does not always marry well, however, and the richness of reborn "René" and fruitful "Pomjalovsky" are turned into the lifeless English puddings of "Renny" and "Brown."

Many critics have felt that *The Years* is a "dead" novel; one of these was Leonard Woolf, who was sure that art and politics should not be mixed—as Virginia Woolf tells us in *A Writer's Diary*.[15] *She* was not so sure, and she worried about the problem, thinking of words as "sticky things" that wouldn't coalesce properly and of the artist who gave in to the state's demands for propaganda as cheating the public by giving it "bread made with plaster." She, like Antigone, was made for loving not hating, but still she asserts that her values are higher than the state's. For British male readers *The Years* may be bitter bread, but it is honest and made with the sweat of her brow. The only sensible words uttered in the great war, Eleanor thinks, were Nurse Cavell's "Patriotism is not enough." But the statue of Cavell, with these words in small lettering at its base but the contradictory "For King and Country" written out large above, was another "cover-up" or pargetting of the truth. The purpose of the statue, said a writer in *The New Statesman*, was to insult the Germans, not to honor Nurse Cavell, who had given her life to help British and French soldiers escape from Belgium. She looked "like an advertisement for a complete nurse's outfit," he added; "a monument so conceived could not be a success, for compromise in art is never successful."[16]

When Peggy says that the statue "always reminds me of an advertisement of sanitary towels" (*Years*, p. 336)—the nurse in the symbolic statue at the top holding out hands draped in cloth—she shocks her Aunt Eleanor. (Was Woolf the first woman novelist to mention menstruation?) As a fusion of sexual and political meanings, this "moment" in the novel is the second of three. The first is the crippling of Rose's imagination by the pervert near the pillar-box. (The suffragettes borrowed Parnell's tactics by blowing up pillar-boxes as symbols of the state; they were red and, in shape, ambivalently male/female; they bore the King's [or Queen's] initials.) Rose, later, becomes violent in her cause, is imprisoned and forcibly fed, and yet in the war she fights for the same state that jailed her. The third "moment" occurs simultaneously with the second. While Peggy is dining with Eleanor, North is being initiated by Sara, with their ritual object "the hair of the Jew in the bath," over which Sara the Sibyl prophesies to North the potential poet-priest and converts his disgust into a recognition of common cause with the outcasts and scapegoats of the world. As a poet North is primitive, but at Delia's party he asks where are the "Sweeps and the Sewermen, the Seamstresses and the Stevedores": there are only Duchesses and Dons, Drabs and Drones. (Sara had said, "No idols.") He doesn't believe in "joining societies, in signing manifestoes" (p. 404). "If they want to reform the world, he thought, why not begin there, at the centre, with themselves?" (p. 405); "and we who make idols of other People . . . only add to the deformity, and stoop ourselves" (p. 380).

While North's initiation proceeds, with Sara riddling and laughing like the

Delphic oracle, Eleanor the washing woman plays Hygeia to her niece, Peggy the doctor. Woolf remembers from Jane Harrison that in antiquity the arts of healing derived from the arts of bathing and purification. Both scenes explode with the sexual and political shock waves, as the relations between Eleanor and Sara, two childless aunts, and their niece and nephew reach mythic proportions. Eleanor's furious ripping of a picture of Mussolini is a surprising act, but more probing is Sara's insisting that North relate his reading of Marvell's poem to "Abrahamson in the tallow trade" and to his own brotherhood with the poor, the Jews, the conspirators. "The Garden" celebrates solitude, but Sara is trying to tell North of her own struggles to retain her individuality and "stain . . . the unstained hand" by joining the "conspiracy" (p. 341).[17]

Abrahamson is a fellow worker in North's own trade of "purifying" hides and fleeces; he transforms mutton fat (from around the kidneys) into candle light and washing soap—another example of the dirt/cleanliness, dark/light imagery of the novel. Ritual purification and sacrifice are also suggested; the biblical Abraham's willingness to sacrifice his son Isaac softens God's heart into asking for a ram instead, and the ram's horn or shofar, blown after fasting and purification, celebrates the beginning of the Jewish New Year. In her own life Virginia Woolf shared her bath with a Jew and a socialist, feeling a feminist common cause with the oppressed more intensely as the fascism of the thirties spread.[18] Now, as we read *The Years*, we see a prophetic anticipation of the holocaust in the references to Jews, from the opening suggestion that Mrs. Levy's life and death were richer, despite poverty, than those of her genteel visitors, to the sexual overtones of Abrahamson's hair in the bath. Throughout, the diaspora of the Pargiters is connected with the diaspora of the Jews; as they split apart they also come together in a conspiracy of rebirth and renewal. Sara, shabby scapegoat that she is in her own family, sings her little song about "the Queen of England" asking her to tea: "and which shall it be; the gold or the rose; for all are in holes, my stockings, said she" (p. 370). The parallel in Virginia Woolf's own life is her refusal to accept an honor from the British empire. The way Nicholas and Sara mock one another, "Sara singing her little song" and "the professor preaching his little sermon," seems to Eleanor admirable and loving; one imagines a similar affectionate mockery between Leonard and Virginia Woolf. Her *Three Guineas* and also *The Years* say to the world, "scapegoats of the world, unite"; "outsiders" all, these have already loosened their chains. Women, Jews, workers, homosexuals together can transform their diaspora into a conspiracy for "Justice and Liberty."

The Kettle That Would Not Boil

One of the most movingly presented motifs in the novel is that of the female as the vessel of life. The clearest symbolic form of the motif is Rose Pargiter's brass kettle embossed with roses and having a serpentine spout (the serpent is the most ancient symbol of the Mother Goddess.) The characters are defined in their relation to it. As Rose dies, the kettle won't boil but Eleanor patiently fiddles with the wick; the dreamy Delia wants to know if a kettle *must* boil; Martin declares often how much he hates it, defining his own relations with women (as a man who pays for love) in his song of the King of Spain's daughter, wondering to himself what the "silver nutmeg tree" means. The Great Mother's symbols are transformational; she changes the body into a vessel; hers are the magic kettle, the ever-boiling pot of folktales, the cauldron of incarnation, birth, and rebirth; also the cave, Hel or the underworld, and grave jars. Neumann writes:

> . . . the vessel lies at the core of the elementary character of the Feminine. At all stages of the primordial mysteries it is the central symbol of their realization. In the mysteries of preservation this symbol is projected upon the cave as sacral precinct and temple—the "sheltering structure" of the vessel gives its form to the grave, the underworld dwelling, as it does to the dwelling house on earth— the collective of village and city is a symbol of the Feminine. Their establishment originally began with the marking of a circle, the conjuring up of the Great Round, which reveals its female nature equally well as containing periphery or as womb and center.[19]

Each section of the novel has a central vessel; cups, glasses, bowls, and jars are provided by women. Even the least likely, Celia, has a bowl of rose petals. Despite thirteen broken glasses Delia provides more goblets for the last ritual libation of the book. The pink jars and bowls of Rose's death-chamber suggest blood and milk, nourishment and death, as does little Rose's pink frock worn on the day her mother dies, and the day of her sexual initiation. Eleanor in mediating between her mother's dying and Rose's fears pauses, becomes a Greek goddess—"she raised her arms slightly, as if she were carrying a pitcher, an earthenware pitcher on her head" (p. 43)[20]—and the dog's bowl with its yellow liquid takes on a classical significance. The jug "stained pink by the setting sun," bringing Delia at her mother's deathbed to "some borderland between life and death," foreshadows the "empty milk jugs" outside her door later signifying the violence of her life. Digby stands at Rose's funeral "with his top-hat held like some sacred vessel." Had they loved each other as Eugénie and Abel? we ask as Rose thinks of Digby on her deathbed, and the incest theme (also in *Antigone* and *The Ring*) later haunts Maggie and Martin, cousins, who think they might be brother and sister.

The moon motif identifies money with chastity; consistently coinlike, the moon suggests the only value woman has in a patriarchal world, that of private property. Oddly enough, the only similar use of the motif I know is in Oscar Wilde's *Salomé*, where the heroine is scapegoat also for a decadent patriarchal world: Salomé sees the moon as a silver coin, "a little piece of money."[21]

The Antigone motif beginning in the burial chamber "Abercorn Terrace" extends to young Sara's bedroom where she reads Edward's translation of the scene where Antigone is buried alive. Sara sleeps and sings throughout the novel; she is the "divine voice" of the oracle, unconscious and spontaneous, crying "No idols." She, the hunchback, says we are all "cripples in a cave," and the novel is full of deformities from Abel Pargiter's crippled hand (which derives from Lord Larrian's in Meredith's *Diana of the Crossways*) to the noseless flower-seller and the child of Eleanor's "Jews" who has six toes on one foot. Abel Pargiter fears Sara and cannot bear deformities in children. The crippled mind is that of Edward the classicist who cannot tell North what the chorus says in *Antigone*. What the chorus does, of course, is to curse the old men who use big words.

The water symbolism bears a similar theme; the rain purifies, as Eleanor purifies the drains and sinks of the slums. The Pargiters quarrel over the bathroom, and Eleanor is ashamed of it as she tries to sell the house; Rose remembers slitting her wrists there, and she returns from an excursion as a suffragette for a ritual bath. Eleanor shares with North her joy at her shower bath; Edward's corruption is suggested by his being unable to "pull the string of the shower bath" (p. 409). "Why can't he flow?" North asks. "Why's it all locked up, refrigerated? Because he's a priest, a mystery monger . . . this guardian of beautiful words." The river and the Round Pond are central to the landscape, and the theme of renewal through water runs through the whole novel like the motif of the Rhinemaidens. The ode to mother water (pp. 47-48) is an astonishing piece of writing and contains all the themes of the novel:

> The fine rain, the gentle rain, poured equally over the mitred and the bareheaded with an impartiality which suggested that the god of rain, if there were a god, was thinking Let it not be restricted to the very wise, the very great, but let all breathing kind, the munchers and chewers, the ignorant, the unhappy, those who toil in the furnace making innumerable copies of the same pot, those who bore red hot minds through contorted letters, and also Mrs. Jones in the alley, share my bounty.

Cleanliness is not only mythical and magical, it is a witty evocation of British life. As Rose dies she worries about the washing bill for the clean tablecloth; little Rose's nurse doesn't notice her fatal trip to Lamley's shop because she is talking to "Mrs. C. who came every week with the washing"; Rose wears a dirty pink frock because the clean one hadn't come back from the wash; Colonel Pargiter gives his mistress two sovereigns "out of his litle gold case" for the washing; and later Crosby trundles across London with Martin's laundry to hear his complaints about a scorch on his silk pyjamas. The dirty linen seems related to "pargetting" or covering up. Eleanor imagines that people think her "an old maid who washes and watches birds," but she is the purifying Mother Goddess looking for the owl and hearing all the birds that symbolize, again, the Great Mother. The birds don't speak to her in Greek as they did to her creator; they say things like "Take two coos, Taffy" and fill the novel with song. In fact the novel so wittily gives us clouds and birds that we expect a *Lysistrata*. But Woolf, a female Aristophanes, gives us instead the reasons why Englishwomen did not unite in withholding their favors from men to stop all wars. In *A Room of One's*

Own she had blamed the mothers and grandmothers for not educating their daughters, endowing women's colleges. In *The Years* she tells us why our more recent ancestresses did not change the world.

The Oxford scenes are instructive here. The actual sources are in Joseph Wright's biography and Mrs. Humphry Ward's *Recollections.*[22] Robson is a working-class professor like Wright, and his pride in his mother and her portrait (p. 72) are taken directly from the biography. Kitty thinks he's "the nicest man" she ever met and is jealous of Nell and full of self-pity, feeling limited by her gentility from ever accomplishing anything. In "Two Women," a review of Lady Stephen's *Emily Davies and Girton College*, Woolf had written: "From the huge middle class few women rose to eminence, nor has the drabness of their lot received the attention which has been bestowed on the splendours of the great and the miseries of the poor"; and "Half occupied, always interrupted, with much leisure but little time to themselves and no money of their own, these armies of listless women were either driven to find solace and occupation in religion, or, if that failed, they took, as Miss Nightingale said, 'to that perpetual day-dreaming which is so dangerous.' Some, indeed, envied the working classes, and Miss Martineau frankly hailed the ruin of her family with delight."[23] The same essay says sharply, "It is difficult to be sure, after all, that a college don is the highest type of humanity known to us" (p. 204)—which anticipates both Old Chuffy and Edward.

Another source for Kitty's tea with the Robsons, which in working-class style includes a large plate of fish, is the visits of the Woolfs to members of Margaret Llewelyn-Davies's cooperative Working Women's Guild, described vividly in *Beginning Again.* Here Leonard Woolf tells of his wife's untiring labor in politics at the "grass roots" level. He attributes his own conversion to socialism to the slum settlement work he did with Virginia's cousin, Marny Vaughan— compare Eleanor's work in *The Years.* He describes Margaret Davies as Woolf describes Eleanor:

> . . . . she was able to inspire thousands of uneducated women with her own passion, both for "Sweetness and light", also for liberty, equality and fraternity. [She had a quality which can] only be described as a kind of virginal purity of mind and motive which—I am afraid it sounds rather absurd, but is nonetheless true—made her a kind of Joan of Arc to her cohorts of Lancashire and Yorkshire housewives in her crusade against ignorance, poverty and injustice. [*Beginning Again*, p. 103]

Her devotion to her father and her combination of classical Greek and fresh English features bring her even closer to the fictional Eleanor. She quoted Maude Royden in a pamphlet written in the thirties: "Nothing will persuade me that the world is not ready for an ideal for which I am ready." She asked women to see to it that "no military training or military corps of any kind are allowed in the schools, whether openly avowed or disguised as physical exercises," and declared: "It is shocking beyond words when boys are put through bayonet practice; and the idea that military discipline is valuable morally belongs to the capitalist world."[24]

Other bits of the portraits of women in *The Years* are supplied from Mrs. Humphry Ward, the author of *Robert Elsmere*, who built the Passmore Settlement Houses and was one of the first examiners at Somerville College but was too genteel to send her own daughter there. In an unsigned review of Mrs. Ward's *Recollections*, Woolf praises her recreation of Oxford, where "she gradually became acquainted with all the academic gods and goddesses; and her account of Mark Pattison and Mrs. Mark, afterward Lady Dilke, of Jowett, Pater, T. H. Green, Creighton, Freeman and J. R. Green, all of whom were her friends."[25] It was typical of Woolf's attempt to understand the age that she should try to see it through the eyes of a woman with whom she was unsympathetic. Kitty's Grosvenor Square house recreates another section of Mrs. Ward's life.[26] Woolf called her later review of the biography "The Compromise"; in it one sees the source of Kitty's failure to read history seriously:

> None of the great Victorian reputations has sunk lower than that of Mrs. Humphry Ward. Her novels, already strangely out of date, hang in the lumber-room of letters like the mantles of our aunts, and produce in us the same desire that they do to smash the window and let in the air, to light the fire and pile the rubbish on top. Some books fade into a gentle picturesqueness with age. But there is a quality, perhaps a lack of quality, about the novels of Mrs. Ward which makes it improbable that, however much they fade, they will ever become picturesque. Their large bunches of jet, their intricate festoons of ribbon, skilfully and firmly fabricated as they are, obstinately resist the endearments of time.
>
> Of Mrs. Ward's descent there is no need to speak. She had by birth and temperament all those qualities which fitted her, before she was twenty, to be the friend of Mark Pattison, and "the best person," in the opinion of J. R. Green, to be asked to contribute a volume to a history of Spain . . . She will marry a Don; she will rear a small family; she will circulate Plain Facts on Infant Feeding in the Oxford slums; she will help to found Somerville College; she will sit up writing learned articles for the Dictionary of Christian Biography; and at last, after a hard life of unremunerative toil, she will finish the book which fired her fancy as a girl and will go down to posterity as the author of a standard work upon the origins of modern Spain. But, as every one knows, the career which seemed so likely, and would have been so honorable, was interrupted by the melodramatic success of Robert Elsmere. History was entirely forsaken for fiction and the Origins of Modern Spain became transmuted into the Origins of Modern France, a phantom book which the unfortunate Robert Elsmere never succeeded in writing.
>
> It is here that we begin to scribble in the margin of Mrs. Ward's life those endless notes of interrogation. After Robert Elsmere—which we may grant to have been inevitable—we can never cease to ask ourselves, why? Why desert the charming old house in Russell Square for the splendors and expenses of Grosvenor Place? Why wear beautiful dresses, why keep butlers and carriages, why give luncheon parties and week-end parties, why buy a house in the country and pull it down and build it up again, when all this can only be achieved by writing

at breathless speed novels which filial piety calls autumnal, but the critics, unfortunately, must call bad? Mrs. Ward might have replied that the compromise, if she agreed to call it so, was entirely justified . . . Without her novel-writing thousands of poor children would have ranged the streets unsheltered. It is impossible to remain a schoolgirl in the Bodleian for ever, and, once you breast the complicated currents of modern life at their strongest, there is little time to ask questions, and none to answer them.

It is tempting to imagine what the school girl in the Bodleian would have said to her famous successor. "Literature has no guerdon for bread-students, to quote the expressive German phrase . . . only to the silent ardor, the thirst, the disinterestedness of the true learner, is she prodigal of all good gifts." But Mrs. Humphry Ward, the famous novelist, might have rounded upon her critic of twenty. "It is all very well," she might have said, "to accuse me of having wasted my gifts; but the fault lay with you. Yours was the age of seeing visions; and you spent it in dreaming how you stopped the Princess of Wales' runaway horses, and were rewarded by 'a command' to appear at Buckingham Palace. It was you who starved my imagination and condemned it to the fatal compromise."[27]

One of Mrs. Ward's stories may be the source for the song of the little Londoners at the end of the novel with its garbled Greek accents. She tells of a little London boy and his parents embarrassed by just such a gaffe before the famous Oxford professor of Greek.

The portrait of Lucy Craddock in *The Years* (with Kitty's "How I loved her") is paralleled in Virginia Woolf's recollection in *A Writer's Diary* (with the same words) of the death of her own Greek teacher, Janet Case. From Woolf's *Letters* (p. 1242) we learn that she had confessed to Janet Case her half-brother's sexual advances, and that the teacher had already been disgusted at his fondling of Virginia over her Greek. In the *Diary* (p. 275) Woolf wrote, "How great a visionary part she has played in my life, till the visionary became part of the fictitious, not of the real life." In an uncollected obituary notice signed "an old pupil" and appearing on the same page as notice of the death of her nephew Julian Bell in Spain (*The Times*, July 22, 1937, p. 16) Woolf called Case "a noble Athena" who broke down "the tradition that only men acted in the Greek play."

> When she left Cambridge she settled in London and for many years earned her living by teaching in schools and in private houses, a great variety of pupils, some seriously to pass examinations, others less seriously to read Greek for their own amusement.
>
> Undoubtedly if the pupil were in earnest Janet Case was a highly competent tutor. She was no dilettante; she could edit a Greek play and win praise from the great Verrall himself. But if the pupil were destined to remain an amateur Janet Case accepted the fact without concealing the drawbacks and made the best of it. The grammar was shut and the play opened. Somehow the masterpieces of Greek drama were stormed, without grammar, without accents, but somehow, under her compulsion, so sane and yet so stimulating, out they shone, if inaccessible still supremely desirable. And then the play was shut, and with her generous tolerance for youth and its egotism she would let herself be drawn into

argument, made to discuss modern fiction, since she had said that Euripides reminded her of Meredith; made to thrash out the old problem of artist and teacher, since she had said that Aeschylus reminded her of Wordsworth. And so by transition, rising naturally from the play, last night's party was reached, and the frock that was worn and the talk that was talked at last night's party, until even she could stretch her one hour no farther but must cycle off, with her little bag of text books, to teach another pupil, perhaps in Islington, perhaps in May-fair.

In a pencilled note written a few days before her death she recalled how Lady D. "used to come to her lesson like a nymph scarcely dry from her bath in a gauze wrap--and used to say 'My good woman' in an expostulatory tone when I objected to an adjective not agreeing with its noun or some such trifle." The words, with their humorous appreciation both of the nymph and of the noun serve perhaps to explain why it was that she, who was both so sound a scholar and so fine and dignified a presence, never held any of those posts that might have given her an academic position and saved her from the stress of private teaching. She enjoyed too many things--teaching a real scholar, and teaching a real world-ling, going in and out of pupils' houses, noting their characters, divining their difficulties--she enjoyed them all too much and music and acting and pictures to concentrate upon one ambition.

The little house at Hampstead where her sister taught children, and friends came, and old pupils brought her new problems to solve, made a happier setting for her buoyant and unfettered spirit than any college.

Woolf loved the worker as well as the scholar:

Her Greek was connected, naturally, seeing that she was the niece of Sir James Stansfield, the reformer, with the life, with the politics of her day. She found time for committees, for the suffrage, for the Women's Cooperative Guild, of which her friend, Margaret Llewelyn-Davies was secretary; for all causes that were then advanced and in dispute. In her way she was pioneer; but her way was one that kept her in the background, a counsellor rather than a champion, listening to the theories of others with a little chuckle of merriment, opening her beautiful veiled eyes with a sudden flash of sympathy and laughter but for herself she wanted no prominence, no publicity. She was contemplative, reticent, with-drawn . . . Her life was . . . a last lesson, in gaiety, courage, and love.

An Opera for the Oppressed

Like its companion "novel of fact" *Night and Day*, *The Years* is fully orches-trated as an opera. *Night and Day* is structured on Mozart's *The Magic Flute* and built on the same Masonic scaffolding and architectural imagery as the opera. While *Night and Day* is scored for flute and piano, lovers' duets and quartets, comic recreations of Papageno, Sarastro, and the Queen of the Night in the characters of Ralph, Mr. Hilbery, and Mrs. Hilbery, it seriously means to mock the theme of *The Magic Flute*, which is patriarchy's most exquisite celebration of itself as civilization, by invoking a less severe and more feminine alternative.

Night and Day is shaped in the circle of Dante's *Divine Comedy* in thirty-three chapters of classical eighteenth-century prose, whose most characteristic note is its imitation of Mozart's "triple accord," the speech of the narrator and the characters being punctuated by a deliberate rhythmic penchant for saying things three times.

The Years is romantic, Wagnerian, loosely structured on *The Ring*, shaped in a Dantean downward-moving spiral within the burning circle of London, and full of allusions to Purgatory and Hell. It is Virginia Woolf's *Twilight of the Gods*, with the old order crumbling and the new not yet achieved. The jacket for the first American edition pictures London from above, with Big Ben dominating the landscape and set at four o'clock. The doomed old gods of the novel, as of the opera, are capitalism, the state, and the domestic *lares and penates* of the patriarchal family. The orchestration is bigger and brassier, a sort of Wagnerian contest between the single voices and massed street noises, from men crying "old iron" to organ grinders, newsboys, and loudspeakers. The instrumentation is very brassy indeed, from cornets and drums to automobiles' horns. Against the noise of history on the march, London on the move, the single voice soars and falters, breaks, tries again, lifts itself above the chorus, sings with the mass, repeats itself, in various accents and inflections, demanding, as *The Ring* does, despite everything despicable in human history, our human passion for "joostice and liberty." Less lyrical than *The Waves* (her *Parsifal*), *The Years* skillfully blends mythic leitmotifs with realistic detail. The ear which hears the downhill tramp of the world the Victorian patriarchs made from 1880 to 1937, has perfect pitch; it cringes, but it records accurately the cries of the rich and the poor, the reformers and the professors, the failures and the successes. In the end, with Eleanor in her red and gold cloak, radiant as the sun that has been her symbol (usurped from her father) we welcome the dawn with the unintelligible song of the children of the future:

> Etho passo tanno hai,
> Fai donk to tu do,
> Mai to, kai to, lai to see
> Toh dom to tuh do—
>
> Fanno to par, etto to mar,
> Timin tudo, tido,
> Foll to gar in, mitno to par,
> Eido, tedo, meido—
>
> Chree to gay ei,
> Geeray didax . . .
>
> [pp. 439–40]

Our ears cringe at the accent, Latin words and Cockney English mixed with echoes of Greek. But Eleanor, Woolf's Brünnhilde, has faith in the working classes' song of freedom. No false note of nostalgia intrudes; no utopian pretense of class comradeship mars the clarity of vision. There has been "no speech," "no peroration." The nameless children of the caretaker in "harsh" voices, "hideous" accents, ring in a world that only those ancient Valkyries, Eleanor and Maggie, can recognize as "beautiful." Eleanor flings the curtains open, ending, as the *Götterdämmerung* does, on a note of hope. A large symphonic sound in red and gold,[28] *The Years* treats the triumphs and terrors of a family whose fortunes decline with British imperialism. Dissonance and discord mark their last meeting, which also spirals downward from the top floor to the basement of a Bloomsbury flat. The dawn viewed from the downstairs windows, Woolf is telling us, is red. (Eleanor is off to the East again, perhaps to Tibet or India.) It is both a prophecy and a wish.

It seems to me that Virginia Woolf uses *The Ring* in two ways. She takes *The Ring*'s structure and technique, the interweaving of motifs and the story of the downfall of the old gods for money and the renunciation of love, and at the same time she suggests that the Wagnerian ideas, with their own superman hero and anti-Semitism which heralded the doom of the nineteenth and twentieth centuries, betray the theme of freedom the music itself expresses. This was, aesthetically, a perfect choice of structure; and with the underpinnings of Dante and Sophocles, her dialectic of descent does not despair. The sun goes down, in such scenes of sunset splendor and sunset sadness as are hardly to be found in our literature, only perhaps in French painting of the period. But, she asserts, the sun also rises and she is a woman. Mistress of all the mythologies and mysteries, the meanings of our ancient symbology, Woolf makes the magic mumbo-jumbo work rationally. She had brilliantly reversed the role of the dread Queen of the Night from Mozart's *Magic Flute* in *Night and Day*, to make woman, mother, radiant with daylight, love, and abundance, denying the opera's and the ancient Masonic myth's associations of evil, sexuality, and death with women. In *The Years*, she does even more for the women of England than her most hostile critics have thought. As *Night and Day* celebrates the joyful eccentricities of her aunts and her mother and sister, *The Years* celebrates their less lovable sisters, the women who had her least natural sympathy ("They're not like us," the old schoolboy rhyme runs, "Miss Beale and Miss Buss")—and frames in fiction the maddening, puritanical life and work of her Quaker aunt's *Light Arising: Thoughts on the Central Radiance*.[29] The sun is a woman, says *The Years*, and the moon, a coin, hard and bright, cold and silvery, represents male obsessions with woman's chastity—for money is associated with the male from the opening sixpence with which Abel Pargiter rewards Martin, to the sixpence worth of song for which Martin pays the children at the end. *Three Guineas* asserts it uncompromisingly—money and private property are male; they cause war and fascism and belong to what Woolf calls in *A Room of One's Own* the childhood of life in the patriarchy. It is Nicholas the homosexual, the exile, a victim like women and Jews, a scapegoat of this patriarchal system, who sees that the human race is in its infancy.

What a radical novel *The Years* is, and no wonder men don't like it and women do, that it was a best-seller, a popular novel—and a critical failure. The common readers have given it their approval. Perhaps they have felt unconsciously its slap in the face to sexist interpreters of the collective unconscious. Entrenched academic critics have sensed that Woolf's eye and her ear have recorded the crashing and banging, the trombones and barrel organs, of their patriarchal ideas and ideals, slipping "downhill all the way," a culture "blaring itself to perdition." Wagner's *Ring* is popular too, with "ordinary people" and women. Men don't like to be blamed for the sins of their fathers. As she declares in *Three Guineas*, she was an outsider to it all: ". . . as a woman, I have no country. As a woman I want no country. As a woman my country is the whole world" (*TG*, p. 166). But like her heroine Woolf is less disposed to destroy than to patch up: "this drop of pure, if irrational emotion she will make serve her to give to England first what she desires of peace and freedom for the whole world." Fiercely pacifist, Woolf will never mount barricades: ". . . the daughters of educated men then should give their brothers neither the white feather of cowardice nor the red feather of courage, but no feather at all; . . . they should shut the bright eyes that rain influence, or let those eyes look else-where when war is discussed . . ." (*TG*, p. 166).

The critics' failure to "hear" Woolf's novels, although they "see" them so well that they have concentrated on her ability to render words as painting, comes in part from ignoring the fact that her college was Covent Garden Opera House.[30] Her Bayreuth essay expresses a longing to imitate music with words, to build a structure to house the human longing for sublimity as Wagner had done. Woolf wanted a form for the novel that would dispense with the conventional plot (love and marriage, rags to riches). She longed to *compose* her novel, to score arias, duets, trios, quartets, as for voices and orchestra; above all to bring forward the chorus. What was done musically by the great composer, Dame Ethel Smyth—whose formative influence on Virginia Woolf in the thirties was, I feel, of decisive importance aesthetically—was what Woolf longed to do in her writing. Smyth wrote for the voice and the chorus; she used leitmotifs and Wagner's concept of the music-drama in an attempt to write for the people, not just an elite of music lovers. She had a proclivity for repetition and restatement. *The Prison*, her opera-symphony that directly influenced *The Years*, uses two ancient Greek melodies as well as popular tunes ("The Last Post"). It is noble, idealistic, and spirited—crying, after suffering, "Now let there be banners and Music!" And Ethel Smyth inscribed the five bars of this line of music to Virginia, in a copy of *The Prison* which she gave her.[31] Sara's song, "Red Rose, thorny Rose, brave Rose, tawny Rose," sung all through the novel with variations, is sung in the last section, to a shower of rose petals. But Ethel Smyth and Virginia Woolf recognized in each other quite contrary spirits, one reason, perhaps, for the strong influence.

In *The Years* Woolf has expressed her fear of her friend's violent nature in the less savory characteristics of Rose, whose image of herself as "Pargiter of Par-giter's Horse" is similar to Dame Ethel's self-image as the daughter of a general in the Royal Artillery. A good friend of Emmeline Pankhurst, Dame Ethel was the composer of "The March of the Women," battle song of the suffragettes. Imprisoned, she conducted the march from her jail cell with a toothbrush. Like

Rose Pargiter she became a patriot during the war, supporting the very govern-ment she had fought, not refusing its honors as Woolf and Margaret Llewelyn-Davies did. The odd scene in the novel in which Rose buys violets for Sara, then knocks her against a wall (calling her a "damned liar" as Sara later remembers), suggests the combination of affection and violence that characterized the friend-ship of the composer and the novelist.

"In another moment you would have felled me to the ground with your fist," Woolf wrote to Smyth of an argument they had in the street (*L*, 5, p. 70). Before they met Woolf had admired Smyth from a distance, not only as a great com-poser but as a fiery feminist and forthright autobiographer. Reviewing *Streaks of Life* (Longmans, Green, 1921) she remarked upon Ethel Smyth's "extreme courage and extreme candour" and her "astonishing vitality."

> Dressed in coat and skirt, tie and collar, Miss Smyth looks the militant working professional woman—the woman who had shocked the county by jumping fences both of the field and of the drawing-room, had written operas, was commonly called "quite mad," and had friends among the Empresses and char-women.[32]

Strident she could be, but never sentimental; reading the memoirs Woolf experienced "one of the pleasures which makes the thought of our own descent into the abyss of age tolerable." Later, having courted Dame Ethel's affections, Virginia Woolf found herself, she felt, in the clutches of "a giant crab." And their correspondence, now in the Berg Collection, shows them to be mutually admir-ing and critical. Ethel called Virginia a "frozen falcon" for her still, alert way of listening to music and called her "4d for 9d" because "she asks a lot and gives a little."[33] But the most interesting aspects of their relationship were the younger woman's hunger for knowledge about the composition of music and their shared love of writing.

In their letters Woolf always compared her friend to roses, while Smyth compared Woolf to a wave. The shower of rose petals over Rose Pargiter in "Present Day" is a tribute to Ethel Smyth, and indeed Rose/Ethel seems to rep-resent the Englishwoman "Soul of the '90s" perfectly. Although Kitty and Martin criticize, for "force is always wrong," Rose has the last word, her per-sonal and active courage being one of the things that must have attracted the confirmed pacificist.

In her exemplary study of the evolution of *The Years* from *The Pargiters*, Grace Radin has analyzed the even more socialist and feminist text of the novel, the explicit and disturbing lesbian passages. Like Louise De Salvo's edition of *Melymbrosia*, one of the versions of *The Voyage Out*, Radin's study raises questions about censorship and self-censorship on the part of anti-establish-ment writers. Contemporary readers may become "pargetters" themselves when they read *The Years* with alternating chapters of *The Pargiters* as well as Grace Radin's study. Did Woolf imagine when she left these masses of manu-script behind her, that her readers would become pargetters, patching up and plastering together the fictional and factual parts of the text? Since Woolf deconstructed and disembowelled the novel herself, she puts the reader into the position of re-constructor. We are there as readers playing the part of the ancients trying to piece together the scattered parts of Echo's body. And since repetition, Echo's art, is so significantly the signature of Woolf's style, especially in *The Years*, it is perhaps fitting that the role of modern readers and critics is that of pargetters and collectors of Echo's scattered remains.

The 1910 section of *The Pargiters* reads like a debate that might be going on among present-day feminists. Rose, a male-identified feminist, works for votes for women but does not question the patriarchal system. Maggie and Elvira, internationalist outsiders like Woolf herself, are isolated and ignorant of the problems of poor women. They are not even aware that it is against the law to disseminate information about birth control. When Rose explains that most women haven't got three guineas to consult a Harley Street gynecologist, they propose writing to the *Times* to demand free contraception for all. (The standard three-guinea gynecologist's fee might suggest that behind *Three Guineas* lies the idea that women's ultimate weapon against war and fascism is to refuse to bear children.) Maggie doesn't want a vote because "Englishwomen in politics are prostitutes. Every patriarch has his prostitute. She comforts him and then asks for favors." Maggie and Elvira have a crude Freudian analysis of Rose's ferocious brand of feminism: "her powers of expression have . . . been atrophied by a hideous childhood experience." Since it was Woolf, not Smyth, who was molested in childhood, this passage is interesting.

Elvira tries to imagine Rose in the arms of a young man, but is shocked into speechlessness when Maggie tells her that Rose loves women. "But whereas . . . I could think of Rose with equanimity in the arms of a man . . . the other thought is loathsome; just for ten seconds. But in the one case, you see Maggie I covered them with syringa petals. In the other—I didn't cover them (at all)—I saw them, naked; which seems to prove Maggie, that (the nature) of the act itself is a mixture of the ridiculous and the repulsive; or am I wrong?" (*TP*, IV, pp. 69-70). Grace Radin suggests that lesbian love appears naked of the trappings of sentimental romance because it has had no literature like heterosexual love to strew flower petals on the lovers' bodies. Elvira says "when you said Rose flung herself into the arms of Mildred in a greenhouse, a shock; horror; terror . . . something that lights up the whole of the dim past of the human race." Indeed. And quite possibly the past of the writer herself. While these passages do not appear in *The Years*, they do explain why Rose is showered with rose petals at the end of the novel. The expunged flower, syringa, is the mock orange used in bridal wreaths. Syrinx was one of Diana's nymphs who turned into a reed to escape being raped by Pan. The reed was made into a flute, a clear reference to Ethel Smyth, the author of *Female Pipings in Eden*, which offers a myth of the origins of women's music. This troubling passage suggests that the family ("the whole of the dim past of the human race") denies lesbian love rituals, ceremonies, and its own literature and prophesies the eclipse of Ethel Smyth's fame.

Echo's refusal of Pan enraged him so that, the myth tells us, he had her body torn apart and scattered. But each part continued to sing from its hiding place in the earth, even imitating Pan's pipe. Perhaps one threatened maiden was sing- ing to the other, as Eliot's mermaids sing each to each. At any rate, the scattered parts of the body of Virginia Woolf's manuscripts continue to sing, long after their author is dead.

Despite the deletions, aesthetically *The Years* is a success. Woolf's tools are so polished and sharpened that we are scarcely aware of the work that has made it shimmer with sound and color. Only afterward do we apprehend its ethical imperative, its affirmation of the human spirit. For, as Clive Bell says of French painting, it has "the maximum of elegance compatible with sincerity." She, like French painters, wanted to give pleasure as long as it was compatible with tell- ing the truth. Bell compared Woolf's style to Constantin Guys', who found motifs for brilliant paintings in the "spectacle of contemporary life." Guys "never condemns, satirizes or denounces," "neither pities, prattles nor ap- proves"; Bell calls the style the two artists share "graphic impressionism."[34] It is the combination of what Woolf calls "the appropriate form" with an austere ethic that gives her fiction its classic stature. She explained:

> When we speak of form we mean that certain emotions have been placed in the
> right relations to each other; then that the novelist is able to dispose these emo-
> tions and make them tell by methods which he inherits, bends to his purpose,
> models anew, or even invents for himself. Further, that the reader can detect
> these devices, and by so doing will deepen his understanding of the book.[35]

The freedom is in the form, then. Our experience of pleasure comes from the artist's hurdling of aesthetic barriers, truthfully orchestrating and painting her feelings about those years. In the process then of "detecting these devices" of form, we deepen our understanding of the content. This is the kind of aesthetic both Roger Fry and Christopher Caudwell would, from their antithetical posi- tions, applaud. The content of this novel happens to be as radical as its form. But, as Clive Bell would have pointed out, where the tradition of an art over the centuries has been a radical stretching of the form, a series of revolutions, the most revolutionary artist is, historically, also the most traditional. *The Years* will seem to future observers of English fiction the most natural novel of the thirties, a classic in the English novel of manners and morals, one that criticized society in new forms. As Eleanor would say, it "fits." *The Years* is a red rag and a red flag, a bandage and a banner, plastering the wounds of the old world while heralding the birth of a new. It murders the patriarchal family to dissect it, and it also is a fit memorial to Woolf's comrades, reformers and radicals, in the 1917 club.

The Years might well be considered a fictional companion volume to George Dangerfield's *Strange Death of Liberal England.* Dangerfield writes in his preface:

> The year 1910 is . . . a landmark in English history, which stands out against a
> peculiar background of flame. For it was in 1910 that fires long smouldering in the
> English spirit suddenly flared up, so that by the end of 1913 Liberal England was
> reduced to ashes . . . the true pre-war Liberalism—supported, as it still was in
> 1910, by Free Trade, a majority in Parliament, the ten commandments and the
> illusion of Progress—can never return. It was killed, or killed itself, in 1913.[36]

Like the social historian, who saw that England's decline hinged on its failure to
deal with the rights of women, the rights of the Irish, and the rights of the
workers, Woolf weaves the same materials into fictional form. (There are also
evident parallels with Shaw's *Heartbreak House*, which the author says he conceived in a house in Sussex where he met Virginia Woolf and fell in love with
her.)[37] The theme of the search for "justice and liberty," first expressed by
Delia's dream of sharing a platform with Parnell, not only recurs with Rose
battling in the by-elections for women's rights and with Eleanor and Kitty at
their cooperative committee meetings, but is echoed by individuals and groups
from all classes, anti-fascists, Rennie the French patriot, Jews, Trafalgar Square
orators, the women who defend Nicholas's right to be a homosexual. When North
says in the "Present Day" section that all they talk about is politics and money,
he suggests the deeper theme of the novel, that the solutions to the economic
and political problems are really social. And although we have seen brave
attempts at reform, they've all been doomed to failure. Eleanor cannot patch up
all the poor hovels in London; Delia marries the class enemy of Parnell and all
he stands for; Rose, like many of Mrs. Pankhurst's followers, abandons her
feminism for patriotism and is knighted for her work in the war. ("She smashed
his window," Martin jeered at her, "and then she helped him to smash other
people's windows.") The failures are failures to unite; one cause is not enough to
change the world.

Woolf did not bring to a conclusion her portrait of the downward spiral of
British life until the mid-nineteen-thirties, the time of the "Present Day"
section. I find it odd that both Quentin Bell and Leonard Woolf used the images
of "twilight" and "hell" when writing of their own experience of living through
this period and yet neither saw that Virginia Woolf had immortalized that twilight, that hell, in *The Years*. In the novel, as in the history of England from 1880
to 1937, the feminists, socialists, pacifists, Irish rebels, Jews, anti-fascists, are
each fighting separate battles. ("Not black shirts, green shirts, red shirts—
always posing in the public eye; that's all poppycock.") *Three Guineas* was
Virginia Woolf's attempt to articulate a unified intellectual position that would
connect them all; very few would share her *whole* vision and its forthright attack
on the patriarchal family as the origin of all oppression. North sees it:

> This is the conspiracy . . . this is the steam roller that smoothes, obliterates,
> rounds into identity; rolls into balls . . . *my* boy, *my* girl . . . they were saying.
> But they're not interested in other people's children, he observed. Only in their
> own; their own property; their own flesh and blood, which they would protect

> with the unsheathed claws of the primeval swamp, he thought, looking at Milly's
> fat little paws, even Maggie, even she. For she too was talking about my boy, my
> girl. How then can we be civilised, he asked himself? [p. 378]

If it were a question "of 'my' children, of 'my' possessions, it would be one rip down the belly; or teeth in the soft fur of the throat" (p. 380). Those interlocking bonds between private property and the patriarchal family must be broken, Woolf suggests in the novel and shouts in *Three Guineas*, before we can begin to "live differently." North's personal solution, to "write little books," is sneered at by his sister Peggy whose life is spent in a hospital patching up the bodies of the sick and the hurt. They are all "pargetters," plastering the cracks in the house of British culture in one way or another, most of them knowing full well that it will fall despite their efforts. The artist is the master plasterer; her materials are whitewash and dung, vision and reality. She makes a picture of our life as "cripples in a cave"; her memory is both moral and magical; we are made to see the truth of our wretched lives, but to keep on going forward despite it. The extraordinary dialectic in the novel between dirt and cleanliness, between the man who spits in his bath and the Crosby who scrubs it, the dirty drains of the slums and Eleanor's passionate plumbing of them, the squalor of the streets and the shining safety of Eleanor's high moonlit bathroom, mimics both the artist making order out of chaos and the fundamental rhythm of women's lives. The novel shows us men making money, making war, making love, making books, and making a colossal mess—and women cleaning up after them. Only a woman like Virginia Woolf could conceive of the metaphor of the artist as charwoman to the world. Not that she is in the least sentimental about charwomen; Crosby is as much at fault for making Martin feel like God as Martin is for playing God. In "Royalty" Woolf prophetically remarked on

> the most insidious and dangerous of current snobberies, which is making the
> workers into Kings; [it] has invested the slum, the mine, and the factory with
> the old glamour of the palace, so that, as modern fiction shows, we are beginning
> to escape, by picturing the lives of the poor and daydreaming about them, from
> the drudgery, about which there is no sort of glamour, of being ourselves.[38]

The Years is, more than anything else, a tribute to the vision of Victorian women reformers like Eleanor Pargiter, to the generations of spinster social workers like Margaret Llewelyn-Davies and Jane Addams who devoted their lives to the cause of immigrants and working people.

❧ 3 ❧

Pargetting The Pargiters

Virginia Woolf's novel *The Years*, I argued in the last chapter, may be *heard* as an opera for the oppressed, may be participated in by the reader as a modern ritual drama of purification, deriving from Greek ceremonies of the death and rebirth of the year, and at the same time may be read as a realistic anti-fascist political novel of the thirties.

In suggesting these perspectives I have noted the influence of Dante, Sophocles, and Wagner and called attention to the triple note of insistent repetition and to the structure of the novel as a helix within the burning circle of London. I have also indicated sources for certain characters and ideas in Caroline Stephen, Margaret Llewelyn-Davies, Mrs. Humphry Ward, Jane Harrison, Janet Case, Ethel Smyth, and Joseph Wright. From her interest in Wright and his *Dialect Dictionary*, the several meanings of the word "pargetter" were seen to be available to Virginia Woolf as she wrote. The pargetter may be one who embellishes the outside of a house—or the patcher-up of chimneys in those "caves of mud and dung," the houses of families, using a mixture of lime and cow dung—or one who covers up the truth or tells lies. Woolf's use of the word as a surname suggests both a moral and physical ambivalence in a novel about the patriarchal family, perhaps a combination of whitewash and filth, a true "whited sepulchre." The themes of cleanliness and dirt, on the spiritual and physical plane, combine and conflict so that London seems both dead and buried—and alive and well.

Before the reader can say "poppycock" to all this critical pargetting, let me add a further gloss on the word "poppycock," which recurs throughout the novel. From Virginia Woolf's delight in the preserving of folk expressions, we may speculate that she knew the origin of "poppycock" and its relation to her theme. The American slang word was used to describe long-winded congressmen in the nineteenth century and derived from a Dutch word meaning "soft, loose dung." The patriarchal house, that cave of pargetting, is mocked, and we are reminded of the curse of the chorus in *Antigone* against the old men who use big words. "I sometimes would like to be learned myself," Woolf wrote, "about sounds and dialects" (*AWD*, 178).

The notes that follow continue my explorations into this rich and complex novel.

Red—and Gold

Woolf has deliberately tried to make us see red—and has been successful, to judge from the critical response. This brilliant exercise in sliding signifiers deconstructs semiotic systems. It is not simply that the rendering of color in *The Years* is a direct representation of its theme. The reds and golds do "mean" sunset, imperialism, blood, sacrifice, love. But the color is so united with the form, the opera's coruscation with the opera house, that we do not immediately apprehend the pattern although we know it is there. Like Eleanor we seek it, and the bloody, yellow-smeared butcher's paper collides with the red gilt chair; nature red in tooth and claw combines subliminally with red-uniformed guardsman and red lipstick. The color red both rhapsodizes and warns. It is a danger signal, an equivalent of the sirens and loudspeakers that wail throughout the book. But it is also the color of the roses with which the weary revelling Pargiters greet the rosy dawn. It holds the political power of the red flag simultaneously with the red rag on a truck full of explosives. The yellow/gold also has a moral scale of equivalents ranging from good to evil; from autumn, sunlight, and harvest to money and power, royalty, phoniness, sin, and sexuality. Emblematic as the colors are, they do not have the same kind of meaning as the colors in Marvell's "The Garden," which North and Sara read as they discuss the problem of solitude and society. The gold and glitter as pomp and circumstance are matched by the golden spangles on a dress and golden bubbles in the wine. The use of color is the aesthetic equivalent of the use of motifs in music; the themes and variations on "money and love," "justice and liberty" are so subtly varied that the effect is a tone poem. The reader senses the sunset glow; only subliminally does one connect the "gilt claw" of Eugenie's chair with Abel Pargiter's deformed hand, the "paws" of Gibbs the huntsman, Milly's "paws," and North's vision of the family "with the unsheathed claws of the primeval swamp." (That chair has a remarkable similarity to Virginia Woolf's mother's chair as she described it in *Moments of Being*.)

Red is the color of calamity but also of fertility. Everything in *The Years* is suffused with such a ruddy glow, from the "Rigby red" hair to the very dog, that the novel leaps with flame, shouting "Stop!" urging "Go!" at the same moment. In her essay on Sickert's painting, Virginia Woolf wrote: "in the eyes of a motorist red is not a colour but simply a danger signal. We shall very soon lose our sense of colour . . . colours are used so much as signals now that they will very soon suggest action merely . . . " (*CE* II, p. 233). The writer "signals" us in *The Years* as ambiguously as Wagner's Siegfried motif resounds. It calls out "justice and liberty!" but it also smashes the anvil; the signal is anarchist and anti-intellectual as well as libertarian. We find it frightening as well as thrilling. (My critics think I have made too much of a "Marxist" out of the middle-class Virginia Woolf. A Red Virginia is surely, however, a nice contrast to the pale lady of other portraits).

During her painful revising of *The Years* Virginia Woolf was also collecting materials for her biography of Roger Fry. Here the color red served as a leitmotif. His memories of a childhood garden scene with an old forked apple tree, like Kitty's in *The Years* —and his passion for the vivid red poppies that grew there—are used by Woolf as biographer to show Fry's fascination with seduction and passion. The red is contrasted with a Quaker mildness to suggest a conflict between the artist and his family, and it serves as a symbol of his rebellion. Woolf quotes Fry on their visit to Delphi, "I've always hated families and patriarchalism of all kinds . . . I have so little family feeling, so little feeling that it's by the family that one goes on with the future" (*Roger Fry* [London: Hogarth, 1940]). But she shrewdly noted that this feeling, like her own, went hand in hand with a passionate devotion to his sister.

In "Pictures" Woolf wrote of how writers need to nourish the eye:

> That still-life, they proceed, pointing to a jar of red-hot pokers, is to us what a beefsteak is to an invalid—an orgy of blood and nourishment, so starved are we on our diet of thin black print. We nestle into its colour, feed and fill ourselves with yellow and red and gold until we drop off, nourished and content. Our sense of colour seems miraculously sharpened. We carry those roses and red-hot pokers about with us for days, working them over again in words. (*The Moment and other Essays* [N. Y.: Harcourt, 1948], p. 177)

It is not only the vivid rendering of the red that pleases us here but the itch of the artist to render the effects of another art. Can this be done in words? she thinks, and tries. In her early essay on Wagner (1909) she had mourned " . . . we are miserably aware of how little words can do to render music. When the moment of suspense is over, and the bows actually move over the strings, our definitions are relinquished, and words disappear in our minds. Enormous is the relief, and yet, when the spell is over, how great is the joy with which we turn to our old tools again!" She is intrigued by the opera, by the way "sound melts into colour, and colour calls out for words, where, in short, we are lifted out of the ordinary world and allowed merely to breathe and see—it is here that we realize how thin are the walls between one emotion and another; and how fused our impressions are with elements that we may not attempt to separate."[1] She was fascinated by the problem of rendering sound and color in words and wished that someone would write a book about "the flirtations between music, letters, sculpture, and architecture, and the effects the arts have had upon each other throughout the ages" (*The Moment*, p. 173). This book will surely have a chapter on *The Years*.

Knowing the capacity of great operas to combine poetry and song with "sublime" orchestral feats, Woolf imitated the collaboration of composer and librettist in her novel. Its last section was to be called "Music" or "Dawn." The lesson of *The Years*, she wrote in 1934, "is that one can use all kinds of 'forms' in one book" (*AWD*, p. 215).

As Ethel Smyth in her opera *The Prison*, a "dialogue of the soul," had used Henry Brewster's poem and mixed the vernacular and early Greek tunes with her own Wagnerian style, so Virginia Woolf wrote as well "a dialogue of the soul

with the soul" (*AWD*, p. 205) with intermixture of modes. Smyth's opera, a quest
for emancipation, asks "Who are our Saviours?" and answers that the secret of
the "free" soul is to "disband" the self and release the ego. "The thing is to free
one's self," Woolf wrote in 1933, "to let it find its dimensions, not be impeded"
(*AWD*, p. 206). The moods of "pastoral" and "sunset calm" that mark *The Years*
also characterize *The Prison*. "Let there be banners and music" is the triumphant cry of the Soul, unceasing in its search for "justice and liberty."[2] In
both *The Years* and *The Prison*, death is not the enemy, as in *The Waves*, but the
friend, the lord of dispersal of the self in a great timeless diaspora, the bringer
of "peace" in the trumpeting dawn that ends both works. Writing *The Years*
made Woolf feel "above time and death" (*AWD*, p. 217); it was an answer to the
diminishment she felt at the deaths of so many friends. Since an audience must
collaborate to make the work of art live (this was Ethel Smyth's attitude also),
The Years would not be "lit up" by the response of her dead friends; it was thus
"less porous and radiant, as if the thinking stuff were a web that were fertilized
only by other people's . . . thinking it too" (*AWD*, p. 207). Her cousin Ralph
Vaughan-Williams's *London Symphony* (1914) is also clearly an influence, using as
it does themes of shabbiness and cruelty and sounds of Westminster chimes, the
cry of the lavender seller and the bells of a cab, as opposition to a classical structure. His own thoughts on the death and resurrection theme with an undercur-
rent of folk tunes may be heard in *Five Variants on Dives and Lazarus* (1939).

The "Overtures"

The section of lyrical prose that begins each "year" of the novel reveals, in com-
pressed form, the sensibility that could play so vibrantly back and forth
among painting and music, urban realism and pastoral myth, contemporary
scholarship and nineteenth-century fiction dealing in social criticism. These
passages work like overtures that introduce the motifs we will hear developed
in the body of the work: fleece, sheep, and clouds; rain (as ritual purification or
washing); sunset or twilight; the colors red and gold; the birds; the contrast of
upstairs and downstairs; street music; the moon as a polished coin; the triple
note. Some of these we have pursued through the extent of the novel; now we
may consider the patterns of their interweaving within each dated section.

The line introducing the action of "1891"—"For it was October, the birth of
the year"—may be explained by Woolf's reading of Jane Harrison, who points
out that the ancient Greek agricultural year began in the autumn and that the
origin of Greek drama lies in the early ceremonies of the "Death and Rebirth of
the Year-Spirit." She argues that to the Greeks, the years "are not abstractions,
divisions of time; they are the substance, the content of time," that "this notion
that the year is its own content . . . haunted the Greek imagination" (*Themis: A
Study of the Social Origins of Greek Religion* [Cambridge, 1912], pp. 185–86.)
The notion of clock time as male in its abstraction and antithetical to emotional
life is sounded by Virginia Woolf most clearly in *Mrs. Dalloway*, where Big Ben

dominates and bullies the characters' lives and the Lady Margaret clock is always late, trailing after "her lap full of odds and ends." But *The Years* quite clearly takes Harrison's view of the year, *annus*, as a ring, a revolution, its acting out in art of the Mother/Son ritual of the death and rebirth of the year as the origin of collective life and the collective conscience. Art, Harrison argued, sprang from religion with a connecting bridge of ritual, dance, and song. Each section of *The Years* contains a ritual death: the deaths of Rose Pargiter, Parnell, Eugénie, Digby, the King, and Abel Pargiter; of Antigone; of Crosby's dog; of Charles, the promising brother of North and Peggy killed in the 1914 war. In 1917 the bombs are "killing other people," and Kitty's friend from her Oxford youth, who was going to be a doctor, is also killed. The ritual deaths happen off-stage, as in Greek tragedy, and the Pargiters learn of the deaths from news brought by a messenger. In each section there are also ritual songs and dances.

The most haunting maiden-trinity scene is Eugénie's bonfire at the birthday party in October, birth of the year, for Maggie: the three women, mother and two daughters, dance around the fire. Then the mysteries are interrupted by the alien male voice of Abel Pargiter. Later Eugénie in a mysterious scene, dancing with her two daughters, is abruptly interrupted by her husband. The ritual of the fire burning the old year and opening the new year is prominent in Jane Harrison. Eleanor's knotted handkerchief is a symbol of the Cretan mother-goddess in this system. In *Mythology* Harrison describes Athena as the goddess of cleanliness, connecting Eleanor and the owl, and Hera as "the Year incarnate," both death and life, represented by Homer as a jealous wife, but in reality "the turbulent nation princess coerced but never really subdued by an alien conqueror." She saw Homeric religion as patriarchal, individualistic, and heroic, as opposed to the collective visions and ecstatic sexuality of mother-goddess worship.

In the 1907 "overture" the moonlight burnishes and silver-plates solid objects; the farmers going to market are like "tribes migrating in search of water, driven by enemies to seek new pasturage." London is "the fiery gauze of the eternally burning city"; the flowers and fruit fill Covent Garden "as with some celestial laundry." The sound of "the eternal waltz" is "like a serpent that swallowed its own tail" (the symbol of the Great Mother) "since the ring was complete from Hammersmith to Shoreditch." There are trombones, bands, red silk canopies, yellow clocks, and "the Serpentine, red in the setting sun." In 1908 the March wind reddens noses, blows out color, "even a solid ruby in a Bond Street window," "yelling its joy in destruction," sweeps up papers "blood smeared, yellow smeared." Matty Stiles in the damp basement with the "stain on the ceiling" of Eugénie's house (with a red "sold" sign on it) growls "Let him ring, ring, ring" at Martin standing "between the canaries' cage and the dirty linen." In 1910 there are red geraniums in the West End, Queen Alexandra with a pink carnation, clouds "staining windows gold" and the Thames "a muddy gold" with "barges with black tarpaulins and corn showing." In 1911 the sun turns the sea "like the skin of an innumerable-scaled fish, glittering gold." Everything is golden, in France, in London, yellow clocks, fires, and corn. In 1913 the sky is "like a grey goose's wing from which feathers were falling all over England"; there is snow, silence; "a sheep coughed." "The snow cast a hard white glare upon the walls of the bathroom, showed up the cracks on the enamel bath, and the stains on the wall," as Eleanor shows Abercorn Terrace to a house agent with a dirty neck who "indicted their cleanliness" and says "lavatory accommodations" instead of "baths."

In 1914 the fields are "red with clover," "up went the rooks as if flung by the bells," and London is "a rough sea of sound." During the war in 1917 there is only a searchlight raying around the sky, pondering "some fleecy patch," and in 1918 only "the bleat of sheep, the croak of rooks," and the growl of traffic. In "Present Day" there are gilt leaves, gold sky, clouds, sheep, a "red gold fume," "red brick villas," and people's faces with a "red glow" "as if lit from within."

The Sheep Motif: A New Version of Pastoral

The playful elegance in these overtures, with fleecy clouds in the countryside above peacefully grazing sheep, has the wit of an eighteenth-century French painting. London at the center is always a ring of fire, while the innocence, the indifference, of these pastoral images suggests the concluding word of this novel full of war and violence: "peace." The country/city contrast enlarges the landscape, spatially and temporally, introducing reverberations of allusion that include Blake's lamb, Handel's "we like sheep," and the Lamb of God— sacrifice, purification, and slaughter. North is the modern rustic shepherd, tending sheep in Africa, writing letters about sheep to his aunts. Behind the motif, too, are Woolf's beloved Samuel Butler on a sheep farm, Jane Harrison's chapter on "Dian's Fleece" and the ritual purification in her *Prolegomena*, and Olive Schreiner's *The Story of an African Farm*.

To tunnel out a cave behind even one aspect of the sheep motif is to discover still more richness in Woolf's linkage of painterly appeal with myth and ritual and political vision. Virginia Woolf met Olive Schreiner in 1909 and wrote to Violet Dickinson about "the sumptuous Jewess" playing Brahms or Schumann (*L* I, p. 394). Schreiner was not Jewish but many English people made the same mistake, assuming that Jews had a monopoly on sexuality and vitality. Olive Schreiner's *Woman and Labour* (1911) was "the bible" of the feminist movement; her *Trooper Peter Halkett* (1897) was a masterpiece of allegorical anti-Boer War protest literature. Like Virginia Woolf's *Three Guineas* it employed "propaganda of the eye," using a photograph of white men leering at the spectacle of hanged blacks in much the same way that Woolf used photographs of British patriarchs to make her point about the origin of fascism in the family. In March 1925 in *The New Republic* Woolf reviewed the edition of Schreiner's letters published by her husband and Havelock Ellis. *The Story of an African Farm* was a "remarkable" book, she wrote; "Olive Schreiner was one half of a great writer; a diamond marred by a flaw." Of the novel Woolf said,

In its brilliance and power it reminds us inevitably of the Brontë novels. In it, as in them, we feel ourselves in the presence of a powerful nature which can make us see what it saw and feel what it felt with astounding vividness. But it has the limitations of those egotistical masterpieces without a full measure of their strength. . . . She was driven to teach, to dream and prophesy.

Woolf admires "her convictions, her ruthless sincerity, and the masterly sanity which so often contrasts on the same page with childish outbursts of unreason." But

it is impossible not to feel for her something of the pity and respect which all martyrs inspire in us, and not least those martyrs who are not required to sacrifice their lives to a cause, but sacrifice, perhaps more disastrously, humor and sweetness and sense of proportion. But there were compensations; the cause itself—the emancipation of women—was of the highest importance, and it would be frivolous to dismiss her as a mere crank, a piece of wreckage used and then thrown aside as the cause triumphed onwards.

Olive Schreiner's pseudonym, Ralph Iron, rings out behind the men crying "Old iron" throughout *The Years*. The images of iron trees and iron steps link with the "hammer, hammer, hammer" of the Siegfried motif and the anvil at Oxford. In *The Story of an African Farm*, Waldo, the idealistic young German sheepherder in Africa, tests God with a sacrifice of his mutton chop. God does not send fire; the sun melts the fat; the ants crawl over it. He feels like Cain. His "God hates me" grows into "I hate God." He is broken-hearted and unable to tell his deeply religious father of his pain. This is Schreiner's allegory of the "intense loneliness," the "intense ignorance" of childhood. This scene seems to foreshadow both the painful scene from Rose's childhood and the ugliness of the mutton meal North shares with Sara. Rose goes to bed terrified after a man exposes himself and leers at her in the twilit street. She tries to count sheep, "but the fifth sheep would not jump. It turned round and looked at her. Its long narrow face was grey; its lips moved; it was the face of the man at the pillar-box, and she was alone with it" (*Years*, p. 40). Many years later Rose can confess slashing her wrists in the bathroom in anger at her brother's making her take the blame for a microscope broken by his friend, but she, like Waldo, cannot confess the childhood pain that was full of guilt. The sheep marks the scene of sexual initiation as, later, in the bloody sacrifice North and Sara share, it marks North's initiation into London society and community responsibility after his African exile and his fears as a warrior. Cassandra-like, Sara presides over his ritual cleansing. In the house where "the bells don't ring and the taps don't run," the mutton bleeds into the well and Sara reminds North that she had called him "coward, hypocrite" for going off to war (p. 321). An apple and a banana continue the ritual of sexual and communal initiation. North recites "The Garden" from memory, and they debate the issue of social responsibility and personal freedom. The orphic Sara creates a drama out of "the hair of the

Jew in the bath." He washes away the sins of the world and is their scapegoat in
the sacred drama they enact. Sara chants her "Waste Land" speech about the
"polluted city," telling him that she was forced to "stain the hand, the unstained
hand," to join the "army of workers," the Jews, the "conspiracy" (p. 341). She
shows him the way. Poverty and the diaspora of the family have made the condition of women like the condition of the Jews. As outcasts and scapegoats they
have "joined the conspiracy" to work toward a better world. North is now a
member of what she names in *Three Guineas* the society of outsiders. The Jew's
bath water gurgles down the drain; the organs, trombones, and singers are
silent in the "curious pale red" twilight. Later Maggie's artist's eye on the
objects in the shabby room gives it the aura of a Greek temple where something
important has just happened. What has happened is that the sphinx-like Sara
has asked North a testing question, initiating the next generation of artists.
"He's killed the king . . . so what'll he do next?" North answers, "Comedy . . .
contrast . . . the only form of continuity" (pp. 345–46). It's the right answer;
North goes off to the party "as if he were riding to the relief of a besieged garri-
son across a desert." He is the incarnation of the Year-Spirit.

One of the working titles for *The Years* was "The Caravan" (others equally
revealing were "Ordinary People" and "Sons and Daughters"). It suggests the
migrating shepherds in the Old Testament, which, besides Dante and Renan,
Woolf read carefully while writing. She was also reading Byron, and I think that
the Cain and Abel story, both Biblical and Byronic, are at work behind the
book's attempt to deal with the origins of the patriarchal family and the violent
images associated with it. Abel Pargiter's name suggests that he is the inheritor
of Abel's values—and that he covers up the truth. If we read with Byron's eyes,
Cain is the rebel and representative of all laboring men who want knowledge
and liberty, and Abel is seen not as victim but as patriarchal slaughterer. Cain is
a farmer, an inheritor of matriarchal values. He offers the fruits of the earth as
his sacrifice, but the Father-god, unlike the Mother-goddess, demands blood.
Byron called the *Cain* a "mystery," and the English mystery plays that interpret
this story often emphasize the nomad/settler opposition, with Cain offering a
sacrifice of fermented corn. This suggests some kind of folk connection between
Cain and John Barleycorn, from the English version of the Year-Spirit rituals
(appearing in the novel as the London sign with the ever-pouring bottle).[3]

It is worth noting that at Sara and North's ritual dinner, neither the
slaughtered lamb nor the apple and banana are particularly appetizing. Perhaps
the recurring "No idols" means that human beings should not sacrifice at any
altar, patriarchal or matriarchal, that there is no savior but the self.

In its search for the beginning of things, *The Years* is, in a sense, epic. Woolf
often used the image of an abyss to convey the foreignness of the male mind and
her sheer terror at the way it works, but here it is followed by her making a
bridge to cross it. *A Writer's Diary* conveys the sense of risk and high adventure
involved in writing out her own female perceptions. Edward Said has suggested
that the modern novel is characterized by this same bold anti-dynastic approach
(although he does not connect this with Woolf or women writers). Said's defini-

tion of the novel as a "ceaselessly changing triangle of encipherment, decipherment and dissemination," which comes from the collectivization and universalizing of the authorial voice in collaboration with readers' reading, seems particularly applicable to *The Years*. His suggestion that the modern novel is concerned with the lateral and dispersed elements of the family, rather than the linear and sequential ordering of time, is also useful in this connection—as is his noting that the modernist search for "beginnings," often in an act of "transgression" against God and the father, leads to repetition—the aspect of Virginia Woolf's style that is certainly the most intriguing. "Repetition is reality," said Kierkegaard, "and it is the seriousness of life." Hopkins, analyzing himself, suggested that repetition or "oftening, over-and-overing, aftering" was the childless author's imitation of genesis. The echoing insistence of the triple note in *The Years* conveys both messages, the feminist radical's need to get back to the beginning of the patriarchal patterning (where it seems to find the "inaugural act" in the sacrifice of the lamb) and the author's own need to speak collectively, to cry out for the responding voice of the reader answering "back" or "with" in a kind of prayer for "peace."[4]

Speaking in Tongues

In "Present Day" Peggy explains the reluctance of the caretaker's children to speak. "The younger generation," she says, "don't mean to speak" (p. 429). Nor need they speak to mean. Their song when it is sung seems to respond to North's reverie (p. 424), his vision of a vast plain with sheep cropping and "babbling" incoherently. He feels himself drifting "into silence, into solitude," as a voice asks "which is the worst torture . . . that human beings can inflict . . . " Maggie's laugh says "no idols." Then there is the sense of release of sound of "the chorus, the cry, the chirp, the stir, which salutes the London dawn" (p. 425). When the children speak they speak in tongues (as Joanna Lipking has pointed out). We need no further evidence than *Three Guineas* to explain Woolf's obsession with Paul's exclusion of women from a direct voice in the church, but perhaps that is the "worst torture . . . that human beings can inflict"—isolation and exclusion from a human communal vision. The reader, I expect, is meant to feel excluded, a rhetorical device Virginia Woolf had used effectively in *A Room of One's Own* and *Three Guineas*. The anguish of being excluded from language and culture she explained vividly in "On Not Knowing Greek."

There has always been debate among Christians about whether the pentecostal miracle lay in the tongue of the speaker or in the ear of the hearer. But George Cutten, in *Speaking in Tongues*, suggests that these ecstatic utterances often contained a preponderance of Greek and Latin sounds, were rhymed and extremely alliterative. An outbreak of this phenomenon often accompanied a people's sense of historical disaster, of upheaval and persecution—all characteristics suggested by the children's singing in *The Years*. Historically, political

and religious persecution of women, children, peasants, and leaders of evangelical sects, like Mother Ann Lee, have produced ecstatic speaking in tongues.
The secret meetings of the sects, the use of wine, and the sense of ecstatic
release in dancing and singing also imply a connection with the ancient Eleusinian mysteries. Cutten points out too that modern speakers have often repeated
sounds three times, in a state of rapture or joy.[5]

The problem of individual freedom and social responsibility with its attendant ambiguity is aptly caught, then, as the reader struggles with the text. How
are intellectuals going to respond to the difficulties of the children's song, to the
new culture, the new art, to the working class? Will we let them eat cake, as
Delia does (and more cake than we would give our own children)? pay them and
send them away, as Martin does? keep our distance, like Peggy? smile benevolently, like Eleanor? We can say "very nice," like old Patrick, or confess our
ignorance, like Hugh Gibbs. What is to be done? I imagine that she is suggesting that they deserve, as the brilliant light falls on "the petals and the bread
crumbs" (p. 432), both bread and roses.

Notes on the "Two Enormous Chunks"[6]

Crosby's voice is rendered by simple repetition, without the third releasing or
varying note which sounds for the other characters. Does this mean that
Quentin Bell and other Woolf critics are right when they call Woolf a snob? I
don't think so. "Step up, step up," she says to the two working-class children
she brings to Kew Gardens during the war. She says it again; it marks her class
and mimics the march of the soldiers and the "tick, tick, tick, tick" of the drum,
military and ominous. Her dumb diction is determined by forty years in the
basement of Abercorn Terrace.[7] She is annoyed by the obedience and sobriety
of Alf and Gladys, remembering Martin "out of sheer devilry" smashing a milk
bottle. The gardens are blazing with red and yellow flowers; the faces of the
soldiers are red and shiny. Here Virginia Woolf has done what she saw that
Wagner could do in music. The *motifs*—the color red, the human voice and the
street noises in contest, the female vessel of nourishment and upper-class male
violence—combine so that we scarcely notice we've been made to see red, to
hear the drumbeats. As Crosby cries "Don't meddle with them birds, Alf!" he
is pecked by a goose; her efforts at talk are rebuffed. We move to a train full of
red-faced soldiers; the headline "Three British Cruisers Sunk" is balanced by
news of the birth of triplets to the wife of the postman at Andover. An officer
with red lips says "Good, Good, Good" to his girl, "little clipped words." In
Leicester Square "there was a bottle of beer that poured and stopped, then
poured again." (The libation continues although its source is forgotten.) "The
sky glared as if a red and yellow canopy hung down over it." Night falls but the
sky "glared yellower and redder" over the theater where Eleanor forgets the
war and believes that "the innocent man is the villain," an underlining of the

"scapegoat" motif. The moon motif recurs: "It was so clear that the craters showed on it like engravings on a beautifully polished silver coin." How consistently the moon shows its metallic face throughout the novel ("money and love," the value of chastity to males). Eleanor, like Crosby, remembers—not a milk bottle but a coffee cup and "soldiers are guarding the line with fixed bayonets"—what her present consciousness calls an "absurd thought" about England in danger. The speed of the empty bus at night, another mother and child alone as at Kew, the "lamps glaring," the "claret-and-buff painted walls of the public-house" give us the feeling that we have been here before; we have heard this story; it is all familiar and ordinary. Eleanor looks up at her new home, "three windows on the very top next the roof." "Her milk was standing outside"—we think of Rose and Delia. ". . . she had only to light the gas ring and the kettle would be boiling in five minutes. Warmth, light, comfort, sprang into being at a touch." Here Woolf's genius is astonishing—the passage of time has been rendered in the change from gas lamps and coal fires and the ancient samovar of a kettle to "modern conveniences." They are ordinary details; their temporality has a mythic resonance. We remember Eleanor and her mother's old brass kettle, chased with roses, the tea ceremony, the impossible wick and how it seemed as if the kettle would never boil. Rose Pargiter's untimely death and the refusal of the eternal female symbol to "boil" create the common Woolfian ambiguity about the death of the mother. Eleanor has survived. Physical motherhood is a mystery to her. She is a "mother" to the slums, and her new kettle boils over. Only Crosby's letters are interesting to her—"a volley of sound, as if she were talking." "Below was the yellow light that never ceased, the glare of London." The list of war dead names a man she knew; "how could I have stopped him? she said aloud."

Oddly, the galley proofs refer to the postman's wife and her "twins"; a few lines later Eleanor reads "triplets. It was odd—birth; destruction. She saw the three red faces under a flannel hood. The triplets seemed to throw a shaft of light into the future." She has drawn a "red ring" on her calendar around the Friday she means to leave for India, the East. But the passage most resonant with the novel's lyric leitmotifs is about Eleanor's bathroom:

> She went into the bathroom. It gave her a thrill of pleasure. It was lined with gleaming white tiles; the taps shone silver; jars and brushes stood on a shining glass shelf. She lit the geyser; water instantly began to steam into the pure white bath. At Abercorn Terrace it always ran cold, she remembered. She began to undress. Yes, she thought as she slipped off her clothes and hung them on a silver hook, this is luxury, a hot bath. And to think, she thought, taking the pins out of her hair, that if I'd had a quarter of a millionth part of that money—she saw Rigby Cottages again and the sunflower with a crack down the middle. I could have . . . But what's the use of thinking? . . . She was stark naked; the window had no blind. She stood looking into the dappled iridescence of the moon-lit sky, which seemed to make her bathroom whiter, cleaner, more dazzling in its purity than ever; and then she stepped in.[8]

Washing and wishing, Eleanor remembers the coldness and inadequacy of the bathroom of her Victorian youth. The themes of chastity and cleanliness return; she regrets that the money went to the men, for her fantasy was to be plumber to the masses, provider of cleanliness to the lives of the poor and dirty. Good plumbing made good citizens, the Victorian reformers believed, and even Shaw and many Fabian socialists felt that a London with good sewers and drains would be a London without poverty or evil. Stubbornly ingrained in Virginia Woolf, from her Puritan and Quaker heritage, was not so much the belief that cleanliness was next to godliness as that dirt darkened the possibility of full humanity. Her early letters to her future husband, Leonard, contain as much excitement about drains and water closets as about love and marriage. Eleanor, performing her ritual act of purification, seems to cleanse the city with herself. Margaret Llewelyn-Davies, immortalized in both *Night and Day* (as Mary Datchet) and *The Years* (as Eleanor) had begun her brilliant reformer's career by agitating for decent plumbing in the slums.

There is a brief wartime section in which the searchlights are "great spokes" and the sky is "fleecy" and Eleanor fumbles in the dark to find Maggie and Renny's house, "number thirty," in the back of Westminster. The reader wonders if the basement dinner, the blackout and bombs that follow in the novel have some connection with an earlier scene at a "number thirty" in the top of a Westminster house where Eleanor's father fumbled "with the hand that had lost two fingers" the neck and shoulder of his mistress, Mira. Further on, the galleys give us Crosby amid sirens wailing and guns booming that the war is over, seeing Kitty in mourning. The next section brings together Kitty and Edward and memories of their youth. The trees are in mourning like Kitty; we learn that Edward now will inherit her father's chair, her father's house at Oxford, at the same moment that Kitty, who married Lord Lasswade to escape from the male world of Oxford dons, learns that her house and lands now pass to her son. Wild ducks, a cuckoo, "a musical wooden clapper," the lake ruffled by "gold scales," a "silver shield of water" set the uncomfortable scene. Edward, the pedant, corrects Kitty. It's not a cuckoo but a thrush, "that's the wise thrush . . . that sings each song twice over." The whole scene is set for the awakening of Brünnhilde by Siegfried. But what a Siegfried Edward makes, his only relation to the hero being his ability to understand the birds! She mourns at the performance of Siegfried that it is Edward who understands the music while she daydreams of Alf, the farmer's boy, and Nell Robson's brother, two more romantic, rustic "heroes." He thinks she's "too rough, too abrupt." She's glad not to have suffered under his edition of Sophocles as she suffered under her father's history of his Oxford college. They pass an officer in red, "blocks of bright-red and yellow flowers." Kitty returns to Grosvenor Square and tea with Eleanor, the "great silver kettle" riding like a ship between them. When Eleanor tells her how Nigs cried when she married ("Nigs" was Vita and Harold Nicolson's nickname for their son) she feels guilty about her brutality. There is a fire, hothouse flowers, a portrait of herself that Kitty despises. They talk about "people wanting power." Eleanor's "eye rested on the gilt basket of flowers by the door. She smiled. No, she could not possibly tell Kitty what they had been talking about. Power, patriotism, love, sex and all the rest of it." Kitty remembers the powerful men and women who have been here. She finds it hard to give up her own power, "now that I'm pensioned off like an old servant." Below them "the horns hooted; the cornet wailed; it was disturbing; unrestful. Like a piece of jangled music," and Kitty adds "what a mess they made of it."

Kitty and Eleanor look down on the London street, the one hating London, the other loving it. The sunset theme returns; "All round them were the great ring of houses, red gold in the evening haze." Eleanor rejoices that a shabby old woman gives a coin to the cornet player. Eleanor then begins a journey into the underworld of London, gazing at a "gold-spotted dress" in a shop window, glancing "automatically into the basements as she walked," into Soho where "they sold red rubber tubes." The contrast between the contraceptives and her mother bearing ten children, her father keeping a mistress, "the lady with yellow hair," moves in her mind. There is a barrel organ, people with "rosy faces." "It was absurd to let all this stir, potency, fecundity, run to waste, it was pouring past unused." She eats alone in a restaurant with red and pink lights, where a girl applies lipstick from a tube. The meal is a mess of "pink blobs"; "she sat there listening to the thudding of the doors; to the violins scrambling over the notes so that they missed the tune. She listened. There was no tune; it was only a scramble of bungled notes." Miriam's postcard with Italian white oxen, North's letter about sheep, and the arrangement of objects make her think of the Bergsonian durée, eternal flux, eternal oneness. "If there were a pattern, she mused, what would it be? If accidentally scattered objects, were yet in order? . . . if this fork, this knife, this flower and my hand—she laid it on the table—were thought together by another mind, so that what seemed accidental—vegetable, animal, metal—were in fact all one?" The couple silent over their food depresses her and the sentimental music, but "listening to music, even to cheap music, always until it became boring, ran things together." It makes the connection she was trying to make from the fork to the flower, the flower to the spoon. She blames "some rich man" for the badness of her dinner and the ornamental decor, remembering the simplicity of an olive jar in Italy compared to "glass beads on pink lamp-shades." The experience fills her with distaste for mankind. The pavement is "stained red with ruby light" from a gilded picture palace; the "thick red lips" of "film stars kissing" make her think of the gentle Nicholas, whose kind is put in prison. Young men "bawling out a coarse, defiant song" have "the faces of beasts." Here Valhalla seems to tumble down before our eyes. A big shop is being pulled down, its scaffolding "violent and crazy." "It was tumbling and falling, pitching forward to disaster. The crazy lines of the scaffolding, the jagged outline of the broken wall, the bestial shouts of the young men, made her feel that there was no order, no purpose in the world, but all was tumbling to ruin beneath a perfectly indifferent polished moon." As she disappears down into the Tube we expect that she will come up again, that there will be a sacrifice, a purification, a rebirth. In the last brief section she sits on her shower bath with North; this seems like the ancient mother and son ceremonies. Horns hoot at him in London traffic, red and green lights. He is like the young god, just back from Africa, thinking of "hides and fleeces." Eleanor wants him to stay; he wants to go back—"they all romanticized solitude and savagery" except Nicholas.

These discarded galleys, the Götterdämmerung scene in particular, show us Eleanor as the Great Mother-Maiden affirming with Bergson the unity and simultaneous flux of life, death, and rebirth. She goes underground like Hecate, next to be seen with a risen "son" in the bubbling stream of the shower bath. The whole scene, burnished red and gold, like Covent Garden in full blaze for the last act of *The Ring*, suggests the great bonfire of traditional myth; the burning away of the rubbish heap or "bone-fire" before the fire is the "good" fire of joy. All the scenes are lit by red and yellow light—a sunset symphony of the Great Mother's birds, from the goose pecking little Alf to the cuckoo and the thrush matched by the military drum, cornet, and out-of-tune violins. The human voice sings out against this dreadful din, and Woolf is in full command of the huge Wagnerian cast. She cut these passages out like a gardener pruning a tree. But the branches still have blossoms worthy of the tree.

Mary Augusta Ward (Mrs. Humphry Ward)

As a final note on *The Years* I want to comment on two women whose work stands behind the composition of *The Years*, Margaret Llewelyn-Davies and Mrs. Humphry Ward, representing the conservative and radical traditions of women reformers.

While it is essentially the *ambience* of Mrs. Ward's "Young Days at Oxford" that suffuses Woolf's Oxford scenes, Mrs. Ward was an important person in her life if only as a representative of the family's high-minded friends, the kind of woman, social worker, reformer, preaching novelist, that Virginia Woolf was determined not to become. One of Mrs. Ward's novels was called *Eleanor*, and she recorded her Oxford life in *Miss Bretherton* and *Lady Connie*. She complained that women's education was so bad that everything had to be "relearnt" before it could be of use to her. Like Kitty and Lucy Craddock, "what I learnt during those years was learnt from personalities; from contact with a nature so simple, sincere and strong as that of Miss Clough . . . and from a gentle and high-minded woman, an ardent Evangelical, with whom . . . I fell in love, as was the manner of schoolgirls then." Her father was classical master at the Oratory School (her uncle, Matthew Arnold) and she describes Mark Pattison with his "cackling laugh" like Old Chuffy's "hyena" laugh in the novel. Edward's vision of Kitty in a white and blue dress (p. 51) in front of the Morris wallpapers suggests Mrs. Ward's description of herself papering the walls of Somerville College with Morris papers and collecting blue and white china. Mrs. Ward relates being told she had "an original mind" like Kitty but being unable to use it because of the social demands on a woman's life. The "lilac and laburnum" of the novel are in the *Recollections*, and Mrs. Ward describes the "atmosphere of tension" around Jowett: "With him there were no diversions, none!—no relief from the breathless adventure of trying to please him" (p. 128). Her own "doctrine of social pity" derived from Renan (Eleanor reads Renan in *The Years*), whom she met at Oxford where he called the university "a deserted Paradise" and "the type of living death" because there was no intellectual life as in France, and the Fellows were all off shooting and hunting (p. 174). She also writes about the visit of Lowell, the "American professor" and his wife (he was Virginia Woolf's godfather), and they are like the Fripps in the novel. Mrs. Ward also writes a good deal about Parnell and the Irish. She was in the House to hear her uncle William Forster denounce Parnell and his response in 1883. There are some lyrical passages about the love of the North from Laura Tennant Lyttelton's letters which are similar to Kitty's (feelings) in *The Years*. She writes admiringly of the austere radical John Morley's *On Compromise*, but obviously Woolf felt Mrs. Ward had compromised the purer life of a Spanish historian for the social life of a London celebrity and best-selling sentimental novelist, and Woolf even entitled her review "The Compromise." The novel shows us a Kitty compromised by her marriage and social life, lustrous still and a moonlike Diana in her old age, but losing even the Northern land she had married to win, to the male property line in the end. Mrs. Ward herself had been the figurehead for male hostility to women by heading the Anti-Suffrage League, publishing in *The Nineteenth Century* a list of prominent women who opposed the reform. Beatrice Webb (who later recanted) and Virginia Woolf's mother were among those who signed; Mrs. Stephen was mocked mercilessly by the feminist George Meredith, who hoped she would educate her daughters for a freer life. In her letters to Margaret Llewelyn-Davies Virginia Woolf wrote mockingly of both Beatrice Webb and Mrs. Humphry Ward and the self-indulgence and righteousness of those who professed to "love their kind" as social workers. On March 2, 1915 Woolf wrote, "Did I tell you that I have decided to write all the novels of Mrs. Humphry Ward and all the diaries of Mrs. Sidney Webb? It will be my life work. (Leonard has not yet laughed at any of these jokes though I think them rather good.)"

Margaret Llewelyn-Davies

Margaret Llewelyn-Davies[9] (1861–1944), a major figure for thirty years in the Women's Cooperative Movement, was christened Margaret Caroline, but eventually took to herself the family name Llewelyn which had been given to her six brothers at birth. Her mother, Mary Crompton, came from a Unitarian family of progressives and her father, a friend of F. D. Maurice, was a Christian Socialist and rector of Christ Church, Marylebone. Margaret, unlike Virginia Woolf, was educated at Queen's College, London, and Girton (her aunt, Emily Davies, was one of the founders of Girton College.) Her striking beauty complemented her commanding intellect and she was equally at home acting in the Greek play at Cambridge with Janet Case and volunteering as a sanitary inspector in Marylebone. She joined the Cooperative Society in 1886, was elected secretary of her branch in 1887 and by 1889, when she moved to Kirkby Lonsdale in Westmorland, she was elected general secretary of the Women's Cooperative Guild. Under her direction and with the help of her lifelong companion, Lilian Harris, Miss Davies developed the guild as a self-help organization with educational, social, and political goals. But, more important, she trained working-class women to make their voices heard on national and international issues of pacifism, feminism, and socialism. During her tenure, the Guild vigorously supported women's suffrage, struggled for and succeeded in establishing a minimum wage for women and girls within the co-op movement, and campaigned strongly for the rights of mothers and housewives. *Maternity: Letters from Working Women* (1915), *The Women's Cooperative Guild* (1904), *The Woman with a Basket: The History of the Women's Cooperative Guild* (by C. Webb with an introduction by M. L. Davies, 1927) and *Life As We Have Known It* (with an introduction by Virginia Woolf, 1931) as well as her many pamphlets and public speeches, made Margaret Llewelyn-Davies into an important figure in the national and international Cooperative Movement. During the twenties and thirties most of her energies were spent in the peace movement as well as encouraging trade between the English and Russian Cooperative Movements and as secretary of the Society for Cultural Relations between the U.S.S.R. and the British Commonwealth.

Looking back at her life of social commitment in the foreword to *The Woman with a Basket*, she felt that her most important work was in organizing married working women to take an active part in politics and to demand their rights to health care, children's welfare, divorce, and wages. These voiceless and neglected working women soon moved from personal politics in the struggle for maternity rights with the men in the movement to a struggle for the vote and for peace. Margaret's statement in 1931 that "the most immediate revolution required is the complete abolition of war and of the fear of war," shows how strongly she and the Woolf of *Three Guineas* were political allies.

The lifelong friendship between Woolf and Davies was built on family connections, feminism, socialism, and pacifism. The two couples were also friends and often visited each other. Woolf's letters are full of references to Lilian Harris, as Davies's are to Leonard Woolf, though, of course, when Leonard was working on his history of cooperation, his relation to Margaret took precedence and she wrote of her concern for Virginia's health. What strikes me about Margaret's letters is that they confirm Woolf's concept of a "conspiracy" of women, the essence of the conspiracy being pacifism. She thought that Leonard was wasting his talents editing the liberal *Nation* and *New Statesman* and discussed with Virginia the issues raised at the Cooperative congresses. In a 1938 letter, Margaret recalled her brother Maurice's visit with his fiancée to the Stephens at St. Ives (perhaps he lurks behind *To the Lighthouse* as he does *The Years*), she wonders what Virginia's niece Ann will be besides a Communist, and says, "I think the idea that by creating 2 Empires on the Mediterranean we shall get peace, is chimerical." Margaret's forthright criticism included a remark that she didn't cotton to Clive Bell's mind—"I don't believe I should ever think anything he did was worth doing," and when Virginia sent the "poetical" Fredegond Shove to work for the Cooperative Guild in 1915, Margaret replied, "Why are the cultured so limited and finicky?"

While the letters of Virginia Woolf to Margaret Llewelyn-Davies are most interesting as documents describing Woolf's active political involvement with the Cooperative Working Women, they also show that Davies was the source for Mary Datchet in *Night and Day* as well as for Eleanor in *The Years*. On January 23, 1916, Woolf wrote:

> I become steadily more feminist, owing to The Times, which I read at breakfast & wonder how this preposterous masculine fiction keeps going a day longer without some vigorous young woman pulling us together and marching through it—Do you see any sense in it? . . . And now they'll give us votes . . . I wish I could borrow your mind about 3 days a week.

She returns to the work of the Women's Guild for comfort when she feels that all efforts at changing the world are doomed to failure. On August 17, 1919, Woolf wrote that Margaret ought to come and see the family portraits she had bought at the Monks House Sale, paintings by an early Victorian blacksmith: "For myself I don't ask anything more of pictures. They are family groups & he began the heads very large, & hadn't got room for the hands & legs, so these dwindle off till they're about the size of sparrows' claws, but the effect is superb—the character overwhelming"—which anticipates the portraits Kitty sees at the Robsons'. *The Years* is again anticipated in the same letter as Woolf wishes that Margaret and Janet Case and the Webbs and Coles and others more frivolous might gather on her lawn so that she could observe them from her window "dissolving and combining in patterns in the distance."

Their families had been close; Virginia's sister Vanessa had been attracted by one of Margaret's brothers, but earlier generations had been related, and Adrian and Karin Stephen's daughter Ann ("6 ft. and means to be a doctor") married Margaret's nephew Richard. The two childless aunts wrote to each other very seriously concerned with the fate of niece and nephew. The letters show Woolf's admiration for her niece's desire to combine medicine and politics. Ann seems to be a source for Peggy in *The Years*. One of Margaret's brothers was named Maurice and they objected strongly when Margaret with Virginia's encouragement tried to collect the family letters and papers. Woolf consulted her friend while doing research for "Professions for Women" and *Three Guineas*, and Miss Llewelyn-Davies wrote to tell her that *The Years* was the last book her Greek teacher, Janet Case, read aloud to her sister. Margaret, like Eleanor in the novel, had built cottages in her youth and encouraged (influenced by Ruskin and Morris) arts and crafts; she sent Virginia some needlework from the cottages and was teased about her idealism. The themes of keeping the family history and of admiration for "the younger generation" recur in the letters; they share examples of "repression" in women of their own class—as

Peggy asks Eleanor if she was "suppressed" in her youth. ("Repression" is villain in this novel; Rose and Edward become violent and dried-up because of it. Woolf is not against homosexuality, only its repression. Nicholas, who is open, is admirable and not a woman-hater at all.) In 1922, Woolf wrote to Margaret that she was going to make a speech at the Guild, "honouring the greatness of Margaret Ll. Davies," and in 1934 there is a reference to "an idiotic Polish Count" whom Leonard is helping out of prison for writing "silly indecent poems": "How can the young be so silly and egotistical. Shelley is at the bottom of it—but they write in the style of Mrs. Hemans save for indecency." In 1938, Margaret Llewelyn-Davies, that visionary woman who inspired Virginia Woolf's creation of the heroines in her two novels of "fact," wrote to her regarding *Three Guineas*: "to read the first sentence was like a Himalaya poppy—or the murmur of innumerable bees in immemorial elms—or beauty born of murmuring sound or the satisfaction given of a music phrase and other things— the style was so delicious. Of course the book would appeal to me no end on account of peace and anti-humbug and justice," and she thanks Virginia for writing "that letter for us about another Congress—I am sadly afraid Leonard won't like it—nor things we have written," as the women became more isolated in their pacifism.

Operatic, realistic, dramatic, domestic, *The Years* is for me, finally, the female epic. It is Woolf's answer to *The Waste Land* and *Ulysses*, siding with the despised Jews and women of Eliot, bursting with the "content" she felt Joyce lacked to fill up his form. It is a communal and anti-heroic Odyssey with Nausikaa as its heroine. Eleanor, that militant but non-violent maiden, washes away the sins of a war-torn world. She rises from her tomb—"that Hell" at Abercorn Terrace—bringing fresh air, light and water out of the Victorian gloom. *The Years* is yet another subversion of the patriarchal genealogical imperative of English fiction. If *Night and Day* does this by "thinking back through our mothers," *The Years* accomplishes its anti-fascist end by thinking sideways through our sisters. Its horizontal leap from Victorian to Modern, in uneven time periods, not the standard decades, emphasizing relations of cousins and aunts and nephews, not fathers and sons, privileging spinsters over mothers, spatializing time in family rooms, marks *The Years'* response to the Victorian voice of paternal authority. We read and hear the novel as one long series of interrupted discourses, the interruptions themselves marking the daughters' emergence from the tyranny of the father's voice.

⌒ 4 ⌒

Liberty, Sorority, Misogyny

> Jug, jug, jug.
> I sing like the nightingale whose melody is
> crowded in the too narrow passage of her
> throat.
>
> —*The Waves*

In *A Room of One's Own* Virginia Woolf explicates a Marxist-feminist theory of literary criticism. "Masterpieces are not single and solitary births," she wrote, "they are the outcome of thinking in common, of thinking by the body of the people, so that the experience of the mass is behind the single voice."[1] She was discussing Shakespeare as the product of history and imagined that Shakespeare's sister, the great woman artist, would arrive when women had had intellectual freedom for several generations. In *Moments of Being* she went even further: "There is no Shakespeare, there is no Beethoven; certainly and emphatically there is no God; we are the words; we are the music; we are the thing itself."[2]

Behind these fierce assertions is the hostile and threatening assertion made by men to feminists of Woolf's generation that women have produced no geniuses, no Shakespeares, no Beethovens, no Rembrandts. Woolf always looks at the writer in historical context, at the conditions of women's lives: "Intellectual freedom depends on material things" (*Room*, pp. 162–63). We are bound to follow her example when we look at her work. It is in the history of her family that we may find the source of her philosophy. The Stephen men and the men of her circle were shaped by institutions, Cambridge University and the secret society, the Apostles, which affirmed their being as the "intellectual aristocracy" of England.[3]

In order to catapult women into history Woolf analyzed the notions of liberty, equality, and fraternity of her forefathers and her friends. Female liberty, equality, and sorority were her goals. In imagination and in action she met misogyny full-face. Her birth image in the passage from *A Room of One's Own* is only one of many vaginal creative spaces (a room of one's own is the most famous), which she asserted as a response to phallocentric culture. The virginal vagina was the place and the space for the production of female culture. Women could not be the producers of culture while reproducing humankind, she felt, and history bore her out. Her task was further complicated by the fact that the misogynists were of two types. The old bullies like James Fitzjames Stephen who thundered about separate spheres and angels in the house were replaced in her own generation and the one before it by a homosexual hegemony over British culture.[4] Woolf did not attack homosexuality itself, nor do I.

But male superiority and the valorization of homosexual over heterosexual love, learned at Cambridge in the study of Greek and reinforced by the philosophy debated in the meetings of the Apostles, resulted in a subtler and more dangerous kind of woman-hating. These men had class and cultural power, an old-boy network with connections in government, diplomacy, education, publishing, and the literary journals. They were not, like homosexuals of more vulnerable classes, the natural allies of women, fellow outsiders. It was working-class men Woolf called upon to be the allies of women in their struggle against patriarchal imperialism and capitalism in *Three Guineas*. But then it was clear to her that "outsiders" needed not only rooms of their own but institutions of their own—buildings, universities, libraries.

In "A Society" Woolf made the most radical assertion of the idea that the production of culture and the reproduction of children were incompatible. Her sorority determines that the only way for women to take control over the production of culture is to find some way for men to bear children. If they are occupied with producing children, then women may produce books. One way that phallocentric culture imprisons women is to enforce guilt.

In *Between the Acts* Woolf rejects Swinburne's recasting of the swallow and the nightingale myth from its original claim of the power of sisterhood over the patriarchal family to a misogynist nagging whine intended to produce guilt. Weighted with this male-imposed guilt, Woolf shows, the married woman cannot begin to bond with her sisters. Into the mouth of the nightingale Swinburne puts a seductive threat: "Thou hast forgotten, O summer swallow/but the world will end when I forget."[5] The nightingale forecasts universal doom if the killing of a male child in revenge for his rapist father's action is forgotten. But the speaker is the rape victim. She has forgotten her own rape and the cutting out of her tongue by her brother-in-law. Her sorrows are not to be sung, the male poet tells us. Woolf rewrites the poem in order to straighten out priorities. *Between the Acts* tells us that "what we must remember" is the rape; "what we must forget" is the male rewriting of women's history.

Woolf's feminism marks the representation of women throughout her fiction. Spinsterhood, for her, is the measure of success. Her artists and reformers, from Lily Briscoe to Eleanor Pargiter, Mary Datchet to Lucy Swithin, are women without men. The virgin mothers, Mrs. Ramsay and Clarissa Dalloway, are women who refuse men, even their husbands. Betty Flanders, widow, recalls in *Jacob's Room* gelding her cat with relish, in memory of her former suitor. Miss Kilman and Miss La Trobe represent varieties of lesbian existence.

Rachel Vinrace experiences male sexuality as rape and dies. In Woolf's most traditional novel, Katherine Hilbery marries an outsider for intellectual freedom
and escape from her class and family. She is not sexually attracted to Ralph, and
they acknowledge that their companionate marriage will be made possible by
the single women who will shoulder their burdens of both family and social
responsibility.

Female heterosexuality is most often represented in Woolf's fiction as victimization or colonization. Those women who accept the ideology of female submission in patriarchal marriage are silently condemned. Mrs. Ramsay's insistence
on marriage and traditional roles results in the death of her son in battle and of
her daughter in childbirth; we see the unhappy results of the marriages she
arranged. The patriarchal family is violently assaulted as the source of fascism in
The Years. Marriage is a primitive form of private property, North thinks. We
will never be civilized as long as we wallow in the "primeval swamp" of marriage; if it is a question of *my* children, *my* property, "it would be one rip down
the belly; or teeth in the soft fur of the throat."[6] Sara's relationship with Nicholas
the homosexual is presented as eccentric but ethical. If the historian had only
Woolf's novels from which to deduce the position of women in England, she
would be forced to conclude that marriage was a primitive institution in decline;
that many women perceived male sexuality as rape; that lesbianism and homosexuality were widespread; that spinsterhood, aunthood, sisterhood, and
female friendship were women's most important roles; that motherhood and
wifehood were Victorian relics. Peggy, exhausted from sitting up late with a
woman in childbirth, is a new woman professional. "All her patients said that,
she thought. Rest—rest—let me rest. How to deaden; how to cease to feel; that
was the cry of the woman bearing children; to rest, to cease to be. In the Middle
Ages, she thought, it was the cell; the monastery; now it's the laboratory, the
professions" (*The Years*, p. 355).

The Years asks the question, Is there a pattern? and *Between the Acts* gives a
sociobiological answer. The origin of aggression, war, and oppression is in the
origin of the species, in the drama of the battle of the sexes. Isa and Giles fight
like the dog fox and the vixen before they make love. Giles is a male animal. He
kills the snake with the toad in its mouth. With blood on his shoes, he fornicates
with Mrs. Manresa like an ape attracted to a female in heat. Is there another
plot? Will the author come out of the bushes and invent a new story not enacted
in the village pageant or in the lives of the audience? The question is whether
Miss La Trobe can imagine the beginning of the human drama without a violent
power struggle. So far it is clear that the survival of the fittest is in conflict with
the survival of the creative woman. She can only refuse to reproduce, refuse
wifehood and motherhood. Chastity is power. Chastity is liberty.[7] Marriage, to
take a phrase from Woolf's contemporary socialist feminist Cecily Hamilton, is
a trade.[8] And since women have no control over the means of production in their
trade or the means of reproduction, their only access to dignity is the sexual
strike.

In three essays published roughly a decade apart and in her last novel Woolf dealt both directly and indirectly with the political implications of female sexuality and male violence against women. The reception of these texts is a corollary of their thesis. "A Society" was published in *Monday or Tuesday* in 1921 and never reprinted because of the hostility of male critics. In *A Room of One's Own* (1928) the author tries to hide her feminist impulses behind the skirts of several narrators and plants her darts at the patriarchy in between passages of fine writing, meant to seduce and solace the male reader. E. M. Forster and his ilk could then, by avoiding her ideas, praise passages of description and create Virginia Woolf the lyrical formalist, minor mandarin, for generations of critics to analyze. *Three Guineas* (1938) plays no games and lost her what was left of her audience. It was met and is still met by male abuse. Finally, I would like to discuss these issues as they appear in *Between the Acts*, published after Woolf's death. All four works are formally experimental, suggesting her unease with tradition and her radical feminist need to overthrow patriarchal forms. "A Society" is a propagandistic and personal essay much like the papers delivered by young men at the meetings of the Cambridge University secret society, the Apostles, where a serious philosophical or moral issue was debated with humor in simple language but according to G. E. Moore's rigorous philosophy of truth-telling. "A Society" pretends to be a short story, but the message drowns the characters and the plot, and it is more like Wollstonecraft's *Maria; or, The Wrongs of Woman* than Katherine Mansfield's *Bliss*.

A *Room of One's Own* appears to be a set of lectures given at Newnham and Girton. Nonacademic and nonscholarly, they revive as characters Mary Beton, Mary Seton, and Mary Carmichael from the old ballad in a shockingly feminist rhetorical strategy which excludes the male reader and directly addresses the female reader.[9] But to capture the uniqueness of Woolf's form in *A Room of One's Own*, one may say that it is an elegy written in a college courtyard for the lost traditions of women's culture, a plea for women writers to "think back through our mothers" encased in a litany of the names of those mother-writers. As Woolf tells her beads to the tune of the ballad of the victims, she names the survivors and heroines. As she lays and slays the ghost of Milton, she captures and revives the ghost of Jane Ellen Harrison, the great classical scholar, in "the voice of some terrible reality leaping."[10]

Three Guineas is even more complex in form. Disguised as an anti-fascist pamphlet in an age of pamphlets, propaganda, and thirties protest literature, it is written in the form of replies to three letters asking for money to support good causes. The author replies as "the daughter of an educated man" in an address that confronts the writers of the letters with the narrowness of their individual demands for social change. But the essay also demonstrates the revolutionary dictum to organize one's own class in that it addresses only other daughters of educated men. Contemporary readers expected a radical protest against the atrocities in Spain and got instead a harsh, angry polemic denouncing capitalism, imperialism, anti-feminism, and patriarchal culture in general.

Three Guineas is a classic in the form of epistolary polemic. Like letters written in exile or in prison, it is in style and content part of the literature of the oppressed. One may certainly argue that the daughters of educated men were not as oppressed as blacks or the working class. But Woolf defines this oppression and seeks an alliance with them. Though we have been unable to convince Woolf's publishers to include her original photographs in reprints of the book, they are an important part of the propagandistic effect. For the reader expecting more photographs of atrocities in Spain, Woolf's photographs of the patriarchs of England in their professional garb were a shock. *Three Guineas* (its title defining the class of her audience as *Three Pounds* might appeal to another class) is, of course, a play on Brecht's *Threepenny Opera*. Besides naming the exact amounts sought by those who want to salve the consciences of intellectuals, the title is an economic metaphor for her arguments. Unlike *A Room of One's Own*, with its supposed lecture form, *Three Guineas* is buttressed by forty-three pages of formidable footnotes. This rhetorical strategy infuriated academic readers like Queenie Leavis, who called *Three Guineas* "Nazi dialectic without Nazi conviction."[11]

The book is more than a work of art. It is a major contribution to political science. Woolf's argument that the origin of fascism was in the patriarchal family (not in Italian, German, or Spanish nationalism or class) is a thesis still too bold for any but the most radical of feminists to take seriously. Recently, however, the same argument has been made in Lina Wertmuller's revolutionary film *Seven Beauties* and in Maria-Antonietta Macciocchi's brilliant essay "Female Sexuality in Fascist Ideology." I suggest that Woolf's pamphlet was influenced by Brecht and his definition of the relationship between prostitutes and a pimp. Woolf's language is much the same. Macciocchi argues that "the body of fascist discourse is rigorously chaste, pure, virginal. Its central aim is the death of sexuality: women are always called to the cemetery to honor the war dead, to come bearing them crowns, and they are exhorted to offer their sons to the fatherland." She quotes Eleanor Marx: "That is why we, for the most part socialists, affirm that chastity, although sacred, is unhealthy . . . we consider chastity a crime."[12]

The thesis made explicit in *Three Guineas* provides the plot and tensions of all four works under discussion here. Woolf came from a culture and a family obsessed with female chastity, and she was obsessed with their obsession. While she consistently attacked this idea and recognized the fascist component in the repression of sexuality, it is a poignant and ironic measure of how one's politics can be more radical than one's life to note that she seems to have lived most of her life in physical chastity, and the powerful and moving images for her own creative processes are of the chaste imagination retreating to a nunnery. Macciocchi claims that "the Nazi community is made by homosexual brothers who exclude the woman and valorize the Mother."[13]

The Cambridge Apostles' notions of fraternity surely appeared to Woolf analogous to certain fascist notions of fraternity. And Woolf's model of sorority as a

parallel concept to the Apostles' model of fraternity had to confront male concepts of female chastity and brutality and violence against women, as well as its
own lack of an institutional power base.

In *Between the Acts,* Woolf again follows Brecht in a classical Marxist dialectic
expressed in the pageant of British history set near Roman ruins in wartime
Britain and insisting on the participation of the audience. As Evelyn Haller
argues, there is an underlying feminist appropriation of Egyptian mythology to
counter the Anglo-Saxon myths of war and aggression.[14] But the form of
Between the Acts is dramatic. I believe that what Woolf was trying to do in the
novel was to write the modern version of a lost Greek play—Sophocles' play on
the myth of Procne and Philomela. This story of rape and sisterly revenge set in
wartime is the theme that structures *Between the Acts* with its recurrent images
of the swallow and the nightingale.

I said earlier that these four formally innovative and explicitly feminist works
of Virginia Woolf's were written in response to the misogyny of her family and
her culture. Macciocchi identifies the elements of homosexual brotherhood,
brutality, and violence against women, the adoration of motherhood and the
simultaneous repression of sexuality. The Brechtian political thesis that women
consent to play angel in the house and encourage war, which Woolf attacks in
Three Guineas, suggests the underpinning for certain ideological components
in the work of the Stephen family in nineteenth-century England.

Victorian violence against women and the institutionalization of that violence
in fraternal organizations like the Cambridge Apostles stirred Woolf's imagination. Her declaration to Dame Ethel Smyth that "women alone stir my imagination" was only half the truth. For women were dispossessed of culture, and it
was Woolf's revolutionary goal to storm the gates of Cambridge to steal the
secret of what sociologists call "same-sex bonding," that brotherhood which
appeared to own the means of production of culture—in law, politics, literature, and life. The men of the Stephen family were dependent on the consent
and support of their women in this enterprise.

Woolf was working against the work of her grandfather, James Stephen, Permanent Under Secretary for the Colonies and architect of imperialism under
seven changes of government, and professor of modern history at Cambridge;
her uncle Fitzjames Stephen, codifier of English law and Indian law, judge of
the High Court, and conservative political philosopher; Fitzjames's son, J. K.
Stephen, Virginia's first cousin, "bard of Eton and of boyhood," misogynist poet
and famous parodist, thought by some to be a likely candidate for the role of Jack
the Ripper; her father, Leslie Stephen, compiler of the *Dictionary of National
Biography*, a powerful political tool in the Victorian definition of English history
as the biographies of England's great men. (Woolf wryly remarked that there
were no lives of maids in the DNB.)

But she had also to exorcise the work of her female family as collaborators in
the making of nineteenth-century British patriarchal ideology. Virginia Woolf's
aunt Caroline Emelia Stephen was the author of a monumental history of sisterhoods, an anti-feminist piece of propaganda that perceived and argued force-

fully that all separate organizations of nuns and nurses (even women's colleges) were a dangerous threat to the patriarchal family.[15] Woolf scholars have known of Julia Stephen's signing of Mrs. Humphry Ward's anti-suffrage petition and Meredith's warning to her of the dangers to her daughters of a self-chosen role as "princess to a patriarch." But Martine Stemerick has recently documented and discussed Julia's neglected and unpublished manuscripts, essays on women and agnosticism and on the servant question that clarify her unswerving conservatism and anti-feminism.[16]

Julia Stephen's *Notes from Sick Rooms* valorizes nursing as woman's highest role.[17] Caroline Stephen, on the other hand, rejected and severely criticized district visiting and the charity of ladies bountiful like Mrs. Ramsay in *To the Lighthouse* as unprofessional and productive of an unwholesome sense of moral superiority in women.[18] But Caroline's role in her history of sisterhoods was exactly like her brother Fitzjames's in the codification and clarification of whole fields of English law. She argued for professionalization of nursing and social work as efficient occupations with clear duties, training, and paid workers. Like her father, James, who built a huge bureaucracy in the Colonial Office (supposedly satirized by Dickens in *Little Dorrit* as the Circumlocution Office),[19] and like Fitzjames, who synthesized centuries of contradictory laws, Caroline Stephen was part of the unacknowledged family plot to take over the institutions of England. There is no more perfect example of the rise of the middle class and its imposition of Clapham Sect morality and the work ethic in place of a lazy, indifferent aristocracy. The Stephens were a progressive force in the interest of the power of the rising middle class.

But Julia Stephen's idealization of nursing derives from a different and more traditional upper-class culture. She was a doctor's daughter and nurse to her mother, family, and friends. She trained her daughter Stella in the same role, but Virginia abhorred these trips to the sickrooms of the slums, complained bitterly, and rejected the role for herself, with the exception of caring for her dying father. Her observations were keen, however, in her comments on Florence Nightingale and in the portraits of Mrs. Ramsay and of Eleanor Pargiter in *The Years*, whose devotion to the poor has the same mystical visionary aspect as Caroline Stephen's Quaker philosophy. But Woolf's most telling comment is Peggy's remark in *The Years* that the statue of Nurse Cavell reminds her of an advertisement for sanitary napkins. Cavell, the nurse-martyr, was executed by the Germans in Belgium. She was in no sense a nationalistic female self-sacrificer and claimed, "Patriotism is not enough!" But when her statue was erected in London, her death was used as propaganda against the Germans, and the slogan "For God, King and Country" was added in large letters.[20] The linking of menstrual blood and the blood of the wounded soldier, sanitary napkins and bandages, supports the anti-war theme of the novel and suggests how difficult it is for women to dissociate themselves from war. Macciocchi, who agrees with Woolf's argument in *Three Guineas* that fascism is inseparable from patriarchy, describes as distinctly fascist the male enforcement of woman as the ideal nurse, which encourages a sadistic passion in the nurse like the mystical desire for blood in a Saint Theresa. She notes that the Italian fascists created this role for women in the image of the Red Cross nurse, which reached its peak in Rosselini's film *The White Ship*, "a filmscript of pure repressive fascist mystique."[21]

There is one other woman in her family against whom Virginia rebelled: her first cousin, Katherine Stephen (1856–1924), principal of Newnham. Woolf associated her cousins, the two Stephen sisters, with the most frightening aspects of evangelical patriarchal Christianity. She told Ethel Smyth that Hyde Park Gate preachers made her shudder with horror in memory of her cousins' brutal attempts to convert her in her youth. She thinks of their God as a rapist: "He's got a finger in my mind." How, we may ask, did the daughter of the man who ferociously attacked John Stuart Mill, who made it his business as a judge to hang women suspected of murdering their husbands, who railed against the emancipation of women, mocking Millicent Garrett Fawcett, and who was hounded out of office as the "mad judge" for prejudicing the jury in the case of Mrs. Maybrick—how did she become principal of a woman's college?[22] Whatever the answer, we may assume that when Virginia Woolf gave her lectures at Cambridge her cousin became one of the Marys of *A Room of One's Own*.

The Stephen women were collaborators in their own oppression, but they also found ways to assert their independence, Katherine in a career in women's education, her sister Dorothea in the study of Eastern religions, and Caroline Emelia Stephen in her break with the evangelicals, her conversion to Quakerism, and her Quaker books *The Vision of Faith* and *The Light Arising: Thoughts on the Central Radiance*. According to Quaker historians, she single-handedly revived the moribund English Society of Friends and found a personal solution to the patriarchal and authoritarian philosophy she had found at home, especially in espousing pacifism.[23] Caroline's Quaker pacifism, which is the source of the pacifism of Virginia Woolf that rankles so many readers of *Three Guineas*, may be seen as a form of bourgeois feminist withdrawal from the struggle against patriarchy. The mysticism that characterizes Woolf's fiction and Caroline Stephen's religious essays is an imaginatively fulfilling substitute for mounting the barricades, a passive-aggressive protest against the violence of the men in their families, which violence they then describe as a characteristic of the male sex.

But women are even more crippled by madonna-worship than men, as the lives of women artists tell us. In the case of Woolf, this, coupled with the public and private misogyny of the men in her family, led to her definition of herself as an outsider and to her repeated equations of both freedom and creativity with chastity. Though she did relent in her pacifism enough early in the Second World War to advocate defense from the enemy, she could not bring herself to the brink of actual fighting, for that would be tantamount to changing her sex. Suicide, in some sense, is perhaps the only solution masochistic enough to satisfy the pacifist when the politics and violence of war become too much to bear.

The legacy of Stephen misogyny went back to James Stephen of the Colonial

Office. His son Leslie described him as a "living categorical imperative." And one of his colleagues said he was "a transcendental Quaker with a tendency to Popery."[24] But Catholicism offended a "patriarch of his standing" (to use his own words) because of its worship of the Virgin Mary. When he saw the Pope in Rome, he wrote that his face had a "benevolence and mental feebleness as becomes a promulgator of the Immaculate Conception." And in Brussels in 1852 he was disdainful of a Saint Nicholas procession with "the goddess and her child turned into two deplorable dolls" as "the old heathen worship in a new dress." He certainly idealized motherhood, but not in any form from which the father was excluded. James Stephen was the chief ideologue of British "benevolent" imperialism, described by Henry Taylor as the most powerful man in England, yet his public behavior was "profoundly subordinate." Stephen was a tyrant at home, and Leslie remembers him dictating to his mother and sisters with a Miltonic tread. But to the feminist imagination Virginia Woolf's grandfather was more than a petty patriarchal tyrant over his family. He was actually the architect of an ideology of oppression that used the model of patriarchal domestic tyranny as a basis for colonial imperialism. His concepts and metaphors have become embedded in our language and thought, and his policies as hallowed as Biblical precept. The press called him "Mr. Mother-Country Stephen," for it was he who coined the phrase "the mother country." It was he who made the policies that bound the British colonies in a domestic metaphor that was to determine their relations for more than a hundred years, to yoke whole nations in a position from which to rebel was to insult sacred motherhood itself. The rebel was then a moral outcast, a bad son. It took a brilliant patriarchal mind to conceive of such a notion for maintaining social control, enforcing dependency, and demanding unquestioning obedience from subjects whose role was defined as that of children.

"No reasonable man would ever affirm broadly and generally," he wrote in 1850, "that a mother country ought at some time or other to part with her colonies . . . England ought never to give up a single colony." The Canadian course (which he had directed) was the right one, "cheerfully relaxing the bonds of authority." The rest of the colonies were "wretched burdens to this country, which in an evil hour we assumed, but which we have no right to lay down again. We emancipate our grown-up sons, but keep our unmarried daughters, and our children who may chance to be ricketty, in domestic bonds. The analogy is a very close one."[25] Mr. Mother-Country Stephen was one of the patriarchy's geniuses. He despised Catholics for pagan mother-goddess worship but tapped the same human impulses for political ends with enormous success. Queen Victoria herself seems to have grown in girth throughout the century to meet the demands of Stephen's majestic mother-image.[26] The matriarch, the maternal embodiment of the mother-country (we see her in Woolf's obituary of Lady Strachey and in her portraits of Lady Bruton and Dr. Bradshaw's wife in *Mrs. Dalloway*), seems to have been the invention of a patriarch. We must never underestimate the power of a man and his metaphor. How clever it was to invest the philosophy of imperialism with the theology of the patriarchal family. Women were burdened with guilt and implicated in exploitation at the most fundamental psychic levels. The master-servant relation, even more clearly defined by James's son, James Fitzjames Stephen, as the relation of a father to his wife and children, was then enforced by their women in relation to colonial subjects and servants. This ideology of imperialism, based on the structure of the patriarchal family, needed woman's consent to dependency and rewarded her with power over her servants.[27]

It should come as no surprise then that both Julia Stephen and Caroline Emelia Stephen were eloquent explicators in print of the necessity of a woman's power over her servants, that she rule autocratically and with a very firm hand. Virginia Woolf's lifelong struggle with the rejection of the matriarchal role and her savage attacks on the patriarchal family in her novels and essays is also not surprising. The letters and diaries reveal a socialist feminist in agonies over the servant problem, for she had none of the matriarchal confidence of her Aunt Caroline and her mother in a benevolently powerful role. And yet, figures of sympathetic charwomen appear in her novels, and they are related to the middle-class reformers like Eleanor in *The Years* (a figure much like Caroline Emelia Stephen), who cleans up the slums and is a mystical figure of the artist as charwoman to the world. But Woolf's rebellion against the matriarchal subjection of servants of her mother and her aunt did not, interestingly enough, result in the idealization and romanticizing of servants. In fact, Crosby in *The Years* is portrayed as an example of that cultural gap we discussed earlier. Long after her masters and mistresses have abandoned the patriarchal family, she remembers and tries to enforce the old roles.

Perhaps the best example may be found in Louise De Salvo's edition of *Melymbrosia*, one of the earlier versions of *The Voyage Out*.[28] On board ship, Mrs. Chailley comes to Rachel to complain that all the sheets are worn and torn and that she has been put in a tiny, noisy cubicle next to the boiler. Rachel says she'll try to get new sheets and have the servant moved to better quarters. But Mrs. Chailley is not pleased by this response. She wishes Rachel's mother were still alive to put her in her place and demand that she mend the sheets and stay near the boiler room where she belongs.

It should now be clear that under the influence of James Stephen's philosophy, the model of the patriarchal family was used in dominion over the colonies and then by upper-and middle-class women to define relations with servants. At home unmarried women like Caroline Stephen nursed their aging parents, their own broken health an exact counterpart to the broken spirits of colonials under the yoke of the mother country, where love and obedience were expected. Caroline's struggle for freedom and self-reliance paralleled the struggles of the colonies. Rejecting the matriarchal role of denigrator of sisterhoods and definer of mistress-servant relations, she chose a single life in a Quaker community as an alternative to life in the patriarchal family. This was a great achievement given the dependency and self-hatred born of her position in the family.

If we accept the notion that women were one of the largest colonies under

Victorian British imperial domain, we can understand the metaphor of enforced infantilization and how it oppressed women and colonial Africans and Indians. The unpaid labor of such women was as necessary to the functioning of the patriarchal family as was the slave labor of the colonies to the expansion of the British empire. Mr. Mother-Country Stephen put it exactly when he said that they kept their unmarried daughters in domestic bondage. Modern feminists are often frustrated in their attempts to understand why Victorian middle-class women so often failed in their rebellions. I suggest that the master-slave relationship, enhanced by a domestic metaphor unassailable in its demands for loyalty and love, is at the root of the problem. A way out for Virginia Woolf was to define herself not only as the "daughter of an educated man" but also as the niece of a nun. Caroline managed not to offend her father's memory by joining the sisterhood which captured her youthful imagination, but she found community among the Quakers.

She is directly responsible for Woolf's vision of sisterhood and is duly thanked in *A Room of One's Own* for her legacy of £2,500 (the others received only £100 apiece): "Indeed my aunt's legacy unveiled the sky to me, and substituted for the large and imposing figure of a gentleman, which Milton recommended for my perpetual adoration, a view of the open sky" (p. 59). The ghost of "Milton's bogey" is laid for Woolf by the visionary example of a maiden aunt and her money. Caroline is transformed in *A Room of One's Own* from a nun wrapped in her shawl in religious retreat in Cambridge to a horsewoman as mythical as Percival in *The Waves*: "My aunt, Mary Beton, I must tell you, died by a fall from her horse when she was riding out to take the night air in Bombay." The narrator claims that she got her legacy at the same time as women got the vote: "Of the two—the vote and the money—the money, I own, seemed infinitely more important" (*Room*, p. 56).

Even the title of *A Room of One's Own* derives from Caroline. Katherine Stephen boasted that she had converted her aunt to the cause of women's education by showing her the students' private rooms at Newnham.[29] Privacy, for women like Caroline and Virginia, who had lived in Victorian patriarchal families (and those of us who live in them now), was a holy state akin to the state of grace for Christians, a goal to be fought for. On one of her visits to Cambridge in 1904, Caroline had introduced her niece to the great classical scholar Jane Ellen Harrison. It was an event of great importance for Woolf's fiction; she was a role model in scholarship and life, proving that women could master and understand Greek (even if, like Woolf, they struggled alone with their texts and with a tutor like Janet Case instead of in a university class with their peers). The narrator sees on the terrace at Fernham a vision of the woman genius: "As if popping out to breathe the air, to glance at the garden, came a bent figure, formidable yet humble, with her great forehead and her shabby dress—could it be the famous scholar, could it be J___ H___ herself? All was dim, yet intense too, as if the scarf which the dusk had flung over the garden were torn asunder by star or sword—the flash of some terrible reality leaping, as its way is, out of the heart of the spring" (*Room*, p. 26).

Was "the terrible reality leaping" the idea that chastity, outsidership, and poverty were the conditions of life for the woman of genius? Famous as Jane Harrison was in her field, she never held a professorship at Cambridge, was harassed in print and in person by some classics professors, and died in poverty in 1928. The sky was unveiled for Woolf by the lives of these women. The star or sword that broke through the veil was a sense of continuity, that women are responsible for passing on freedom to the next generation.

A Room of One's Own does just that. Like most of Woolf's fiction, it is an elegy. As I said earlier, it is an elegy written in a college courtyard for all our female dead, the reformers, the pioneers, the artists, buried like Shakespeare's sister, in unmarked graves at places like "the Elephant and Castle." The essayist begins by trying to place herself in the patriarchal tradition, with a prayer to "Saint Charles" Lamb. Lamb had come to the college a hundred years before to read the manuscript of Milton's "Lycidas." She, too, longs to see the revisions, and also those in another of the library's manuscripts, Thackeray's great fictional elegy, *Henry Esmond*, given to the library by Leslie Stephen and revealing his improvisational style and his method of dictating to his daughter. The realization that geniuses made mistakes and revised their manuscripts would be important to an aspiring writer to demystify the process. *Esmond* was also important in another way. Millicent Garrett Fawcett in *Woman's Suffrage* (p. 12) celebrates its denunciation of petty "household tyrants" as a landmark in the history of the struggle for women's rights. Woolf may not enter the library (the library of her brothers, cousins, father, uncles, grandfather) because she is a woman. "That a famous library has been cursed by a woman is a matter of complete indifference to a famous library." Woolf's curse joined the chorus of curses, perhaps, from working-class men and women and all the "ordinary people" and common readers also excluded from the library. Woolf vows to reject male literary tradition as she descends the steps of the library in anger: "Never will I wake those echoes, never will I ask for that hospitality again" (*Room*, p. 12). If she rejects Milton's elegy as a model, and even the "memento mori" mood of Thackeray's elegiac novel, self-described as "grave and sad," the *Bildungsroman* of youth at Trinity College, with its appealing, almost Proustian remembrances, how then will she proceed?

Obviously she will have to invent the female elegy. Woolf mourns the death of Judith Shakespeare in the voice of the anonymous female balladeers. She may have stolen Thackeray's digressive elegiac form, but it is molded anew. The lugubrious mourning of the agnostic Leslie Stephen and her uncle Fitzjames's fixation on hellfire and eternal punishment are rejected in her memorial service for Judith Shakespeare. And she rejects too that Victorian "Women Must Weep" of Kingsley (used, incidentally, as the title of *Three Guineas* when it was published as an anti-war essay in the *Atlantic Monthly* in America, where it was better received than in England) for a position much like Caroline Stephen's Quaker rejection of mourning as unbecoming to those who have real faith. Woolf predicts Judith's resurrection:

> Now my belief is that this poet who never wrote a word and was buried at the crossroads still lives. She lives in you and me, and in many other women who are not here tonight, for they are washing up the dishes and putting the children to bed. But she lives; for great poets do not die; they are continuing presences. . . . [*Room*, p. 171]

The origins of Woolf's character are obscure but may be detected in her half-serious "Acknowledgements" prefacing *Orlando*, where one finds the name of William Black, the now-forgotten popular Victorian Scottish novelist, known as the successor to Sir Walter Scott for his romantic historical fictions. In 1883, the year after Virginia's birth, he published a delightful novel, obviously aimed at young women readers, called *Judith Shakespeare*, in which he said "the awful figure of Billy" was well in the background. Center stage is Shakespeare's daughter, Judith, the disinherited rebellious younger daughter, who rejects marriage to a proper suitor and is attracted by a stranger from London to whom she gives her father's manuscript of *The Tempest*. It is then published in an unauthorized edition and brings down her father's wrath. The novel has a father-daughter plot that is a form of homage to Shakespeare himself. Black's Judith cannot read or write and is forbidden to enter her father's workroom. She steals the keys and sits in the barn with her best friend, Prudence, laboriously trying to read the great plays. When *The Tempest* appears, Shakespeare is furious, and Judith is struck down by an incapacitating illness in guilt and fear at his wrath. One can see how the daughter of Leslie Stephen may have responded to such a story, and one may guess why Woolf's Judith Shakespeare became Shakespeare's *sister*, not his daughter. Judith's ignorance of reading and writing and her passion to be an artist express Virginia Woolf's own ironic definitions of reading and writing as radical acts and of the "daughter of an educated man" as one who is dispossessed of culture.[30]

Louise De Salvo's analysis of Virginia Stephen's 1897 diary has documented what feminist readers had already suspected.[31] Reading, writing, and studying *were* radical acts for the young woman. When she fell ill, they were precisely the activities forbidden her by her family and the doctors, the activities she had found were a way to keep her sanity. She identified the liberty of intellectual endeavor with men, and no wonder. She often fell ill from the stress of what we might call the "theft" of her father's manuscripts. In 1897 Leslie wrote to her brother Thoby that he would not come up to Cambridge to vote on women's membership in the university, despite many pleas from women to do so. Virginia had been forbidden to read and write, and her request to attend classes at King's College denied. Leslie said that he had bought her a spade and set her to making a garden in the shaded stony soil in back of Hyde Park Gate. The subject of degrees for women was a topic on which Thoby might make his name in his debating society, Leslie suggested—while his daughters were digging.[32] The reader as a radical (the disobedient daughter), the writer as a feminist revolutionary (usurping her father's job) came to birth that year and kept a journal.

She then imagined "the common reader" as her audience and her ally against
patriarchal academics and institutions, from the early story "A Society" to
"Anon and the Reader," the manuscript she was working on when she died. *The
Voyage Out*, in which Rachel learns to read, like many first novels, is a reading
list of the author's influences. Rachel dies from such knowledge as she gains from
books, of woman's plight. St. John Hirst reads Sappho in chapel. It is Swinburne's Sappho that he reads, a violent and bloody male fantasy about lesbianism, and his reading is linked to the sinister figure of a nurse.

Sappho, however, is the woman reader's heroine, and the object of her
search in "A Society." One of the sisterhood (a group of young women set out to
explore why men have destroyed civilization, written bad books, and made war
and weapons while insisting that women simply reproduce) goes to Oxbridge to
find Sappho. Castalia (named for her purity) is disguised as a charwoman and
compares the Sappho expert, Professor Hobkin, to her aunt's cactuses. His
life's work is a book six or seven inches thick, most of which is not by Sappho but
is his defense of her chastity, which has been denied by a German professor.
The dispute about Sappho's chastity centers on "the use of some implement
which looked to me for all the world like a hairpin."[33] Sue declares that Professor
Hobkin cannot possibly be a real scholar if he is only concerned with such a silly
issue. "Probably," she says, "Professor Hobkin was a gynaecologist" ("Society,"
p. 21). Castalia is sent back to Oxbridge to investigate further and returns pregnant. She is triumphant at the loss of her chastity. Unlike Judith Shakespeare in
A Room of One's Own, she does not contemplate suicide but produces a
daughter to inherit the society's concerns. And unlike the professor's book on
Sappho, the debate on whether to expel Castalia for impurity is short and sweet.
"What is chastity, then?" they ask, and Poll answers that "chastity is nothing but
ignorance—a most discreditable state of mind. We should then admit only the
unchaste to our society" ("Society," p. 25). They move on to Judith's scientific
study of two other aspects of female sexuality, artificial insemination and the
elimination of the need for prostitutes. Both could be used to deprive men of
their power over women.

There are ways in which Woolf's women's club resembles meetings of NOW,
Redstockings, the Women's Caucus of the MLA; or, considering its political
goals, it best reminds us of the socialist caucus of the Women's Studies Association, where women share the radical aims of Woolf's 1917 club. When they question the capitalist system, they learn how much men despise them. And they
are told that not since Sappho has there been a first-rate woman artist. Woolf's
explanation was socialist, for since Sappho women have never enjoyed the social
conditions necessary for the freedom of the artist. But she shared with many
members of her sex in the late nineteenth and early twentieth centuries the
desire to find the real Sappho, not Professor Hobkin's Sappho and certainly not
the Sappho of his German colleague.

Some feminists actually sat down with the German professor, von Wilamowitz-Moellendorff, who was probably the man Woolf meant. Her friend Ethel
Smyth, the composer, tells a delightful story in her memoir, *Streaks of Life*,

which appeared in the same year as "A Society," reviewed with high praise by Woolf herself. Dame Ethel tells of meeting the Sappho scholar, a treat for women like herself, who had little Greek and had been dependent on Swinburne and Gilbert Murray for a glimpse of the great poet. Wilamowitz-Moellendorff showed her a hitherto unknown poem of Sappho's that he had just deciphered. "Incidentally, he informed me that in his opinion Sappho was the most maligned of women, that she was really a sort of High School Mistress, and the famous passions merely innocent 'Schwarmerei' between her and her pupils. Luckily it is open to those who have no Greek to reject this depressing reading of 'burning Sappho.'"[34]

The modern cult of Sappho for daughters of educated men, women artists, feminists, and lesbians began with their reading of Swinburne and was followed by a rejection of his version and a search for the real Sappho. This cult reached its peak in Paris before the First World War. Ethel Smyth had made a "Three-Legged Tour of Greece"; Natalie Barney and many lesbian artists had also gone to Greece to find their heroine and to recreate Sappho's school. The modern inhabitants of the isle of Lesbos were not sympathetic to their aims, and the amazons returned to make a new Mitylene in the French republic's green and pleasant land. It was in these salons that women artists began to flower and islands of sorority began to surface in the cities of the patriarchy. The isle of Lesbos stirred their imagination, and Virginia Woolf's "Friendships Gallery" was only one of many lesbian utopias.[35] Compton Mackenzie's 1928 novel *Extraordinary Women* is a comic satire on the cult of Sappho and the new women's island utopias. The chapters are headed with quotations from the poet, and Olimpia Leigh, the composer, who sounds suspiciously like Ethel Smyth, has set all of Sappho's poetry to music.

Radclyffe Hall was a member of these same circles. Woolf did not think *The Well of Loneliness* was a great book, but urged by Vita Sackville-West, she joined in support of the lesbian artist during the obscenity trial for the novel. Woolf's creation of Shakespeare's sister in *A Room of One's Own* derives not only from William Black's popular novel but also from the intellectual cause célèbre surrounding Radclyffe Hall, who was known to be the descendant of Shakespeare's other daughter, Susanna Hall. The homosexuality of Shakespeare's sonnets was of course a major part of the defense in the obscenity trial. Stephen Gordon in *The Well* is christened Mary Oliva, a "man's soul trapped in a woman's body," like Shakespeare's Olivia. Is it this Olivia whom Chloe likes in *A Room of One's Own?*[36]

In the official biography of Virginia Woolf, Quentin Bell described his aunt as a "sexless Sappho." Feminist readers objected at the time, but we have come to think he might be right. When the women return to their society much later, one of them remarks, "It is now well-known that Sappho was the somewhat lewd invention of Professor Hobkin" ("Society," p. 31). If the classics professors are merely gynecologists *manqué*, the women of the society have gained enough education to outstrip them, and after the war they can laugh together over "old Hobkin and the hairpin." But they have lost their innocence. Reading has radicalized them. When the story opens, Poll, who has been left a fortune provided she will read all the books in the London Library, bemoans her fate: "Why, why, did my father teach me to read?" ("Society," p. 12). After the war Castalia complains bitterly that if they hadn't learnt to read

> "We might still have been bearing children in ignorance and that I believe was the happiest life after all. I know what you're going to say about war," she checked me, "and the horror of bearing children to see them killed, but our mothers did it, and their mothers, and their mothers before them. And *they* didn't complain. They couldn't read. I've done my best," she sighed, "to prevent my little girl from learning to read, but what's the use? I caught Ann only yesterday with a newspaper in her hand and she was beginning to ask me if it was 'true.' Next she'll ask me whether Mr. Lloyd George is a good man, then whether Mr. Arnold Bennett is a good novelist, and finally, whether I believe in God." ["Society," p. 36]

It is significant that Woolf's sorority, unlike our modern counterparts, does not study the history of women. Its object is to understand why men have not produced good people and good books, why the male sex has made war and capitalism and imperialism. The sisterhood is very sorry to conclude after years of study and the presentation of many papers that "our belief in man's intellect is the greatest fallacy of them all" ("Society," p. 37). Like generations of men, they have defined a good member of the opposite sex as "honest, passionate and unworldly" ("Society, p. 35). "What could be more charming than a boy before he has begun to cultivate his intellect?" ("Society," p. 38). But the daughter of those great nineteenth-century Stephen professionalizers puts the blame for man's mistreatment of women squarely on the shoulders of the professions. Leslie Stephen had made the profession of journalism respectable and powerful in its "higher" forms and left behind "those 68 black books," the *DNB*, as a monument to the fathers. His brothers Fitzjames had done the same for the legal profession with his digests, his manual for the conservative politician, *Liberty, Equality, Fraternity*, and his role as judge. Caroline Emelia Stephen had spearheaded the professionalization of nursing and social work. Virginia Woolf identified this process of professionalization with the subjugation of others. Her grandfather had built a bureaucracy in the Colonial Office which kept down the natives. Fitzjames made it very clear that physical force was necessary to control the working class. In *Liberty, Equality, Fraternity*, he declares that women and the working class must be kept down forcibly in order to show the colonies how rebellion will be treated. Those seemingly outrageous demands Woolf makes on professional women to transform their professions were the result of a political analysis of the rise of the middle class in her own family and the corruptions of power which go with professionalization:

> They teach him to cultivate his intellect. He becomes a barrister, a civil servant, a general, an author, a professor. Every day he goes to an office. Every year he produces a book. He maintains a whole family by the products of his brain—poor

devil! Soon he cannot come into a room without making us all feel uncomfortable; he condescends to every woman he meets, and dares not tell the truth even to his own wife; instead of rejoicing our eyes we have to shut them if we are to take him in our arms. True, they console themselves with stars of all shapes, ribbons of all shades, and incomes of all sizes - but what is to console us? . . . Oh, Cassandra, for Heaven's sake let us devise a method by which men can bear children! It is our only chance. For unless we provide them with some innocent occupation, we shall get neither good people nor good books. . . . ["Society," pp. 38-39]

"A Society" is even more fundamentally subversive than a modern version of *Lysistrata*, when read as mockery of the institutions of the men of her class, Cambridge University, and the secret society of her friends, her husband, her brother, her uncles, and their cousins, the Cambridge Apostles. If the Apostles were the "Cambridge Conversazione Society," Woolf's fictional females formed a London conversazione society. There are no restrictions on the number of members of this sorority. The Apostles limited themselves to twelve. But Woolf is anti-elitist, and fourteen women come and go. Besides Cassandra, Castalia, and Poll, we meet Ruth, Clorinda, Rose, Jane, Fanny, Helen, Sue, Moll, Eleanor, Jill, Elizabeth, and Castalia's daughter, Ann. When Poll, the prototype of Woolf's common reader, complains about the books in the London Library, the remark is significant because the London Library was founded by Apostles in an age when a more radical sense of brotherhood held them together and they also built East End settlement houses for boys and founded workingmen's colleges. Virginia Woolf taught at Morley College and supported the London Library, for public libraries were necessary to educate her "common reader." She developed what her husband called her "London Library complex" when she expected E. M. Forster to invite her to be the token woman on its board. But this effort failed, he said. They wanted no woman, and cited as precedent Leslie Stephen's annoyance with the previous woman, Mrs. Henry Green, the novelist.

"A Society" is Woolf's attempt to penetrate the mysteries of male secret societies like the Apostles and to offer a parallel sisterhood of intellectual inquiry and social conscience. The wrath it provoked is unaccountable unless one takes seriously the British male's paranoid fear that woman's loyalty to her own sex was a real threat to male hegemony and the patriarchal family. The fraternity functioned as primary male bonding and demanded loyalty above a man's loyalty to his family. It allowed attacks on authority but still reinforced the patriarchy. By the late nineteenth century, the Apostles served to find wives and professional jobs for their members, though they still idealized homosexuality and the "Greek view of life."[37]

This old-boy network that Fitzjames Stephen proudly claimed as the backbone of British imperialism and his son J. K. Stephen called "the intellectual aristocracy" in his "Defense of the Compulsory Study of Greek at Cambridge" had no parallel "old-girl" network.[38] There were no girls' schools teaching the superiority of the female sex, no sororal organizations claiming future loyalty to one's sisters over the claims of family, no power or place to be shared as a reward for loyalty to one's own sex, no woman-designed cult of female chastity or idealization of lesbianism as the highest form of love, no female philosopher of the stature of G. E. Moore to shed sweetness and light on female friendship. If such female friendship networks existed, and they did, they did not bear the hallmarks of an institutional stamp of approval, and they did not serve as exchanges of power, money, and careers. Plato was revered for loving his students. Sappho was reviled for loving hers. To separate the real Sappho from centuries of scholarly calumny, as the feminist Elizabeth Robins wrote, was the goal of women like Woolf. In their London Lesbos the women were hampered by Professor Hobkin and his hairpin.

The knowledge of Greek was the key to power, J. K. Stephen argued when he coined that phrase, since used by historians and biographers to describe his class and family, "the intellectual aristocracy." Woolf felt that not knowing Greek—not knowing Greek in groups of schoolboys, in gangs of Apostles, only knowing Greek alone or with a tutor—meant no female intellectual aristocracy. "The voice of some terrible reality leaping" was Jane Harrison's voice, piercing through the classics back to the matriarchal religious cults.

I believe that the Apostles as a fraternal organization were the descendants of freemasonry and European guilds and youth organizations, that the overt homosexuality and woman-hating of the late Victorian Apostles as inadvertently revealed by Paul Levy in his recent book were corruptions of the revolutionary ideal of fraternity.[39] The cultural gap is evident in Woolf's attempt to articulate a revolutionary ethic of sorority when fraternity had declined into decadence, into being merely a club for jobs and preferment. As a socialist she urged women writers to think back through their mothers. As a feminist she urged them to think sideways through their sisters. It goes without saying that they should know Greek, and they should know Greek in groups. They should recover Sappho from the lewd professors.

Virginia Woolf continued to propose sisterhood, to speak in "a little language unknown to men" which we might call "sapphistry" in *Night and Day*, *A Room of One's Own*, "Professions for Women," *The Years*, and *Three Guineas*. In *Jacob's Room* and *Mrs. Dalloway* she attacked the notion of fraternity and its collaboration with patriarchy, capitalism, and imperialism. She tried to work out the sororal idea for the last time in *Between the Acts* but admitted its failure at the end of the novel.

"Lempriere will settle it," Lucy Swithin says, as the Olivers try to understand the origin of the phrase "Knock on wood," in Pointz Hall before the Second World War. Lucy needs a classical dictionary, and Woolf and women like Dame Ethel Smyth depended on one as well. What Lempriere settles is the origin of the superstition in the Greek myth of the giant Antaeus. The moral of that myth is that patriarchy, like fascism, functions only with women's consent. Antaeus, the Libyan giant, son of Terra and Neptune, boasts that he will erect a temple to his father with the skulls of his enemies. Hercules tries to kill the killer, but he revives whenever he touches his mother, Earth, and Hercules has to crush him in his arms in midair. If we accept that description of Antaeus building a temple to his father with the skulls of his enemies as a definition of the patriarchal culture of heroism, war, and violence, we can see how angry Woolf was about the war and women's inability to stop it.

Both Fitzjames Stephen and his son, J. K. Stephen, were known as giants and nicknamed "the Giant Grim" and "the genial giant." Fitzjames made his name by building a patriarchal temple. Simultaneously and anonymously he published in all the major journals of the day vicious reviews of Dickens's *Little Dorrit* because he believed his father was being satirized in the "Circumlocution Office."[40] In *Liberty, Equality, Fraternity* he denounced Mill's idea of liberty and defended the patriarchy against feminism and egalitarianism. The "genial giant" advocated violence against women and the working class in his misogynist poems and essays. Even Leslie Stephen wrote a "Mausoleum book" for the patriarchy in the *Dictionary of National Biography*.

But there is another metaphor in the novel that even more effectively evokes the image of sorority. It is an amazon's war cry from the supposedly pacifist Virginia Woolf, buried in the book in all the references to the swallow and the nightingale. But unless women "know Greek" in a sense, they may miss the message. In "The Voice of the Shuttle" Geoffrey Hartman joins the Greek fathers in analyzing the myth of Procne and Philomela as a story in which "the truth will come out." He universalizes the story as saying that the artist will not be silenced and suggests that in these universal terms the myth is an archetype.[41] In *Three Guineas* Woolf says that in the profession of literature, no one rules "that metaphors shall only be used by one sex." Let us see how the other sex sees that story.

Lempriere tells us that, like *Between the Acts*, it was a war story. Pandion gave away his daughter to Tereus as part of the spoils of war. Procne wept bitterly at the separation from her sister, Philomela. Procne bore Tereus a son, Itys. Tereus then went off again, raped Philomela, cut out her tongue, and left her on an island. Philomela wove the story of that rape into a tapestry and sent it to Procne, who rescued her sister and in an awful rage at the violation of sisterhood attacked the patriarchy itself in revenge: she killed her son and served him to his father to eat. The gods turned the sisters into the swallow and the nightingale and Tereus into the hoopoe, a bird that fouls its own nest.

Geoffrey Hartman is not alone in misreading the tale's message of sorority and revenge for rape. In *Between the Acts* Woolf ironically lets Bart adapt Swinburne to his own concerns: "Oh sister swallow, O sister swallow,/How can thy heart be full of spring?" Swinburne's nightingale in "Itylus" castigates her sister for not feeling guilty about murdering her son; she remembers "the voice of the child's blood crying yet" but not the voice of the shuttle and her own rape. Swinburne's suggestion that both sisterhood and revenge are unnatural reveals his failure to understand the implications of the myth, as Woolf's development of the theme will show.

The "voice of the shuttle" in *Between the Acts* is a newspaper account of the

gang-rape of a girl by soldiers. Isa sees herself as the violated girl and her hus-
band as the rapist: "The girl had gone skylarking with the troopers. She had
screamed. She had hit him . . . What then?"[42] Isa struggles toward sisterhood.
She gets no vicarious erotic pleasure from thinking about the rape victim.
While her husband is in the greenhouse seducing Mrs. Manresa, she stands
outside with William Dodge, singing "songs my uncle taught me" (Between the
Acts, p. 64). She rejects the role of the virgin mother and encourages herself:
"Hear not the frantic cries of the leaders who in that they seek to lead desert
us. . . . Hear rather . . . the brawl in the barrack room when they strip her
naked" (Between the Acts, p. 183)—an exact equation of politics and war with
rape. But she is bowed down by the weight of fruit from the family tree and its
burden of family injunctions, "what we must remember, what we must forget"
(Between the Acts, p. 182).

Isa is a prisoner in her father-in-law's home. She is Irish and subject, like
Ireland to England, to that old colonial tyrant, Bart Oliver. She does not kill her
son and serve him to his adulterous father. She does not avenge the girl victim
or herself. She goes to bed with the enemy. But we should have known, for
Woolf's description of Isa runs, "She never looked like Sappho" (Between the
Acts, p. 22). Sappho remembers "At my age/Why does the swallow of heaven,
daughter/of King Pandion/bring news to plague me?" Isa and the other wives of
England are recolonized, resubjugated by war. They lose their liberty and
sorority. Misogyny triumphs over the patriarchal family as war triumphs over
Europe. The giants are loose again, building temples to their fathers with the
skulls of their enemies. Women cannot resist reviving their wounded—and the
civilians are knocking on wood.

In 1930 Woolf had imagined that the Working Women's Cooperative Guild
and other women's political groups would create international peace and the
world would be safe for socialism and feminism in what she called "the sisterhood of nations."[43] By 1941 she saw that fascism had appropriated the ideology of
brotherhood. And sorority was suppressed as it always has been during most
wars, except in the service of men.

The representation of women in Woolf's last novel makes an inexorable
point.[44] The primitive poems of Isa, scribbled in an account book, are a wife's
work of art. It is all she can manage as a domestic prisoner, and cannot be compared to the power of Miss LaTrobe's pageant and her ambitious plans for
rewriting Genesis. Woolf reaches further back in history than Shakespeare's
sister for Miss LaTrobe's character. She is the sister of the anonymous writers of
the Bible. And Lucy Swithin imagines herself as a powerful woman, Cleopatra,
under the influence of the lesbian artist's vision. Lucy represents Caroline
Emelia Stephen's Quaker mystical belief in the oneness of the universe; she
heals and mends like an ancient goddess. One wonders at Woolf's point in
naming the painted life force Mrs. Manresa, for Manresa is the place in Spain
where Saint Ignatius wrote his Spiritual Exercises, devoted to the Virgin Mary.
But in her new feminist Pantheon there is even room for Venus.

In Miss LaTrobe Woolf has ended the sorority's search for Sappho sketched out in "A Society." She is not a poet but a playwright in her modern incarnation. Her lovers are not students but actresses. She has left her island home to teach her audience their own role in history. There are lessons in the novel for the modern sisterhood of scholarship, for the feminist literary critic of *A Room of One's Own*, for the Outsiders' Society of *Three Guineas*. One lesson is that if we allow male critics to universalize our stories—as Swinburne retold the myth of Procne and Philomela, and Geoffrey Hartman claims that reading the myth as the story of the artist and the truth rather than as a sister's revenge for the rape of her sister is "higher" or "deeper" than the story of the power of sisterhood— we will be domesticated and subjugated into the loss of our own history. After all, J. K. Stephen warned his brothers in the study of Greek that if they did not retain their knowledge, it was their own fault if they ceased to be an "intellectual aristocracy." In *Between the Acts* Englishwomen are even further than they were in "A Society" from securing sorority as a political principle. The novel makes it impossible to imagine that they could ever form an intellectual aristocracy, even if they wished to. Women's consent is necessary for men to go on making war and making love as if it were war. Isa consents, but Miss LaTrobe does not. She is a rather shabby Sappho, with no school to sustain her, no daughter to console her. But at least she is not Professor Hobkin's Sappho. She is the woman artist's honest portrait of the woman artist.

❦ 5 ❦

Virginia Woolf and Her Violin: Mothering, Madness, and Music

When Julia Stephen praised her daughter's youthful writing she felt ecstatic, Virginia Woolf recalled in "A Sketch of the Past": " . . . it was like being a violin and being played upon." This metaphor, with its consciousness of the mother/daughter erotic and its conception of the unawakened artist as a stringed instrument that waits for the expert hand to lift the bow—is, I think, perhaps the perfect figure to express the relationship between the woman artist and a mother/mentor. The subject of this essay is the *mental* nurturance of the woman artist by the woman chosen to fill the place of the absent mother. She is the one who rescues one from silence, who tunes the trembling strings and brings forth the song. It is a romantic, Coleridgean figure of speech, but then Virginia Woolf's great romance was with her dead mother, and one of the bonds she felt with Dame Ethel Smyth, the composer, was a shared adoration of their absent mothers. For our purposes in this essay, the violin is too small and too specifically related to Julia, to resonate across the many, lifelong and varied mother/mentor relationships that sustained Virginia Woolf as an artist. As Dame Ethel would say, lifting her baton, we shall have to sound a deeper note. Let us try the cello.

There was only one violin mistress in Virginia Woolf's life, a figure described often in musical terms, bringing harmony and rhythm into family life. Leslie Stephen bellowed and roared and moaned and groaned, and he didn't care for music. Escaping from the cacophony of a motherless Hyde Park Gate, Virginia Woolf matured as an artistic instrument under the bows of a series of women, mother/mentors, whom we may call the cellists in her life.

One of the remarkable things about Virginia Woolf is how willing other women were, and some dedicated men, to play cellist to her cello. And it is also notable that in these unequal friendships she was never seduced, betrayed, or abandoned. Patrons and patronesses of the arts have often been fickle, unreliable, or cruel. One thinks of the black novelist Zora Neale Hurston, whose white patroness insisted on being addressed as "godmother," and kept the artist like Cinderella, providing only one pair of shoes at a time, so that Hurston was forced to work as a domestic on and off all her life.[1] But Virginia Woolf was luckier than Zora Neale Hurston. The color of her skin and of the banknotes of her aunt Caroline's legacy exempted her from certain kinds of suffering and from humiliating dependencies that liken the artist/patron relationship to that of the professional prostitute and her rich lovers. Woolf wrote of Harriette Wilson.[2]

> Across the broad continent of a woman's life falls the shadow of a sword. On one side all is correct, definite, orderly; the paths are strait, the trees regular, the sun shaded; escorted by gentlemen, protected by policemen, wedded and buried by clergymen, she has only to walk demurely from cradle to grave and no one will touch a hair of her head. But on the other side all is confusion. Nothing follows a regular course. The paths wind between bogs and precipices. The trees roar and rock and fall in ruin.

Her own experience of life on the other side of the sword, the life of an Aphra Behn, a Harriette Wilson, or a Zora Neale Hurston, was only in illness and madness, an experience, she told Ethel Smyth, that was "terrific."

She perceived very young that there were two modes of life for a Victorian girl of her class, to nurse or to be nursed, to care for invalids or to be an invalid. Her mother and her half-sister, Stella Duckworth were deeply involved in district visiting alleviating the miseries of the poor in the tradition of ladies bountiful. Like Mrs. Ramsay in *To the Lighthouse*, Julia Stephen found scope for her desire for power in a conservative philanthropic exercise that was properly ladylike. As Louise De Salvo shows in her study of Virginia's 1897 diary, she dreaded being dragged along on these missions of mercy.[3] Woolf has given us a fine portrait of the female philanthropist in action in the opening chapters of *The Years*. And Eleanor Pargiter sees what life on the other side of the sword is like as she compares the honest and loving experience of a daughter at her mother's deathbed among the East End Jews to her own mother's pale, cold, clean passing away. Since she read her father's *Mausoleum Book*, Woolf knew how much he resented his wife's nursing and how much he needed it, how jealous he was of Julia's long nursing visits to her dying mother, in which patient and nurse seemed to be the only people in the world to each other.

The world of the sickroom is a little empire and the nurse is queen. For Victorian women like Julia Stephen it was an outlet for desire for power and an arena for behavior that was not subservient to a husband. In this relationship and her relationship with servants, she could give the orders. Her *Notes from Sick Rooms* (1883) was written with authority, for Julia was a doctor's daughter and daughter/nurse to her ailing mother for many years.[4] "I have often wondered," she writes ingenuously, "why it is considered a proof of virtue in anyone to become a nurse. The ordinary relations between the sick and the well are far easier and pleasanter than between the well and the well." Is she a little guilty about enjoying her power over the ill and the patient's dependency? Obviously relations between equals did not come easily to her. She could play "princess to a patriarch," as Meredith described her relationship to Leslie Stephen, or angel in the house to her poor patients in St. Ives. Julia considered nursing an art and, interestingly enough, she remarks that "the art of being ill is no easy one to learn, but it is practised to perfection by many of the greatest sufferers." The invalid and her nurse are both *artists*, and she firmly advises the nurse to hide all troubles for the sake of the patient, even to "lie freely." One is reminded of Virginia's "lying" letters to Violet Dickinson about her brother Thoby's recovery after he had died, for Violet had been struck down by the same disease. She had learned from her mother that the nurse, the liar, and the artist are one person. And Julia is very firm and funny on the subject of crumbs in the sickbed.

But it is not to be assumed that Julia's version of the twin arts of nurse and patienthood was accepted by most members of her class. Her sister-in-law, Caroline Emelia Stephen, in *The Service of the Poor* (1871) argued that nursing was not indeed "proof of virtue" but evidence of religious and moral egotism and vanity. Nursing and social work ought to be paid professions, not forms of philanthropy subject to the whims of the rich. Julia did not care much for Caroline, the *Mausoleum Book* tells us. She had one area in which her authority was unquestioned and perhaps found it hard to hear a reformer question her motives.

One of Caroline Stephen's efforts in *The Service of the Poor* was to shift women's past burdens of caring for the poor, the sick, the insane, and prostitutes on to some other back. What ethics, she asked (and she had a lifetime of nursing her own parents to add to her authority) could claim that these people were more deserving of the sacrifice of the lives of thousands of women, than the happy, rich and good? There is nothing morally superior about those in pain, suffering, and poverty, she wrote, and therefore there is nothing morally superior about those whose lives are devoted to alleviating their ills. This is a rather shockingly rational reproof to sickbed sentimentality.

Virginia's illnesses began at her mother's death. In "On Being Ill" (1930) Woolf uses the same images she had earlier used to describe Harriette Wilson's life, life on the other side of the sword, with nature in chaos, roaring trees, and precipices: ". . . what wastes and deserts of the soul a slight attack of influenza brings to view, what precipices . . . a little rise of temperature reveals, what ancient and obdurate oaks are uprooted in us by the act of sickness, how we go down into the pit of death and feel the waters of annihilation close above our heads. . ."[5] For Virginia Woolf, the art of being ill was essentially the art of letting go, as for Julia Stephen the art of nursing was the art of taking complete control.

After her mother's death, she again assumed the position of the quivering violin but no Julia came to play a tune. Stella Duckworth nursed her and fell ill herself and died. Virginia stood watch at the deathbeds of her father and her brother Thoby, at the miscarriages and lyings-in of her sister Vanessa. She rallied as an expert nurse for Vanessa when Julian Bell was killed in Spain and later when Leonard was seriously ill. But one's impression is that she was the patient more often than nurse and played invalid with Leonard as nurse a good deal more than she wanted to. Her "madnesses" and suicide attempts confirmed these roles. As she told Ethel Smyth, the loss of control, the spewing forth of anger at loved ones, and the hallucinations were often useful for her art. She had many examples in the family of genius-related madness, most notably her grandfather James Stephen, Permanent Under Secretary for the Colonies, professor of Modern History at Cambridge, and ecclesiastical biographer. Like Virginia, he was abstemious and fastidious, ate little, and periodically over-worked himself until he went mad. He always recovered and claimed for him-self "the power of going mad" as if he had a kind of control.[6]

Nature had given his father a hair shirt, said Leslie. And he was "a living cat-egorical imperative." He was "thin-skinned," the family phrase for madness and genius combined. Like all the Stephens after him (including Virginia Woolf) he loved the poetry of Cowper with its religious compulsion and "mad genius." In Caroline Emelia's edition of her father's letters we can see much that Virginia inherited from the old puritan with the beautiful nose and "unremitting vigi-lance," with his demand that women *ought* to be beautiful and his concern with the moral significance of dress. Leslie Stephen remembers his tramp and his tread as he dictated to his daughter, wife, and sister, Miltonic and morose. He described Wordsworth as the happiest man he'd ever known because he was "surrounded by idolaters in his own house." Strongly criticized by the press for his colonial policy, he regarded himself as a lonely outsider: "The hostility it has been my lot to encounter has always tended to awaken in me a sort of morbid self-esteem." James Stephen often felt "oppressed by myself" as an "unwel-come, familiar and yet unknown visitor." He felt as if he were "two persons in one, and were compelled to hold a discourse in which soliloquy and colloquy mingled oddly and even awfully." Like his granddaughter, he kept a diary asking what he had accomplished, castigating himself. "I might as well have asked the old elms for their annual biography." In his periodic madnesses, he had his wife and sister and daughter to mother his mind and nurse him back to health, to deal with that devilish doppelgänger, his conscience. Even "madness" was a Stephen family art, practiced with the ascetic control of the Clapham Saints.[7]

The doctor whom Sir Leslie Stephen chose to consult about his daughter Virginia was Sir George Savage. Sir Leslie had his share of problems with mad-ness and must have thought deeply on the subject. After the suicide of his violently mad nephew in 1892, his brother Fitzjames descended into harmless madness and died in 1894. Within a year, Leslie had written a huge biography of his brother in which the deaths of both father and son were hallowed as history. Stephen brushes aside the fact that Fitzjames had been hounded out of office for prejudicing the jury in the Maybrick Case.[8] He also had the madness of his daughter by his first wife, Minny Thackeray, to consider, and to weigh what effect Laura's behavior had on the other children. The deaths of Julia and Stella, the resident nurses in Hyde Park Gate, would naturally disquiet the inmates. Vanessa did not choose to be an artist/nurse but an artist/artist. What was

Virginia to do? Playing artist/patient did not bring her mother back. Her break-downs brought the advice of England's most distinguished "neurologist," Dr. George Savage.

Because of the continuing debate among scholars over the nature of Woolf's madness and Leonard Woolf's responsibility for her treatment, it seems to me that we might clear a little smoke from the battlefield by examining exactly what her doctor thought about mental illness and by trying to imagine what ideas she herself formed in her youth of her body, her mind, and their illnesses. Nothing dates faster than medical knowledge and it would be unfair to blame Savage for the sins of his age. But one can get a sense of the appalling cruelty and ignorance of the treatment of the insane in late Victorian England by comparing Savage's *Insanity and Allied Neuroses* (1884) with the wise and compassionate work of Woolf's sister-in-law Karin Stephen in *Psychoanalysis and Medicine* (1935). What intervened and changed the theory and practice of the treatment of the mentally ill was the work of Freud, published in England by the Woolfs' Hogarth Press. Why, many people have asked, didn't the Woolfs consult a Freudian analyst? The answer, I think, lies in the family's perception of the nature of Virginia's illness and the doctor's perception of it. They had strong evidence to support a belief in hereditary Stephen insanity, and, believing in genetic or physical causes, they also believed in a physical treatment, food, rest and no mental work. They did not believe that an effort of will or imagination could cure what appeared to be a neurological disposition to madness. There was probably also an unspoken assumption that this disposition was a natural accompaniment of her genius. And if rest and food had "cured" her before, why shouldn't it work again?

Savage's *Insanity and Allied Neuroses: Practical and Clinical* was first published in 1884. It was the standard medical text on the treatment of the mentally ill in Victorian Britain. It was reprinted in 1886, revised in 1890; reprinted in 1893, 1896, 1898, 1901, and 1905; and a new and enlarged edition appeared in 1907. Sir George Savage was one of the leading men in the field, an M.D. and M.R.C.P., superintendent of Bethlehem Royal Hospital, a consultant at Guy's, and joint editor of *The Journal of Mental Science*. In his preface to *Ten Post-Graduate Lectures*, which Savage delivered at the Royal College of Medicine, Sir Clifford Allbutt calls him "one of the happiest, wittiest, kindest, and, in his own subject, most experienced members of our profession." He had already, like his colleague Sir William Gull, served the Stephen family well in treatment of the difficult case of J. K. Stephen. He was well-versed in all the legal and social aspects of insanity and recommended private rest homes for his well-to-do patients.

"Among special predisposing causes," Savage explains, "heredity stands first in importance. . . .The torch of civilisation is handed from father to son, and as with idiosyncrasies of mind, so the very body itself exhibits well-defined marks of its parentage."[9] He gives many examples to support his opinion that "insanity by inheritance" is the "most dangerous" kind of mental illness. "Perhaps," he ventures, "the suicidal tendency is one which appears to be most directly and distinctly transmitted . . . the same family tendency to self-destruction, the same inability to bear reverses philosophically, the same unrestrained motor impulse to end their troubles has manifested itself."[10] Leslie Stephen does not describe his nephew, J. K. Stephen, as a suicide and one cannot be sure that Virginia Woolf knew of the manner of his death in a rest home, but her family knew, and must have been made anxious by her symptoms. He makes very clear that a doctor ought to be consulted on the advisability of marriage and childbearing in cases of hereditary insanity. Instead of blaming Leonard Woolf for too little originality and self-confidence in his care of Virginia, let us try to imagine the young husband in an interview with the famous neurologist, hearing, perhaps in shocking detail, the description of the case of his wife's first cousin. If the sexual disappointment of the honeymoon caused a second suicide attempt, with what fortitude and fear did Leonard Woolf face a future as a monk and a nurse?

Virginia's first attempt to kill herself came after a long sojourn as nurse at her father's deathbed. Dr. Savage claims that Bedlam was full of women whose grief at the deaths of loved ones they had nursed turned into guilt at having been unable to prevent them from dying: "Good examples of what is meant by the effect of grief in producing insanity are frequently seen in the wards of Bedlam. . . ." Seldom can one see more clearly the changing position of women in society than in the pages of Savage's text. His wards, he says, are full of grief-stricken women, hundreds of Hecates worn out from watching at the gates of death. And then there were the governesses, confused and collapsed in a state he clearly describes as hysteria (and all mental illness in women was then ascribed to their sexuality). At one point, doctor or no, he reveals a rather unscientific belief in witches:

> All the manifold tales one hears of miracles, all the tales of ghosts, many of the instances of the thought-reader and spiritualist, are, in my opinion, the result of cases of hysterical insanity. The old idea that wherever any trouble was present there was sure to be a woman, is confirmed, in my opinion, by the fact that whenever strange manifestations take place which are beyond the sphere of observation by our senses, there will be found a girl with hysterical history or otherwise distinctly neurotic.[11]

He recommends force-feeding the woman who refuses to eat and for "neurasthenic" women he orders two hours of massage a day, milk every hour, and electrical stimulation. (This is the origin of the milk-cure that so upset Virginia.) In the course of his work in asylums, Savage "noticed a marked increase in the number of female general paralytics seen in the middle classes." But, he remarked, "women seem to be more readily cured, and are more liable to recurrences of insanity." "That there is an excess of female lunatics," he declared categorically, "might be expected from the greater nervous instability of women living at any one time in England, to the greater tendency of insanity to recur in women, and to the greater tendency of mothers to transmit insanity to their female children."

With such a spirit of scientific objectivity to guide him, Savage also made social observations and pronouncements that ought to have appealed to the author of *Jude the Obscure*:

> I have constant examples in Bedlam of young men, who, having left the plough for the desk, have found, after years of struggle, that their path was barred by social or other hindrances, and disappointment, worry and the solitude of a great city have produced insanity of an incurable type.

In fact, one of the major concerns of his book is to speak against both the education of working men and the education of women. In her teens, Virginia Stephen had found an extremely effective weapon against depression and anxiety: reading and study. And these were precisely the things forbidden her by the doctors. Books were the cure, not the cause, of her anxiety. Not only did Savage hunt witches, he put the whole weight of his medical authority down on the side of those who opposed the education of women. Indeed, what sensible parent reading the expert would have the heart to expose a daughter to such danger:

> A strong, healthy girl of a nervous family is encouraged to read for examinations, and having distinguished herself, is, perhaps, sent to some fashionable forcing house, where useless book learning is crammed into her. She is exposed, like the Strasbourg geese, to stuffing of mental food in over-heated rooms, and disorder of her functions results. Or if a similarly promising girl is allowed to educate herself at home, the danger of solitary work and want of social friction may be seen in conceit developing into insanity. It is in this manner that the results of defective education become often apparent in the case of the weaker sex nowadays. [12]

Savage's warning was based on an abundance of lily-livered young ladies having hysterics in the asylums. (When Virginia fell ill in 1897, the doctor's advice was to replace her pen with a spade. Books were forbidden and she was ordered to make a garden.) Some of Savage's geese obviously gave him a good deal of amusement. His remarks on the "imagination as the most attractive side of mania," his pleasure in the patients' punning, rapid verbal associations, and verse-making show another side to his character. And he tells the story of a patient who could be a cousin to Rhoda in *The Waves*, or her inventor. There was, Savage says:

> a patient who associated all her ideas of moral qualities with colour and was brilliantly imaginative. Everything that was good and pure was white and upright or straight, perfection to her mind being a square of perfect whiteness. Unfortunately she looked on me as a black round. [13]

It is difficult for the modern reader not to take the side of this prototypical Rhoda and the stuffed geese, and to dismiss Dr. Savage's opinions as circling around in the dark. But he was ahead of his time in insisting, on the basis of his observations and against the opinions of his colleagues, that there was such a thing as male menopause, because he had observed it often among professional men. He was a pioneer in studying the relations of syphilis to insanity. In 1907, he wrote "The feeling undoubtedly exists that insanity is one of the most transmissible of all diseases, and this has weighed, and still weighs, heavily on the lay mind."[14] Genius, he said, was associated with danger and claimed that auditory hallucinations in particular were inherited (Virginia heard the birds speaking Greek and King Edward shouting obscenities in the bushes). Patients who came from "neurotic stock" were more likely to "go out of their senses" periodically, but not necessarily "out of their minds." He associated much mental illness and depression with the aftermath of influenza, and here we may note the particular care which Virginia required during and after bouts of the flu. He felt that an inflammation of the nerves occurred during influenza and that it was a dangerous time for those with a hereditary disposition to insanity. I think that this explains much about Virginia Woolf's perceptions of her illness, as well as those of her family, husband and friends.

Between 1919 and 1920, George Savage gave a series of post-graduate lectures at the Royal Society of Medicine. Among the cases he discussed was that of a soldier returned from the front, who, like Septimus Smith, felt pursued and shunned by everyone. "He told me after," Savage writes, "he heard them coming and threw himself from the window, and though he lived for a few hours, he died."[15] One often thinks of Holmes and Bradshaw in *Mrs. Dalloway* as drawn from Savage and his colleague Sir William Gull. Woolf's savage attack on psychiatrists as the social police of society would have had a likely source in Savage's own pronouncements on the over-education of men of the artisan class. And she may well have imagined them in ruthless pursuit of her cousin, J. K. Stephen.

The point of this discussion has been to establish a reasonable basis for imagining Virginia Woolf's conception of the illnesses of her body and her mind, to see how she sought out what she called "maternal protection" from women all her life. She chose her "mothers" and her nurses carefully, the one prerequisite for the role being the absolute antithesis of motherhood, chastity. The plot of these relationships is like the plot of "An Unwritten Novel"; Minnie Marsh, spinster, turns out to be a mother, begetter of stories, "the unborn children of the mind, illicit, none the less loved." Like Minnie Marsh, this figure of inspiration for art is a virgin mother, a madonna:

> wherever I go, mysterious figures, I see you turning the corner, mothers and sons; you, you, you. I hasten, I follow . . . . if I fall on my knees, . . . if I go through the ritual, the ancient antics, it's you, unknown figures, you I adore; if I open my arms, it's you I embrace, you I draw to me, adorable world.[16]

How does this rhapsodic writing relate to its inspiration, a woman sitting opposite the narrator in the train with a twitch, an itch between her shoulder blades?
Her imagined virginity is the source of the artist's "making-up". She, like the
waves themselves in the first draft of *The Waves*, is one of many mothers, drop-
ping their babes on the shore, life itself. This virginity and its miraculous
motherhood meets its mate in the virginity of the author and gives birth to
books. "But when the self speaks to the self, who is speaking? The entombed
soul, the spirit driven in, in, in to the central catacomb; the self that took the
veil and left the world—a coward perhaps, yet somehow beautiful, as it flits with
its lantern restlessly up and down the dark corridors."[17]

This soliloquy and colloquy of the selves in the central catacomb is similar to
Woolf's grandfather's self-described mental processes. The source of creativity
is not generativity or sexuality but purity. Woolf's lesbian imagination conceives of her own artistic process as an immaculate conception. The annuncia-
tions were not trumpeted by angels but spoken by the series of real women who
mothered her mind.

Clara Pater, her Latin teacher; Janet Case, her Greek teacher; Violet Dickinson, who read her first essays and got them published; Caroline Emelia
Stephen, "Nun," her Quaker aunt who helped her into the discipline of work
and left her a legacy of economic freedom to do it; Margaret Llewelyn-Davies,
who brought her into the world of the Cooperative Working Women's Guild to a
lifetime commitment to feminism, pacifism, and socialism—these were the
formative influences on Virginia Woolf's mind. From them, she learned the
self-discipline of study, the classical structures that form the architecture of her
novels, the value of intellectual work, the use of Quaker visionary experiences
and "rational mysticism," and a politics based on a pure, ideal ethics. These are
the saints of her sanity and her survival. They stand in her imagination like
statues in the central catacomb like the "saints in the light" of her Clapham Sect
ancestry, haloed by lives of "single blessedness" or virgin martyrs to the causes
dear to her. Their portraits appear in her work as "conspirators" for the freedom
of their sex, as founders of what she called "the women's republic." Clara Pater
appears as a music teacher in "Slater's Pins Have No Points" and the progress of
her pupil, Fanny, is similar to the narrator's in "An Unwritten Novel." Gossip
has made her suspect that Julia Craye was unhappy because she was unmarried.
"No, Miss Craye was steadily, blissfully, if only for that moment, a happy
woman . . . obstinately adhering, whatever people might say, in choosing her
pleasures for herself." Julia blazes, kindles, burns "like a dead white star" and
kisses Fanny on the lips.[18] Janet Case is recalled as Lucy Craddock in *The Years*
and Woolf wrote her obituary. Violet Dickinson is celebrated in "Friendships
Gallery" and Ellen Hawkes has described her "gift of self" to Virginia in
"Woolf's Magical Garden of Women."[19]

Caroline Emelia Stephen was undoubtedly the most important of Woolf's
early mother/mentors. She, too, was the subject of a spoof biography, which has
been lost. Virginia wrote her obituary, which attempted to repair the damage
done to her aunt's reputation in her father's *Mausoleum Book*. *A Room of One's*

Own takes its title as well as its theme of an aunt's legacy directly from Caroline's life. In 1904, at the Porch, her aunt's Cambridge cottage or "nunnery," Virginia Stephen the professional writer was born. She was recovering from illness and a suicide attempt after her father's death. Between them, the two Quaker spinsters, Violet Dickinson and Caroline Stephen, wove a professional life of work for the lost young woman. Violet encouraged her to write reviews and got them published through a friend at the *Guardian* (church weekly). Caroline insisted she train and discipline herself as an historian and together they collaborated with Maitland on the biography of Leslie Stephen. She learned then the value of writing and keeping diaries and letters, that life was "fully lived" if it was written down. And she imagined the life of a historian searching out domestic history in the story of Rosamond Merridew in "The Journal of Mistress Joan Martyn" (1906) as a corrective to the history of great men in her father's *Dictionary of National Biography*.[20] It is not too much to say that Virginia Woolf's "moments of being" were born of her aunt's mystical illuminations in *The Light Arising: Thoughts on the Central Radiance* and that she is that mysterious "lady at a table writing" who appears so often in Woolf's writing.[21]

Margaret Llewelyn-Davies first appears as Mary Datchet in *Night and Day* and later as a source for Eleanor Pargiter in *The Years*.[22] Both characters reflect the central radiance in figures of light, lighthouse, and sun.[23] She, like Caroline Stephen, reinforced Virginia's pacifism and encouraged her socialist feminism.

Margaret Llewelyn-Davies, Caroline Emelia Stephen, Violet Dickinson, Clara Pater, and Janet Case were the first and formative figures in the mothering of Virginia Woolf's mind. They were the cellists whose sensitive, chaste, and hardworking bows could draw forth the music from Virginia's cello. They could be trusted not to violate her sense of self and to encourage by their example the growth of "the self that took the veil and left the world." Caroline Stephen's Quaker doctrine of silent worship and the search for "inner light" taught her the methods of "rational mysticism," self-reliance, and self-discipline that became the core of her working life as an artist. Her teachers and friends gave her "maternal protection" and praise. We can see them as a "string section" of talented and happy women in an orchestra of nuns, imposing music, order and harmony on the life of a youthful writer, tormented by guilt, grief, and self-destructive despair. Work, as Mary Datchet says in *Night and Day*, is what saves one.

Virginia's relation to and with her sister Vanessa is emotionally more primary and less an intellectual process than that with her mother/mentors. And her relation with Leonard Woolf was more complex but not as inspiring or creative. He nursed her and cared for her health with the strict obsessive discipline of her mother in the sickroom. She needed his praise and approval of her work, his partnership in the daily hard work and decisions of publishing life at the Hogarth Press. His approval relieved her anxiety. His harsh, ascetic rational behavior was a source of great security, and his moral beauty was impeccable. There was a monk in "Monk's House." But he did not, alas, make her feel like a violin being played upon. Woolf was serious when she told Ethel Smyth, "women alone stir my imagination." She thought that if her father had lived, his life would have entirely ended hers. But did she ever allow herself to think what would have happened if her mother had lived? Neither the writing of books nor the marriage to a Jew would have been possible. The life with her Greek translations, reading, concerts, arguments with Bloomsbury men, would not have been possible. A proper marriage to a proper young man of Julia's choosing . . . ?

As it was, Virginia's choice of Leonard for a husband was as brilliant a move in the protection of those central catacombs where her art came to virgin birth as was possible. The only parallel that comes to mind is the marriage of Beatrice Potter to Sidney Webb. The class background of Miss Potter and Miss Stephen was essentially the same. Middle-class marriage with its servilities, civilities, and humiliations would have ruined the careers of both. Each woman chose a partner over whom she had the upper hand, economically and socially, an outsider, below her in class and status, and passionately in love with her beauty. Beatrice and Virginia made it clear to Sidney and Leonard that they were not attractive physically, and the women's money made it possible for the men to devote themselves full-time to Labour politics. Marriage, Beatrice told Virginia, was the "waste pipe" of the emotions, and an old family servant would do as well. Their freedom depended on a spartan life, childlessness, and the continued adoration of their husbands. Both women achieved more than was possible for any more fully "married" woman of their class. The "penniless Jew" and the Cockney intellectual were not only the agents of their wives' freedom. They were able, within such marriages, to do exactly the work they chose to do. These "partnerships" were liberating for both parties. Virginia Woolf had in her marriage a nunnery with a knight in shining armour to guard it. Her suicide notes are not quite like a message to an old family servant. Rather, they are like an invalid parent's message to an unmarried daughter who has spent years of her life nursing her. They are a "nunc dimittis" to the faithful nurse, urging him to take his reward of a full and happy life. And certainly, it appears that he did. She absolved him of guilt, and guilt, it appears, he felt none. A happy love affair appears to have followed, and one of the finest autobiographies of modern times.

One thing is pretty certain. The person who mothered Virginia Woolf's body, ordered her daily life, and watched over her illnesses, was not eligible for the post of mothering her mind. Leonard was neither inspiration nor ideal audience for her work. If she was a musical instrument, he was a meticulous and expert craftsman, keeping it in order, replacing strings, polishing the wood, keeping it out of the damp and the draughts, applying rosin to the bow. But Leonard did not play the instrument. He was a harsh and demanding judge of execution and performance, a jealous guardian of her health, not a role to be minimized in any sense. But the distance between them is like the distance between Bertram and Sasha in "A Summing Up." Bertram doesn't understand Sasha's "soul," that "creature beating its way about her and trying to escape." The soul, Sasha thinks, "is by nature unmated, a widow bird; a bird perched aloof on that tree."[24]

Katherine Mansfield was certainly an important influence on Virginia Woolf. And here again, the question of sexuality is crucial. Woolf at first recoiled from a woman she felt behaved like an amorous street cat. But as soon as Katherine was dead, she was made an honorary virgin in Woolf's mind, and appears in Woolf's *Diary* in a white veil, wreathed in orange blossoms in bridal purity. Virginia's love for Vita Sackville-West is also a special case, for it was truly sexual, and Vita had real children to mother and a husband to care for and had primary sexual needs herself. She was not the selfless nun who could mother Virginia's mind and minister to her demands with the kind of unconditional love Virginia required. There was, I think, much more of a professional camaraderie than has been suggested, and a real respect for each other's craft. But ultimately it was ethics that interfered. On the issues of politics and promiscuity, Vita did not pass the purity test. Her flirtation with fascism and her list of lovers locked her out of the orchestra, though they did not lock her out of Virginia's heart.[25]

But Woolf's relationship with Vita Sackville-West is the only one in which she was willing and able to play mother to another woman's mind and to give the intellectual nourishment she had so often taken from her own mental "mothers." It is significant that her love affair with Vita was her most fully sexual experience. When Vita reviewed *A Room of One's Own* (*The Listener*, Nov, 1929) she was understandably enamored of the idea of the androgynous mind of the artist, but, she promised the reader, "Mrs. Woolf is too sensible to be a thorough-going feminist." One may imagine that Vita's lessons began with a refutation of that assertion. Though Virginia Woolf felt aggrieved at her lack of formal education, she found that, compared with Vita Sackville-West, she was a learned woman. And, to her credit, she tried to influence Vita as she had been influenced. We know that Virginia Woolf spent a great deal of time and energy over the years advising young writers and reading endless piles of manuscripts as an editor at the Hogarth Press. But little attention has been paid to this mothering role of hers. In the case of her influence on Vita, it may be seen most clearly in Vita's most explicitly feminist (and Woolfian in structure) novel, *All Passion Spent* (1931).

The novel is the story of Lady Slane's liberation after the death of her husband at the age of ninety-four, as she moves from Mayfair to a cottage in Hampstead. Her first trip on "the tube" is her "voyage in" and her fantasy of freedom is marked by a parenthetical punctuation of the tube stops from Leicester Square to Hampstead. Dedicated to Sackville-West's sons, Benedict and Nigel, the novel is an apology for a woman who gives up her art for her marriage: "Other people would point to their marriage as a perfect marriage; to herself and Henry, severally, as the perfect wife and husband. They would say that neither had ever 'looked at' anybody else. They would envy them, as the partners in an honorable career and the founders of a satisfactory and promising dynasty" (*APS*, 161). Lady Slane is apt to blame mothers for their complicity in the misery of daughters and their maintenance of marriage: ". . . as for her mother's heart, that might have been a railway terminus, so many shining threads ran up into it out of sight." (APS, 150). Perhaps Lady Slane is speaking her author's feelings of motherlessness, the feelings that waked such a maternal response in Virginia Woolf. In getting engaged, Lady Slane had pleased her mother, "she had performed an act of exceeding though joyful virtue." It was a world where "matriarchy ruled . . . and thus, she thought, might a Theban mother have tried her daughter before sending her off to the Minotaur" (APS, 153).

Virginia Woolf appears to be the mother/mentor behind this one glimpse of a feminist Vita Sackville-West. Marriage is mocked, and many passages in the novel suggest Virginia Woolf's speech "Professions for Women," given the same year: "Is it not for this function that they have been formed, dressed, bedizened, educated—if so one-sided an affair may be called education—safeguarded, kept in the dark, hinted at, segregated, repressed, all that at a given moment they may be delivered or may deliver their daughters over, to Minister to a Man?" (APS, 154). The repetitions of the following passage are again reminiscent of "Professions for Women":

> It would not do if Henry were to return one evening and be met by a locked door. It would not do if Henry, short of ink or blotting paper, were to emerge irritably only to be told that Mrs. Holland was engaged with a model. It would not do, if Henry were appointed governor to some distant colony, to tell him that the drawing master unfortunately lived in London. It would not do, if Henry wanted another son, to tell him that she had just embarked on a special course of study. It would not do, in such a world of assumptions, to assume that she had equal rights with Henry. For such privileges marriage was not ordained. [APS, 156]

Vita's very different experience leads her to say "there was an air of freemasonry among men, based on their common liberty, very different from the freemasonry among women, which was always prying and personal and somehow a trifle obscene." Virginia's experience had been the opposite, and the female bonding of her mentors had been examples of feminist freemasonry in social work, study, suffrage, and religion. It was the men of her circle in Bloomsbury whose relations were "personal" or "obscene." Lady Slane's marriage has been like being shot out of the terminus of her mother's heart into the destination of her husband's:

> Her love for him had been a straight black line drawn right through her life. It had hurt her, it had damaged her, it had diminished her, but she had been unable to curve away from it. All the parts of her that were not Henry Holland's had pulled in opposition, yet by this single giant of love they had all been pulled over, as the weaker team in a tug-of-war. Her ambitions, her secret existence, all had given way. She had loved him so much that even her resentment was subdued. She could not grudge him even the sacrifice he had imposed upon her. Yet she was not one of those women whose gladness in sacrifice is such that the

sacrifice ceases to be a sacrifice. Her own youthful visions had been incompatible
with such a love, and in giving them up, she knew that she gave up something of
incomparable value. [*APS*, 164]

Lady Slane's life had been like Vita's, in short, not like Virginia's. The novel is
both a confession and a fantasy of feminist freedom in old age when all passion is
spent. Lady Slane complains, "He had decoyed her into holding him dearer
than her own ambition. She has used up her "maternal protection" on her
husband" [depicted like the professional men in *Three Guineas*]. "She had
seen him always in a *processional* life, threatened by bombs, riding on an
elephant through Indian cities." For male processions to be effective, Woolf
suggests, mobs of women and ordinary men must applaud and stare. Vita's
allegiance was there, and despite her lesbianism, she was not at heart a feminist, nor was she bonded to women in primary allegiance as Woolf was. This
novel is a tribute to Woolf's teachings, a fantasy, not a reality.

We can see in the relationship of Lily Briscoe and Mrs. Ramsay in *To the
Lighthouse* that it is not easy for the artist to find a mother/mentor. Lily longs to
go back to the womb in the most explicit way, and to merge with the mother.
But Mrs. Ramsay does not encourage her art, her work. In fact, she wants her to
marry, to minister to men. She is an inspiration to Lily, who adores her. But
Lily gets more good out of old Carmichael, who does not lie or flatter, than she
does from Mrs. Ramsay. But then, Lily is a painter. She is an "active" artist (as
responsive as Vanessa Bell, whom Virginia thought of as self-sufficient and
independent).

The writer, Virginia thought, plays a passive role. Romantically, she is an
instrument waiting to be played, like Coleridge's Aeolian harp, waiting for the
muse, holding herself in readiness to Keats's negative capability. And this condition demands collaboration, the wind, the world, another person. Its analogue, of course, is illness. In "On Being Ill," Virginia Woolf describes the
"astonishing" spiritual change she experiences, "the undiscovered countries"
disclosed "when the lights of health go down." Illness is a "voyage in" for the
artist, a trip into those silent catacombs where the self withdraws and takes the
veil. The experience is so remarkable that "it becomes strange indeed that illness has not taken its place with love and battle and jealousy among the prime
themes of literature. . . ."

> Those great wars which the body wages with the mind a slave to it, in the soli-
> tude of the bedroom against the assault of fever or the oncome of melancholia,
> are neglected. . . .To look these things squarely in the face would need the
> courage of a lion tamer; a robust philosophy; a reason rooted in the bowels of the
> earth. Short of these, this monster, the body, this miracle, its pain, will soon
> make us temper into mysticism, or rise, with rapid beats of the wings, into the
> raptures of transcendentalism.[26]

Only Proust, she feels, deals with the drama of illness. But English lacks the
language of physical pain: ". . . let a sufferer try to describe a pain in his head to

a doctor and language at once runs dry." As women writers need "a little language unknown to men," so writers on illness not only need a language "more primitive, more sensual, more obscene, but a new hierarchy of the passions; love must be deposed in favour of a temperature of 104°; jealousy give place to the pangs of sciatica; sleeplessness play the part of the villain, and the hero become a white liquid with a sweet taste—that mighty Prince with the moth's eyes and the feathered feet, one of whose names is chloral."

Illness, she claims, is a confessional; one may tell the truth and return to childhood. Reading is a new experience—one may be "rash" in reading Shakespeare intuitively. The kind of reading one does in bed is the reading of an outlaw, "with the police off duty." Illness makes one an outsider to rational, busy, daily activity. It is thus analogous to art and also to the political and ethical "outsidership" she describes in *Three Guineas*. But writing about sickness is difficult because of the commonality of human suffering. So she avoids "turning the old beggar's hieroglyphic of misery into volumes of sordid suffering." But the mark of that "beggar's hieroglyphic" is on all Woolf's work, the deformed old men and women, flower-sellers, organ-grinders, the crippled, and the maimed who stand on the street corners of her novels to remind us of "those barracks of pain and discipline."

Suffering requires solace. Only women can give it, and only certain dispassionate women at that: "Sympathy nowadays is dispensed chiefly by the laggards and failures, women for the most part (in whom the obsolete exists so strangely side by side with anarchy and newness), who, having dropped out of the race, have time to spend upon fantastic and unprofitable excursions." The sick person, like the artist, is a "deserter" from the battlefield of life. She does not believe that we are all alike under the skin, that "however far you travel in your own mind someone has been there before you."

Illness is an opportunity to strike out for virgin territory: "There is a virgin forest in each; a snowfield where even the print of birds' feet is unknown. Here we go alone, and like it better so." Here she contemplates the indifference of nature and the non-existence of God. "Surely, since men have been wishing all these ages, they will have wished something into existence; there will be some green isle," and she finds comfort in "the snowfield of the mind, where man has not trodden." Creativity is clearly a convent, a clean well-lighted cell of one's own, the perfect white square that Dr. Savage's patient longed for. It is a nunnery like Caroline Stephen's retreat, "The Porch," a catacomb in which to cloister the imagination, a snowfield on an inaccessible glacier. If this cloister is to remain unsullied, "maternal protection" is necessary from male aggression, male sexuality.

Life on the other side of the sword is terrifying. The sword is like the scimitar James sees as his father in *To the Lighthouse*. It threatens like the fantasy in "The String Quartet":

> He followed me down the corridor, and, as we turned the corner, trod on the
> lace of my petticoat. What could I do but cry 'ah!' and stop to finger it? At which

he drew his sword, made passes as if he were stabbing something to death, and cried, "Mad! Mad! Mad!"[27]

This fantasy is brought on by meeting a relative at the concert, and "the ties of blood" require the narrator to speak. Perhaps it is the "mad" J. K. Stephen plunging his sword into the nursery loaf which incites the fantasy, as well as the thought, "the worst of influenza is its after effects . . ."

In *Psychoanalysis and Medicine: A Study of the Wish to Fall Ill*, Karin Stephen, a Freudian, regards illness as a defense mechanism of the psyche, and often an extremely useful one. "Praise for health and blame for illness do not belong here," she says, and "moral indignation is surely out of place in the science of medicine." She urges her students not to deprive the patient of his symptoms. For they were created in order to avert a danger of which the person is terrified. Civilization, she says, echoing Freud, is based on repression. Repression cannot solve conflicts but only shelve them. "The foundation of psychogenic illness always dates from the early conflicts between desire, disappointment and fear in childhood." She does not minimize the suffering involved but claims that "the healthy person is one who has bought stability and freedom from anxiety cheaply enough to outweigh his losses by his gains."[28] Karin Stephen does not go so far as to regard this capacity to fall ill as the work of the artist but she does say, "A neurosis is, indeed, a very remarkable human achievement which proves the extraordinary capacity for renunciation possessed by mankind, but it is an unnecessary heroism and is based ultimately on groundless fear," and "the renunciation of sex becomes tolerable and possible in so far as it can draw strength from sexuality itself." The asexual person "draws comfort at a deep unconscious level from the fantasy of a sexual experience so mighty and awful that the body has died under it." This represents "the most utter abandonment to passive love" and is expressed in the female Christian phrase, "Behold, the handmaiden of the Lord." But the self-hatred engendered by guilt is often "the deep motive of suicide." Karin Stephen's Freudian approach helps to explain Woolf's need for "maternal protection" and her open seeking for it, her feeling that life was a heroic struggle and that women like Ethel Smyth in their mothering saved her from "instant dismemberment by wild horses." Rachel Vinrace dies, we sometimes feel, in *The Voyage Out*, because Helen Ambrose denies her complete maternal protection. She does not save her from Mr. Dalloway's kiss, or even reprimand him. She kisses Terence over Rachel's head after they have all tumbled in the grass in that "rape of Persephone" scene, making clear that she will not play the perfect Demeter.

But in the last decade of her life, Virginia Woolf had a mother/mentor to match her early teachers, Ethel Smyth. And Ethel helped her to release all her anger at male aggression which she finally "spat out" in *Three Guineas*. In *Melymbrosia*, the earlier, more political version of *The Voyage Out*, Woolf wrote, "Music is a tiny tin sword which was clasped into their hands to fight the world with, if other weapons failed."[29] Ethel Smyth returned this weapon to

Virginia Woolf, and taught her how to fight, as earlier she had literally taught Mrs. Pankhurst and the suffragettes how to throw rocks. She taught Virginia Woolf how to let loose her righteous anger. Dame Ethel could conduct real orchestras as well as tune up the imaginary cellos of Virginia's art. In "The String Quartet" Woolf had described the effect: "Flourish, spring, burgeon, burst! The pear tree on the top of the mountain. Fountains jet; drops descend." With Ethel Smyth on the scene, there was a perpetual pear tree on top of a mountain. Virginia courted Ethel by calling her a pear tree, in an image very like one in Katherine Mansfield and also in a sketch by Pater. It meant memory, virginity, motherhood, music.

Ethel Smyth entered Woolf's life on a wave of praise for *A Room of One's Own*. In Ethel's first surviving letter, she asks to see Virginia (Jan. 28, 1930) for advice on a feminist talk she is about to give for the BBC. She says that her object is to drive home "what women should do if war ever again threatens." She wants to broadcast advice to women, "Stow patriotism and simply say you will strike." This is, of course, the theme of *Three Guineas* (1938) and one might say that Woolf learned to let her anger loose from an expert feminist fighter.[30]

Virginia and Ethel shared their love for their dead mothers. Ethel wrote:

> with me and I think many women the root of love is in the imaginative part of one—its violence, its tenderness, its hunger . . . the most violent feeling I am conscious of is . . . [her dots] for my mother. She died thirty-eight years ago and I never can think of her without a stab of real passion; amusement, tenderness, pity, admiration are in it and pain that I can't tell her how I love her (but I think she knows). Now you can imagine how much sexual feeling has to do with an emotion for one's mother![31]

Virginia agreed that both Ethel's mother and her own were "adorable." But the essence of their relationship was a discussion of the career each artist made with the help of a series of mother/mentors, those women who mothered their art. They discussed in detail what it meant to be a "daughter" and an artist. Daughterhood is the universal female condition. It was also a role which each artist played with a series of women in order to insure "protection" for that convent of the mind where creativity was centered. Virginia told Ethel that she provided "protection" and saved her psychiatrist's fees, that she could "confess" to her the story of the molestations of her half-brothers as she had earlier confessed to her Greek teacher, Janet Case. Their friendship was a fight from beginning to end over who was to mother the other, over whose daughter-need was the greatest. Virginia could be cruel and ungenerous. Ethel called her "four pence for ninepence," and Virginia withdrew from Ethel's self-pity and fury at the rejection of her music by the establishment, hating what she called her "eldritch shriek." But Virginia wanted to have her cake and eat it too, in posterity. Most of her criticism and mockery of Ethel is in letters to her nephews, Julian and Quentin Bell. And yet she flirted outrageously with Ethel and begged for love.

Ethel had been lucky in her friendships. Her success as a composer was due to the care of women in Leipzig where she studied—Lisl von Herzogenberg, the wife of her composition teacher, Lily Wach, Mendelssohn's daughter, and Clara Schumann. They urged her not to marry, to encourage her talent, spoiled her and encouraged her, played her music, discussed her technique with Brahms, trained and trusted her—as if she were their own youthful selves, the composer each had longed to be. The list of Dame Ethel's mother/mentors is endless, from Lady Ponsonby to Mrs. Pankhurst, as well as a series of sisters and their husbands who sponsored and supported her. Women had recognized genius in both Woolf and Smyth, and they had given them the teaching, discipline, and love which they needed to survive. Their names for each other were "the Snow Queen" and "the Old Buccaneer." It was a battle over who was to play mother and who daughter, when both were needy. They compared notes on the ministrations of their past muses. Virginia gave Ethel the strength to write her last volumes of memoirs and her opera/oratorio, *The Prison*. Ethel inspired some of *The Waves* and *The Years*, but most especially the anger of *Three Guineas*.

In one of Virginia's love letters, she describes Dame Ethel as a burning bush in a sexual portrait which strikes one as anticipatory of the plates in Judy Chicago's *The Dinner Party*. Ethel is

> a quickset briar hedge, innumerably intricate and spiky and thorned; in the centre burns a rose. Miraculously, the rose is you; flushed pink, wearing pearls. The thorn hedge is the music; and I have to break my way through violins, flutes, cymbals, voices . . . to this red burning centre . . . I am enthralled that you, the dominant and superb, should have this tremor and vibration of fire round you—violins flickering, flutes purring; (the image is of a winter hedge)— that you should be able to create this world from your centre . . . [VW, *Letters*, vol. 5]

But Virginia retreated like the "cowardly" narrator of "An Unwritten Novel," from rescuing her Brunnhilde from the ring of fire. The image of female sexuality, the labyris of roses and music is exquisite, feminist and, perhaps, frightening. But it is Woolf's clearest expression of her vision into "the heart of the woman's republic."

The "tiny tin sword" of music became as vigilantly virginal as Joan of Arc's and Woolf a militant maiden in *Three Guineas*. She sought other mothers, teasing Vita Sackville-West about being attracted to the "old maid" who loved poetry in Edith Sitwell. The last of Virginia Woolf's mother mentors was Dr. Octavia Wilberforce. But Octavia was confused by Virginia and did not understand her needs. She did not know Virginia's history or how she herself stood in a long line of chaste mother/mentors. Still engaged as "daughter" to her own mother/ mentor, Elizabeth Robins, she did not see herself as a savior for Virginia. Part of the problem surrounding Virginia Woolf's suicide resides in this misunderstanding.[32] Leonard Woolf's autobiography expresses his relief that Virginia was in Dr. Wilberforce's hands. Virginia told Vita that she loved Octavia, and she was making a "sketch" of her life. But Octavia was busy with war work and her patients. She visited Virginia socially, not professionally, as a dutiful response to Elizabeth Robins's request, and told Virginia the story of her life with much discomfort and unease. Though she brought milk and butter, she brought no mothering nor, until the night before Woolf's suicide, was she sought as a doctor. She did not know the history of Virginia's mental instability, nor was she cognizant of her medical history.

There was little Dr. Wilberforce could do under the circumstances. She herself was ill at the time. What had happened was a failure of the support system Virginia had devised for herself of mother/mentors. Octavia Wilberforce did not understand what was expected of her. She wrote Elizabeth Robins in detail on every conversation and consultation she had had with Virginia. And, in the process, she absolved herself of any guilt or blame. Virginia had asked for permission to have lunch with Clive and a publisher. Octavia agreed with Leonard that it would be too much for her. What Virginia had wanted was a motherly voice to permit her to have a treat. When she didn't get it, her "tiny tin sword" was no match for the voices in her head, and she threw herself into the arms of "Mother Water." Virginia Woolf had worn out the possibilities for unconditional love. She had failed to recognize the daughter in Ethel Smyth and to give back some of the mothering she had received. She had failed to recognize that the woman-bonding she called for in *Three Guineas* had been effectively squelched in a patriarchal war. It was no time for music and the instruments were out of tune. She went down to the sound of German bombs and German planes smashing the orchestra of her mother country.

ᏫᏋ 6 ᏫᏋ

The Niece of a Nun:
Virginia Woolf, Caroline Stephen,
and the Cloistered Imagination

> Often down here I have entered into a
> sanctuary; a nunnery; had a religious retreat;
> of great agony once; and always some terror:
> so afraid one is of loneliness: of seeing to the
> bottom of the vessel.
>
> —DVW 3:196

> The continued metaphors in which their
> [the Quakers'] philosophy is expressed,
> taken from the wind and light, waters, chains
> of bubbles and other sustained forces, solve
> all personal energy into one suave stream.
>
> —VW, 1908, review of H. Fielding Hall's
> *The Inward Light, Contemporary Writers* 46

The Erotics of Chastity

Virginia Woolf's model for female power derived from chastity had two
sources; the life of Queen Elizabeth (an early and lifelong interest of the woman
named "Virginia")[1] and the example and history of nuns, including her aunt,
Caroline Emelia Stephen, a great Quaker theologian. Woolf's work, like her
aunt's, based religious and political stances on a celebration of celibacy and
remade male repressive ideology into a feminist ideology of power.

Caroline Stephen's major work before her conversion to the Quaker religion
was *The Service of the Poor* (1871),[2] a history of sisterhoods. There is no more
heartrending example of the plight of Victorian womanhood than the tortured
ambivalence of this book. The young woman's passion to escape the patriarchal
family into a sisterhood was harnessed into many years of study, firsthand
research, and writing what became powerful propaganda against sisterhoods, a

book used to convince "daughters of educated men" that such salvation was selfish. Celibate women living separately in convents, she says, are a dire threat to the patriarchal family, which needs for survival the unpaid cheerful labor of its unmarried daughters. With what personal pain and almost erotic longing for escape into a self-governing world of women does Caroline Stephen argue against the desire for freedom from family constraints. Chafing at these bonds herself, she was an extremely effective spokeswoman for patriarchal protestant-ism. Her harshest criticism was for the bonding of women into groups. It was many years before she found a personal solution that would not dishonor the memory of her father—the mixed religious meetings of the Society of Friends, where class and sex boundaries could be transcended without threatening the structure of the family, where she could experience community and also estab-lish a private life in a nunnery of one. These breeding grounds for a female col-lective haunt the imagination of her niece, Virginia Woolf, in her dream of "a woman's republic," her idealization of girls' schools and women's colleges because she had never experienced this bonding, her work in women's suffrage, the Women's Cooperative Guild, and the Women's Service League and Library. In "A Society" she created a sisterhood of intellectual inquiry that fore-shadowed her lifelong friendships with women. In *A Room of One's Own* she outlined a strategy of the collective voice of women artists united over history, and in *Three Guineas* she sketched the utopian woman's college of the future, where the possibilities of sisterhood might be explored and tested, and called for an "Outsiders' Society" where female marginality could be exploited for col-lective political purposes.

In *Three Guineas* Virginia Woolf eroticizes the idea of chastity as the romantics eroticized the idea of liberty. What an idea—the erotics of chastity—but it can be traced in the writings of nuns like Saint Teresa and the image of the chaste virgin warrior in the life of Joan of Arc and in the adoption of that Amazonian image by Christabel Pankhurst and the British suffragettes. The sexualization of politics and the valorization of chastity at the end of the suffrage campaign have been dismissed by historians as hysteria, but there is no question that they infused the suffragettes with an enormous feeling of power and intimidated men far more than the espousal of free love by other feminists.[3]

The chosen state of celibacy has been elevated by some women to the status of freedom, since it represents escape from the bonds of family. The inviolate body suggests youth and life when compared with the body of Victorian mother-hood, battered by childbirth. Both Annie Thackeray (before her marriage to a man much younger than herself) and Caroline Stephen lecturing to university students on the joys of spinsterhood, suggest that the chaste life with female friends allows a woman her own work and her choice of emotional ties. It was a form of rebellion against the patriarchal family, and the idea of that rebellion was itself erotic. Virginia Woolf's choice of a Jewish "outsider" husband in a companionate marriage with no children and her attacks on the patriarchal family in her novels, especially *The Years*, make her own inheritance of this female tradition clear.

In "Toilers and Spinsters" (1873) Anne Thackeray wrote, "May not spinsters climb up craters, publish their experiences, tame horses, wear porkpie hats, write articles in the *Saturday Review*? They have gone to battle in Topboots, danced on the tight-rope, taken up the Italian cause, and harangued the multitudes. They have gone to prison for distributing tracts; they have ascended Mont Blanc, and come down again." Money, Annie argued, was more important than virginity. In "Living Alone," a lecture given at Newnham College in 1906 and published in *The Light Arising: Thoughts on the Central Radiance* (1908), Caroline Stephen described the "austere charm" of the single life. "We cannot be finally freed from loneliness except by encountering it. It will be subdued only by those who dare to meet it with a hearty embrace," she wrote. The imaginative power to outline your own life is not a misfortune, she told the students. The family protests at first when a daughter begins to break ties, but "An admonition or two, a gently affixed label of eccentricity, and the thing is done." "The hermit," she wrote, "is impervious to many an arrow which scatters dismay among the flock." Like Virginia Woolf in *A Room of One's Own*, Caroline demands a feminist territorial imperative. The single woman has "an open space in the labyrinth of life," and she encourages the young women to claim it: "That there is in the human mind a power of making the 'iron bars' of our cage into a hermitage, and the empty spaces around us into a sanctuary, we all instinctively feel; but it needs some reflection to understand what is the spell by which such transformations are to be wrought." In *A Room of One's Own* Virginia Woolf also uses this image of the cage and bars to describe the space in which the feminist historian can investigate men's opposition to women's freedom.

Woolf's erotics of chastity is deeply feminist and is even, perhaps, a screen for her lesbian imagination. What she has done is to take the Victorian ideal of female chastity, which was patriarchal culture's enforced imprisonment of women's bodies and minds, and created in *Three Guineas* a modern ideal of "intellectual chastity."[4] Intellectual purity is then equated with intellectual liberty. This concept, once stated, leaps backward onto that Victorian beast, men's obsession with female chastity, and transfers the concept to the mind. This new chastity of choice suggests power, both mental and physical, and has ascetic beauty and fierce attraction. The single women in Woolf's novels represent aspects of the powerful privileging of purity in her imagination, as the deaths of Rachel Vinrace and Judith Shakespeare represent women's loss of freedom in heterosexual relations, marriage or rape. Lily Briscoe's artistic integrity seems to derive from her refusal to marry, and Mary Datchet, Eleanor Pargiter, and Lucy Swithin are almost high priestesses of virtue rather than heroines. Perhaps the most interesting case is that of Clarissa Dalloway, whose honor seems to have derived from her failure to be Richard's sexual partner.[5] As virgin mother, Clarissa lives the life of a nun in her attic room, her narrow white bed. Her "virginity preserved through childbirth" and the memory of her blissful love for Sally make Clarissa a very attractive figure. She may lack "something central which permeated" in her relations with her husband, but she is erotically inflamed by memories of Sally, by Miss Kilman's threat to steal her daughter, and by listening to the confidences of other women. She is the lesbian who marries for safety and appearances, produces a child, cannot relate sexually to her husband, and chooses celibacy within marriage, no sex rather than the kind she wants. Denial of desire is easier than living Miss Kilman's life, she feels.

It is interesting regarding Clarissa's celibate marriage that, in Caroline Stephen's history of sisterhoods, one of the groups studied is the *Clarissan* nuns, an order of women who were married but signed vows of celibacy with their husbands, lived at home, and were secret nuns. They performed good works without threatening the family by living in groups.

On the Clarissans, the Third Order of Saint Francis, Caroline Stephen quotes her father's *Essays in Ecclesiastical Biography*. (Virginia Woolf read her grandfather's essays when she was fifteen.) As lay nuns, the Clarissans were allowed to hide the scapulary and cord; they needed only the "tacit consent" of their husbands to their vows of celibacy. As "poor ladies" the Clarissans cared for the insane and "fallen women." Woolf also felt the appeal of the secret life of a nun under the protection of marriage, and her Clarissa is like "a nun withdrawing." Clarissa's call is even clearer in her relationship with the "insane" Septimus Smith. There is really only a difference of degree between Septimus's voices and Clarissa's, between her desire for celibacy in marriage and his. The historical relationship of nuns to the mad, the ill, and prostitutes is an interesting one, outsiders caring for outsiders.

The erotics of chastity has parallels in politics, in religion, and in speech. In Woolf's thought pacifism is privileged as morally superior to war and imperialism, unassailably correct by any standards. Mysticism has the same aura in religion. Mysticism is nonhierarchal and private, a harmless creed with no hatred.

Caroline Stephen's mystical writing—*The Light Arising: Thoughts on the Central Radiance, Quaker Strongholds*, and *The Vision of Faith*—constitutes a subversive female discourse, and it strongly influenced Virginia Woolf.[6] If pacifism is the purest political stance, mysticism is the purest religious concept. It allows access to the community of saints without the dogmas and disciplines of organized religion. Objecting to the *language* of piety as spoken and written by patriarchal priests, Caroline Stephen advocated communal silence and the direct utterance of spiritual experience, unfettered by form, of Quaker testimony. Though she claimed she was not a feminist, her effort is godmother to Woolf's search for a feminine sentence. Caroline's weariness with the language of men is symptomatic of her century, her class, and her family.

Caroline wanted to revive a religious image of her father, the author of ecclesiastical biographies, in direct opposition to the portraits of power painted by her brothers, Fitzjames and Leslie, in the studies of him as colonial administrator and professor of modern history. The men created an image of the master of the language of imperialism in their portraits of James Stephen. When Fitzjames and Leslie were safely dead, she collected her father's letters to show him as master of the language of piety.[7] Instincts of filial piety and filial rebellion were at war within her until her old age. She could not blot out her brothers' pronouncements, but she could suggest revision. It is clear from Virginia Woolf's letters that Caroline was concerned with truth-telling in biography, and she struggled with Maitland (and the young Virginia) to no avail over the prettified portrait of Leslie Stephen that neglected to sketch in his temper and his emotional bullying of women.[8]

Caroline's brother Fitzjames literally "laid down the law" in his legal digests, his political essays, and his reactionary response to John Stuart Mill, *Liberty, Equality, Fraternity.* His legal language of controversy, argument, aggressive denunciation, and judgment, with its Old Testament thundering about punishment, damnation, and law and order, was male discourse of immense and ferocious authority.[9] Even Leslie Stephen's essays were authoritative male discourse, argumentative and assertive. The *Dictionary of National Biography* is a patriarchal masterpiece in its exclusion of women and of men who did not fit the pattern of power. Sitting on the library shelves, the volumes of the DNB are a horizontal monument to phallocentric culture.

The spinsterhood of silence in Caroline Stephen's work is a rejection of male discourse. She was weary of words as weapons, though she was obviously powerfully convincing enough to turn the Society of Friends away from evangelical preaching and back to simplicity, silent worship, and "inner light." Fitzjames and Leslie not only were argumentative, they were highly emotional. What Virginia may have found at The Porch to heal her sorrow and self-destructive desires was a calm and very rational peace. Listening, that highly developed female art, was offered by Caroline to her niece as a method of spiritual survival, the first step in learning to trust oneself that the artist needs. "We talked for some nine hours; and she poured forth all her spiritual experiences. . . .All her life she has been listening to inner voices, and talking with spirits" (L 1:299).

Ex cathedra: Caroline, Cathedral, and Cloister

> Stop shaking. Imagine her.
> She was a cathedral.[10]

These are the words the poet Denise Levertov addressed to herself at the end of her elegy for Muriel Rukeyser. The form of feminist elegy is itself transformative. The political poet does not mourn; she organizes herself and the reader to move beyond the despair of "We've made / our cathedrals, / had our chance, / blown it." to respect for Rukeyser's work, its commitment to social change, the clarity of her imagination. The traditional elegiac tone of lugubrious mourning is rejected. The poet wears white, not black; seeks light, not darkness. So the poem celebrates the life of the poet and imagines the political and poetic work as a permanent monument, a cathedral.

Levertov succeeds in imagining her sister poet by leaving off lamentation and forcing the ancient elegiac form to give over its grieving for a celebration of spiritual liberation. Much of Virginia Woolf's work began as elegies for her own dead. The ghosts of her loved ones haunted her imagination, and she played god, the writer, resurrecting them into fictional life.

The extraordinary revival of interest in the life and work of Virginia Woolf has, I believe, a single source—the political themes of her novels and the ethical and moral power of her writing, both essays and fiction.

Despite their distaste for idolatry in all its literary forms, and because of their own struggles against the canon and canonization itself in our cathedrals of learning, feminist critics have been reluctant to build a female church or to erect statues to our sainted literary mothers. Saint Virginia herself would have been appalled at shrines or pilgrims on bended knee. But now that we have examined the social and political themes of her novels, the attacks on capitalism, patriarchy, and imperialism that are the backbone of her work and the reason our generation calls her blessed, let us return to those other "isms" that so infuriated the radicals of her own day—her pacifism and her mysticism. Why does she insist on equating feminism with pacifism in *Three Guineas*? How can she be a mystic and as materialist as a marxist at the same time? Did the same hand that wrote *The Years* write *The Waves*?

We may see this conjunction of revolutionary materialism, a tremblingly violent pacifism, and a simultaneously erotic and sublimely chaste mysticism in the intellectual response to modern fascism of two other important figures, Simone Weil and Walter Benjamin.[11] The saintly trinity of self-defined outsiders rejected their bourgeois origins—the German Jewish intellectual was torn between the Kabbalah and *Das Kapital*; the French Jewish pacifist was torn between physical labor for the working class and Catholic mysticism, and the English daughter of middle-class evangelical professional reformers called herself a Jew and yet attacked patriarchy in all its forms. Their studies of power and violence are invaluable to us; their ethical purity is unassailable. Their suicides—seemingly so socially determined as political acts—fill us with humility and rage. Did they mean to be scapegoats in self-slaughter or martyrs to fear of fascism? Walter Benjamin predicted their predicament in "Ministry of the Interior": "The more antagonistic a person is toward the traditional order, the more inexorably he will subject his private life to the norms that he wishes to elevate as legislators of a future society. It is as if these laws, nowhere yet realized, placed him under obligation to enact them in advance at least in the confines of his own existence" (*Reflections*, 69). Having given up family, class, country, they could administer the interior of their own minds under an ethical imperative too pure, severe, and ascetic in its mysticism and pacifism for the real world.

This place, this space, was for each a refuge of silence, an inner cathedral. Woolf described herself as retreating to a nunnery when she wrote, and she extolled as high virtue for professional women the ideal of "intellectual chastity." Simone Weil was equally enamored of silence, and her concept of the inner void that must be experienced to achieve spiritual purity is remarkably like Woolf's room of one's own in the soul and Walter Benjamin's "ministry of the interior." Unlike existentialists, these three mystical "Marxists" came to reject action and choice for "waiting," "attention," meditation, and mystical moments of illumination.

Their intense austerity and emphasis on personal purity and the search for truth seems self-destructive to us now, though it has a rare ascetic authority. As the whole of Europe seemed to immerse itself in the destructive element, their vows of silence, poverty, and intellectual chastity bear personal witness to the idea of goodness. Pacifism in the face of fascism may seem to us, as Christopher Caudwell said, a bourgeois luxury, and perhaps only an alternative for the middle-class intellectual, but it was an honorable alternative. Yet pacifism was also part of the politics of the weak, the spiritually oppressed. Its first premise is untenable for the revolutionary—that is, that the powerful will stop destruction and violence once they see the error of their ways, that one can make a rational appeal to warriors and politicians in the midst of battle. (Trotsky said the powerful would ignore all rational appeals for peace unless they came from a united working class.)

Even their mysticism was nonviolent. No frenzied ecstasies or joyful dancing unto the Lord, it was a "rational mysticism" the three outsiders shared—a mysticism based on ethics and morality, a vision of history and socialist community.

For Virginia Woolf this rational mysticism had a specific and real origin. *The Waves* is haunted by the vision, mystical and mysterious, of a "lady at a table writing." This "mystical eye-less book" is also a mystical I-less book, the one in which ego is most diminished by the writer as minister of the interior. Here she celebrates that memory makes us moral and that community is collective memory.

The lady at a table writing was a real person, Virginia Woolf's aunt, Caroline Emelia Stephen, as she appears in a photograph in her last book of essays, in her plain gray Quaker dress and cap, writing at a window overlooking the garden in her Cambridge cottage called "The Porch" after George Herbert, her antechamber to heaven.[12] The young Cambridge Quakers to whom she was mother-mentor (in fact she wrote to one student of her "inward motherhood") called Caroline Stephen "Nun." It was an appellation she earned through years of struggle, torn between duty to the patriarchal family and the desire to join a sisterhood. Much as the young Virginia Stephen mocked her aunt's celibate mysticism, it was an attitude she herself adopted more and more as she grew older, even to the equation of writing with the notion of retreat into a nunnery.

Virginia Woolf succeeded in imagining her aunt Caroline Emelia Stephen (1834-1909) not only in the obituary she wrote at her death[13] but in the figures of Eleanor Pargiter in *The Years*, Lucy Swithin in *Between the Acts*, and "that odd little priestess of humanity," Sally Seale in *Night and Day*, fifty-five and carrying on her father's work with her crossed crucifixes and her dedication to the cause.

Even the maiden aunts in *The Voyage Out* and Hirst's Aunt Lucy who works in the slums of Lambeth—an anti-intellectual who celebrates the inner life of feeling and faith—owe something to Caroline Stephen.

Woolf's comic life of her aunt does not survive, but we may imagine that its genre was a feminist utopia, like her portrait of Violet Dickinson, another Quaker spinster, composed at the same time. These "antibiographies" were a relief from the real work of helping Maitland with his biography of Leslie Stephen and were anticipatory of *Orlando* and *Flush*. Woolf later envisioned her aunt as "the lady at a table writing," the self-cloistered nun she compared herself to as she equated celibacy with creativity and withdrew into her room of her own for mystical visions, moments of being that are remarkably like Caroline Stephen's experiences of "inner light" as she described them in *Quaker Strongholds* and *The Light Arising: Thoughts on the Central Radiance*. In bad times Woolf could tell herself to stop shaking, to imagine her aunt's life as a Quaker "nun," a spiritual cathedral of mystical vision and rational peace.

After nursing her father until he died in 1904, Virginia Stephen had a breakdown and attempted suicide. Her cure was effected by Violet Dickinson and Caroline Stephen. She wrote to Violet from The Porch: "This is an ideal retreat for me. I feel as though I were living in a Cathedral Close, with the big bell of the Quaker's voice tolling at intervals."[14] Between them, the two Quakers set Virginia to work as a writer and got her reviews published in the *Guardian* (church weekly). Her first lesson in becoming the historian Caroline wanted her to be was to help with Leslie Stephen's biography. What is interesting is that her letters at the time show her as her father's champion against Caroline's negative view of her brother, whereas in Woolf's later memoir she criticizes her father for the same faults Caroline had seen.

At first glance the life of Caroline Emelia Stephen seems to be one of those "lives of the obscure" Woolf wanted to write. There were, she pointed out, "no lives of maids in the *DNB*." There were, however, some lives of Quakers, and they were written by Caroline. What is amazing to the student of history is Leslie Stephen's portrait of his sister in *The Mausoleum Book*[15] as an utter failure. He invented a reason for the failure of her life—unrequited love—a mythical Percival who dies in India. Leslie's motives were not malicious, one feels, but simply an example of a rather good male Victorian mind utterly unable to comprehend the value of a woman's life if it did not revolve around marriage and motherhood. Like her niece Virginia, Caroline produced books instead of babies. They were "little," said Leslie. In their diminution he perhaps found some satisfaction, since his own works were so big.

Of her single-handed revival of the almost extinct English Society of Friends he says nothing. In a querulous tone he blames her loss of health on travel for the Quaker cause. But Caroline's health was lost, alas, not as a Quaker martyr but as a dutiful Victorian daughter and sister, nursing at the sickbeds and deathbeds of her family. She collapsed after three weeks of caring for Leslie and Laura after Minny's death, and Leslie complained that her nurse and doctor carried her off to her own house in Chelsea—as if she had no right to a house of her own and work of her own, after so many years as nurse to her parents.

Quaker historians have recorded that Caroline Emelia Stephen was their foremost religious thinker in the Victorian period.[16] *Quaker Strongholds* and *The Light Arising*, as well as her talks and travels, her essays, and her personal influence in Quaker meetings in London, Cambridge, and Malvern, saved the Society of Friends. The Quakers had been deeply affected by evangelical trends and had lost contact with the purity of their origins. She wrote as a convert and revived the spirit of the early Quakers. She was in her own way a great Victorian theologian, insisting that an agnostic could have faith and live a good life, explicating "rational mysticism" and achieving such a reputation that she was elected to the ministry, only to start a movement to abolish ministers.

Leslie was not proud of his sister's achievements. He blamed religion for her ill health and was contemptuous of her "taking up with the Quakers." He misnamed her book "Strongholds of Quakerism," the -ism of which makes it sound like quackery, irrational and eccentric, and called it "another little book of hers." Yet some historians claim it had a "very great influence both within and beyond the Society of Friends," and it still does.

Leslie's sketch continues, "But even in 1877 she seemed to be broken in spirit. She had no power of reaction. She was hardly even 'a reed shaken by the wind,' she was more like a reed of which every joint has been crushed and which can only float down the stream." (Leslie's reed image suggests the Syrinx/Pan myth and its sexual connotations, clues to his characterization of Caroline as frustrated.) For Caroline Stephen the break with the Clapham Sect evangelicalism of her father and brother Fitzjames, then being, as Rufus Jones says, "more or less forced intellectually to take an agnostic position by her brother Leslie," was exhausting. Silent worship with the Quakers gave her "indescribable relief." "What I felt I wanted in a place of worship was a refuge, or at least the opening of a doorway toward the refuge, from doubt and controversies, not a fresh encounter with them. Yet it seemed to me impossible that anyone harassed by conflicting views of truth, with which just now the air is thick, should be able to forget controversy while listening to such language as that of the Book of Common Prayer. It seems to me that nothing but silence can heal the wounds made by disputations in the region of religion."[17]

Hardly the words of a helpless, spineless reed. Caroline's conversion was an out and out rejection of the disputatious patriarchal religious controversies of her two quarrelsome brothers. But to Leslie she was Silly Milly, criticized by Julia as too fond of her brother. He admitted that she still makes "a few pathetic little attempts to turn her really great abilities to some account." Perhaps Leslie's most perverse judgment was made on a working life that began with a monumental history of sisterhoods, *The Service of the Poor* (1871) (Leslie did confess that this was one work of hers he could call "able."). Caroline's study was an exact counterpart to her brother Fitzjames's codification and professionalization of the law and to Leslie's professionalization of the higher journalism and biography. She argues for the professionalization of nursing and social work and against private philanthropy. Torn by the desire to join a convent herself after her first reading of Florence Nightingale's study of Kaiserwerth, she uses the writing of the book to convince herself and her readers that all female desire to live in sisterhoods is spiritual vanity and a very serious threat to the power of the patriarchal family.

The second important phase of Caroline Stephen's life was her philanthropic work with Octavia Hill, her work with an organization to help servant girls, and the building of Hereford Houses in Chelsea in 1877 as artisans' dwellings. The architect was Elijah Hoole, who later built Toynbee Hall. In the archway over the twenty-eight-flat building she placed a stone with words from Psalm 112, "Unto the upright there ariseth light in darkness." The interesting point about Hereford Houses, aside from their design for light, air, and privacy, was the installation of a shower bath and washhouse on the roof.[18] Obviously Eleanor Pargiter in *The Years*, surrounded as she is by the imagery of light, with her charity work and the building of houses with the stamp of the sunflower, and her excitement over her shower bath, has a source in Caroline Emelia's life and work. One of her strongest concerns was with the relations of mistress and servant, which we may interpret as matriarchal and antidemocratic, but she won the devotion of her own maid, Leah Gwillam, who wept in Virginia's arms at Caroline's cremation and confessed that her mistress had called her "bearkin." The servant question hounded Virginia all her life—simple matriarchal benevolence was out of the question, and the extraordinary portraits of charwomen and servants in her novels are a continuation of a theme about which both her mother and her aunt were concerned.[19] After her Quaker conversion in 1879, Caroline Stephen gave up social work for spiritual labor and began her second career as a writer and speaker for the return to silence and the experience of inner light in the Friends' worship.

There were other political questions on which Caroline remained as conservative as the stance of her book on sisterhoods. With her cousin Albert Dicey, she opposed Irish home rule, and through him she spoke for the Anti-Suffrage League. Her last essays on "Women and Politics" in the *Nineteenth Century* in 1907 and 1908 must have occasioned some interesting debates with her niece Virginia. She argued that the vote would be too burdensome a responsibility for women and then outlined a plan for a national consultative chamber for women acting as another second chamber, modeled on the Women's Yearly Meeting of the Society of Friends.[20] This is a very radical idea.

Caroline Stephen's work, thought, and life, in their combination of the radical and the conservative, constitute a perfect study of the plight of Victorian womanhood. She became an invalid after long years of nursing her parents as a dutiful daughter. The rest of her life, from late middle-age to old age, freed her for work of her own, for fame and friendship, and for the role of mother-mentor to a generation of Cambridge Quakers. Alternating between debilitating illness and intense periods of writing and speaking, she left to her niece a legacy of the value of silence, inner light, and the absolute authority of one's own mystical experience. One cannot dismiss her economic legacy, for Woolf tells us in *A Room of One's Own* that it "unveiled the sky" to her.

The achievements of the invalid Quaker visionary were noted by Virginia Woolf in her obituary, which seems to be a private rebuttal of her father's portrait of a mystical old maid in *The Mausoleum Book*. Caroline Stephen taught a simple method of spiritual exercises, of clearing an inner chamber (a room of one's own in the soul) to prepare the way for visionary experiences in which daily life was lit up to incandescence. It was a method of spiritual self-reliance in which no exterior aids were invoked except the need to wait receptively in silence.

Caroline Emelia Stephen was a woman of ample girth. She was not beautiful, high-strung, or fussy about food like her brother Leslie and her fastidious father, who had strong ideas about the duty to be beautiful and to dress well. What she may have suffered in a family that so prized physical beauty goes unmentioned. Her father was described as a "wild duck," distinguished but erratic. But Caroline was an ugly duckling. If Leslie could criticize Julia Stephen's classic nose, what did he say of his sister's, which was large and prominent? Virginia's youthful candor described her aunt's tear-stained "pendulous cheeks" as she visited her dying brother. In her book on sisterhoods Caroline had written, "I cannot wonder at the longing to join a religious sisterhood which is secretly cherished by many young women." But she warned that the romantic attraction of a nun's habit was only "the outward livery of religion." One of her first essays was "Thoughtfulness in Dress," published in the *Cornhill* in 1868. With what joy did she finally embrace the plain gray dress and cap of the Quakers, a nonthreatening nun's habit; she did not object when nicknamed "Nun" and even signed her letters so. While Virginia Woolf was initially embarrassed at being the niece of a "nun," the relationship was an enabling one, and she gained a good deal from it. She herself was troubled by clothing, and women like Ethel Smyth, who had adopted a protective and eccentric uniform of baggy tweeds and three-cornered hats, were annoyed at Woolf's anxieties. The nun's habit or Quaker dress is a form of transvestism even more protective than wearing men's garb; it signals celibacy and demands respect.

Virginia Woolf wrote of her aunt:

> One could not be with her without feeling that after suffering and thought she had come to dwell apart, among the "things which are unseen and eternal" and that it was her perpetual wish to make others share her peace. But she was no solitary mystic. She was one of the few to whom the gift of expression is given together with the need of it, and in addition to a wonderful command of language she had a scrupulous wish to use it accurately. Thus her effect on people is scarcely to be decided, and must have reached many to whom her books are unknown. Together with her profound belief she had a robust common sense and a practical ability which seemed to show with health and opportunity she might have ruled and organized. [*Guardian* (church weekly) 21 April 1909]

Woolf's biographical portrait of her aunt is a complete revision of her father's dismissal of his sister in *The Mausoleum Book*. While Leslie described an old maid destroyed by the loss of a mythical lover, Virginia describes the "maternal" qualities of the creative spinster, an echo of the quality of "inward motherhood" that young Quakers found in Caroline Stephen. What Leslie saw as a wasted life of a will-less crushed reed, Virginia saw as having "the harmony of a large design."

Rufus Jones, the Quaker historian, treated her as one who *had* actually ruled and organized: "One of the most important events in the history of English Quakerism . . . was the convincement of Caroline E. Stephen to its faith. The influence of her exposition of its central ideals and practices was very great both within and beyond the Society." He described her conversion when "the old faiths and forms did not meet her personal spiritual needs, nor speak to her condition":

> Caroline Stephen, with her fresh experiences, soon became the foremost interpreter in the Society in England of Friends' way of worship and of the type of religion they were endeavouring to maintain and express. She fortunately cared little for the traditions of Quakerism; she held many of the accumulated forms lightly, and yet she was gifted to penetrate to the heart and living secret of the faith which she had accepted. She belonged by bent and experience to the order of the mystics. She had seen truth at first hand, had received a direct revelation, and, according to her own testimony, she had been able to "sink into the innermost depth of her being" and "become aware of things which are unseen and eternal." She was, furthermore, a woman of broad culture, of rare insight, a beautiful personality, possessed of a graceful literary style, and thus she was able to do the work of interpretation which so few Friends of the time could hope to accomplish. [21]

"What she did," the Quaker historian wrote, "more clearly and emphatically than anyone else at that time was to call the attention of Friends to the richness of their own inheritance, and to help them to see and realize the immense inner possibilities of their faith." She calls her readers to experience "the central glow of Light and Love," to find the "spiritual radiance" within themselves, a radiance she described as like the sunshine shed upon shadowed family life by her mother and by her aunt Emelia. She had struggled for years to find this light among the Clapham Saints and evangelicals, to no avail. Though her father felt he was one of the "saints in the light," he was a deeply unhappy and dissatisfied man, with a puritanical sense of outward election that masked his inner turmoil. Caroline rejected the outward forms of piety. As Rufus Jones says, "She interpreted worship better than any other modern Quaker writer had done, she raised silence to a new significance and she gave 'spiritual radiance' a new and living meaning." He found her too inward-looking, too individualistic, for his own Quaker emphasis on democracy and cooperation, but he had to admit that her mystic visions were a great inspiration to many Victorians lost in the maze of materialism and religious controversy.

In *Three Guineas*, when Woolf demands vows of intellectual chastity and poverty for new women professionals, she significantly leaves out a vow of obedience. The Quakers have used "civil disobedience" as a way of remaining true to their pacifist principles and confronting the conscience of leaders of the state. Caroline Stephen's own rebellion began with an articulation of the idea of "filial disobedience" (though she would have been shocked at these words). In *The Service of the Poor* one finds both the suppressed passion to become a nun and the suppressed violence of the daughter at home chafing at the bonds of family. She argues there against convents because of the irreversible authoritarian nature of a vow of obedience, which offers a girl protection but no individual freedom. "I wholly disbelieve," she cries passionately, "in the competence of one human being to discipline the soul of another."[22] "It is a statement perfectly consistent with Woolf's views. But, one wonders, did Caroline Stephen include in her creed the competence of fathers to discipline the souls of daughters? Is it consistent with her views on mistresses and servants?

The Service of the Poor contains several such slips that suggest Caroline's rebellion had already started before she finished the book: "Who is there who would not escape from a multitude of care, anxieties and sorrows, as well as lose much happiness, if it were possible altogether to obliterate family life?" she asked.

The very mention of the *obliteration* of family life as a possibility suggests a violent response to her own life of self-sacrifice and an appeal to other women who have felt the same annihilating urge. It is here that she appeals to the martyr in women, urging them to stay at home precisely because it is more painful. Sentiment then swallows all: "For what booklearning is to be compared with the intellectual exercise of association with educated men? What training in the world can be so valuable to a woman as the daily intimacy of family life with her father and brothers?"[23] Thus speaks the classic "daughter of an educated man" to her sisters. There were many kinds of training more valuable to women, as she herself was to find. Caroline Emelia Stephen is undermined by her own rhetoric. The problem of woman's relation to paternalism is posed as a rhetorical question. But it can be read as a straightforward query once you dispose of the notion that to answer it is unthinkable effrontery on the part of the daughter of an educated man. If in her philosophy no one has the right to discipline the soul of another, it is a short step to questioning paternal and fraternal intimacy as the alternative to professional training.

The Service of the Poor makes an effort to define charity as social work and to remove religion from the debate. Works of charity should not be used by women as acts of worship, for this encourages pauperism in the poor and spiritual pride in the ladies. "You do not pay a daughter to wait upon a mother, nor a father to bring up his children," she writes in defense on the "natural" claims of the family. But "to find the right way of employing single women is a problem of some difficulty." It would be wrong, she suggests, to use sisterhoods "as a remedy for the preponderance of women, as if women ceased to exist when they retired into them, and as if the one object to be aimed at with regard to single women was to get rid of them." This was a social question of some importance, but she was not to be distracted: "If good single women are really the salt of the earth, society can ill afford to spare them." On vows of poverty, chastity, and obedience, Miss Stephen is equally logical: "If poverty, celibacy, and dependence are good things in themselves, so that women ought to be encouraged to choose them, then riches, marriage, and independence are comparatively bad things, and women ought to be encouraged to renounce them."

In "taking up with the Quakers" Caroline Stephen got to have her cake and eat it too. She had a nun's life without a vow of obedience. Caroline Stephen paid her dues with a patriarchal history of sisterhoods. Like Miranda in *The Tempest*, she was her father's best student. Her reward was not a mainland marriage but an island of her own. She "migrated," she said, like a bird, and her niece Katherine reports she often said that if one did not have "a family of one's own," one should live like a bird of the air.[24] With the Foxes at Falmouth she attended her first Quaker meeting. She described in a letter the peace she found: "It is as if my painted roof had been smashed and, instead of the darkness I had dreaded, I had found the stars shining."[25] The image is a beautiful one, but as violent as her earlier imagination of the "obliteration" of family life. To smash the painted roof is obviously an image of destruction of that "cathedral" of her childhood with her father. The painted roof was the prison of the patriarchal home. Her escape to freedom left one less Victorian "madwoman in the attic." That Virginia Stephen had shared this knowledge with her aunt is revealed in her similar metaphor, that her aunt's legacy had "unveiled the sky" to her.

When Caroline Stephen wrote "to have been my father's child was like having been brought up in a cathedral. In his presence the very atmosphere seemed full of awe and reverence,"[26] the daughter's voice is dutiful but edged with pain. It was dark and gloomy in that cathedral, and she went to her mother for "sunlight." She nursed her father in his bouts of madness and acted as his amanuensis. Her brother Leslie remembers his father's Miltonic tread as he dictated to his daughter.

It was Milton's God, ferocious male patriarch, whom Caroline rejected when she smashed the painted roof of evangelical cathedrals that literary and religious fathers offered their daughters as places for worship. Virginia Woolf was obviously moved by this image, and in *A Room of One's Own* she explicates it: "Indeed my aunt's legacy unveiled the sky to me, and substituted for the large and imposing figure of a gentleman, which Milton recommended for my perpetual admiration, a view of the open sky." The ghost of "Milton's bogey," the patriarchal God and the patriarchal father, is laid for Woolf by the visionary example of a maiden aunt and her very practical legacy.[27] Caroline's father had behaved like a bishop and made his home into a cathedral. She had escaped—smashed the painted roof—and from her chair at the window of The Porch she dispensed peace and blessing. It was only a nunnery of one, but its purity and freedom were the models on which Woolf imagined a *society* of outsiders, the collective version of her aunt's vision—not a convent but a union, of the daughters and nieces of those Victorian women who dared to smash those painted roofs. If one could "unveil the sky" above the home and above the church, it was possible to imagine unveiling the sky above the roofs of courts, universities, parliaments, and war offices.

The Language of the Light

From Caroline Stephen, Virginia Woolf learned to speak the language of the light. Her mysticism, "agnosticism with mystery at the heart of it" was a particularly suitable philosophy—one could hardly call it a religion—for the daughter of a Cambridge-educated man with such an emotional attachment to the rational as Leslie Stephen and the wife of a Cambridge-educated man with such an edgy and psychological attachment to the rational as Leonard Woolf. Those mystical meditations on life and death, the Jungian suggestions of a collective unconscious in Woolf's novels—one thinks of the "Time Passes" section of *To the Lighthouse*, what Suzette Henke calls "the communion of saints" in *Mrs. Dalloway*, and the whole of *The Waves*—are essentially rational. The author and her characters are always tapping on the door of personal and collective memory, and ghosts from the past answer them. In *Between the Acts* Lucy Swithin (like Caroline Emelia Stephen) is absorbed by the prehistoric, and Miss La Trobe plans to set her next play at the dawn of human life. The author was experiencing "inward motherhood," like Caroline Stephen with the young Quakers, and wanted to give birth to the *first* characters.

Since her own mother was so "central" to her memories, as she says in "A Sketch of the Past," it is not surprising that in her memoir Woolf should revise her aunt's metaphor to fit her own case: "Certainly there she was, in the very centre of that great cathedral space which was childhood; there she was from the very first" (MB 81). Virginia Woolf describes her mother as "one of those invisible presences who after all play so important a part in every life . . . well, if we cannot analyze these invisible presences, we know very little of the subject of the memoir; and again how futile life-writing becomes" (MB 80). In her revision of Caroline's confessions (where one can see the connections between the cathedral, "Milton's bogey," the patriarchal God, and her father, and her dream of smashing the painted roof and unveiling the sky) Woolf is equally revealing. For Julia is called a madonna, an "obsession" worked out only by writing *To the Lighthouse*. Women very seldom smash the painted roofs of their mothers' houses, but they can abjure idolatry, as Martine Stemerick says, by recognizing that their idol has clay feet, as Woolf effectively does in *To the Lighthouse*. Caroline Stephen was one of those "invisible presences" that unveiled the sky to Woolf. Milton's bogey may have been blocking her vision, but it took another woman to help her up from her knees before the statue of the virgin mother that dominated the "great cathedral space" of her childhood.

I believe that Virginia Woolf took the central figure of the lighthouse in her novel exorcising her mother's ghost from an eloquent passage in Caroline Stephen's essay "Divine Guidance," in *The Vision of Faith* (49):

Have you ever seen a revolving lighthouse at night from across the sea, with its steadfast light alternately hidden and displayed? Have you watched the faint spark as it glows into splendour for a few seconds and then fades away again into darkness? And have you considered how the very fact of its intermittency is the means by which it is recognized and its message is conveyed? It is a light given not to read by, but to steer our course by. Its appearances and disappearances are a *language* by which the human care that devised it can speak to the watchers and strugglers at sea. That care does not wax and wane with the light; but in its unchanging vigilance it provides a means of communication which no unaltering beam could afford . . . speaking to us in a language understood by the trusting heart alone.

The language of the light and the language of the lighthouse are clearly the language of hope, an agnostic's faith that "human care" will help us understand the mysteries of life and death. Mrs. Ramsay's identification with the pulsing of the lighthouse beam is both erotic and domestic as she merges with the forces of life and death in *To the Lighthouse*. The lighthouse itself is a well-worn symbol of philanthropic and religious groups. The language is a common one, but Woolf transforms it without reference to a specific god into a mystical language of her own. The intermittence is like Morse code, alternating rhythms of light and dark, life and death, but signifying safety in the end.

There is much in Caroline Stephen's mystical writing that appealed to Virginia Woolf—her concept of "faithfulness to the light," her argument that grief should be "confirming, cleansing, raising, making free," and above all her devotion to silence. Her description of her own "illuminations" resembles Woolf's "moments of being": "There is something in the unsought, undreamed of harmonies, which from time to time shine through the ordinary course of struggling life, which seems to tell of a melody continually accompanying that course, though mostly hidden by its clamour" (*Vision of Faith*, 41-42). Caroline's "inward revelations" did not make her feel elite or elect, and she cautions against those dangers, for she had her visions but passed them on. Late in life (1907) she wrote that "to give up the hope of radiating is very much like giving up life . . . If words are failing us, it is surely because Light is spreading, and prayer is no longer to be confined within the banks of language but is suffusing all life." The language of the light was both female and democratic; one might even say it was a spiritual demotic. She was Woolf's first teacher of how to transform silence into women's words, a discourse to oppose to the languages of the patriarchy.

Caroline Stephen was not without humor. "It is the *artificial* element in religion that I want to get rid of," she said; "perhaps the starch without which it would collapse into a limp heap." Her natural and untutored (or perhaps detutored) approach to religion was like Woolf's approach to scholarship in "On Not Knowing Greek." In "The Faith of the Unlearned," Caroline advocated thinking, not reading, and said that one should look at life steadily from the standpoint of the inexperienced human spirit. There was no point in gathering crumbs from the table of philosophy: "The trouble is that other people's thoughts are apt to act the part of the scriptural patch of new cloth on an old garment, whereby 'the rent is made worse'" (*Vision of Faith*, 137). This philosophy fell on willing ears, for an autodidact like Woolf, deprived of formal education, needed the defense of the power of one's own inner voices. Caroline's figure was a useful one for a novelist—she points out that Scheherazade stopped her ears with wool to block out other voices so she could tell her own stories.[28] Catherine Smith reports that 82 women were among 650 authors granted imprimatur by the Quakers between 1650 and 1700. There was a respected place for women in the Society of Friends. Caroline Stephen's search for female predecessors in religion with her history of sisterhoods and her biography of Caroline Fox and for the roots of radical Quaker thought in its origins is a precursor to Woolf's concept of "thinking back through our mothers" for women authors.

In *The Light Arising: Thoughts on the Central Radiance*, Stephen wrote of "intimations," of "apparitions and visions and dreams and voices," and wondered how to interpret these signs. She cited William James (he was one of her admiring readers), speaking of "touches of the very 'finger of God' [Woolf found god's finger threatening]—whispers of the inspeaking 'still small voice'— gleams of the innermost radiance" (176). Quaker practice preserved sanity, for after a vision one was to wait and then consult other Friends. Caroline quotes Sir William Gull (often consulted as a psychiatrist by the Stephen family) in connection with the idea of conferring with others: "The human mind needs ventilation." Her perception of visions and voices (a notion that must have appealed to Woolf) was not that they defined the visionary as a superior authority: "But mystery, like music, in itself neither proves nor authorises, but appeals— and for the moment at least exalts—as with the pledge of a beauty not belonging to earth" (179).

"Rational Mysticism" is a brilliant essay. By excluding from her subject history, theology, and psychology, Caroline Stephen grounds her work in experience and "inner light," and an "Inward Monitor" of experience that is the self. By this definition it is clear that both the daughters of educated men and the sons of uneducated men can be mystics. Intermittence, as in her figure of the lighthouse, is an important element, but so are language and the value of certain words, though she is opposed to theorizing. She believes that mysticism is accompanied by "practical efficiency and shrewdness." But, like other women mystics, she insists that reason must be combined with illumination to reach wisdom. The power to sink into the depths of one's own mind she compares to "the power to flee to a City of Refuge" (20). She is very English and Victorian in declaring that ethics, not ecstasy, is her aim, and she wants no association with the occult.

On silence Caroline Stephen is equally eloquent, for intellectual controversy in the Stephen family had upset her: "Words can always be opposed. You cannot oppose silence" (64). Silence is a woman's weapon against patriarchal arguments and a form of passive resistance, but it is also a form of stern self-discipline in Quaker worship; it is the *gathering* of the silent that is important. "War and Superfluities" is an eloquent pacifist piece, in Victorian religious language a precursor to the socialist pacifism of *Three Guineas*. Her footnotes attack the stockpiling of weapons, deliberate panics, and the keeping of too many servants and remind one of the power of Woolf's footnotes. "Living Alone" and "The Fear of Death" are descriptions of the joys of spinsterhood and an argument against mourning. She explicates George Fox's idea of inner light, rejects paid ministry, affirms the pacifist position, and insists on a return to silent worship. "A true mystic believes that all men have, as he himself is conscious of having, an inward life, into which, as into a secret chamber, he can retreat at will" (32). Inner light was, then, a room of one's own in the soul.

"In this inner chamber he finds a refuge from the ever-changing aspects of outward existence. . . . He finds there, first repose, then an awful guidance; a light which burns and purifies; a voice which subdues," Caroline explained. Mystics are "indisposed to discipleship. . . . They sit at no man's feet, and do not . . . greatly care to have anyone sit at theirs." "Faithfulness to the light" is not the same as obedience to conscience, for conscience can be morbid and is never an absolute guide. "God created the animals but left it to each one to develop its own fur or feathers" (47).

Although public worship among Friends is pledged to silence, everyone can speak. "It is sometimes as part-singing compared with unison. The free admission of the ministry of women, of course, greatly enriches this harmony. I have often wondered whether some of the motherly counsels I have listened to in our meetings would not reach some hearts that might be closed to the masculine preacher." With a heartfelt eloquence she tells of her own spiritual struggles. Before she became a Quaker, Caroline Stephen felt like "a moth dashing itself against an iceberg." In the midst of Babel she praised the "thrice-blessed power of silence," and in a day of extravagance in dress she spoke of the "mute eloquence" of plain dress as a language that expressed quiet, gentleness, and purity.

I have quoted Caroline Stephen at length here because of the difficulty of getting her books. Clearly her work belongs to the great tradition of English women mystics. And I think we need search no further for the origins of Virginia Woolf's pacifism and mysticism, for we have caught a glimpse of one of the "invisible presences" in her life. In "A Sketch of the Past" Woolf wrote that the influence of Bloomsbury on her was minor compared with the influence of her mother. It was also minor compared with the influence of her aunt.

As a feminist critic I had avoided the subject of Woolf's mysticism, and of *The Waves*, feeling that acknowledging her as a visionary was a trap that would allow her to be dismissed as another female crank, irrational and eccentric. I was drawn to her most anti-capitalist, anti-imperialist novels, to Woolf the socialist and feminist, logical, witty, and devastating in argument. But Catherine Smith has raised an important issue in her study of Jane Lead, the seventeenth-century mystic.[29] Smith asks us to study mysticism and feminism together "to learn more about the links between envisioning power and pursuing it." She argues that "idealist analogues of transcendence may shape political notions of sexual equality as much as materialist or rationalist arguments do." To study both traditions together—and certainly Woolf's writing embodies both—would teach us about "the structure of vision in feminist politics." Smith concentrates on the figure of Sophia or "the woman clothed with the sun," in women's mystical writing. If there is a feminist collective unconscious, this figure was passed down to Woolf from her aunt Caroline and lives in Eleanor Pargiter and Lucy Swithin. With the vision comes a female language of the light, a language of silence—acts of light and acts of silence.

Caroline Stephen laid out very carefully a structure of vision that included a pacifism and a mysticism that could be embraced by the socialist-feminist. Virginia Woolf did learn from her aunt how to speak the language of the light—it was a "little language," unknown to most men, perhaps best achieved in that combination of soliloquy and colloquy in *The Waves*. Is it possible to see the structure of *The Waves* as a Quaker meeting, as interior monologues in which each character comes to terms with death and grief? Was the most successful Bernard, that rational mystic? Caroline Stephen had one enemy she struggled against all her life as the daughter of an educated man: the power of religious words—the Bible and the Book of Common Prayer—to oppress and suppress individual religious feeling. Sermons, the set pieces of preachers, and the traditional forms of protestant worship seemed to imprison her. Silence set her free.

What Woolf learned from her aunt was that that crippling and debilitating label—"daughter of an educated man"—stamped on the foreheads of women of their class was not indelible. It could be erased and a new identity established. Caroline repressed her desire to join a convent, served her parents until they died, then braved her brothers' wrath and led the British Quaker renaissance. Woolf learned to harness her grief for her art and to forge an identity as the niece of a nun, one who had forgone sisterhood at the command of a patriarch but managed an old age in a nunnery of one. Woolf learned to turn her lack of education to advantage; she trained herself to trust memory and inner voices. Her journey to a nunnery was shorter than her aunt's, but the example of her achievement was crucial to her own development as an artist. Virginia Woolf found that cloistering her imagination promised a secret and profound creative life. Her inner room of her own was a clean, well-lighted nun's cell like the "cathedral close" of Caroline's house in Cambridge.

When Woolf left The Porch in 1904 for a new life in Bloomsbury, she was, in a sense, "born again," but not in the sense of her evangelical Clapham sect forebears—nor did she join the Quakers. She remained an agnostic, a rational mystic. She came to terms with her father's death and discarded the identity of "daughter of an educated man" for a new identity as "niece of a nun." While we can see her pacifism and mysticism in the context of other European leftists like Simone Weil and Walter Benjamin, we can also see their derivation in the life and work of her aunt, which was part of the British female mystical tradition. A nunnery was not a negative space for Virginia Woolf, and quite clearly she felt that mental chastity (the lack of attachment to patriarchal or imperialist institutions) would make her free. Let us imagine her not as a cathedral, not even as a plain Quaker meetinghouse, but as a room of her own. Like Walter Benjamin,

she was engaged in a "ministry of the interior," establishing in her own mind a
model for a future state where socialism, feminism, and pacifism, would be possible in the collective.

> What is the meaning of life? That was all—a simple question; one that tended to
> close in on one with years. The great revelation had never come. Instead there
> were little daily miracles, illuminations, matches struck unexpectedly in the
> dark.

To the Lighthouse

As readers we are continually struck by the archetypal imagery of Woolf's
novels, the light/darkness contrasts, the sea, the sounds of birds, the voice/
speech/silence images. In his study of early Quaker sermons, Phillip Graves
analyzes these images as a rhetorical strategy of the Quakers.[30] Unlike other
religious writing or sermons, the Quakers did not explicate biblical texts or logi-
cally explain doctrine. The speaker poured forth an abundance of archetypal
images in plain language to a point where "metaphor has transcended its normal
function, and instead of merely indicating a point of resemblances between two
differentiable entities, it has totally merged them."[31] Jackson I. Cope describes
the technique of "an incredible repetition" with a result that was "not ungram-
matical but agrammatical." The effect of this literature is a great affirmation of
life and faith. Woolf's prose style has all these characteristics in common with
the Early Quakers and her Aunt Caroline's writing. There is an authenticity and
sincerity combined with verbal simplicity and purity of speech or writing that
comes from "hearing voices" and experiencing the "inner light" of visions.
Woolf often described the difficulty of writing when her voices were racing
ahead of her. The Quakers esteemed the role of listening in silence, and it is
here that the writer is like the Friend who then relates her inner experiences to
the meeting. The relation of the writer and the reader (the common writer and
the common reader speaking a common language) I have described elsewhere
as an experience of "the Collective Sublime," a political act on the part of Woolf
as a socialist writer. But clearly there is a mystical analogue for her acts as well.
The experience of waiting in silence for the word in a collective "gathering,"
then the extraordinary importance of the spoken word, is one Woolf wants to
imitate in her relationship to her audience. The power of her writing is in the
reader's response to archetypal imagery—the pulse of the lighthouse, Ralph
Denham's vision of the birds besieging the lighthouse, the match in the crocus
in *Mrs. Dalloway*, the vision of ancient women beating carpets in *Jacob's Room*,
Eleanor's sunflower in *The Years*.

From a feminist perspective it is clear that women mystics drew authority from
the Spirit, rather than from the Father or the Son. The pen was so clearly like the
penis, as Gilbert and Gubar have demonstrated, that one is tempted to see the
Quakers' spatial concepts of the "Inward Light" and the Word, received passive-

ly by the silent self in an "inner chamber" as the equivalent of the authority of the pen/penis in female physical terms. The inner chamber receives the light as Mary received Christ from the Holy Spirit.[32] Virgin motherhood or "inward motherhood," or the writer as nun, is then a strategy of power for the woman mystic or artist. It is a chaste vagina, the room of one's own in the soul, to be sure, but then creativity is much like an immaculate conception. One could, by embracing these concepts, subvert the patriarchy without having to take up male aggressive attitudes, words, or arms. These concepts naturally appealed to women and working people, in a world where language was an aggressive weapon for argument and controversy and for the wielding of power. Chastity then becomes erotic in these mystical terms because in union with the light and the word the soul experiences enormous power. This English concept is very different from the sexuality expressed in the writings of Saint Teresa, but it resembles Joan of Arc's experiences.

Very interesting work has been done on the ethnography of speaking and on Quaker speech that sheds light on Virginia Woolf's fiction. Maurice A. Creasy studies the spatial terms of contrast by which the Quakers expressed belief, inward and outward, spiritual and carnal, as well as mystery and history.[33] If the origin of the peculiar language of the Quakers was in a revolt against rhetoric that matched the Puritans' revolt against royalty, two kinds of "authority" were being challenged. Plain speech and plain dress (which was also a language) challenged the hegemony of the priesthood and of the rich and learned. The marginal, working people and women, were claiming that God speaks directly to all people. One must wait in silence to hear this voice—it is an inner light that claims only the authority of one's own experience. In a logocentric society the Quakers esteemed silence. They were tired of Latin obfuscations and valued only the heartfelt utterance of spiritual experience in one's own words, not the words of a religious text. After their initial building of the society, they did not attempt to make converts, but strove to live simply and give good example by their lives.[34]

If we look at *Three Guineas* in these terms rather than as another 1930s antifascist pamphlet, the political anger and utopian idealism it exhibits seem to come from the female mystical/political tradition. Like the Quaker philosophy of Caroline Stephen, *Three Guineas* attacks war, the pompous dress of men in power, the university, the established church, and the professions. Its radical break with the pamphleteering tradition is the identification of fascism with the patriarchal family. Otherwise the Outsiders' Society could be the Society of Friends. Louise Bogan, reviewing *Three Guineas* (*New Republic*, September 1938) claimed that Woolf demanded "a moral pattern so severe that it has never been adhered to by anyone who was not by nature an artist or a saint." Virginia Woolf was both an artist and a saint. The moral vision she gives in her novels is that of a rational mystic who calls for human community from her cloistered imagination.

7

Taking the Bull by the Udders: Sexual Difference in Virginia Woolf— A Conspiracy Theory

> PENTHEUS:
> And is it a Wild Bull this, that walks and waits
> Before me? There are horns in thy brow!
> What art thou, man or beast? For surely now
> The Bull is on thee!
>
> DIONYSUS: . . . He hath
> Unsealed thine eyes to see
> What thou shouldst see.
>
> —Euripides, *The Bacchae*, trans.
> Gilbert Murray, 1910

> It has been with a considerable shaking in
> my shoes, and a feeling of treading upon a
> carpet of eggs, that I have *taken the cow by
> the horns* in this chapter, and broached the
> subject of the part that the feminine mind
> has played—and minds as well, deeply
> feminized, not technically on the distaff
> side—in the erection of our present criteria.
> For fifteen years I have subsisted in this to
> me suffocating atmosphere.
>
> —Wyndham Lewis,
> *Men Without Art*, 1934

Reviewing *A Room of One's Own*, Rebecca West saw Virginia Woolf "braced against an invisible literary wind" blowing from the direction of Bloomsbury. She saw this "uncompromising piece of feminist propaganda" as the "ablest" written in a long line of feminist pamphlets from Millicent Garrett Fawcett in the middle of the Victorian age until the actual winning of the vote in 1928. And so indeed it must be seen, as a product of thinking back through those Victorian mothers in the context of the history of those pamphlets. Vera Brittain in *Lady into Woman* (1953) remarked that *A Room* "took propaganda back to high literary levels," after the "lively and tendentious" literature of the suffrage movement (216). It is an exact demonstration of Woolf's own socialist thesis in *A Room* that "masterpieces are not single and solitary births" but are "the outcome of many years of thinking in common, of thinking by the body of the people, so that the experience of the mass is behind the single voice" (68-69). Woolf's voice is not single in this essay, but collective, and she speaks for seventy years of struggle. Rebecca West praised Woolf's courage, which "defied a prevalent fashion of the day among intellectuals."[1] Dame Rebecca pointed out that "before the war conditions were different. The man in the street was anti-feminist, but the writers of quality were pro-suffrage." Her explanation defines the change as "due to the rising tide of effeminacy which has been so noticeable since the war. The men who despised us for our specifically female organs chastised us with whips; but those to whom they are a matter for envy chastise us with scorpions."

Wyndham Lewis and Rebecca West agreed on little. Here are voices from the Right and the Left calling the Bloomsbury Liberals effeminate and blaming them for the "feminization" of British culture. Apologists for Bloomsbury's pacifist ethos of friendship have ignored its rampant anti-feminism, the chill wind that froze the author of *A Room of One's Own* into isolation. But it is my contention that what is called "feminization" is really another form of patriarchal power—a homosexual hegemony over British culture derived from the values of the Cambridge Apostles and King's College and antifeminist with a difference—scorpions, not whips. This hegemony, in the Gramscian sense,[2] was as oppressive to women like Virginia Woolf as the whips of her uncle Fitzjames had been to Millicent Garrett Fawcett. It is a mistake to call this cultural softening "feminization," when the homosexuals who exercised this power were loyal to the patriarchy. Wyndham Lewis might have more correctly said "sodomization" as an example of the "erection of criteria" for art that were less robust than he wished, though that is as offensive a term as his own.

Virginia Woolf felt that cold wind of Bloomsbury antifeminism and in *A Room of One's Own* she gathered a collective counter BLAST (with apologies to Mr. Lewis) in the breathing together of women in a conspiracy to huff and puff and blow down the walls of Cambridge and deflate its chief villain, Oscar Browning.[3] Oscar Browning was conveniently *not* Lytton Strachey or Morgan Forster, but he was their philosophical father. In puncturing that pompous over-stuffed boy-loving patriarch, Virginia Woolf symbolically attacked her "friends," and rid herself of the illusion, surely dispelled by Desmond McCarthy's attack on her and all women artists in *The New Statesman*,[4] that the elite gay men of her world were allies with women in oppression. They may have been pouting, self-pitying patriarchs, but they were patriarchs nonetheless.

"Taking the bull by the udders" (a phrase dropped in a letter) is one of those astonishingly "lupine" locutions in Virginia Woolf's writing, so funny, outrageous, and "true," for the woman reader, that they haunt the imagination. Like a Freudian slip, her deliberate verbal "mistakes" seem to tap a primal spring in the unconscious. In the role of asides or jokes in letters, these slips reveal that she is aware that she writes from within the prison-house of patriarchal language. Woolf's jokes, slips, and asides are signals to the woman reader, who laughs in recognition or nods in assent over the page, that we are together, woman reader and woman writer, conspiring against the power of patriarchal language. As the comedian needs our laughter to continue mocking authority, Woolf needs her audience's assent and she courts us unashamedly to participate in the plot against phallocentric language.

This conspiracy of woman reader and woman writer is literally a "breathing together" as we rock or are rocked to the rhythm of her words. In *A Room of One's Own*, the con-spirators are also the in-spiration for her talks to women students. In this chapter, which, like Woolf's, is a written version of a talk, I want to explore with you the ways in which she makes sexual difference an asset for women, makes the male the other, defines his language as different from the natural, normal speech of women together, and asserts the superiority of women's speech as a demotic and democratic instrument of communication, as opposed to the egotistical male "I" that lies like a "shadow" across the page, "a straight dark bar" (*A Room of One's Own*, p. 123) on the prison-house of language. For our texts we will take "taking the bull by the udders" a seemingly casual spoken phrase recorded in a letter; "A Woman's College from the Outside," an essay written at the same time as the lectures that compose *A Room of One's Own* and also concerned specifically with women's education; and a section of "The Pargiters," originally intended to be part of *The Years*. My concern is with Woolf's role as a feminist literary critic, her experiments with a female grammar and with a rhetorical strategy that I have called "sapphistry,"[5] which masters the principles of classical rhetoric and subverts them at the same time.

Sexual difference for Woolf is not a simple matter of male and female, power and desire. Lesbianism and homosexuality are equal others, and androgyny is a privileged fifth sexual and literary stance. In her life as in her work, celibacy is also singularly important in her own sense of sexual difference.[6]

One may argue, moreover, that class difference extends her five-finger exercise to the other hand. For the salient subtext in every Woolf novel is the voice of the working-class women, the heroic charwomen mythologized into a collective Nausicaa washing the dirty linen of the patriarchal family, her perpetual subject. The caretaker's children, who sing for their supper at the end of *The Years* speak in tongues with the hard "k's" of a Greek chorus, a prophecy of the British mother tongue's responsibility for the exploitation of her colonial children. If women speak to each other in "a little language unknown to men" because of the male control of language, Britain's future workers, the Indians, Africans and West Indians of her former empire, speak to each other in pidgins and creoles, languages less "little," but equally "unknown" to the powerful. Their music, their art, may be a mystery to the elite, but it is a culture of its own. *A Room of One's Own* may appear to be merely a primer for valorization of female difference, but its eloquent peroration to the absent women washing up the dishes, assuring us that Shakespeare's sister will be born of the uneducated classes, declares that it will also serve as manual for the subversion of class difference and racial difference.

Her Sister's Voice

In this section I want to suggest that Virginia Woolf deliberately fashioned for herself a role in which reading, writing, and speaking were feminist and radical acts, a role in which she, as novelist and as feminist critic, became *her sister's voice*, as Procne read the text of Philomel's woven story in the tapestry, and spoke for her against the patriarchy. Biographical accounts of Virginia Woolf's speaking voice stress her weakness and describe a high-pitched whinnying sound. Hearing her voice on a BBC tape that Nigel Nicolson played at the Woolf Centenary Symposium in Texas, I, like the rest of the audience, was shocked by the difference between this voice and the hesitant hysterical voice I had expected. Virginia Woolf's voice was a deep, rich, fruity contralto, bordering on the baritone. Two features stand out on this tape—the authoritative self-confident commanding tone of the born leader and public speaker, and the rhythmical musical range from low to high of the writer who loves the sounds of words. They roll off her tongue in accents betraying her class, of course, but also in liquid syllables suggesting a bubbling spring of laughter counterpointing her cool control. The voice is so sure of itself, so eminently sane and healthy that it banishes forever the biographer's hysterical invalid. (When this paper was read at the Berkshire Women's History Conference, 1984, at Smith College, Cora Kaplan responded with the point of view of English working-class women. To them, Woolf's voice on the tape represents class privilege, Kaplan argued, and the class identification outweighs any sense of gender solidarity for those women.)

Woolf's own odd phrase, "taking the bull by the udders," which I have taken as my text here, may possibly have been a simple reaction to Wyndham Lewis's attack on her as a lesbian when he said he was "taking the cow by the horns." One is amused that, inadvertently, Lewis had conjured up an image of the horned goddess, Hathor, the cow goddess of the ancient Egyptians, crowned with the moon. As Evelyn Haller has convincingly argued, the Egyptian myths surrounding the worship of Isis inform Woolf's thought as fully as *The Odyssey* informs *Ulysses* or the image of Byzantium occurs in Yeats.[7] Anthropologists have even suggested recently that on the grand nurturing figure of the "Many Breasted Artemis" in Ephesus the "many breasts were not breasts at all but bulls' scrota sacrificed every year to the Asian *magna mater* Kybela, goddess of fertility, and hung on her statue."[8] But of course that association of the bull with mother goddess worship was first made clear by Woolf's great role model and mentor, Jane Ellen Harrison, in her *Prolegomena to the Study of Greek Religion* (1903). According to Harrison, the maenads used the bull, the phallus, and the thyrsus or ivied rod in their worship of Dionysus, in order to partake of male power and to deny the division between male and female. Both projects engage the narrator of *A Room of One's Own*. Dionysian worship included tearing apart "the Bull of God" with bare hands. The bacchantes left their children and nursed wild animals. Part of Dionysus's power seems to have been his sexual ambiguity; and the transvestism of Pentheus in order to spy on women's rites leads to a death as horrible as Actaeon's for a similar deed. So a bull with udders is suggestive of ancient women's rituals, the acting out of female power and desire, and a Dionysian collapse of difference that privileges the female as *A Room of One's Own* does.

In Woolf's letter, she attributes to her sister her own rewriting of Wyndham Lewis's phrase. "Taking the bull by the udders" is such a rebellious verbal gesture, thumbing its nose at the phallus, that Woolf denies responsibility for saying it. "Not for attribution," she seems to say. Or "off the record," as politicans say when they tell the truth. It's not my tongue that uttered it, not my hand that wrote it, Woolf the ventriloquist seems to claim in her attribution/misattribution of these words to her sister, Vanessa Bell. Why, we ask, can Vanessa's voice say the unsayable, talk back to His Master's Voice (as we may call the Patriarchal power over language)? The answer is part of Woolf's lifelong myth of difference from her sister, a difference, for her, as powerful as actual and symbolic sexual difference. Woolf's companionate marriage protected her celibacy, but her deepest emotional relationships were with women. "Women are my line," she was continually telling her sister:

> You will never succumb to the charms of any of your sex—What an arid garden the world must be for you! What avenues of stone pavements and iron railings! Greatly though I respect the male mind . . . I cannot see that they have a glow-worm's worth of charm about them—the scenery of the world takes no lustre from their presence. They add of course immensely to its dignity and safety: but when it comes to a little excitement—![*Letters* 3, 281]

Vanessa, constructed by Virginia as the "normal woman" to whom she was "other," was married, a mother, and had sexual relations with several men (including homosexuals). She was what all men want women to be (as Woolf said of the Angel in the House). Although she often dares her own anti-phallic discourse, putting anti-phallic discourse in her sister's mouth on this occasion, Woolf doesn't risk male disapproval ("She's a feminist; she's a sapphist; she's a man-hater.") By putting these words in the mouth of a "womanly woman," she gets to say them loud and clear and be protected from male displeasure at the same time. A woman like Vanessa Bell couldn't possibly suggest castration, the male reader thinks. The lover of men, the mother of sons, she is not suspect. By this rhetorical ventriloquism, Woolf as a feminist is able to express in the voice of one of the patriarchy's pet women the wish to castrate the symbol of male power. Thus the "normal" woman becomes her political sister, is "on her side" and joins in her feminist protest. The difference is erased. She is then not really "other," or different from her sister. They are bonded by a mutual attack on men.

Part of Woolf's self-made myth of difference from her sister, is not only

Vanessa's "real" womanhood as opposed to her own largely unacted lesbian identity, but her division of the artist's body into the verbal and the visual. As Woolf conceives and enforces these roles in a lifetime of letters to and about her sister, she and Vanessa are one body in her continually reiterated desire to merge with her sister as Lily Briscoe wants to be one with Mrs. Ramsay ("like waters poured into one jar"). Vanessa, the painter, is the eye and the hand, and she, the writer, is the ear and the mouth. If we did not have Quentin Bell's biography, but only Virginia's letters, we would see Vanessa as Virginia verbally constructed her, completely inarticulate, deaf and dumb, except with a brush in her hand, a child in her lap, or a lover in her arms. Obviously, the real Vanessa Bell was not inarticulate, but Virginia Woolf continued to create her as a modern Mrs. Malaprop.[9]

Woolf commonly attributes to her sister the mixing of two old saws or folk sayings, some of which are very funny, and obviously the invention of someone who wants to be her sister's voice, someone who is inventing a role and writing the dialogue. Writing the script of her sister's life in this small way, Woolf enacted her desire to control what she had no control over, and simultaneously *spoke for* Vanessa as the representative of all the common women she felt she was writing for and to, as a feminist. The mistakes attributed to Vanessa, the mixed truisms, one feels, are meant to suggest that Vanessa, by mistake, stumbles on a deeper wisdom than the verbally adept can ever command. Her slips tap into a deep reservoir of old wives' tales and women's folk wisdom not available to the sophisticated (and by extension, more shallow,) writer. Vanessa Bell certainly played her role well in her sister's script. The following quotations are from one letter to Virginia in response to *To the Lighthouse*: "I don't flatter myself that my literary opinion is really of any interest to you. . . ." "In fact, I think I am more incapable than anyone else in the world of making an aesthetic judgment on it." "I am very bad at describing my feelings." "I don't feel capable of much analysis." "I daresay you'll think all I've said nonsense. You can put it down to the imbecile ravings of a painter on paper." (*Letters*, 3, 572–573). Simultaneously Woolf glorifies her sister as the dumb goddess mumbling the oracular wisdom of the ages, a Cassandra in Sussex, and reaffirms herself as artist/god, because she has put the unverbalized into words, written the script for the prophetess. Vanessa is Everywoman, stuttering out of her historical silence and Virginia then is legitimately women's spokeswoman. (It is astonishing to read Angelica Garnett's *Deceived With Kindness* in relation to this myth, for aside from a few very brief affairs, Vanessa's life appears to have been as "virginal" as Virginia's, in keeping with the Stephen family myth of virgin motherhood.) "Anonymous" is always a woman and *she* speak for anonymous. Through this rhetorical strategy, she satisfies the feminist's desire to be her sister's voice, and it is only another bold leap from blood sisterhood to political sisterhood.

The actual phrase "taking the bull by the udders" revises the old imperative to meeet difficulty head-on, to bravely confront a powerful adversary, to take the bull by the horns, an aggressive action not commonly associated with women. The bull is the ancient symbol of the phallus, representing male power and sexuality. The horns symbolize the genitals and also can be dangerous and deadly to the attacker. Traditionally, a person who takes the bull by the horns is coming to grips effectively with an enemy or an obstacle. Woolf's language implies the removal of the horns (castration) which deprives the bull of his power to kill. The horn is also a speaker, an instrument to project the voice, the sign of phallic control over language. She silences it, cuts it off, udders it, utters it. She does not say " we will share speech." She says—"You will be silent. I will speak." (One wonders why we use a reference to a bull's excrement to mean exaggerated speech or lies.) Is the lie (all fiction?) a prerogative of male speech? The silent replacement of the bull's genitals with udders leaves him not only castrated but "cowed." He can be milked; he is maternal. The bold act of taking the bull by the udders mean not only depriving him of evidence of phallic power, horns and genitals, but replacing them with organs of nurturance. (The Bacchae, according to Jane Harrison, are nurses to the figure of Dionysus, the bull.) The phrase asks the question "How can I deprive the fathers of their phallic power, their threatening masculinity?" and answers itself, "by turning them into mothers." In other words, (bull—horn—genitals) = (cow—udder—?). What is *absent*, where the *difference* lies, is in female genitality—yet another instance of Woolf's reverence for female chastity. She give us a mythical androgynous beast, a bull with udders. In real life this is what Woolf did to her husband. She married the only virile and intensely masculine man in her circle, Leonard Woolf, and cast him in the role of the bull with udders, the maternal male. He is a nurturing figure throughout their married life, appearing in her letters and diaries as a version of the Lady with the Lamp, maternalized, "uddered," the Husband with the Glass of Milk.

The verbal act of castrating/silencing the bull seems to me analogous to the myth of Procne and Philomel (which Woolf revises in *Between the Acts*).[10] The rapist cuts out the tongue of his female victim so that she cannot speak of his sexual crime. This phrase deprives the phallic voice of its power to speak/kill but replaces it with the power to nurture. The female version replaces one power with another, while the male version not only does violence to the female, but cuts off her power to relieve the hurt by telling her story. She saves herself by her skill in weaving, which is a kind of telling. Her sister is her reader. And the reader-sister speaks and acts for the silenced and oppressed sister. So Virginia speaks for Vanessa as Procne speaks for Philomel. The narrative voice in Woolf's novels is the voice of the sister/reader/speaker; she is the swallow who sings for all the silenced nightingales: "I am my sister's keeper." She is the tongue of the tongueless ones.

Geoffrey Hartman, following Plato, has described Philomel's cry against oppression the universal "voice of the shuttle." I have argued that the weaving of the tapestry is a specifically *female* art which is "read" by a specifically female person, just as the violence Procne's husband does to her is a rape of her female body. The voice of the shuttle is gendered voice. But what concerns me here is the role of Procne as *reader* of her sister's text, translator of the invisible (to men) stitches in the *peplos*, secret sharer of a "little language unknown to men," the language of weaving: ". . . a native loom she found,/And hung the warp; and weaving on the white/With crimson threads, set forth her piteous plight" (*Metamorphoses*, 133–34). Procne reads and is struck dumb; in horror, she disguises herself (significantly) as a follower of women's biennial "Bacchic rites" with vine leaves in her hair and dressed in a fawn skin (like the savage virgin sisterhood of Bacchantes). She disguises Philomel in the same costume with an ivy mask and rescues her from her prison in the forest. As a huntress, she contemplates cutting out her husband's eyes, tongue, or penis, but decides to punish the patriarchy, kills her son, and serves him to his father to eat so that the father's body becomes "his son's unhallowed tomb" (136).

Procne, reader and actor, is her sister's severed tongue, which "strangled utterance made": "The remnant twitched; the tongue with muffled sound/ Muttered its secret to the blackened ground,/And writhing still, like a cut snake, it tried/To reach her where she stood, before it died" (133). Like many feminist critics after her, Virginia Woolf was the reader of the "scraps, orts and fragments" of women's texts and lives, of the oppressed, raped, and silenced. *Writing/writhing* is a kind of feminist poetics, for the "cut snake" reminds us of Apollo's killing of the python at Delphi, the silencing of women's cults and culture. In *A Room of One's Own* she is Procne to the Philomel of Judith Shakespeare. Procne's voice is sometimes undeniably venomous, "like a cut snake"; sometimes "strangled." She does desire to castrate the rapist, to kill. She cannot restore her sister's virginity or sew the severed tongue back to its root. She can flaunt the severed head of her son in the face of her horrid husband; she can deny him his fatherhood.

I would suggest that the brutal cutting out of woman's tongue in the Procne and Philomel myth represents more than the rapist's desire to silence his victim. For the tongue is not only a verbal instrument, it is a sexual instrument, an organ of pleasure as well as an organ of speech. It challenges phallic supremacy at both levels. Woman's tongue is a threat to the Phallus as law, and to the phallus as penis. Woman's culture, her oral powers, both verbal and sexual, are here strangled. Procne's disguise as a Bacchante suggests man's fear of female rites and cults which threaten phallic power, his fear of a sisterhood that extends beyond the blood sisterhood of Procne and Philomel. What lurks beneath this myth except man's desire to suppress lesbianism and a woman's culture which ignores the phallus?

In 1928, the same year that Woolf gave the lectures that form *A Room of One's Own*, Djuna Barnes published *Ladies Almanack*, a celebration of lesbian salon culture in Paris. At Dame Evangeline Musset's funeral, Natalie Barney's lesbianism and her self-sufficient female art are represented by the survival of her tongue in the ashes of her funeral pyre. Her community of women artists enact a version of ancient female rites recalling their attempt to recreate a new Mytilene on the outskirts of Paris:

And when they came to the ash that was left of her, all had burned but the Tongue, and this flamed, and would not suffer Ash, and it played about upon the handful that had been she indeed. And seeing this, there was a great Commotion, and the sound of Skirts swirled in haste, and the patter of much running in feet, but Senorita Fly-About came down upon that Urn first, and beatitude played and flickered upon her Face, and from under her Skirts a slow Smoke issued, though no thing burned, and the Mourners barked about her covetously, and all night through, it was bruited about that the barking continued, like the mournful baying of Hounds in the Hills, though by Dawn there was no sound, And as the day came some hundred women were seen bent in Prayer. [Djuna Barnes, *Ladies Almanack*, 1928, 1978 Harper and Row, p. 84]

Susan Lanser characterizes Barnes' writing as "speaking in tongues." The woman artist and the lesbian are imaginatively one. Sappho's school and the lesbian salons of Paris in the twenties are versions of Woolf's dream of female community. Her "little language unknown to men" suggested sexual skill as well as verbal skill. In the next chapter we shall see how Woolf seduces the reader with a disguised but nonetheless powerful appeal to "untie the mother tongue." *A Room of One's Own* is another version of *Ladies' Almanack*, as *Ladies' Almanack* is a version of *A Room of One's Own*. Both celebrate women's community and art; both ask 'what relation does women's writing have to her body and her sexuality?' One might compare several passages from Woolf's text with Barnes' narrator's lament:

Nay—I cannot write it! It is worse than this! More dripping, more lush, more lavender, more mid-mauve, more honeyed, more Flower-casting, more Cherub-bound, more downpouring, more saccharine, more lamentable, more gruesomely unmindful of Reason or Sense, to say nothing of Humor . . . [*Ladies' Almanack*, 46]

Ovid's description of Philomel's tongue as a "cut snake" reminds us of the protruding tongue of the Gorgon's head. Jane Harrison argued (in *Prolegomena*) that this representation on a shield was made to frighten off enemies. The tongue of the Gorgon often suggests another of the snakes that form her hair and the head is, by analogy, representative of frightening female genitalia, with the tongue as an exaggerated clitoral threat. Mary Douglas argues in *Natural Symbols* that "the human body is always treated as an image of society and that there can be no natural way of considering the body that does not involve at the same time a social dimension. Interest in its apertures depends on the preoccupation with social exits and entrances, escape routes and invasions. If there is no concern to preserve social boundaries, I would not expect to find concern with bodily boundaries . . . abandonment of bodily control in ritual responds to the requirements of a social experience which is being expressed" (70). The cutting of the tongue/snake by the Thracian savage, Tereus, as he rapes and commits incest, is an act of war or boundary-breaking against Pandion, the sisters' father, and Athens. Her triple rape is revenged with an even more violent and horrific breaking of body taboos when Procne serves Tereus his son's body to eat and brandishes the child's head severed from the body as Philomel's tongue was severed. The references in the myth to the bacchantes' costume suggest that when men and the state render voiceless woman's religious cults, dread violence against the patriarchy results. What we may remember in regard to the representation of female violence and revenge in the Greek plays and myths is that this revenge is imagined by the male artist. We have little surviving early female writing, aside from Sappho's cry, "Why do you trouble me, Pandion's daughter, swallow out of heaven?" Classicist Teri Marsh argues in an unpublished paper that the portraits of violent women in Greek male art come from the idea of power as a closed system, where men cannot imagine sharing power without diminishment and project on to women a violence beyond any evidence of historical reality, as Euripides represents the Bacchae as capable of tearing wild animals and men limb from limb with their bare hands. The playwright is imagining what women ought to do by his own patriarchal standards, not women's actions, when their culture and religion has been suppressed.

In *A Room of One's Own* we hear the swallow ("Mary Hamilton") singing of the nightingale (Judith Shakespeare). Woolf produces and reproduces a woman reading practice here. Our collaboration in this process is surely why the book has become the one standard text in Women's Studies classes. Throughout this book we have looked at Woolf's strategies for subverting patriarchal language. In *A Room of One's Own* she seduces the female reader into collaborating in this erotic and political project by offering reading between women as a bond of kinship to replace patriarchal ties. As Peter Brooks argues, "desire is always there at the start of a narrative, often in a state of initial arousal." Nowhere is this more true than in *A Room of One's Own*. All the suppressed desire of *Night and Day* finally surfaces.

The Triologic Imagination

In *A Room of One's Own* Virginia Woolf deconstructs the lecture as a form. The lecture was another version of the discourse of male domination. "Lecturing," she wrote, "incites the most debased of human passions—vanity, ostentation, self-assertion, and the desire to convert." "Why not create a new form of society founded on poverty and equality?" she asked. "Why not bring people together so that they talk, without mounting platforms or reading papers or wearing expensive clothes or eating expensive food? Would not such a society be worth, even as a form of education, all the papers on art and literature that have ever been read since the world began? Why not *abolish* prigs and prophets? Why not invent human intercourse?" (*The Death of the Moth*, 227–34).

The lecture as conversation (between women) rather than the dictation of the expert to the ignorant, is enacted in *A Room of One's Own*, as she puts that protesting "But" in the mouths of the supposedly silent student audience before uttering a word in her own voice. She abolishes the prigs and prophets, the absent father, the absent grandfather, the absent male professor. As *abolitionist* of the slavery of the listener to the speaker, she echoes her grandfather, abolitionist of the English slave trade, and her father, would-be abolitionist of the servitude of the Cambridge don to the Church of England. As she shows us by her use of pronouns that the lecturer's "one" is not impersonal, gender-free, and universal, but male, she also shows us that the "lecture" as "a form of education" is a one-way street. Communication is not reciprocal: when he stands they sit; when he speaks they listen. *A Room of One's Own* invents human intercourse on a model of female discourse, as a conversation among equals. By what narrative magic can she do away with the whole authoritarian patriarchal structure of domination in the system of academic lectures? Has she really rid herself of those four deadly sins, those debased passions roused by the power of the podium? She does limit her own authority in that she only speaks as herself and not the collective "Mary" when she speaks as a writer and as a reader.[11]

In *Three Guineas* Woolf suggests refusing to lecture as a pacifist's political act, because of the university's collusion with the war-machine. She calls the system of lecturing "vain and vicious," and then qualifies this in a footnote which I will quote at length because it addresses two issues of concern to us today, the illiteracy of students and the viciousness of literary criticism:

> No one would maintain that all lecturers and all lectures are 'vain and vicious;' many subjects can only be taught with diagrams and personal demonstrations. The words in the text refer only to the sons and daughters of educated men who lecture their brothers and sisters upon English literature; and for the reasons that it is an obsolete practice dating from the Middle Ages when books were scarce; that it owes its survival to pecuniary motives; or to curiosity; that the publication in book form is sufficient proof of the evil effect upon the lecturer intellectually; and that psychologically eminence upon a platform encourages vanity and the desire to impose authority. . . . Again, the violence with which one school of literature is now opposed to another, the rapidity with which one school of taste succeeds another, may not unreasonably be traced to the power which a mature mind lecturing immature minds has to infect them with strong, if passing, opinions, and to tinge those opinions with personal bias. Nor can it be maintained that the standard of critical or of creative writing has been raised. . . . None of this applies, of course, to those whose homes are deficient in books. If the working class finds it easier to assimilate English literature by word of mouth they have a perfect right to ask the educated class to help them thus. But for the sons and daughters of that class after the age of eighteen to continue to sip English literature through a straw, is a habit that seems to deserve the terms vain and vicious; which terms can justly be applied with greater force to those who pander to them. [*Three Guineas*, 155–56]

But *Three Guineas'* use of female epistolary form is a deliberate last attack on authority in narrative, almost postmodern in its insistence that the righteous tone of authority in political pamphlets is a literary form of fascist dictatorship. The personal form of the letter is a mockery of demagoguery, a woman's politics of persuasion. The looseness and discursiveness of the letter form allows her to replicate women's sexuality with her textuality. It is the anti-authoritative un-bound book.

While the rhetorical strategy of *Three Guineas* does involve three correspondents, it is not a "triologue" like *A Room of One's Own*, for only the male who wants to stop war is fully realized as a character, though there is some tricky ventriloquism in the opening pages when she asks Mary Kingsley to speak for all educated men's daughters to explain the difference between male and female views of war, regretting that there is no "absolute point of view," a pun on her own writing practice and the politics of war. In a few pages one woman addressing one man expands to speak to the woman reader, then for the woman reader, then "how are we to understand your problem"? and her we is an extension of "the kitchenmaid's cry." (85) *Three Guineas* articulates a nonaggressive feminist/pacifist polemic of "correspondence" where all the meanings of that word suggesting agreement and harmonious intercourse are related to the community formed by letter-writing. As receiver of the letters she introduces her correspondents to each other, asking them to be answerable to each other as well as to her.

Woolf was not "vain and vicious," we assume, ten years earlier lecturing at the women's colleges, because they were so young and poor, and therefore comparable to the working class in the thirties. But if I, who lecture upon English literature, take her seriously, then I am a cross between a soda jerk and a pimp, providing my "mentally docile" listeners with Miltonic milkshakes and Shakespearean sodas. Even as I lecture about her, she is lecturing me (in the sense of admonishing and chastising me) and she wants to abolish my trade altogether. Her notion of a "conspiracy" between her "common reader" and the writer against professors of literature and critics was not just a pretty rhetorical device, but a serious attack on professionalism, which she saw would be as dangerous to women as it had been to men. So I will try to avoid vanity and viciousness, to keep my feet firmly planted in the margins of this text, to come out from behind the podium and acknowledge your "But, what does 'taking the bull by the udders' have to do with sexual difference and Virginia Woolf?"

While Woolf as a feminist reformer lectured in the Stephen family tradition, she also *spoke* "back through her mothers" with her Aunt Caroline Stephen's informal Quaker talks in Cambridge in mind. But, more importantly, the heroine of this text, the great Jane Harrison, was her role model as a lecturer. When her eccentricity lost her a teaching post at her college, Harrison, as one of the first generation of university educated Englishwomen, went to work studying Greek vases at the British Museum. For fifteen years she supported herself lecturing at the British Museum and at boys' schools. A flamboyant and entertaining speaker, she showed lantern slides of Greek vases to illustrate her talks and had her friends shaking bull-roarers in the back of the room to illustrate the frenzy of the worship of Dionysos. Her colleague Francis Cornford wrote, "Every lecture was a drama in which the spectators were to share the emotions of recognition" (Jessie Stewart, *Jane Ellen Harrison: A Portrait From Letters*, London: The Merlin Press, 1959, 20.) This is exactly the structure of Woolf's lectures. We are not *told* the truth as she sees it, but we participate in the drama of asking questions and searching for answers.

Harrison's most famous lecture told the history of successive cults at Delphi, where "she showed Apollo as a usurper deposing the primaeval prophetess or earth-goddess from her oracular sect" (Stewart, 19). Her great project as a classical anthropologist was to analyze the Olympian Greek gods as patriarchal supplanters of earlier matriarchal cults. Francis Cornford recalled her dramatic presence as a lecturer — "a tall figure in black drapery, with touches of her favorite green and a string of blue Egyptian beads, like a priestess's rosary;" her audiences were spellbound because she was not so much a lecturer as a fellow enthusiast. Eventually, the strain of being an "impostor" made her "disheartened," she says in her memoirs, and she "threw up the lecturing sponge and fled." She was criticized as a show-off and angered the conservative classicists. Professor Ridgeway denounced her as a charlatan who deluded young minds, and Hilaire Belloc was so enraged at her correction of him that he decided she must be Jewish. An outsider like Woolf, she left her a heritage of the woman's lecture as "*imposture.*" A *Room of One's Own* continues the tradition of a woman lecturing as *imposture* in which Harrison and Woolf are linked to other women like Fanny Wright lecturing on racism in America in the early 19th century.

Gilbert Murray, Jane Harrison's colleague and dear friend, wrote: "Her lectures had a combination of grace and daring, of playfulness and dignity, which made them unlike any others." He quotes Mrs. Salter: "She had an admirable dramatic sense and knew just how to lead an audience to expect a particular point and then give them what they expected"—or perhaps did not expect. "One small instance comes back to me. We were gradually led to expect a revelation, and then with a slightly hushed voice Jane heralded as an exquisitely lovely creature, the appearance on the screen of a particularly hideous Gorgon, grinning from ear to ear." Murray himself goes on to praise "the obvious and undeniable beauty of her own speaking and lecturing. A lecture of hers, apart from its matter or its originality, was always a delightful artistic performance. The language and articulation were as finished as they were unaffected. And again to quote Mrs. Salter, 'Jane had an additional advantage in that she could throw herself in as part of the show in a way that is hardly possible for a man. She was always delightful to look at, and I remember among other things how skillfully she used her beautiful hands.'" (Gilbert Murray, *Jane Ellen Harrison*, Cambridge: Heffer, 1928, 9-10).

Woolf deconstructs her own lecture with the opening words of A *Room of One's Own* as she includes the audience in conversation by articulation of their question: "But, you may say, we asked you to speak about women and fiction— what has that got to do with a room of one's own?" The audience, the "you" with its question, comes first. She says she will "try" to explain. She relaxes her authority, gives up the stance of the expert. Her opening sentence is the continuation of an interrupted conversation in which she is only an equal partner. In her written text, she keeps the conversation going. The reader is included in the "you," so the text becomes a three-sided conversation between the woman writer, the women students in the audience, and the woman reader. Without us, we are made to feel, she cannot speak. Our role as readers is to collaborate in this conversation, to conspire with the woman writer and the women students to overthrow the formal rigidity of the lecture as an "educational device." It is not a monologue. It is not even a mock Platonic dialogue, but a *trio-logue*. The woman's text asks the reader to share in the making of the text as the lecturer includes the listeners in her speaking. She abdicates her power of suspense by giving her conclusion first, and in the simplest possible language. "A woman must have money and a room of her own if she is to write fiction." We could rewrite this as an "expert" might say it—"Let us examine the role of gender and capital in the production of culture." If she had opened this way, and there is no doubt, given the hectoring, lecturing tone of the footnote from *Three Guineas*, that she *could* have, we would have a lecture, not what she called "talks to girls." (See the next chapter.)

After tripling the power of her own voice by including her readers and her student audience, she triples it again—"call me Mary Beton, Mary Seton, Mary Carmichael or by any name you please."[12] She is not Virginia Woolf standing on the platform but the voice of the anonymous female victim of male violence throughout the ages. In the text she tells us that Anonymous was most often a woman. On the platform she becomes "Anonymous" in person. She transforms herself in the narrative to the object of her narration.

Once the three-sided conversation is established, its informality and collectivity implicitly mocking the formal egotism of the absent male professor's lecture, her illegitimacy as a lecturer proclaimed, she can say "I." "I have shirked the duty of coming to a conclusion," she confesses. This disingenuous pose disarms us into thinking her far more truthful than any authoritative lecturer. Humbly, she abjures expertise: "Women and fiction remain—so far as I am concerned—unsolved problems." Now she has all her women readers and listeners in the palm of her hand. To "make some amends" for posing as a lecturer, "I am going to do what I can to show you how I arrived at this opinion"; "I am going to develop as fully and freely as I can the train of thought which led me to think this."

Confidences thus exchanged—among women—Woolf moves to the impersonal "one," the two generalizations then proposed (p. 4) are an extrapolation from the single and collective female. "One" is robbed of its impersonality as a gender-free pronoun. "*One* can only show how *one* came to hold whatever opinion *one* does hold. *One* can only give *one's* audience the chance of drawing their own conclusions as they observe the limitations, the prejudices, the idiosyncrasies of the speaker." The linking of the questioning *you* and the responding *I* to make a female *one* reminds the audience of the absent other whose educational process we imitate and remake in female terms. The authoritative, supposedly gender-free impersonal "one" of the male professor, the British authority, is *not* gender-free but male, and made by a conflation of the *I* and *you* of the male lecturer and his male students. We know this because she has "fully and freely"

engendered and gendered her *one* out of herself and some women students. We
know also that the *one* in her title, *A Room of One's Own*, is as female as the *one*
in "Between puberty and menopause *one* menstruates once a month." She is
making the female the universal norm in this title, but she can only do this with
our consent, and we are very well aware that in a mixed audience the assent
would not be granted her, and the response would be of the kind produced by
"Between puberty and menopause one menstruates once a month." But Woolf's
most exciting act in *A Room of One's Own* is its collective narration.

In the March 1929 issue of *The Forum*, Woolf published an essay called
"Women and Fiction" which must have been a draft of part of *A Room of One's
Own*. It is curiously flat and lifeless compared to the book, solely because of its
single omniscient narrator. Reading the essay, one becomes aware that *A
Room's* brilliance is based on its *triologue*, the three-fold narration of speaker,
reader, and audience, as well as the multiple Marys of her own persona. The
essay in *The Forum* is more openly political, complains of the "distortion" of
"someone resenting the treatment of her sex and pleading for its rights" in
Middlemarch and *Jane Eyre*. "This brings into women's writing an element
which is entirely absent from a man's unless, indeed, he happens to be a working man, a Negro, or one who for some other reason is conscious of disability."
But she predicts that women's novels, now that women have the vote, will
"naturally become more critical of society, and less analytical of individual
lives." "We may expect that the office of gadfly to the state, which has been so far
a male prerogative, will now be discharged by women also. Their novels will
deal with social evils and remedies. Their men and women will not be observed
wholly in relation to each other emotionally, but as they cohere and clash in
groups and classes and races."

The Forum exhibits a strong concern with women's education. The previous
issue had an article by the president of Smith College in favor, but in March,
W. Beran Wolfe, a psychiatrist, claimed that unnamed sexual vices were rampant: "They spell out a terrific indictment of women's colleges." He describes
the frustrated scholar "with the feeble glory of a Phi Beta Kappa key" who "projects her social discouragement to the next generation." If she isn't a scholar,
"college teaches her the futility of being a woman, and when she graduates, she
swells the growing number of neurotic women who fill the divorce courts and
mental sanitaria. These women miss the opportunity to learn social and sexual
adjustment during the most significant years of their development, because
women's colleges offer them the sickly pablum of archeology and art appreciation instead of the robust material of human cooperation."

Though *A Room of One's Own* may have seemed a redundant reissue of the
pamphlet literature of the suffrage movement, it is clear from *The Forum* that
misogny was alive and well in 1929. The January issue contained a piece by D. H.
Lawrence, "Cocksure Women and Hensure Men," blaming male impotence on
intellectual women, begging women to obey their biological imperative in a
barnyard lecture on the evil of brains in women.[13]

The Mermaid Muse

In "Professions for Women," her speech before the London National Society for Women's Service in January, 1931, Virginia Woolf, who despised lectures, again gave a lecture to an all-female audience. (The text I use is from the original speech, published in *The Pargiters*.) It was another fishing trip into the female element, into the arms of mother water, a submerged merger of several female selves, "waters poured into one jar." Whether one reads this talk as a description of creativity as amniotic bliss or as an example of a woman writer's "fluid boundaries," it does dramatize the underwater world of a woman writer's imagination, and answers a question that has puzzled feminist critics: "What sex is the muse of the woman writer?" Virginia Woolf's muse is female, and the relation between her two selves (here reason and imagination) is distinctly sexual. The muse of the woman writer, her guide into the unconscious realms of female sexual experience, is a mermaid. Their relationship, the writer as "fisherwoman," and the muse as diver, is distinctly lesbian. Jane Harrison asked in *Prolegomena*, "Who are the Muses?" and answered herself "Who but the Maenads repentant, *clothed* and in their right minds" (464). In the following passage Woolf traces the development of maenad into muse, a process which I suggest is common for women writers.

She gives two scenarios (*The Pargiters*, pp. xxxviii-xxx)—a fishing trip and a reverse striptease. In one she was "letting her imagination feed unfettered on every crumb of her experience; she was letting her imagination sweep unchecked round every rock and cranny of the world that lies submerged in our unconscious being." The "imagination" comes to the surface, floating "limply and dully and lifelessly." When reason says "What on earth is the matter with you?" the naked muse "began pulling on its stockings and replied, rather tartly and disagreeably; it's all your fault." The novelist apologizes for her lack of experience.

In the second scenario, the mermaid darts away into the depths. "The reason has to cry 'Stop!' the novelist has to pull on the line and haul the imagination to the surface. The imagination comes to the top in a state of fury." The novelist replies, "My dear, you were going altogether too far. Men would be shocked.' Calm yourself, I say, as she sits panting on the bank—panting with rage and disappointment." She says it will be fifty years before a writer can use "this queer knowledge" about "women's bodies" and their "passions" in her writing, not, in fact, until "men can be educated to *stand* free speech in women." The use of the word "stand" brands male intolerance as the source of women's reticence. The mermaid is impatient but resigned. "Very well, says the imagination, dressing herself up again in her petticoat and skirts, we will wait. We will wait another fifty years. But it seems to me a pity." She is not sure that men can be civilized or "reeducated" to allow women to be artists. That problem "lies on the lap of the Gods, no not upon the laps of the Gods, but upon your laps, upon the laps of professional women."

Here, as in *A Room of One's Own*, Woolf flirts with her female audience, seductively suggesting that with the support of women readers the woman writer can tell "the truth about the body." This dramatization of the relation between a woman artist and her muse, the rational feminist and the sexually liberated unconscious, parallels Woolf's relationship with Vita Sackville-West—the daring dive, the pull of convention, the hasty retreat and exchange of bad temper.[14]

Woolf then dramatizes a conspiracy of women against the male breadwinner, a conspiracy to win them the right to work. Having aroused her audience, she then cautions patience. She claims that there actually *are* "men with whom a woman can live in perfect freedom," yet she concludes with a romantic description of the working woman's room as an escape from the patriarchal house: "I suspect that the sofa turns into a bed; and the wash stand is covered with a check cloth by day to look as much like a table as possible." The next step is "a step upon the stair. You will hear *somebody* coming. You will open the door. And then—this is at least my guess—there will take place between you and *someone else* the most interesting, exciting, and important conversation that has ever been heard. But do not be alarmed; I am not going to talk about that now." What sex is *somebody*?" What sex is *someone else*? Why is this "alarming"? This lecture as lupine plot, feminist conspiracy, is another seductive *sapphistry*. It stops just short of sedition. It writes a script with missing lines like the ellipses in "Chloe like Olivia. They shared a . . ." The audience (or the reader) supplies the missing dialogue in "the *most* interesting, exciting and important conversation that has ever been heard." Has Chloe come to visit Olivia after the laboratory has closed? Will that "conversation" become a conspiracy? Can a married woman bond with a single woman?

The fishing trip enacted in *A Room of One's Own* and "Professions for Women," the longing for submerged merger and escape and the portrait of the woman artist as fisherwoman, fish, or mermaid—are parts of a continuing drama in Woolf's work that begins with Cam trailing her fingers in the water in scenes VIII and X of *To the Lighthouse*. "They don't feel a thing there, Cam thought . . . Her hand cut a trail in the sea, and her mind made the green swirls and streaks into patterns and, numbed and shrouded, wandered in imagination in that underworld of waters where the pearls stuck in clusters to white sprays, where in the green light a change came over one's entire mind and one's body shone half transparent in a green cloak" (*TTL* 272). In section X Cam tells herself a story, for the sense of adventure and escape that will take her away from the tense Oedipal clash between her father and James. "From her hand, ice cold, held deep in the sea, there spurted up a fountain of joy . . . and the drops falling from this sudden and unthinking fountain of joy fell here and there on the dark, the slumbrous shapes in her mind . . ." (*TTL*, 280, 281). Cam finds not only her "place in the universe" but also her story—telling of a self revealed as powerful enough to conjure up "Greece, Rome, Constantinople" from the underwater world of her imagination. That cloaked submarine self, the half-transparent mermaid, reveals herself as the woman artist's muse, as Cam the

Wicked grows into the no less wicked (and witch-like) narrator of *A Room of One's Own* and "Professions for Women."

In Susan Dick's edition of the holograph draft of *To the Lighthouse* Mr. Bankes sees Cam as "wild and fierce," a "wild villain," but her mother thinks her mind is "vacant" and she cannot be trusted with a message to the kitchen; her mind is a "well, where if the waters were clear they were also extraordinarily distorting" and the words twist as they descend (Dick, 94). Her father criticizes her mother for teaching Cam to exaggerate and links her to her great aunt Camilla who was worse but was also a great beauty. Cam is very important in the draft, as is Mrs. McNab. Here Mrs. McNab *is* "the fountain of life"; as Elizabeth Abel says, she is Cam's "kitchen muse," and Cam's imagination develops in its relation to the words of working-class women. In the draft the children are "Cam the Bad" and "James the Sullen"; "a serious melancholy couple"; Lily is furious that they are "trodden under" and made to "stumble" by Mr. Ramsay. Cam is "shortsighted" and "obstinate." Woolf seems to work out her own ambivalence to her father in an extraordinary scene in the boat where Cam is enraged by her father's tyranny, recognizes his need for her love when he wheedles her about the puppy, and forgives him. He is a tyrant but a "beautiful" tyrant. She says to herself the whole of "The Castaway" and then fantasizes herself as a heroine saving the victims of a shipwreck—"all depended on her catching a fish" (318), a vision that whirls away her anger and her unhappiness. That is, Woolf's version here of the birth of the woman artist is not in the struggle with the Angel in the House, but the primal struggle with the "demon" father in the boat. Though Woolf's plan for the novel was to include a portrait of her father in the boat "clutching a dying mackerel," it is Cam who catches a fish in the holograph. James, interestingly enough, sees a devil in both his father and Cam. Both spirits obviously had to be cast out for Woolf, the angel mother and the devil father. This chapter in the draft of *To the Lighthouse* is analogous to the killing of the angel in "Professions for Women"—with the difference that the woman artist kills the angel in a violent struggle, whereas Cam "submits" to the demon father.

"Her fishing line . . . flew out between her fingers . . ." she had "hold of something thrilling with life, a quivering sharp thread, which went down in & the word . . . then her line seemed to flick with an intense excitement, jerking and vibrating in her fingers" and " . . . with a future which it was dazzling to contemplate" she imagines herself as God creating the world of Egyptians, Greeks, Byzantines, Shakespeare. Then she submits all these questions to her father (319, 320). Cam needs her father's approval and desperately wants to know what he's reading in a little book "with covers mottled like a plover's egg." This green and brown book, eventually revealed as a Greek text, is obviously the dying mackerel. Cam's vision of her father's passionate love of reading quells her anger—"she would like him to approve of her thoughts but not to know them" (232), that is, she seeks unconditional love from the Father-Reader. She predicts the father's disapproval of the writing/reading daughter when she catches the fish. "She was wildly excited. She had . . . felt a bite. She . . . pulled the line in."

There it was a silver green flash in the water. She hauled a mackerel on board . . . and then, because . . . Macalister's boy . . . jerked the hook out & her father saw it & shut his eyes in a spasm of horror, Cam all together shut up; She would not bait the hook again" (349–59).

Woolf continues to work on the father/daughter drama, where fishing and reading and writing are equated. Cam thinks of her agnostic father preaching morals: "they were all sinking in *a waste of waters*," words which will recur in *The Waves* with Bernard's vision of the fin. In the next passage Cam imagines a shipwreck, "how the mackerel felt," and "her own bait sweeping white through the waves," thinking of her father's tyranny and her own "blind ungovernable rage." She imagines drowning men and the roots of the land in the sea; "Wagging her little finger to & fro in the gunwale she acted the effort of the mind to be free" (355). She grasps her finger with her other hand, sees the father escape confrontation by reading. Just as she wants to strike him dead, she imagines the tyrant giving her mother a flower and puts herself in her mother's place.

It is a powerful psychic drama enacted here in draft, but the story of the fisherwoman as writer is even more complex. For in the draft the fairytale that Mrs. Ramsay tells the children is first "The Three Dwarfs" and then "The Three Bears." In the final version only James is told the story of "The Fisherman and His Wife" by his mother, who also directs him to cut out pictures of sharp, phallic objects (like his scimitar father) and a refrigerator, an object of nurturance that is cold. That is, Mrs. Ramsay helps her boy through his Oedipal struggle by teaching him to identify with the hated father and to see his nurturing mother as rejecting and cold, and, through the story, that women are greedy and power-mad. James's experience tells him that this is not true, but Mrs. Ramsay plays her part in the patriarchy with her pointed lessons. Cam is absent from these scenes in the final version, but working them out was necessary for Woolf. Cam tells herself a story in which the fisherwoman would be king and does indeed build an empire in her mind, creates the whole world from her imagination. It is not a flounder that comes out of the sea as an enabler of empowerment, but a mackerel (the father's Greek text). From this misogynist fairy tale about women's insatiable desire for power, James learns that good is male and evil is female. But Cam leaps like a mackerel out of this text into several others, carrying her fishing rod, chasing elusive fish and dreaming of power as a writer. We are reminded of Gunter Grass's *The Flounder*, where feminists put the father fish of the fairy tale on trial for his crimes against women, and Zora Neale Hurston's *Their Eyes Were Watching God*, where Janie liberates herself by fishing.

The mermaid, the fisherwoman, and the fish make up a female underwater womblike world of freedom that Woolf creates again and again. In *The Voyage Out* Rachel escapes from Terence in a mock battle they have had that predicts their marriage. He wins but she escapes: "I'm a mermaid. I can swim . . . so the game's up." (VO, 298). Nina Auerbach claims in *Woman and the Demon* that "Mermaids . . . submerge themselves not to negate their power but to conceal

it." Auerbach's chapter on the angel and demon in Victorian literature explicates Thackeray's drawings of mermaids as well as his texts. Woolf's choice of
the mermaid figure to fight the angel mother and the demon father obviously
draws on a common mythology of empowering woman. As we have seen in
"Professions for Women," the underwater world of the woman artist's imagination suggests a submarine lesbian utopia where desire and writing are in-
timately connected. Woolf called both her sister Vanessa and Vita Sackville-
West "dolphins." In a curious essay written in 1928 after a trip to see the eclipse
with Vita, Woolf shifts her story abruptly back to the London zoo with a vision of
"one lizard . . . mounted immobile on the back of another . . . All human passion seems furtive and feverish beside this still rapture" (CE, IV, 182). Then
follows an extraordinary passage that asserts the superiority of the fish tank to
the world, the variety and "immortality" of fish compared to human beings.
This passage is Cam's book, the conflation of the mottled green book and the
mackerel, the world-creating text of the overweening fisherman's wife who
insists on having her kindgom:

> Tanks cut in the level blackness enclose squares of immortality . . . There the
> inhabitants perform forever evolutions whose intricacy, because it has not
> reason, seems the more sublime . . . The discipline is perfect, the control abso-
> lute; reason there is none . . . Each of these worlds too, which measures perhaps
> four feet by five, is as perfect in its order as in its method . . . The fish themselves
> seem to have been shaped deliberately and slipped into the world only to be
> themselves. They neither work nor weep. In their shape is their reason. For
> what other purpose except the sufficient one of perfect existence can they have
> been thus made, some so round, some so thin, some with radiating fins upon
> their backs, other lined with red electric light, others undulating like white pan-
> cakes on a frying pan, some armoured in blue mail, some given prodigious claws,
> some outrageously fringed with huge whiskers? More care has been spent upon
> half a dozen fish than upon all the races of men. Under our tweed and silk is noth-
> ing but a monotony of pink nakedness. Poets are not transparent to the back-
> bones as these fish are. Bankers have no claws. Kings and Queens themselves
> have neither ruffs nor frills. In short, if they were to be turned naked into an
> aquarium—but enough. ["The Sun and the Fish," CE, IV, 182–183]

I suggest that like Artemis, the savage virgin goddess who is her muse,
Virginia Woolf imagined the woman artist as a fisherwoman. Artemis wove nets
for fishing and hunting as Woolf weaves her tale of the daughter's fish and the
father's book in *To the Lighthouse* and rewrites the tale of the Fisherman and his
Wife to valorize woman's dream of power. Her drama of the underwater struggle between the woman artist and her muse is like her vision of Vita Sackville-
West as dolphinlike in a fishmonger's shop. It is a complete enclosed (female)
world of the fish tank she imagines when limited by the "monotony" of pink flesh
under the tweed and silk. The enclosed perfect and various world of the fish
tank is the novelist's creation of a world in her fiction. God and the eclipse of the
sun cannot mar its perfection or subtract from its immortality. Like Jane Harri-

son's priest in *Alpha and Omega*, she has created her own alphabet, and then ordered it with magic words.

A White Hotel

The lectures we have looked at were public addresses and they show Woolf's rhetorical strategies at their best. Now let us look at "A Woman's College from the Outside," a sketch of Newnham published in *Atlanta's Garden* by the Edinburgh University Women's Union in 1926 (now reprinted in the Complete Shorter Fiction of Virginia Woolf, 1986). Here the chip on her shoulder at never having had a formal education ("From the *Outside*") weighs down Woolf's shoulder and sprains her writing arm. The scene is a "drama in muslin," if we may borrow George Moore's title, in which the woman in the moon gazes on a pure white virginal world of Newnham and its garden bathed in a "vapour" that is the *breath* of women laughing together, issuing from the windows, attaching itself "by soft elastic threads to plants and bushes." The reader feels like an intruder on the rites of "The Wild White Maids" of *The Bacchae*, exhausted by their "long, long dances" and flung about the hillside in just such a trancelike female communal sleep. It is another "*conspiracy*," the breathing of women, sleeping together, laughing together. Their misty breath veils the garden so that the moon may un-veil her face: "As none but women's faces could meet her face, she might unveil it, blank, featureless and gaze into rooms where at that hour, blank, featureless, eyelids white over eyes, ringless hands extended upon sheets, slept innumerable women." The Tennysonian "innumerable" aches with the kind of nostalgia that comes, not from memory of experience, but a wish for the memory of experience. It is the way one would describe a castle in Spain if one had never seen a castle in Spain and always longed for a glimpse of it. It is doubtful if any actual graduate of Newnham would conjure up that virginal mist, the communal nun's bridal veil blanketing the world of the women's college. The "blank, featureless" face of the woman in the moon is mirrored by the "blank, featureless" faces of the sleeping women. Like the white square name cards on the women's doors, the virginal sleeping faces are blank pages— their history has not been written.[15]

The moon sees Angela (it had to be Angela) kiss her bright reflection in the glass, her identity "visible proof of the rightness of things," "a lily floating flawless upon Time's pool," "the bright picture hung in the heart of the night, the Shrine hollowed in the nocturnal blackness." Angela's identity, her being "glad to be Angela," comes from the community of women in which her selfhood can be developed. The shrine of female identity is in the sleeping quarters of the women's college. The dormitory of the women's college is a "white hotel" in which the sleepers are watched by the blank-faced moon—Watch-woman, what of the night?: "Night is free pasturage, a limitless field, since night is unmoulded richness, one must tunnel into its darkness. One must hang it with jewels." The narrative nightwatch of the outsider and her eyeless lunar companion scans names as well as faces in one of the most unabashedly romantic passages ever to come from the ironic pen of Virginia Woolf:

> A. Williams—one may read it in the moonlight; and next to it some Mary or Eleanor, Mildred, Sarah, Phoebe upon square cards on their doors. All names, nothing but names. The cool white light withered them and starched them until it seemed as if the only purpose of all these names was to rise martially in order should there be a call on them to extinguish a fire, suppress an insurrection, or pass an examination. Such is the power of names written upon cards pinned upon doors. Such too the resemblance, what with tiles, corridors, and bedroom doors, to dairy or nunnery, a place of seclusion or discipline, where the bowl of milk stands cool and pure and there's a great washing of linen. [*Books and Portraits*, 6–9]

There she is again, that recurrent figure in Woolf's work, the virgin mother, the moon chaste yet protective, the nunnery and dairy, a-sexuality and maternal nurturance—the insistent note in all her writing, of *sexual difference as sexual abstinence*. (I don't really mean abstinence, but a kind of sexual autonomy associated with the goddess Artemis in the wilderness). Why is this passage on purity so seductive? "Elderly women slept, who would on waking immediately clasp the ivory rod of office . . . reposing deeply they lay surrounded, lay supported, by the bodies of youth. . . ." It is that Mother Superior or Headmistress and her "ivory rod" that rouses an unawakened female desire for a haven under female authority, the rule of the nunnery, the discipline of the headmistress in a community of work, the underlying sexuality of social and political sisterhood. (Shades of Caroline Emelia Stephen.)

Seductive as this sketch is, ending with 19-year-old Angela sucking her thumb in "this good world, this new world, this world at the end of the tunnel," it does not finally work. The reader is neither invited nor coerced into co-narration. Attractive as Angela is, she is only a vision glimpsed in the mirror by the moon and we are not invited to worship at her shrine, our breath does not cloud her mirror. The rhetorical *trio-logue* of the lectures here lacks a third, and it takes three to make a conspiracy. Yet we respond to the clean, white milky ambience of this world without men. We do respond to Woolf's "erotics of chastity,"[16] if we read "chastity" as ownership of one's own sexuality.

The relationship of childlessness to female genius is one that Woolf explores in *A Room*. It is interesting that the essay which fails valorizes chastity, while the one which succeeds celebrates sexuality, though, as I argue in "Sapphistry," it is lesbian sexuality. Feminist critics have analyzed the absent mother in many texts—perhaps we should explore as well the figure of the absent child. Judith Shakespeare is not only a suicide but a pregnant suicide.

Vera Brittain praised Woolf's stress on the difference between the feminist desire for equality with men and adopting male identity. But she was troubled by Woolf's conclusion that women of genius had no children. "Must we then accept the proposition that a woman writer can produce great literature only by subduing her natural desire for children? So long as women writers and artists must sacrifice motherhood in order to fulfill the inexorable demands of a creative gift the feminist revolution remains incomplete" (*Lady Into Woman*, London: Andrew Dakers, 1953, 221).

It is interesting to compare *A Room of One's Own* to the view of a woman's college from the *inside* in Dorothy Sayers's *Gaudy Night* (1936). A Somerville graduate herself, Sayers mocks all the romantic feminist visions of female scholarly community that Woolf's two essays celebrate. [I disagree with Lee Edwards's reading in *Psyche as Hero* (Wesleyan University Press, 1985) which celebrates the novel as a study of women's work and community.] It is unclear if *Gaudy Night* was meant as a deliberate reply to Woolf's book, but it is an effective attack on women's education.[17] In "Shrewsbury College," the shrews are buried by poison pen letters and the excretal brown paint of obscene graffiti on the walls as well as the destruction (by pen) of a feminist scholar's proofs. Interestingly, the draft of *A Room of One's Own* is even more redolent of references to *Antony and Cleopatra* than the printed text. Sayers's title refers to the same text and its ooze and slime and excreta are a deliberate reference to the woman's world of Egypt, and Artemis' arrows are mocked. Woolf wants to know what would have happened if Cleopatra liked Octavia. Dorothy Sayers is sure that women can't trust one another. In *Gaudy Night* the individual rooms are violated as well as the common rooms, and a critique of Woolf's view of women's writing and reading practice is presented in the text's obsession with other forms of women's writing than fiction—anonymous letters, mystery stories, literary and historical scholarship, psychology, love letters, term papers, and the disturbing brown obscenities on the library walls. Harriet's poem is *finished* by Wimsey, just as she does all the research and he solves the crime. The best example of Sayers's attack on female creativity is the scene where Harriet pays Wimsey's nephew's bills by *writing* out the checks, which he *signs*. When women write, the male completes the poem, signs the check. The woman scholar's real insights don't appear and she doesn't dare to express them until she has page proofs of her book. While *A Room* is concerned with thinking back through our literary mothers, *Gaudy Night* asks, "How many great women have had great fathers and husbands behind them?" "Dear me! Being a great father is either a very difficult or a very sadly unrewarded profession" (p. 48). Harriet Vane is less romantic about the sleeping women but surely she mocks Woolf's essay: "On the doors were cards, bearing their names: Miss H. Brown, Miss Jones, Miss Colburn, Miss Szleposky, Miss Isaacson—so many unknown quantities. So many destined wives and mothers of the race; or, alternatively, so many potential historians, scientists, schoolteachers, doctors, lawyers . . . " (p. 92). Woolf's Angelas and Marys here have Eastern European and Jewish roommates. Instead of bowls of milk, Sayers sees shoes and "little heaps of soiled crockery" outside the women's rooms. The dons present a different version of female authority than the Woolfian outsider imagines. Woolf's dream of a lesbian utopia in a woman's college is in Sayers's hands a nightmare of repressed sexuality, jealousy, and hatred. (One is reminded here of Woolf's own phrase in *Between the Acts*, "words the defilers.") In fact, Sayers's most telling response to Woolf is her bitter argument that women cannot cross class in sisterhood. Sayers's villain, the passionate hater of all intellectual women, is the very charwoman Woolf idealizes in all her writing, in this text, the woman who is absent from the lecture because she is washing up the dishes. To Woolf, the women's college is a dairy or nunnery; to Sayers it is a toilet or madhouse. The cleaning woman dirties the walls of the woman's library. Nothing could be further from Woolf's vision of their common cause.

The failure of "A Woman's College from the Outside" is a failure to share narration with her subject and her audience (to give the audience a voice in the text), as well as an imaginative failure, and it underlines the brilliance of Woolf's "sapphistry," her "trio-logue" in *A Room of One's Own*. In *A Room of One's Own* Woolf's narrative strategy builds such a strong collective presence of women co-narrators of her text, a chorus of oppressed and victimized women, that her feminist voice is continually supported by their presence. Mary Beton, Mary Seton, Mary Carmichael, the women students in the audience, the women professors, and the implied women readers—that she seems invincible to the patriarchy. Indeed the platform is so crowded with conspirators that when Woolf says "I" we read it and hear it as "we," and her written "I" has no five-o'clock shadow, no resemblance to the "straight dark bar" on the patriarchal cage.

I have suggested that the male reader is forced to deny the superiority of his gender if he is to read *A Room of One's Own* sympathetically. But I would like to point out some exceptions to this rule, Geoffrey Hartman in "Virginia's Web" and J. Hillis Miller's reaffirmation of its argument in *Fiction and Repetition*.[18] Aside from the absence of references to feminist critics, note that the essays center on the passage in *A Room* that describes a man and woman getting into a taxi. Woolf herself described her fascination with the "rhythmical order" with which she invests the scene. Both men see this passage as descriptive of the source of Woolf's creativity, a recognition of a "force" in nature. Frankly, every woman reader I know sees this passage as Woolf's mnemonic device to force herself out of her feminist and lesbian fantasy world, back to a realization of "heterosexuality makes the world go round." That couple is Woolf's rude reminder to herself that most women are not part of a woman's community but are isolated from each other in relation to individual men. It is a reminder to herself that the male reader is out there, and she placates him with this mysterious heterosexual romance. It signals the female reader—that this is the stuff of reality; that this is the stuff of fiction—a man and a woman getting into a taxi. The scene accentuates her own difference and the difference of her text from the stream of life represented by the rhythmical meeting of the couple in the crowd and its reference to the stream at Oxbridge on whose banks she first began to puzzle out the problems presented by her lecture. This passage is the "little fish" she promised her listeners as their prize. It is in fact two little fishes, one for men and one for women. The men get the red herring of the taxi passage to reassure them. The women, still hungering for the elegant meal served at the men's college, get the reverse of the fairy tale of "The Fisherman and His Wife" which Mrs. Ramsay tells James in *To the Lighthouse*. If Cam the narrator of *A Room* retells the story as The Fisherwoman and her Husband, that tale of male vanity and greed is *A Room of One's Own*. Women's assertion of difference, perhaps in lesbianism, in militant feminism or in celibacy, will alienate them, as Woolf is alienated, from the mainstream, from the order and rhythm of everyday heterosexual life. It is significant that male critics pounce on this passage of romantic heterosexuality, the modern version of the lines from Tennyson and Rossetti which she mocks, as evidence of Woolf's creativity, when it is clear from her letters and diaries that she herself feels (whether rightly or wrongly it is impossible to say) that her own creativity lies in the experience of madness and of difference from men, her sympathy with lesbianism and her sexual abstinence, but also her sense of difference from both heterosexual and lesbian women.

As male writing continually represents women as other, alien and different, *A Room of One's Own* is one of the strongest feminist statements of maleness as other. But, more important, like her novels, the text also represents *heterosexuality as other*, not only by mocking Tennyson and Rossetti's lovey-doveyness as obsolete, but by distancing the couple entering the taxi from herself very subtly by class. Perhaps I am overreading the young woman's patent leather boots and the young man's maroon overcoat, but their "seeming satisfaction" seems to relegate "love" to a class other than her own. The sight of the pair "*seems* to ease the mind." She notes that she is "separate" and "apart from them." There is something equally hesitant and very odd about her statement "One has a profound, if irrational, instinct in favour of the theory that the union of man and woman makes for the greatest satisfaction, the most complete happiness" (102). What the word "irrational" suggests here is that common sense and experience tell one the opposite. The passage suggests doubt. Let us look at what precipitates the taxi passage. It is the fall of a single leaf "like a signal falling, a signal pointing to a force in things which one had overlooked" (100). Woolf then recalls the opening passage of the book where the undergraduate is swept down the river (the Cam?) with dead leaves. Since the taxi scene is a prelude to the assertion "that a woman writing thinks back through her mothers" (101), we are reminded of Woolf's own mother's insistence on the difference between the sexes and Mrs. Ramsay's role as enforcer of heterosexuality in *To the Lighthouse*. Elizabeth Abel, in her argument that "Cam enables Woolf to dramatize the narrative plight of the daughter who thinks back through her father,"[19] points out that Cam's image of her mother is the leaf, which she carries in Part I; and the island, seen by Cam from the sea, is her mother's body: "It lay like that on the sea, did it, with a dent in the middle and two sharp crags, and the sea swept in there . . . it was very small, shaped like a leaf stood on end" (280). The narrator of *A Room of One's Own* is as troubled by the leaf as Cam. When the leaf falls, it is a "signal pointing to a force in things which one had overlooked." The falling leaf is the mother's voice, insistent on the "reproduction of mothering," that women must marry and bear children. In Chapter 19 of *The Well of Loneliness* "a leaf dropped, and she heard its minute, soft falling, heard the creak of the branch that had let fall its leaf," as Stephen is asked by her naive married lover, Angela, whether she can *marry* her.

"Again if one is a woman one is often surprised by a sudden splitting off of consciousness, say in walking down Whitehall, when from being the natural inheritor of that civilisation, she becomes, on the contrary, outside of it, alien and critical" (101). As the pronouns shift here from "one" to "she" instead of "I," Woolf distances herself from womanhood, trying to find a "comfortable" position, moving finally to the concept of androgyny. It is an attempt to flatten out those "two sharp crags" of the ancient duality and opposition between the sexes, to make a new geography of difference which will include bisexuality. Male critics are right to see this passage as the turn of the text, but it is a weak and wavering vision of sexual unity, signalled by the falling leaf, the return of the repressed voice of the mother. "But some of these states of mind seem, even if adopted spontaneously, to be less comfortable than others. In order to keep oneself continuing in them one is unconsciously holding something back, and gradually the repression becomes an effort" (101).

The mother insists on having her page in the daughter's text. The narrator, if we may borrow Joyce's terms, is writing a separatist *manifesto* on women's rights/writes, and it turns into a *mamafesta* on women's duties (for one page.) The leaf signals the textuality of the mother's body ("a woman writing thinks back through her mothers") turning the text for a moment from the literary history of women writers to the family history of mothers and daughters, haunting the text with the double bind—great women writers had no children; mothers have left their daughters no texts.

If the writing daughter catches the falling leaf, what can she write on it? Mr. Ramsay scribbles on geranium leaves. Cam's vision of the island/mother as a leaf is also a vision of the leaf of a book, loose or bound, the blank page of the mother's body, as a text. As the Cumaean sibyl wrote her prophecies on leaves, the daughter writer takes her mother's body as a text. Cam is the legendary maiden from the Aeneid (7.803; ll. 539-828) as well as Camilla, the "wise virgin" of Leonard Woolf's novel. Tied to her father's javelin and dedicated to Diana, she is flung across the river Amasenus. In *To the Lighthouse* "She was off like a bird, bullet or arrow, impelled by what desire, shot by whom, at what directed, who could say?" (84) The name Cam is also an attenuated version of Cambridge, the intellectual home of the Stephen males, and its river. "Camilla/us" is also used by classical writers to mean an acolyte to a priest or priestess. Cam is again for us as women readers the fisherwoman narrator of *A Room of One's Own* and "Professions for Women." Writing the book that is absent from the shelves of the British Museum, the narrator of *A Room of One's Own* is returning to her mother her lost textuality. Cam's observance at the door of the study that books belong to men leads her, as she becomes the narrator of *A Room*, to envision her project as writing the mother's body, interleaving her story in the daughter's text, as Woolf wrote one of her diaries by pasting her pages over the male text of a book.[20] Interleaving the woman's story in the male book of history is the project of *A Room of One's Own*. One of the leaves in the woman's book, its most problematic page, is the single leaf speaking in the mother's voice, of the dangers of separating oneself off from the patriarchy. Women readers share the writer's anxiety at the return of the repressed maternal imperative and join the narrator in struggling with her ghost.

By collaborating in the *trio-logue* of the narration of *A Room*, we readers have validated our own gender-derived reading experience. We have not only gone fishing but learned to reproduce our fishing trip in our imaginations. So empowered, we can also join Virginia Woolf in uddering/uttering the bull. When Woolf un-horns the bull, she un-mans the patriarchy. This message rings through all her writing. When she first suggested in "A Society" (1921) that "some way must be found for men to bear children," she wanted men to alter the destiny of their biology. When she wrote much later in "Thoughts on Peace in an Air-Raid" that "some way must be found to *compensate* the man for his gun," she was still offering to udder those ferocious native English bulls, her brothers. Difficult as this conspiracy is, it must include as well the most serious project facing all feminists, writing not only the bull with udders but the cow with horns, the return of the repressed "phallic mother." The signalling leaf is not only the mother's body but the voice of the nightingale, Philomel's tongue. *A Room of One's Own* gives utterance to her strangled cries.

⌁ 8 ⌁

Sapphistry:
Narration as Lesbian Seduction in
A Room of One's Own

> 'What,' said that good Dame, 'can you know
> about it, who have gentlemaned only?'
>
> —Djuna Barnes, *Ladies Almanack*, 1928
> (rpt. N.Y.: Harper and Row, 1972, 50)
>
> Homosexuality was not only institutionalized.
> It was mythologized in the two discourses
> that occupied practically the entire
> curriculum.
>
> —Noël Annan, "Portrait of the Genius as a
> Young Man" (*New York Review of Books*,
> 1984, 36–37)

The purpose of this essay is twofold: to return to Virginia Woolf's book, *A Room of One's Own* (1929), the circumstances of its material production, its historicity, and to suggest a reading based on its relation to the trial of Radclyffe Hall's novel, *The Well of Loneliness* (1928), for obscenity. In this reading we can identify the heroine of the essay, Judith Shakespeare, as Radclyffe Hall herself, and the narrator, the unnamed Mary (Hamilton) of the old Scots "Ballad of the Four Maries," as speaking in the voice of Mary (Llewelyn), Stephen Gordon's lover in *The Well of Loneliness*. (Woolf's narrative Mary is generic, but it is interesting to note if one doubts the generic power of "Mary" that Lovat Dickson in his biography of Radclyffe Hall, calls Stephen's lover Mary *Hamilton* instead of Mary Llewelyn three times and once calls her Mary Henderson.)[1] The essay as fictive "Mary (Hamilton)'s" gallows' song sings sisterhood in homoerotic tones, slyly seducing the woman reader and taunting patriarchal law just this side of obscenity. The metaleptic echo of the absent name of Mary (Hamilton) is, in Jefferson Humphries' words,[2] a "haunted trope," a ghostly allusion to an absence, and it mirrors the primal absence in the text of women's books on the shelves of the British Museum.

The unverbalized allusion to the narrator of the ballad and the lost beloved of Hall's novel cannot reverberate as an echo without the reader's recognition of the source of the echo. Since the success of *A Room* depends on the reader's collaboration in the conspiracy of its making, the critic's role here is to embody the historical context in which the disembodied voice of Echo can be reconstituted, to collect some of the scattered parts of the woman artist's body. The classical Echo is buried in pieces all over the earth, pieces that shriek and speak when stepped on, endlessly repeating the tag ends of statements as questions. Woolf's Judith is buried at the Elephant and Castle in one piece, or rather two pieces, since she is pregnant, and "she never wrote a word." Her resurrected self is Mary Hamilton, the narrator, who sings her ballad before she is publicly hanged for sexual transgression. Mary (Hamilton) echoes Judith Shakespeare and both voices echo Radclyffe Hall. Woolf's narrative voice is sexually and politically exciting for the woman reader because it simultaneously rings with fear of male reprisal for sexual and verbal transgression, it mourns our martyrs, and it also resurrects them. *A Room of One's Own* is a chamber of echoes, an echo chamber, in which Echo, the woman artist, who transgressed both sexually and verbally in the myth, may cease to seduce the self-loving narcissistic male with his own words, and may speak in *her* own words, having "put on the body which she has so often laid down," as Woolf says of Judith Shakespeare.

The second point I want to explore is the way *A Room of One's Own* lectures women students on the necessity of the female mentor, with the name of Jane Harrison (she had died that April), triumphantly initialed as "the great J. H.," used as another haunted trope, the shabby "phantom" of "terrible reality," which is set against the melodramatic villainy of Oscar Browning, whose name evokes the even more terrible reality of academic homosexual misogyny. The origin of the metaleptic troping of his name is far more complex and personal. Woolf could not fault the Cambridge homosexuals of her own circle, Strachey and Forster or Lowes Dickinson for their misogyny, but she could attack all they stood for in the name of Oscar Browning. Echoing even further back was Woolf's realization through reading Browning's life, that her own first cousin, J. K. Stephen, had been part of Browning's homosexual circle, was a misogynist poet, went mad, and committed suicide. These facts, I suggest, made her, at some level, question the veracity of her father as a biographer, for he had memorialized his nephew as "the Bard of Eton and of boyhood," in his biography of James Fitzjames Stephen. Consequently, in scapegoating Oscar Browning, Woolf worked out her anger at homosexual misogyny, her anger at her father, and her fear that the Stephen family "madness" connected her to her cousin, in that they were both writers and, however it may have been expressed, lovers of their own sex. [This essay is a companion piece to *Taking the Bull by the Udders*, and my references to uddering or uttering the bull, Woolf's de-masculinizing of the male, refer to the argument of the previous chapter.]

In a brilliant essay, "Literary Allusion as Feminist Criticism in *A Room of One's Own*," Alice Fox traces and analyzes Woolf's turning of allusion into a strategy for feminist criticism.[3] She rightly argues that the contemporary educated audience understood and responded to its fundamental feminist attack on patriarchal hegemony over culture, especially in the allusions to Milton, the Manx cat, and the Scots ballad. What I want to suggest here is that allusion or echo cannot function now without the reader's recognition of these allusions and the reader's response. Otherwise, Woolf's horror that she had lost her audience, the "No echo" confided to her diary just before her death, will be true. The critic must help the ghostly echo put on not only a body, but the body she wore in 1928 and 1929. Echo's voice needs both a literary and historical context. No one now reads William Black's historical novel, *Judith Shakespeare*, which so charmed the imagination of Victorian girls like Virginia Woolf. But I believe that it was in reading this "girls' novel" that Woolf first fantasized herself as both the Bard and his sister. Tillie Olsen in *Silences* has reminded readers of the passage in Olive Schreiner's little-read fictional study of prostitution, *From Man to Man*:

> We have a Shakespeare; but what of the possible Shakespeares we might have had, who passed their life from youth upward brewing currant wine and making pastries for fat country squires to eat, with no glimpse of the freedom of life and action, necessary even to poach on deer in the green forests, stifled out without one line written, simply because, being of the weaker sex, life gave us no room for action and grasp on life? [*From Man to Man*, 195]

A Room of One's Own is an echo chamber for readers like Tillie Olsen and Alice Fox, because they follow Woolf's instruction to think back through their literary mothers. But an allusion is not an echo until it rings a bell in the common reader's ear as well.

"Talks to Girls"

> "But my 'book' isn't a book—its only talks to girls."
>
> [*Letters*, 4, 102 (to Ethel Sands)]

A Room of One's Own, two lectures in six chapters, given at Newnham and Girton in October, 1928, is, first of all, a feminist subversion of the form of the academic *lecture*. Unschooled herself, Woolf despised lectures, seldom heard one and seldom gave one, except to audiences of women and working men. Several Stephens had lectured here before her. But no romantic old-girl nostalgia for Cambridge Octobers endowed her visit with a sense of carrying on a great tradition, though her grandfather had been a radical in making "Modern

History" a field and her father's lectures on 18th-century great men were radical with religious doubt and Victorian angst. Her first cousin, Katherine Stephen, Principal of Newnham, had recently died, but I suspect the kinship Woolf felt was to her mystical aunt Caroline Emelia Stephen's informal lectures to young Quaker outsiders, plain, unpretentious and sincere in their presentation.

In her memoirs, Kathleen Raine[4] describes Woolf's "talks to girls" at Girton. Her vivid recollection is of the presence of Vita Sackville-West with Virginia Woolf, descending "like goddesses" with the "divine mana" of their beauty and fame: "In the fairy land of the Girton reception-room, then, members of the Literary Society were gathered for coffee, after Hall; young Eton-cropped hair gleaming, Chinese shawls spread like the plumage of butterflies." The walls were embroidered with birds and flowers in wool on ivory satin, and oriental embroidery was draped over the grand piano. So the setting was as seductive as the speech. Despite Woolf's emphasis on the poverty of the women's colleges, the atmosphere was luxuriously feminine and relaxed. The presence of Vita Sackville-West was not only real but symbolic. *Orlando* had just appeared—a lesbian love letter, including photographs of Vita Sackville-West, and it was *not* on trial for obscenity. When Woolf asked the students to check that Sir Chartres Biron or Sir Archibald Bodkin were not eavesdropping, that they were all women in the room, the obscenity trial for *The Well of Loneliness* was still in progress.[5] The names of the patriarchs, while deliciously fictional in quality, were in fact real. Lesbianism itself was on trial as well as literary free speech, and it was well known that Vita had devoted much energy to organizing support for Radclyffe Hall. The audience would have known of Sir Chartres Biron's role as presiding magistrate in the case, and his refusal to consider "literary merit" as an issue and that Bodkin was Director of Public Prosecutions. In responding to Woolf's command to see that the offending magistrate was not hiding in a cupboard, the audience accepts the plot of the talk, that literary women gathered in a room to discuss women and writing are, at least symbolically, lesbians, and the Law is the enemy. The conspiracy she sets up with her audience is of women in league together against authority.[6] When she told the sad tale of Shakespeare's sister, her audience knew that Radclyffe Hall was descended from Shakespeare's daughter and that the supporters of Hall had tried to use Shakespeare's sonnets as evidence in the trial.[7] Like all great propagandists, Virginia Woolf exploited in her speech the death of a martyr in her cause. That Judith Shakespeare was a fiction did not prevent the audience from seeing her death as a sign of the suppression of lesbianism in the obscenity trial. Judith Shakespeare is certainly the universal figure of the oppressed woman artist, but she was also in the context of the times, "Radclyffe Hall." The informal "talks to girls" was an anti-lecture in form, but it also served as discourse of feminist conspiracy— both, one thinks to connect the non-feminist lesbians (like Vita Sackville-West and the Radclyffe Hall circle) with women's political cause, and to connect all women with the plight of lesbians. Much of *A Room* was meant simply to convert her beloved Vita to feminism, its seductive tone an extension of her love letters. By adopting Vita's lesbian cause (see her letter to *The Nation*, Sept. 8,

1928) in a public lecture, she was seducing Vita into accepting a larger feminism. Appearing with Vita at Girton in October before the final trial (Nov. 9) was
a public statement in a way of her own "sapphism." She often felt that she would
be "hinted at for a Sapphist" for writing this book, but her appearance with Vita
at Girton was more than a hint. The woman artist as seductress of her audience
is also the role played by Miss LaTrobe, the female descendant of the *troub-
adours*, as Radclyffe Hall is the descendant of bi-sexual Shakespeare. In
Between the Acts Sallie Sears points out the play's problem as "seduction gone
awry" when Miss LaTrobe cannot reach her audience.[8] LaTrobe was also the
name of an important abolitionist discussed in the *Life of Wilberforce* which
Woolf was reading to trace her "drop of common blood" with Octavia Wilberforce through her great grandfather's marriage. LaTrobe is in her pageant a
revisionist of English history as well as a lesbian.

Readers of *A Room* are part of a conspiracy, that word Woolf used to define
"us against them" with her sister in the nursery, with Margaret Llewelyn-
Davies and the Cooperative Working Women's Guild. We are all breathing
together in the relaxed anti-academic rhythm of her prose. Soon she has us
breathing hard (when we realize the exclusion of men from this text and begin to
fear their interruption or reprisal)—and then she has us breathing heavily, as
the erotic nature of her verbal enterprise becomes clear. If one who lectures
harbors a discreditable desire to convert (see the previous chapter), one who
give "talks to girls" harbors, and in this case, practices, a similarly powerful
and barely disguised, desire to seduce. In fact, I would argue that for the woman
reader this text is irresistible. I would agree with Sylvia Townsend Warner reading *Mrs. Dalloway*: "I felt like Joseph resisting Potiphar's wife."[9]

I believe *The Well of Loneliness* got its name from the reversal of the name of
a well-known homosexual and lesbian club in London in the twenties, mentioned by Vera Brittain, the Cave of Harmony. Radclyffe Hall and Una Troubridge were frequent visitors and Katherine Mansfield did impersonations
there. The club was named after the club in Thackeray's *The Newcomes*, famous
for impersonations, improvisations, and dirty songs. Hall's impulse may have
been political, with the words "well of loneliness" a realist attack on those
"caves of harmony" where rich, well-connected lesbians in Paris salons and the
international lesbian artistic community were protected from the scorn of family
and society. She may have been speaking for all those hungry Miss Kilmans in
their dirty mackintoshes who were ostracized because of class and poverty
while a Natalie Barney, a Princess de Polignac, or a Vita Sackville-West were
immune.

The Cave of Harmony was certainly a community "room of one's own" for the
intellectual *avant-garde* of the twenties in London, where Jews and radicals
joined cranks, vegetarians, lesbians, blacks, homosexuals, mystics, Quakers,
and poets, according to Douglas Goldring's *The 1920's* and Elsa Lanchester's
recent autobiography (St. Martin's, 1983). Elsa Lanchester, who inherited
Woolf's problematic servant, Nelly Boxall, and claimed she was an excellent
cook, was one of the founders of the Cave of Harmony at 107 Charlotte Street,

along with Harold Scott. They did Pirandello and Chekov as well as hilarious versions of Victorian songs, like "Please Sell No More Drink to My Father." One of Elsa Lanchester's favorite cabaret skits she called "Krafft-Ebing Case #74B Zurich" in which she portrayed "a nun called Blankebin [who]spent her time looking for the foreskin of Christ when he was circumcised." The poet Sylvia Townsend Warner captured the modernist atmosphere of united outsiders as she describes dancing with her lesbian lover to the music of a black saxophone player:

Caves of Harmony

Play, dark musician, play—
How almost human sounds your saxophone!
(Somewhere in Africa
An angry lion tosses up a bone.)

Sambo's a ready scholar
And hides his black skin under a black coat.
Although he wears a collar
Adam's own apple yet sticks in his throat.

Play, dark musician, play—
I see your imitation diamond flash.
(Once in America
Your fathers howled and writhed beneath the lash.)

How leers the blackamoor,
Exhaling his melodious delight!
Music's his paramour;
And yours, and mine, since we dance here tonight.

Play, dark musician, play—
Outdo the beast's roar and the scourged slave's moan.
Ambassador from the U.S.A.,
How almost human sounds your saxophone!

[Sylvia Townsend Warner, *Collected Poems*
(N. Y.: Viking, 1982) 90]

Uniting lesbian and black outsiders in the "almost human" Townsend Warner joins other women modernists, like Peggy Guggenheim, Nancy Cunard, and H. D., in the espousal of the cause of blacks. We often forget that Radclyffe Hall's training was in music and that her feminist hymn to the overthrow of all the patriarchal Jerichos, "Salvation," was set to music and sung by Paul Robeson. She was not only "Shakespeare's sister" but a lesbian Joshua calling for a "mighty noise" to topple the patriarchal walls.

Even more interesting is the connection between the Cave of Harmony and the 1917 Club. Elsa Lanchester recalls that she was the youngest member to meet in the "squalor" of 4 Gerrard Street, Soho, and Goldring quotes John Armstrong's verse: "In nineteen one seven they founded a club/Partly as brothel and partly as pub,/With a membership mainly of literary bores/ Redeemed by a girl in Giotto-pink drawers." The connection between the sexual outsiders and the political outsiders in the two clubs is very clear. I wonder if Virginia Woolf ever saw Elsa Lanchester's signature cabaret act in which she and Angela Baddeley every evening hung a clothesline with laundry across the stage and sat soaking their feet and discussing the day's news as two charwomen, Mrs. Bricketts and Mrs. Du Bellamy. I also like to think that the Pargiters' party in *The Years* takes place in Woolf's old political haunt, the 1917 Club, where Jane Harrison was always asking the young women writers why men made women into symbols and women writers did not.

What, then, will we call it when the woman writer seduces the woman reader? I have suggested *sapphistry* as a suitable term for this rhetorical seduction. It requires complete mastery of the structure of classical rhetoric to subvert powerlessness, acute consciousness of female otherness and difference to even wish to make maleness other and different. ("Been down so long it feels like up to me.") An earnest feminist appeal to political solidarity would not be half as effective as shameless flirtation, Woolf seems to feel. Not only narration but even punctuation is enlisted in her seductive plot: "Chloe liked Olivia. They shared a . . . " Dot dot dot is a female code for lesbian love. The draft of this lecture reveals that before writing "a laboratory," Woolf declared that she "thought of the obscenity trial for a novel." She didn't think much of *The Well of Loneliness* as a work of fiction or truth to female experience. Perhaps her asides and sexual jokes are meant to show Radclyffe Hall a trick or two, how to suggest that women do sometimes like women and avoid both the censor and lugubrious self-pity at the same time.

> I turned the page and read . . . I am sorry to break off so abruptly. Are there no men present? Do you promise me that behind that red curtain over there the figure of Sir Chartres Biron is not concealed? We are all women, you assure me? [*A Room*, 85]

The question marks and ellipses, to which we supply silent assent and fill in the blanks, seal the pact of our conspiracy. The rest of this flirtatious passage ("Do not start. Do not blush.") asserts as the norm that "women like women." Woolf's analysis of the style of Mary Carmichael's new novel is also couched in sexual terms. Her style seems to lack a sense of an ending: "To read this writing was like being at sea in an open boat"; "She was 'unhanding' herself as they say in the old plays." Reading *Life's Adventure*, "I feel as one feels on a switchback railway when the car, instead of sinking, as one has been led to expect, swerves up again. Mary is tampering with the expected sequence. First, she broke the sentence; now she has broken the sequence." It is perhaps not necessary to gloss the open boat as the vulva or the rising and falling without a single climax to female orgasm, to see an example of Woolf's usual references to language in sexual terms. As for "unhanding herself," it certainly can be read sexually. But "Unhand me, Sir," is also the cry of the damsel in danger of male violence, from which she rescues herself. The "expected sequence" is the structure of the novel on the model of male sexual experience. When she breaks it, "Up one went, down one sank." "I tried a sentence or two on my tongue" is also extremely suggestive. If Cixous wanted an example of "writing with the body" it is to be found here. If Radclyffe Hall wanted an example of lesbian writing, "the shortest of shorthand, in words that are hardly syllabled yet," it is here. If Mary Carmichael is to "catch those unrecorded gestures, those unsaid or half-said words" of the language of women, "she will need to hold her breath. . . ." We are, of course, as breathless as Mary Carmichael at Woolf's daring half-said suggestion that fiction is structured on the model of one's own sexual experience. But she leaves us in no doubt about this in her discussion of non-androgynous super-male texts, novels of "unmitigated masculinity":

> Do what she will, a woman cannot find in them that fountain of perpetual life which the critics assure her is there. It is not only that they celebrate male virtues, enforce male values and describe the world of men; it is that the emotion with which these books are permeated is to a woman incomprehensible. *It is coming, it is gathering, it is about to burst on one's head*, one begins saying long before the end. That picture will fall on old Jolyon's head; he will die of the shock; the old clerk will speak over him two or three obituary words; and all the swans on the Thames will simultaneously burst out singing. But one will rush away before that happens and hide in the gooseberry bushes, for the emotion which is so deep, so subtle, so symbolical to a man moves a woman to wonder.

This passage is not only amusing. It seems to me that it took great courage to say this on a public platform in 1928. Woolf's next assertion, that the novel of "unmitigated masculinity" leads directly to "the Fascist poem," foreshadows the analysis of the origin of fascism in the patriarchal family in *Three Guineas*. She calls it "a horrid little abortion." Since writing to Woolf is always a sexual act, abortion as the product of male writing is a significant epithet. (The word is not a common one for Woolf, though she calls Isa's writing in *Between the Acts* "abortive," because she is a prisoner of the patriarchal family and cannot act on the principles of sisterhood.) Then Woolf moves on to her well-known celebration of the androgynous mind of the artist. What I want to point out here is that Woolf's feeling for sexual difference privileges the female and describes the male literary product as a two-headed monster "in a glass jar in a museum in some country town." The typescript (Sussex) makes clear the connection between fascism, patriarchy, and male writing.

Let us look again at the opening pages of *A Room of One's Own*. Woolf identifies herself as a writer of fiction, a "liar"; she invents Oxbridge and Fernham, rejects "I" as unreal, and claims anonymity through the three Marys rather than identity as the descendant of Jane Austen and George Eliot.[10] (Here she outmaneuvers those who would call her a bourgeois feminist literary critic who

merely wants to replace the canon of great men with a canon of great women.)
Later in the text, Woolf quotes a contemporary male critic: "Women rarely
possess men's healthy love of rhetoric," and here, in the first four pages of her
text, she has led rhetoric, in the form of the traditional pedagogical lecture, a
merry chase. Twice she calls the burden of getting up the lecture a "collar." Is
this a reference to Dr. Johnson's dog? (On page 25 she quotes Johnson, her own
character Nick Green on Shakespeare's sister, and a modern musicologist on
women musicians.) Or is it a clerical collar that stirs memory of George
Herbert's poem or of her father, who gave up his professorship at Cambridge
because of his religious doubts? Or is it a trans-vesting into the shirt-collar of the
male professor? Or even the collar of "collar and tie," a slang reference to
lesbian dress?

In view of the fact that Woolf's "Oxbridge" merely conflates the names of two
existing predominantly male universities, her "Fernham" is a puzzle. The
"ham" is obviously from Newnham, but from what female garden or wilderness
does she get "Fern"? For, unmistakably, "Fern" has a feminine feel to it. I suggest that it comes from Gertrude Stein's first novel, *Fernhurst* (1904), an exposé
of lesbianism at Bryn Mawr with Carey Thomas as the model for a dominating
dean and Mary Gwinn, her lover, the English professor who in actual life ran
away with Gertrude and Leo Stein's friend, Alfred Hodder, but in Stein's novel,
remained at Bryn Mawr. Stein took her title from Greenhill-Fernhurst in
England where she had stayed in 1902, defending America to Bertrand Russell.
Carey Thomas was related to Russell's wife Alys, who was also a strong feminist,
and Woolf's brother Adrian married Karin Costelloe, another cousin. Gertrude
Stein's *Fernhurst* was published only recently but Stein had copied a great deal
of it into *The Making of Americans*, which Virginia Woolf read and rejected for
the Hogarth Press (although they did publish Stein's *Composition as Explanation*, 1926).[11] Gertrude Stein had studied at Radcliffe (then the Harvard Annex)
and published papers as a student of William James in experimental psychology. She was among the first women medical students at Johns Hopkins but left
just before taking her degree. In 1898 she had given a speech called "The Value
of a College Education for Women," based on Charlotte Perkins Gilman's
Women and Economics, seeing women's reform movements as puritanical in
the urge to control sexual drives, a project "all sex to destroy." One cannot help
but wonder if Woolf's successful female collective narrative strategy in *A Room
of One's Own* owes some of its brilliance to a reading of the difficulties of the
narrative struggle in *Fernhurst*. In Stein's novel, the opening tirade against
feminism that contradicts her earlier speech introduces a Guest of Honor who
baits the audience with praise in the "technical language of the hearer's profession." The narrator says that this is "dangerous" because it flatters the audience's
illusions. The disgusted narrator mounts the platform herself, to declare that
studying "classics and liberty" does not make it easier for a woman in the real
world—"we college women we are always college girls"—that the women's colleges are structured on male models so that education renders women as power-
less as they were before. Stein's narrator is A Woman Speaking as a Man. Woolf,

of course, refuses the role of Guest of Honor and invites the students and her readers into a co-narration that abolishes the dominating power relations that disturb Stein. The problem with Stein is that she doesn't trust her reader and will not share authority. While her narrator says that the reader "is probably tired of this posing," she means that she is tired of the pose. In her women's college, lesbian relations are structured on domination and submission and Miss Thornton, like any male dean, is the agent of the repression of desire. Stein, of course, was both an insider to the experience of the woman's college and a committed lesbian. Woolf romanticized women's education as a shared sexual experience from within a celibate marriage and while the "ivory rod" of the headmistress, in "A Woman's College From the Outside" represents authority, it is a female authority idealized as "protection," not a form of domination, and Woolf valorized a virginity that Stein would have seen as "puritanically feminist" in the interest of the repression of desire. Woolf's martyred Mary narrative voice allows a collective narration of sexual and verbal transgression that strips the author of her authority. Stein rebels against the patriarchy by appropriating the male voice, the woman speaking as a man, while Woolf speaks as Woman. Yet it is clear that Woolf learned from Stein how to write in the "continuous present."

In *A Room of One's Own* the narrator, divested of "Virginia Woolf," then tells us how she sat on a riverbank and looked at the reflections of a "burning tree" and a weeping willow, cast out her line (the image of the woman writer as fisherwoman which she works out later in "Professions for Women"), and caught a thought, too small a fish to keep. "I will not trouble you with that thought now, though if you look carefully you may find it for yourselves in the course of what I am going to say."

By now we are hooked, like her thought, the small fish. We women readers have been tangled in the net of a narrative seduction by the woman writer. She becomes steadily more feminist. At what point does the reader realize that she has agreed to go on this all-female fishing trip as *Celine and Julie Go Boating* (in the recent French film)? When do we realize that our inclusion in the "we" of this narrative marks the exclusion of the male reader? When the Beadle tells Mary What's Her Name that she may not trespass on the grass, when the Keeper tells her she may not enter the college library, I think we recognize that the text we are collaborating in making is just as clearly marked to men "No Trespassing," "Women Only." She has set up an "Us Against Them" situation; sides are drawn. The reader is excited by the novelty of the woman-to-woman writer-to-reader experience. The voice of the anonymous Marys is justified in its sense of oppression. But does the reader feel justified in her response? True, we have always had to contort and distort ourselves to read male texts, but will we do unto men what they have done to us?

With whom will the male reader identify when he reads *A Room of One's Own*? The sexist homosexual professor, Oscar Browning? The forbidding Beadle at the college gates? The student with the ready-made tie in the British Museum? Professor von X? Surely, she will not lock him out of her book as she is locked out of the university and its library? Ah, I have it, he finds Shakespeare, Shakespeare of the incandescent mind, the androgynous genius. To find a hero, a place for himself in this text, the male reader must deny his own gender and Shakespeare's. To get off the horns of his dilemma he must de-sex Shakespeare, recognize his androgyny, for he cannot identify with the cast of male villains in this piece. The price of male admission to the woman's room of this text is acceptance of the notion of Shakespeare's genius as bi-sexual. He must tacitly agree that the greatest of English writers was not great because he was male—an agreement that takes some of the sting out of the eternal "Why is there no woman Shakespeare"?

In *A Room of One's Own*, Shakespeare saves us from sexism. The woman writer and the woman reader are collaborating on the making of the first modern text of feminist criticism. If they were, in that lecture-room at Newnham or Girton, to exclude men entirely, they would simply reverse sexual prejudice. Woolf merely makes it very difficult for men to claim a place within this text without admitting misogyny. Oscar Browning, Professor von X, and male figures from Napoleon to Mussolini are named and quoted. As Mary What's Her Name quotes them, no liberal-minded male—and who else would be reading *A Room of One's Own*?—can claim identity (at least not openly) with their misogyny. To insert himself into this text, the male reader must read Shakespeare as "man-womanly" and androgynous.

That is also the point of the presence of the Manx cat. After the splendid luncheon at the men's college this "abrupt and truncated animal" changes the "emotional light" for the narrator: "Something seemed lacking, something seemed *different*." In one paragraph (pp. 11–12) she uses the word "different" seven times, comparing the romantic rhythms and sentiments of love lyrics of Tennyson and Christina Rossetti at a college luncheon party before the war to the present moment. The lecturer reads the two love lyrics by "Alfred" and "Christina" as she calls them, bursts out laughing, calls them "ludicrous," and "explains" her laughter by pointing to the Manx cat. On a university platform in October, 1928, Virginia Woolf explodes the narrow Victorian notion of sexual difference implicit in the love lyrics: "Why has Alfred ceased to sing 'She is coming, my dove, my dear?' Why has Christina ceased to respond 'My heart is gladder than all these/Because my love is come to me?'" Her answer is that romance was killed in the war.

But what is the Manx cat doing in this narrative? Does it refer to Bella/Bello calling Bloom a "Manx cat" in *Ulysses*? "The tailless cat, though some are said to exist in the Isle of Man, is rarer than one thinks. It is a queer animal, quaint rather than beautiful. It is strange what a difference a tail makes—" (13). In what tone of voice were there words spoken? Did the women students laugh when she said "What a *difference* a tail (read penis) makes?" Is the "Isle of Man" the men's college, and that "quaint" and "queer" animal on the lawn one of the "old deans and old dons" like "giant crabs and crayfish" she described earlier? Did the young women write in their notebooks "what a difference a tail makes" or "beware of apostolic buggers" or "steer clear of the queens at Kings"?

The Manx cat also arrives in Woolf's text by way of a review she wrote (5 Feb. 1920, CW 149–151) of Aldous Huxley's short story collection, *Limbo*. She quotes his portrait of the eccentric headmaster's wife, Mrs. Crawister, "a lady of 'swelling port' and unexpected utterance, who talks to the bewildered boys now about eschatology, now about Manx cats ('No tails, no tails, like men. How symbolical everything is!')" (*CW*, 150). But Woolf took more than the Manx cat from *Limbo*. Huxley invents two colleges, named Aesop and Cantaloup, and also, in 'Richard Greenow,' he explores gender and writing, as Woolf does in *Orlando* and *A Room*. Richard plays with dolls as a boy and is a "hermaphrodite" writer. His male self is mathematical, a socialist and pacifist. But his female writing self, Pearl Bellairs, writes sentimental fiction and jingo patriotic articles, both of which make money. This division of serious politics and rationality as male and prolific conservativism as female surely prompted Woolf's response in *Orlando* and *A Room*.[12]

The Manx cat's missing tail is a representation of women's missing tales in the men's college setting and culture at large. *A Room* is not simply a declaration of difference from male writing, but a questioning of the difference within difference. She asks not only how is women's writing different from men's, but who speaks for working-class women? How is the lesbian writer to say "Chloe liked Olivia?" As I said in the previous chapter, the idea of the androgynous mind of the artist comes directly after the leaf falls, the ambiguous taxi floats the couple downstream and Woolf expresses her discomfort with notions of sexual opposition and unity. In trying to deal with the maternal imperative, the definition of the feminine as the opposite of the masculine, the imaginary "cooperation of the sexes," Woolf hits on a temporary solution in the idea of androgyny: "Ought not education to bring out and fortify the differences rather than the similarities? For we have too much likeness as it is" (92). Androgyny means erasure of difference. How can she hold both views at once? Androgyny, it becomes clear, is a good idea for overly masculine writers to try, though the opposite does not hold true. That is, the arguments are not logical. She is biased in favor of women. When she says "the book has somehow to be adapted to the body," (81) she means the female body.

If Woolf took the Manx cat from Huxley and contradicted his equation of women's writing with romantic trash and right-wing ideologies, she also took the idea of the Ballad of the Four Marys from her husband and remade it for feminism. Leonard Woolf's *The Wise Virgins* (1914) links the ballad with talk of charwomen and maids in a text where he portrays his own relationship with Virginia quite openly.[13]

Henry Davis, the autobiographical hero, is arguing with his mother and the neighboring Garlands about the wretchedness of servants' lives. But Mrs. Davis and Mrs. Garland turn the conversation to the difficulties of getting good servants:

... for the next quarter of an hour she poured out the lore of servants, their follies, stupidities, and vices; the unmentionable horrors of their bedrooms; their dirtiness, carelessness, ingratitude. She told the tale of Marys and Ellens and Kates; how one had broken a valuable old glass that "my poor brother" had brought from Venice, how one had been discovered "quite intoxicated" on the kitchen floor, and another—this in a whisper—had to be bundled quickly out of the house for disgraceful behaviour, or rather the result of it . . . The two ladies now pulled their chairs together, bent their heads to one another, and spoke in lowered voices. An atmosphere of the scullery and the dirty-clothes basket gathered around them. And through it all to Harry . . . floated only disconnected sentences and the long list of women's names, Mary and Ellen and Agnes and Ethel, that excited and irritated him by vague suggestions and the romance of all they might mean. Familiar and endearing, they seemed to be used with cynical mockery of him in the sordid, greasy chronicles of his mother and Mrs. Garland. Mary, Agnes, Ellen, Ethel! The names sang in his ears with snatches of poetry that came to him again and again. 'Mary Beaton and Mary Seaton (sic) and Mary Carmichael and me.' 'Bertha Broadfoot, Beatrice, Alice and Ermanyard, the lady of Maine, and that good Joan whom Englishmen at Rouen . . .' 'Mary Beaton and Mary Seaton and Mary Carmichael and me.' [*The Wise Virgins*, 19, 20]

Virginia Woolf was just as romantic as Harry (and Leonard Woolf) about women's names. Here Leonard conflates the four Marys with charwomen as Woolf does in *A Room*, as well as conflating, by his ellipses after Joan of Arc, the martyrdom of women, saints, maids, and Mary Hamilton who sings the ballad. Despite their pregnancies the working-class maid and the maid of honor are virginal heroines (wise virgins?) whose deaths are equated with the burning of the Maid of Orleans at the stake for insisting on her visions and voices against the French patriarchal church and "Englishmen at Rouen."

Virginia Woolf's "Mary Carmichael," whose disruptive novel endears her to deconstruction and contemporary feminist critics, also had a source familiar to her readers, but unfamiliar to us now. In 1928 the famous advocate of birth control Marie Stopes published a novel called *Love's Creation* under the name Marie Carmichael (London: John Bale, 1928). Stopes's *Married Love* and her opening of birth control clinics had made her a very controversial figure. Her novel opens with two women in a laboratory, setting the scene for Woolf's Chloe and Olivia.[14]

Marie Stopes's *Love's Creation* was published under her maiden name, Marie Carmichael. "As 'Lewis Carroll' means to the public 'Alice' and not mathematics; so 'Marie Carmichael' means a novel and not sexology or paleontology," her publishers boasted. It does indeed open in a laboratory where the cleaner wishes for the presence of women students. The author kills off the scientist on her honeymoon and her sister, the Womanly Woman, gets the hero, after her husband is abruptly killed off as well (Marie Stopes practiced eugenics in fiction as well as in politics). There is a lot of talk about sexually unawakened women along with evolutionary theory applied to social questions, the whole as much of a muddle as Marie Stopes's mixture of radical birth control theory and conservative politics. Like Woolf's imaginary *Life's Adventure*, the prose style makes one feel like being out at sea in an open boat, but not for the same reason. Given the extreme difficulty of holding a job if you were married after the men returned from WWI in England, Woolf's dream of a married woman working in a lab is utopian.

How to write in a notebook is the subject of chapter two. The scene has shifted to London to the British Museum, a public library which does not reject her as the university library did. The narrator's tone is light and amusing but a "little fish" is thrown out for the students to catch. Explicit instructions are given in how to do research, how to use the card catalogue, and how to collect notes. Her audience is being instructed in how to take her place on the platform and told what questions to pursue as feminist historians. (The difference between lecturer and lectured is erased.) She is no longer standing but sitting— we are all readers and note-takers. Procne is reading Philomel's text; we are reading with her—the original meaning of the word *lecture* is restored, "the action of reading." Both admonition and domination have disappeared. She demystifies scholarship but warns women to wear "claws of steel and a beak of brass" to protect us while we work. Later she says, "The history of men's opposition to women's emancipation is more interesting perhaps than the story of that emancipation itself. An amusing book might be made of it if some young student at Girton or Newnham would collect examples and deduce a theory— but she would need thick gloves on her hands, and bars to protect her of solid gold" (57). She reveals that she keeps a notebook of misogynist quotations. It is labelled "cock-a-doodle-dum" and she keeps it "for reading to select audiences on summer nights." She is under no illusion about the dangers inherent in feminist history or feminist literary criticism. Before a select audience of women students at Newnham and Girton, she reads aloud the contents of this notebook and the list (p. 28) is a rhetorical device used to great effect. I have often read *A Room of One's Own* as the first modern text in feminist history and literary criticism, concentrating on its instructions and demonstrations of "thinking back through our mothers," finding and evaluating women's works and lives. But I had ignored her simultaneous practice of criticism of male texts, her insistence that her student followers look up the letter M in the British Museum, as well as the letter W, to find out why "women do not write books about men," why women are "so much more interesting to men than men are to women?" The seduction of the woman reader by the writer of *A Room of One's Own* has two purposes, to inculcate sexual solidarity by establishing difference and claiming that difference as superior, and the recruitment and enlistment of a new generation of women in the cause of feminist scholarship. The artist, the historian, or the critic have all been assigned their tasks in the conspiratorial "cell" of our "room." Secrecy has not only been sexually suggestive but politically primary. When we leave these lectures we have practically pledged ourselves to "write like women." We have been seduced into sisterhood.

Cock-a-doodle-dum: The Name of the Father

> I am writing about sodomy at the moment
> and wish I could discuss the matter with
> you; how far one can say openly what is the
> relation of a woman and a sod? In French,
> yes; but in Mr. Galsworthy's English, no.
>
> [VW, Letter 2850, to Quentin Bell]

The relation of women to male homosexuals and homosexuals to women is not a subject discussed in the recent histories of homosexuality. Jeffrey Weeks in *Coming Out* and in his fine essay in *The Making of the Modern Homosexual* actually does discuss the other important issue, that of class, as well as the social construction of homosexuality in Britain. The field is a young one, of course, and it is to be expected that homosexuals of the late nineteenth and early twentieth centuries should appear heroic to their historians.[15] But what concerns me here is that for women like Virginia Woolf, the homosexual men of Cambridge and Bloomsbury appeared to be, not the suffering victims of heterosexual social prejudice, but the "intellectual aristocracy" itself,[16] an elite with virtual hegemony over British culture. E. M. Forster, Lytton Strachey, Goldsworthy Lowes Dickinson, and their friends were misogynist in their lives as well as their writing. Virginia Woolf, already exacerbated by her own sense of sexual difference was, I think, confused and disturbed by the woman-hating of her male homosexual friends, and this is the origin of that difficult passage in *A Room of One's Own* on Oscar Browning, which appears to be uncharacteristically intolerant in a writer who produced so many sympathetic portraits of homosexuals in her fiction. The passage results from her anger and sadness at the realization of the loss of these men as allies in her own cause. She had, I believe, thought of them as fellow outsiders, expected them to support her feminism as brothers in oppression. While they supported Radclyffe Hall politically, they clearly despised lesbians and women, personally. They did not see the patriarchal family or the patriarchy itself as the enemy. They did not ally themselves by sexual preference with lesbians or by a sense of sexual oppression with feminists, but by *gender*, with men, and with the power of the patriarchy itself. Why were they not punished by the patriarchy for their own deviance?

The patriarchs often were products of the same educational system at Eton and Cambridge, where "the Greek view of life" was glorified by the most elite secret societies like the Apostles.[17] The sexual relations between men in school appear to have been hierarchical power relations between the strong and the weak and thus reinforcements of patriarchal structures. It does not appear that the homosexuality of these upper-class men threatened the patriarchal family. Lytton Strachey was protected by a large and powerful family. Morgan Forster did not demand that his policeman lover leave his wife and children. The choosing of lovers from the working class or among boys in foreign countries or across an age gap reinforced a power relationship. Men like Harold Nicolson married, produced children, and practiced their homosexuality while supporting a conservative family structure. We have no sociological studies to tell us in what numbers the wives of these men were or were not lesbians. But it would be interesting to know if any evidence exists of dissatisfaction on the part of the wives of these elite Eton and Cambridge men. We have one rather telling Victorian example in the life of Lady Henry Somerset, Virginia Woolf's mother's first cousin.[18] She was married by her family to the already notorious Lord Henry, later forced into exile because of his involvement in a scandal relating to a homosexual brothel. She produced a son and returned to her mother after two years of suffering. Though she obtained a divorce, her child went to her husband's family, and she was socially ostracized. Her own sister would not see her; the attitude in society was that the young virgin was married to the confirmed homosexual in order to convert him to heterosexuality. She was to blame that he preferred his footman; it was somehow her fault. Lady Somerset went on to become the national and international leader of the Temperance Movement, as well as dedicating her time and money to "fallen women" in an institution built on her property. Was this case unusual or common in that class?

If the patriarchy tolerated elite homosexuals because they did not threaten the family, the Forsters and Lowes Dickinsons paid their debt to the fathers by the overt misogyny of their writing. Perhaps unconsciously in the belief that it would please the patriarchs or perhaps to protect themselves from the fathers' wrath, they combined their glorification of Greek love with the denigration of women. Unlike the pro-feminist homosexuals, Edward Carpenter and Laurence Housman, whose conception of sexual freedom was broadly based and political, the men in Woolf's circle saw their sexual practice as separating them from mankind, rather than uniting them in an ideal of social progress. This is true of Radclyffe Hall's tragic vision of "inversion" in *The Well of Loneliness* as well. Weeks suggests that Hall and Una Troubridge applied for membership in the secret homosexual rights organization of George Ives, the Order of Chaeronea, but he may have meant the British Sexological Society.

The papers of both organizations are in the Harry Ransom Humanities Research Center at the University of Texas, as are the papers from both the British and American obscenity trials of *The Well of Loneliness*.[19] The British Sexological Society invited Radclyffe Hall to speak after the trial, but she declined, citing her Catholic beliefs as a conflict with some of the goals of the society. The trial papers deserve a fuller treatment than I can offer here. But it is interesting to note the number of artists who joined the protest. The Americans included Hemingway, Fitzgerald, Dos Passos, Dreiser, Sherwood Anderson, H. L. Mencken, Susan Glaspell, Ellen Glasgow, and Edna St. Vincent Millay. Edna Ferber, like Virginia Woolf, supported the principle, not the book, but allowed her name to be used because, she said, she feared that the New York Vice Society might discover the Old Testament. Robert Nathan wrote "the book is dull and honest and about as immoral as *Pilgrim's Progress*"; and Sinclair Lewis found it "almost lugubriously moral"; Joseph Wood Krutch pronounced "there are no indecent facts."

Virginia Woolf and her fellow writers were not allowed to give testimony at the trial, but depositions were taken from them which are in the trial papers. Woolf stated that she had read the novel and that "In my opinion, *The Well of Loneliness* treats a delicate subject with great decency and discretion."[20] Leonard's deposition is much fuller, and he also reviewed the book favorably in *The Nation*. Among the papers is an anonymously compiled list of lesbian literature, including Gertrude Atherton's *The Crystal Cup*, Sylvia Stevenson's *Surplus*, Rosamond Lehmann's *Dusty Answer*, Naomi Royde Smith's *The Tortoiseshell Cat*, and a 1904 novel by Maurice Hewlett, *The Queen's Quair*,[21] which is annotated as being about the lesbian relation of Mary Queen of Scots to her lady-in-waiting, Mary Beaton.[22] It is about no such thing, but rather a contribution to the controversy of Andrew Lang about the "Casket Letters," suggesting an affair between the Queen and Bothwell. (Hewlett defines a quair as a cahier, a quire of paper, a little book, like "The King's Quair," of Mary's ancestor, which was a diary of his love life. The compiler of the list may have simply extrapolated from the title.) Contemporary historians dismiss the idea and in Antonia Fraser's 1969 biography it is assumed that the papers were forged. Mary Beaton's handwriting was much like the Queen's, because all five Marys were educated together in France. Hewlett's novel repeats the tale of the Queen and her "Maries," "virgins, maids, Maries, demoiselles of honour, or the Queen's *mignons*, call them as you please, your Honour," wrote Randolph, the English ambassador in 1563. This passage is quoted in D. Hay Fleming's *Mary Queen of Scots*, published in 1897. Louise De Salvo's research shows that Virginia Stephen read a biography of the queen, and this seems a likely candidate, with its "call them as you please" echoing in *A Room of One's Own* as "Call me Mary Beton, Mary Seton, Mary Carmichael or by any name you please." Fleming emphasizes the Queen's youthful happiness and freedom with her four Marys. They were fond of adopting male dress and the queen herself, like Virginia Woolf's Orlando, dressed as a man to wander the streets incognito. Woolf's use of the ballad's Marys for her narration of *A Room of One's Own* has complex roots: her reading during that difficult adolescent year, when she longed for friends and companions of her own, as De Salvo notes; the publication of *Orlando*; and the obscenity trial. The ballad of the Queen's Maries was *in fact* based on the story of a Scots lady-in-waiting to Queen Catherine of Russia. *That* Mary Hamilton had a child by Tsar Peter and was hanged. But Woolf would have known the ballad from its attribution in Sir Walter Scott's *Minstrelsy* as a legend of Mary Queen of Scots. Scott took this from John Knox's attack on the queen and her four Maries in his *Monstrous Regiment of Women*. Mary Beaton and Mary Seton were in reality the queen's handmaidens; Mary Carmichael and Mary Hamilton were not the actual names of the other two, who were Mary Fleming and Mary Livingstone.

There was, however, another historical Mary Hamilton, whose story may have surfaced during the meetings regarding the defense for the Radclyffe Hall trial, which both Virginia and Leonard attended. In 1746, Henry Fielding, novelist and judge, published a pamphlet called *The Female Husband: or, the*

Surprising History of Mrs. Mary, Alias Mr. George Hamilton . . . Fielding found her guilty of marriages to three women and ordered her whipped publicly in four market towns in Somerset.[23] The result of all of these allusions and echoes behind the names of her narrators is a muddle and confusion regarding women that exactly mirrors Woolf's experience in the British Museum as a historian bent on "truth." There is no truth about women. What one finds are legends based on legends. The factors that stand out are anonymity and the comradeship in chastity of the queen's Maries, the equation of pregnancy with death, as in the life of her own Judith Shakespeare. The cross-dressing of Mary and her maids, their ability to ride and hunt, was also important, and this, as well as Shakespeare's heroines, also contributed to *Orlando*.

A *Room of One's Own* has another echo of *The Well of Loneliness*, which Angela Ingram points out. The Fernham passage where Jane Harrison appears like a phantom ends an excited description, in denial of the "fact" that it was fall, of the spring garden, dim and intense "as if the scarf which the dusk had flung over the garden were torn asunder by star or sword—the flash of some terrible reality leaping, as its way is, out of the heart of the spring. For youth—."[24] This echoes chapter 38 of *The Well* and its love scene in the dim, sweet garden "and something in the quality of Mary's youth, something terrible and ruthless as an unsheathed sword, would leap out at such moments and stand between them." The star or sword that tears the veil to reveal the leaping reality could be read in many ways. Earlier in this book I described it as a visionary reference to Caroline Emelia Stephen and the female mystics. But it may also be read here as a reference to the lesbian novel. For, not only did Chloe like Olivia; Jane Harrison liked Hope Mirrlees, and they appear to have shared more than their research on the mythology of Russian bears. Surely some of the Cambridge audience would have thought of Harrison in this connection as well as for her great and pioneering role as a scholar.

Although Jane Harrison is given her full name later in the text, here in this emotional passage she is not only ghostly in body but her name is reduced to initials. The use of initials in this text is as complex as the narrative Marys and the ellipses. The absences indicated by anonymity and unsaid words reflect woman's absence from history, but they are also sexually suggestive of women's love of women. We note that "Professor von X" suggests professional misogyny; the von suggests the aristocracy and also plays on England's ambivalent attitude toward Germany between the wars. Mr. A, the novelist, and Mr. B, the critic, lose some of their power over us by their reduction to initials. The absence of their whole names, unlike women's absences, tends to equalize them with women. Robbed of their fame, they intimidate us less as A and B or "old Professor Z." It may be a coincidence that the men are designated by letters at the beginning and the end of the alphabet, but it does make them somehow terminal, and unreal, suggesting a solid chunk of reality in between. By naming them in such a truncated way, she is also verbally castrating them in a sense, like the Manx cat. And Mary Carmichael (who was really Marie Stopes) is fully named in the text as the imaginary novelist. The Marys, with their suggestion of maidenhood and anonymous disguise, are Woolf's literary ladies-in-waiting. She is having a fling as the slightly sapphist author of *Orlando*, queen of the literary world at least for a day, and a "figure" to the students. She is also capitalizing on the obscenity trial for a lesbian novel in a book about women's writing, forever linking the two subjects in her pages.

The most intriguing naming in *A Room of One's Own* is that troubling passage on *Mr.* Oscar Browning.[25] He is, of course, the villain of the piece, and is contrasted to Jane Harrison, who is the heroine. Oscar Browning was seldom called by his full name, still less called "Mr." While not a professor, at Cambridge, he was a permanent Fellow of King's and a considerable figure in his day. He was always familiarly known as "O.B." or "the O.B.," and many rhymes and limericks were in circulation, some by himself, which played on his initials. By transferring the familiarity of initials to Jane Harrison and spelling out Browning's full name and sarcastically repeating the "Mr.," Woolf turns the rhetorical tables. Her purpose is instruction. The women students are being told to choose a female mentor, that male homosexual academics are misogynist. Woolf suggests by the nature of her naming that women keep their distance from male teachers and reserve the familiarity and respect which the nicknaming represents, for their female teachers.

Trying to measure "the effect of discouragement upon the mind of the artist" (p. 54), Woolf cities a dairy company's experiments with Grade A and ordinary milk. The Grade A milk produces a glossy, bold, big rat, and the ordinary milk one that is "furtive, timid and small." The woman writer as rat is an interesting notion, but let us look at her portrait of the Great Discourager. "I will quote," she says to her audience of women students:

> Mr. Oscar Browning, because Mr. Oscar Browning was a great figure in Cambridge at one time, and used to examine the students at Girton and Newnham. Mr. Oscar Browning was wont to declare "that the impression left on his mind, after looking over any set of examination papers, was that, irrespective of the marks he might give, the best woman was intellectually the inferior of the worst man." After saying that, Mr. Browning went back to his rooms—and it is this sequel that endears him and makes him a human figure of some bulk and majesty—he went back to his rooms and found a stable-boy lying on the sofa "a mere skeleton, his cheeks were cavernous and sallow, his teeth were black, and he did not appear to have the full use of his limbs . . . 'That's Arthur' (said Mr. Browning). 'He's a dear boy really and most high-minded.'" The two pictures always seem to me to complete each other. And happily in this age of biography, the *two pictures often do complete each other*, so that we are able to interpret the *opinions of great men not only by what they say*, but by what they do. [55]

Virginia Woolf's mention of the rats was an appeal to the concerns of her audience, for the women's colleges were over-run by rats, and she later quoted newspaper articles to this effect in "Professions for Women" and *Three Guineas*. Woolf remembers the prunes and custard and asks, "What food do we feed women artists upon?" In the biography of Oscar Browning (1927) which she quotes here and his own *Memories of Sixty Years* (1910), the encounter with the notorious gourmand, lover of boys, friend of her uncle Fitzjames Stephen and tutor to her cousin, J. K. Stephen, must have been enough to turn her stomach. One sees her thumbing the index for references to her family. Opposite an unkind reference to the impossibility of Browning's dancing with "Miss Stephen" at Cambridge, because of her "commanding stature," his biographer quotes a sonnet Browning wrote for a dinner of "the Extremes," another under-graduate dining club at King's. This poem is surely the source for Woolf's classic description of the dinner at Oxbridge:

> Fair Goddess, Hater of the Golden Mean,
> Smile on thy sons Extreme, and as they dine,
> Fill them with juicy meats and joyous wine
> Till Moderation, vanquished, leaves the scene.
> Consummate soup with sherry; and between
> The crisped smelts infuse the gay Sauterne.
> Stir up the thoughts that breathe the words that burn
> With foaming grape of amber-coloured sheen,
> Bottled by good Count Robert of Avise.
> Grant us a Gallic entree, sure to please,
> A haunch of venison from the haunts of Herne.
> Through icy creams and devilled savouries.
> Guide us, till half inspired and half distraught,
> Like storm-tossed mariners we reach our port.
>
> [H. E. Wortham, *Oscar Browning*,
> London: Constable, 1927, p. 184]

Wortham quotes "a friend," defending Browning from the charge of being "attracted" to the continual parade of working-class boys and sailors he be-friended:

> I remember, for instance, going to see him in his rooms one evening when he had just returned from Paris, and there on the sofa in the dining-room reposed a shabbily dressed and apparently exhausted youth. He was a mere skeleton, his cheeks were cavernous and sallow, his teeth were black, and he did not appear to have the full use of his limbs. Altogether he was a terrible looking object. I went in and talked to O.B., who was in his inner room. As I was leaving, I asked him who his visitor was. "Oh," he said, "that's Arthur" (or some other Christian name). "He's been a stable boy at Chantilly and was shamefully misused. They starved him to get his weight down and then beat him because he lost his strength. Finally, they threw him out. I found him destitute in Paris, and the only thing I could do was to bring him back with me. He's a dear boy really, and most high-minded." . . . what inspired him, I think, was a sort of Franciscan feel-ing for humanity at large. [*Oscar Browning*, 246-47]

It was not a Christian motive that inspired Woolf to put the picture of Arthur next to the picture of Browning's attitude toward women students so that they might "complete" each other. Browning's biographer also tells the story of "a lecturer at Girton, who was his colleague upon some university examination board, and was irritated with him for giving indifferent marks to the women candidates, wondered sweetly how he had managed to look over the papers so quickly. He replied equally sweetly: "Genius, madam, sheer genius" (231). It was the same sense of his own genius that allowed him to believe that the best of the women could not equal the worst of the men. Woolf was so rankled by Browning's remark that she quoted (misquoted) it again in *The Pargiters*. In the Fifth Essay of *The Pargiters* (the factual chapters which were to have been interspersed between the fictional chapters of *The Years*) Woolf collects and comments on male professors' disdain for women's education. She cites Mark Pattison, Dr. Andrews, Walter Pater—and, as in *A Room of One's Own*, the difference between the male scholars and Lucy Craddock is described in terms of appetite. The "old humbugs" spill soup, drink port, smoke cigars, and put their hands on the knees of young girls. Kitty thinks the professor would know a great deal more about Greek art "if he scrubbed out his bed-sitting room as Lucy Craddock did." "Poor Lucy's little book on the Angevin Kings was treated as the scribblings of an industrious child" (*TP*, 124). She quotes a 1907 life of Walter Pater on a women's college "gaudy":

> . . . in the course of the evening, the lady head of the house dropped her white kid glove in front of Pater; and Pater, at least, thought that she did it on purpose. Therefore, he "instead of gallantly picking it up, walked up and trod on it." Didn't you see *that*? whispered a friend who stood near.
> "Didn't you see how I rewarded the action?" followed Pater. "If I had not remembered how, in spite of the honours heaped upon him by Queen Elizabeth, Sir Walter Raleigh was in the end led out to execution, perhaps I, too, might have made a fool of myself. Believe me, my dear sir, it was an insinuation of the devil that caused this woman to drop her glove."

Three pages later Woolf quotes Oscar Browning's judgment again "that the lowest man is intellectually the superior of the cleverest woman."

Why does she choose Browning as her scapegoat? Clearly Browning's Arthur, the French stableboy, is meant to be connected later to the middle-class Arthur of "Arthur's Education Fund" in *Three Guineas*. Their needs come before any women's, the text suggests. The money and time of tutors, as well as families, is devoted to one Arthur or another. But I think there is a deeper reason for this uncharacteristic outburst. "Let us suppose," *A Room* continues, "that a father from the highest motives did not wish his daughter to leave home and become a writer, painter, or scholar. 'See what Mr. Oscar Browning says,' he would say" (55).

What she read in the biography of Oscar Browning was the text of the patriarchy exposing its phallocentric power as clearly as the pervert exposes himself to Rose in *The Years*, to freeze women's "powers of expression." It was her own father who was the culprit, the Stephen men who wielded this power by their support of men like Oscar Browning. She had been living with the illusion that the homosexual and bi-sexual men of Bloomsbury were women's natural allies and fellow outsiders, that they were all fellow-sufferers from Victorian repression and suppression. The rage behind this outburst comes from the discovery that the name of the father includes the name of the son, even if he is a homosexual or a suicide. The patriarchy protects its own and male bonding seems to transcend all other bonds in society. The names of Angela, Eleanor, and Phoebe on little white cards outside the doors of the women's colleges as in "A Woman's College from the Outside" will fade and disappear, but bronze plaques at Eton and King's College will last forever, as fathers' tributes to dead sons and sons' tributes to dead fathers, despite their misdeeds and misogyny.

Let us reconstruct what happened as Virginia Woolf read Oscar Browning's biography. Very quickly after his brother Fitzjames's death in 1895, Leslie Stephen rushed into print with a monumental biography of the famous conservative, bullying justice, depicting him as a great man. The book also contains a eulogy for Fitzjames's son, J. K. Stephen. Leslie and Julia were very fond of their nephew, "our Jem" and he is praised as "the bard of Eton and of boyhood" as Leslie tells of his untimely death at thirty-three and the family's erection of bronze plaques at Eton and King's College, Cambridge, where both men had been Apostles. He does not mention homosexuality or scandal or the friendship of both men with Oscar Browning.

Wortham's biography of Oscar Browning was also a whitewash. In his attempt to clear Browning's name of the scandal of being fired from Eton, he used the illustrious names of Fitzjames and J. K. Stephen and inadvertently revealed to Virginia, the reader, that her father, the biographer, had left out some important events in Stephen family history. It began with a boating party at Eton in the 1870s, chaperoned by Oscar Browning and his friend Walter Pater. A novel about a lesbian was the cause of it all. Apparently, a lady heard Pater recommend reading *Mlle de Maupin* to one of the boys (who drowned mysteriously shortly afterwards). The novel in question is worth study as a male version of female transvestism. The lady told Annie Thackeray, who told Leslie Stephen. Browning was fired, his defenders say, for academic reasons, but the scandal of his relationship with his students remained alive. To show his support for his fellow Apostle, Fitzjames Stephen allowed his son J. K. Stephen to leave Eton with his master to travel in Germany until the smoke cleared. Browning then went back to King's College as a permanent Fellow, and his student came up to join him. They quarrelled, the biographer reveals, over who was to have the tutorship of the Duke of Clarence, J. K. Stephen being chosen over his master.

It is this relationship that leads Michael Harrison and others to put J. K. Stephen on the list of candidates for Jack the Ripper.[26] Clarence died young, supposedly of the flu. Stephen, confined to a nursing home as mad, by Savage, the same doctor who later treated Virginia, stopped eating at the news of Clarence's death and died three weeks later. The family suppressed the first edition of Stephen's poems, *Lapsus Calami*, which contained the most violent pornographic fantasy about killing prostitutes, "Kaphoozalem." But there is enough misogyny in the revised version to appall any reader. Quentin Bell describes his kinsman as "a massive, powerful, genial figure," "the author of light, ingenious verses." I imagine Virginia Woolf reading this one while preparing her lectures for *A Room of One's Own*. It is called "A Thought" and was published in *Granta*, the Cambridge literary magazine in 1891:

> If all the harm that women have done
> Were put in a bundle and rolled into one,
> Earth would not hold it,
> The sky could not enfold it,
> It could not be lighted nor warmed by the sun,
> Such masses of evil
> Would puzzle the devil
> And keep him in fuel while Time's wheels run.
> But if all the harm that's been done by men
> Were doubled and doubled and doubled again,
> And melted and fused into vapour and then
> Were squared and raised to the power of ten,
> There wouldn't be nearly enough, not near
> To keep a small girl for the tenth of a year.[27]

Woolf's anger at O.B is displaced anger at the Stephen family's misogyny, at the covering up or "pargetting" of family history, of misogyny, homosexuality, and madness.

Recalling J. K. Stephen in "A Sketch of the Past," Woolf saw him as Achilles—"Achilles on his pressed bed lolling roars out deep applause"— though it was as Ajax he was typecast in the Greek play at Cambridge. He was in love with her half-sister Stella, "with his madness on him, . . . [he] would burst into the nursery and spear the bread on his swordstick."

Lapsus Calami meant not only slips of the pen to Stephen's audience, but thrusts of the sword; and recalled Whitman's "calamus" passage and the homosexual following who called themselves "calamites." His pen was not only a penis, but the penis as a weapon for punishing women. "He always brings to mind some tormented bull," wrote Virginia. I suggest that Oscar Browning received the wrath meant for the Stephen men. Woolf also openly rejected an alliance between homosexuals and women, for she had seen how the old boy network protected its own and how homosexuals of her own class asserted their masculinity by oppressing women. She deprived the bull of his horns—Abel Pargiter has a maimed hand in *The Years* and Betty Flanders recalls gelding her cat in memory of a former suitor in *Jacob's Room*. But J. K. Stephen was the family skeleton of a bull she could not udder or utter, for the genius, the madness, and the supposed homosexuality were too close to her own situation for comfort. Her own slips of the pen, like "taking the bull by the udders" are there to remind us of an anti-phallocentric discourse.

"Let Us Now Praise Unknown Women"

The rhetorical strategies of *A Room of One's Own* construct an erotic relationship between the woman writer, her audience present in the text, and the woman reader. Seduction serves the political purpose of uniting women across class. Appealing to educated women who need private rooms for creativity, Woolf asks us to think of the rooms of working women, kitchens, and shops. In *Memories of a Working Women's Guild*, she makes even clearer a feminist solidarity in the demand for space:

> And then that room became a place where one could make, and share with others in making, the model of what a working woman's house should be. Then, as membership grew and twenty or thirty women made a practice of meeting weekly, that one house became a street of houses . . . It was thus that they were to ask, as the years went by, for peace and disarmament and the sisterhood of nations. [*CE*, 4, 146]

In the holograph draft notes for *A Room of One's Own* (Monks House Papers, B.6) after "Chloe liked Olivia. They shared a ____." Woolf wrote:

> The words covered the bottom of the page: the pages had stuck. While fumbling to open them there flashed into my mind the inevitable policeman . . . the order to attend the Court; the dreary waiting: the Magistrate coming in with a little bow . . . for the Prosecution; for the Defense—the verdict; this book is obscene + flames sing, perhaps on Tower Hill, as they compound (?) that mass of paper. Here the paper came apart. Heaven be praised! It was only a laboratory. Chloe-Olivia. They were engaged in mincing liver, apparently a cure for pernicious anaemia.

Woolf feels fearful and complicitous with the author of *The Well of Loneliness*. The paper of her own pages is singed by the flames that burn the banned book.

The only surviving typescript of *A Room*, neither the first draft nor the last, shows a long evolution. Much is made of the contrast between "Chloe liked Olivia" and "Cleopatra did not like Octavia." There was a third college, called St. Miriam's. "Milton's bogey," the patriarchal god, does not appear until the end. Much as she played with the gender of the pronoun "one" in the beginning of *A Room*, she repeats "but" and corrects herself for saying "but" so many times when reading the male writers. "But were 'buts' beginning again? What did I mean by 'but' this time?" (*TSS*, 132). She is much more hostile to male writers than in the published text, writing of Mr. C.:

> Everything seems to be at least ten sizes too big for a living person, I thought, the sentence, surely is getting bigger and bigger; rhetoric is getting nobler and

nobler; one can almost see the poor little ideas going off to the powder closet to be rigged up into brocade and have rouge dabbed on their cheeks. [*TSS*, 130]

After a banquet where the Prince of Wales tells men how many million sprats have been caught in the North Sea she writes:

> I could hardly keep myself from shouting into the loud-speaker, Let us now praise Unknown Women, and demanding that Princess Mary should celebrate the labors of the charwomen and tell us how many steps had been cleaned by them every year . . . [*TSS*, 131]

The brilliance of *A Room of One's Own* lies in its invention of a female language to subvert the languages of the patriarchy. Like her novels, it is about reading and it trains us to read as women. Its tropes figure new reading and writing strategies, enlisting punctuation in the service of feminism with the use of ellipses for encoding female desire, the use of initials and dashes to make absent figures more present and transforming interruption, the condition of the woman writer's oppression, as in the citations to Jane Austen's experience, into a deliberate strategy as a sign of woman's writing. The narrator of *A Room* continually interrupts herself. In following the interrupted text the reader reproduces the female experience of being interrupted and joins Woolf in making interrupted discourse a positive female form. The tyranny of the interrupter is forgotten as the woman writer interrupts herself. I began by insisting on the contextualization of *A Room of One's Own* as historically the last in a series of women's suffrage pamphlets. I will end by suggesting that the literary strategy of interruption in the text is derived from the political strategy of the interruption of male politician's speeches, developed by the suffragettes after Christabel Pankhurst and Annie Kenney interrupted Sir Edward Grey and were thrown in jail. The tactic enraged the men and it was continued successfully throughout the campaign for the vote. Virginia Woolf's lasting contribution to "the Cause" was to transform a feminist political strategy which truly voiced women's rebellion at enforced silence into a literary trope which captures the radicalism of the movement in a classic tribute.

NOTES

Introduction: A Rose for Him to Rifle

1. Virginia Woolf, "The Introduction," in *Mrs. Dalloway's Party*, ed. Stella McNichol (New York: Harcourt Brace Jovanovich, 1973), 37–43.

2. James M. Haule, "'Le Temps passe' and the Original Typescript: An Early Version of the 'Time Passes' Section of *To the Lighthouse*," *Twentieth Century Literature* 29, no. 3 (Fall 1983): 267–311.

3. Julia Kristeva, *Desire in Language* (London: Oxford, 1980), and *Revolution in Poetic Language* (New York: Columbia University Press, 1984).

4. For a feminist analysis of elegy as a genre, see Celeste Schenck's essay forthcoming in *Tulsa Studies in Women's Literature*, 1986.

5. Terry Eagleton, review of *Black Literature and Literary Theory*, New York Times Book Review, Spring 1985.

6. "Still Practice, A/Wrested Alphabet: Toward a Feminist Aesthetic," *Tulsa Studies in Women's Literature* 3, no. 1 (Spring/Fall 1984): 2, 79–97.

7. Woolf continued to think of working women all her life, as in this passage from her diary in Oct., 1940 (*D* 5, 328):

> I was thinking of Mabel's history. Her friend has died. Could I write it, how profoundly succulent it wd be. The cold pear shaped woman: her suppressed country childhood: no its her life with Charles that interests me. He was 'on his own.' Did a good deal of shady dealing I imagine. Lived in lodgings kept by an old lady near Elephant & Castle. Used to eat raw tripe—being from Yorkshire. A typical underworld card. He made a good deal at dog races. He wd take Mabel to race after race. How did they meet? He was life & romance to her. Why didn't they marry? Had he a wife? Every spare day I wd find him a solid red faced grizzled man in his shirt-sleeves—perhaps helping to wash up. His other passion was the Opera. He knew them all by heart. For hours they wd stand in a queue, at the Old Vic &c. She knew all the tunes. What a queer relationship—she so dumb & passive yet following him; maternally proud of him, to races, to plays: following the form of horses; always with something on. I gave him 3 lemons [?]; but I also made her come down here, when he was ill—Lord, the bloodless servitude of the domestic poor! Now she's been "as near death as can be"—the flats toppling on to their shelter. It is something like an Arnold Bennett novel the life of the bastard woman; her subterranean London life, with this 'friend' as she called him. Charles Stanford I think his name was—Charles will do—or wont do—She thought of him as a small impetuous boy. Now his life is over; & no one will know more than I do about Charles & Mabel.

8. Sandra Gilbert, "Woman's Sentence, Man's Sentencing: Linguistic Fantasies in Woolf and Joyce," in *Virginia Woolf and Bloomsbury: A Centenary Celebration*, ed. Jane Marcus (Macmillan/Indiana, 1986); Gilbert and Gubar, "Sexual Linguistics: Gender, Language, Sexuality" in *NLH* 16, no. 3 (Spring 1985), 515–543; and Gilbert and Gubar, "Ceremonies of the Alphabet: Female Grandmatologies and the Female Authorgraph" in *The Female Autograph*, ed. Domna Stanton (New York Literary Forum, 1985).

9. Indiana University Press, 1985.

10. *The Complete Shorter Fiction of Virginia Woolf*, ed. Susan Dick (New York: Har-

court Brace Jovanovich, 1986). "The Watering Place," 285–86. Quotations from notes, 306. See also Lyndall Gordon, *Virginia Woolf: A Writer's Life* (London: Oxford University Press, 1984), 272.

11. Lyndall Gordon, *Virginia Woolf: A Writer's Life* (London: Oxford, 1984), 273.

12. *New Feminist Essays on Virginia Woolf* (London: Macmillan; Lincoln: University of Nebraska Press, 1981), 16–17.

13. *Themis: A Study of the Social Origins of Greek Religion* (Cleveland: World Publishing Co. Rpt. 1969), 482, 485.

1. Enchanted Organ, Magic Bells: *Night and Day* as a Comic Opera

This essay first appeared in *Virginia Woolf: Revaluation and Continuity* ed. Ralph Freedman (Berkeley: University of California Press, 1979).

1. See Robert Moberly, *Three Mozart Operas* (New York: Dodd, Mead, 1967); Brigid Brophy's *Mozart the Dramatist* (New York: Harcourt, Brace and World, 1964); and Robert Craft's essay in the *New York Review of Books*, Nov. 27, 1975. See also Rose Laub Coser, "The Principle of the Patriarchy: The Case of the Magic Flute," *Signs* (Winter 1978).

2. For a critical response, see *Virginia Woolf: The Critical Heritage*, ed. Robin Majumdar and Allen McLaurin (London and Boston: Routledge and Kegan Paul, 1975).

3. *Monday or Tuesday* (New York: Harcourt, Brace, 1921), 14.

4. Sylvia Pankhurst is revered in Ethiopia, where her statue stands to commemorate her work for independence. Leonard Woolf also espoused this cause. Woolf's criticism of the suffrage movement in *Night and Day* should be seen in the light of the socialism and pacifism that always underlay her feminism. Her work for the cause of "adult suffrage," like that of Sylvia Pankhurst and many leftist intellectuals, must be seen as an alternative to the feminism of those women like Sally Seale to whom the "cause" was a personal religion that specifically did not include working men. For a discussion of Woolf's feminism, see my "No More Horses: Virginia Woolf on Art and Propaganda," *Women's Studies*, Virginia Woolf Issue, 1977; "Art and Anger," *Feminist Studies*, Feb. 1978; and Naomi Black, "Virginia Woolf and the Women's Movement," in *Virginia Woolf: A Feminist Slant*, ed. Jane Marcus (Lincoln: University of Nebraska Press, 1983).

5. Rebecca West, "Autumn and Virginia Woolf," *Ending in Earnest* (Garden City: Doubleday, Doran, 1931), 212-13.

6. G. Lowes Dickinson, *The Magic Flute: A Fantasia* (London: George Allen and Unwin, 1920), 9. See also *The Autobiography of G. Lowes Dickinson*, ed. Dennis Proctor (London: Duckworth, 1973).

7. E. M. Forster, *Goldsworthy Lowes Dickinson* (London: Abinger ed., Edward Arnold, 1973 [1934]), 147.

8. Lola L. Szladits, *Other People's Mail* (New York: New York Public Library and Readex, 1973).

9. Brigid Brophy, *Don't Never Forget* (New York: Holt, Rinehart and Winston, 1966), 183. She continues: "with the result that onomatopoeia cannot make good the imprecision of her images." Brophy is very interesting on Mozart as a dramatist: "The literature in opera is like a well-contrived exhibition of landscape gardening or architectural town-planning: it *arranges* the vistas down which we glimpse the objects" (112). The same might be said of the structures of the *Magic Flute*, the Masonic "square on the oblong," and the Dantean circle that arranges our perceptions in *Night and Day*.

10. In the novel Katharine and Mrs. Hilbery are trying to write the biography of the great Victorian poet; Mr. Hilbery is writing about Shelley; Ralph, as his assistant, is writing about law but really wants to write the history of the English village; Cassandra Otway's sister is helping her father write his autobiography; her brother, Henry, has written half an opera; Katharine is writing mathematics; William is writing a poetic

drama and delivers a paper on Shakespeare; Mary is writing "Some Aspects of the Democratic State," as well as feminist pamphlets with Mr. Clacton and Sally Seale.

11. In the opera it represents the ordinary nonheroic man as well.

12. Woolf described Lady Ritchie's style: "Her most typical, and, indeed, inimitable sentences rope together a handful of swiftly gathered opposites" (*Collected Essays* 4, 74). She quotes her aunt: "the sky was like a divine parrot's breast" (75), and *Night and Day* is full of references to parrots, a tribute to Lady Ritchie as well as Papageno. See Carol MacKay's essay on Annie and Virginia in *Virginia Woolf and Bloomsbury: A Centenary Celebration*, ed. Jane Marcus (Indiana/Macmillan, 1987) and her "Only Connect" in *The Library Chronicle* (University of Texas) (Fall 1985).

13. The theme of sisterhood is strong in the novel. Mary's sister cares for their father, making it possible for Mary to live and work in London. Cassandra's sister serves the same function at Stogdon House. Joan will manage to fulfill Ralph's responsibilities at Highgate so that he can be free as well as married to Katharine. Mrs. Hilbery is indebted to her own sister; Katharine to her aunts, and to her cousin Cassandra, who frees her from her engagement to William and plays "angel in the house" to Mr. and Mrs. Hilbery, charming them by playing Mozart so that Katharine can slip away to discover whether she loves Ralph. Katharine also acknowledges her dependence on Mary and her work. While to Ralph Katharine is the "star-flaming queen," to Katharine that role is played by Mary: The light in her room symbolizes the serious work for socialism and feminism that can make possible marriages like that of Ralph and Katharine, and they recognize their indebtedness in the last scene of the novel.

14. Robert Moberly explains the visual pattern as a pyramid (*Three Mozart Operas*, 262-63):

		Virtue		
	Discretion		Beneficence	
Truth				Purity
Reason		Beauty		Nature
Patience		WISDOM		Friendship
Craftsmanship		Strength		Justice
Hard Work	Arts		Forgiveness	Good Will

15. See Jacques Chailley, *The Magic Flute: Masonic Opera* (New York: Alfred A. Knopf, 1971).

16. See Allen McLaurin, *The Echoes Enslaved* (Cambridge: Cambridge University Press, 1973) for a fascinating section on repetition and rhythm in Woolf that compares her writing to the music of Satie. I think the source was Mozart and Woolf's Cambridge was Covent Garden.

17. "That's early Mozart, of course—" "But the tune, like all his tunes, makes one despair—I mean hope . . ." "But . . . Sorrow, sorrow. Joy, joy. Woven together, like reeds in the moonlight" (*HH*, 24).

18. See *ND*, 456, for an evocative picture of an opera house: "The hall resounded with brass and strings, alternately of enormous pomp and majesty and then of sweetest lamentation. The reds and creams of the background, the lyres and harps and urns and skulls . . ."

19. For a fine reading of *Night and Day* and this scene in particular, see Avrom Fleishman, *Virginia Woolf: A Critical Reading* (Baltimore: Johns Hopkins University Press, 1975).

20. Cassandra is the name of the narrator in "A Society," which ends with one of the members saying, "Oh, Cassandra, for Heaven's sake let us devise a method by which men may bear children! It is our only chance. For unless we provide them with some innocent occupation we shall get neither good people nor good books" (*Monday or Tuesday*, 39).

21. *A Room of One's Own*, 53, n. 3. Of the death of Ray Strachey, Woolf wrote: "that very large woman, with the shock of grey hair, and the bruised lip; that monster, whom I remember typical of young womanhood, has suddenly gone. She has a kind of representative quality, in her white coat and trousers; wall-building, disappointed, courageous without—what?—imagination?" (*A Writer's Diary*, 325). Ray Strachey's book ends: "The change in the type of heroine required for 'best sellers' is the real test, and it is not until the 'strong silent hero' ceases to 'dominate' the gentle heroine that the end of the Women's Movement will have arrived" (*The Cause* [1928, New York; rpt. Kennikat Press, 1969], 420). Florence Nightingale's fragment "Cassandra" was written in 1859; both Mill and Jowett advised her not to publish. Woolf sustains this critique, describing women like Katharine and Cassandra in terms of an ineffectual versatility: "Now it was socialism, now it was silkworms, now it was music" (*ND*, 283).

22. Ralph is also very like Leonard Woolf; his voice has "a slight vibrating or creaking sound" (*ND*, 17); he is compared to Ruskin and describes himself as a rebel against "the family system." Katharine calls him "penniless," a melodramatic Dickensian work not characteristic of Woolf's prose style, but exactly the word she uses to describe Leonard Woolf in her letters announcing her marriage to her friends. Ralph lives at the Apple Orchard, Mount Ararat Road, Highgate, in a tower with his rook, which suggests that he is a Jew, botanist, an intellectual, and also perhaps like Noah. There is another mention of Jewishness in the novel. When the aunts come to Mrs. Hilbery to complain of cousin Cyril living in sin, she casts about for an explanation: "'Nowadays, people don't think so badly of these things as they used to do,' she began. 'It will be horribly uncomfortable for them sometimes but if they are brave, clever children, as they will be, I dare say it'll make remarkable people of them in the end. Robert Browning used to say that every great man has Jewish blood in him, and we must try to look at it in that light'" (*ND*, 123). Mrs. Hilbery is always on the side of revolution. When the aunts fulminate about a third son born out of wedlock, to bear the family name, Mrs. Hilbery says, "But let us hope it will be a girl" (*ND*, 122).

23. "Music in London," *Major Critical Essays* (New York: W. H. Wise, 1931), Vol. 2, 275.

24. Robert Moberly calls *The Magic Flute* "the most beautiful and entertaining sermon ever written" (*Three Mozart Operas*, 286). Ford Madox Ford called *Night and Day* "a severe love story" (*Piccadilly Review*, Oct. 23, 1919, 6). Not known for the severity of his own attitude toward love, Ford heard in the novel "the voice of George Eliot . . . who . . . has lost the divine rage to be didactic."

25. For readings of the novel as Shakespearean comedy, see Fleishman, *Virginia Woolf*, 22–24; Margaret Comstock, "George Meredith, Virginia Woolf and Their Feminist Comedy" (Ph. D. diss., Stanford University, 1975); also Comstock's essay on *Night and Day* in the 1976 *Women's Studies* special issue on Virginia Woolf.

26. Quentin Bell quotes from remarks by Virginia Woolf concerning her new novel: "I am the principal character in it & I expect I'm a very priggish & severe young woman but perhaps you'll see what I was like at 18—I think the most interesting character is evidently my mother who is made exactly like Lady Ritchie [Aunt Annie] down to every detail apparently. Everyone will know who it is, of course" (*Virginia Woolf*, 42).

27. Samuel Butler's Notebooks were a source not only for this novel, but for all of Woolf's work. In *Night and Day* it is Rodney who keeps a notebook as Butler's "perfect literary man," as it is Bernard in *The Waves*. See Butler's remark "It is a wise tune that knows its own father," intended to defend borrowing from the classics as a technique of the greatest genius. Also, his passages on unity and separateness seem to me to be the source for Woolf's philosophy". "In the closest union there is still some separate existence of component parts; in the most complete separation there is still a reminiscence of union. When they are most separate the atoms seem to bear in mind that they may have to come together again . . . the two main ideas underlying all action are desire for closer unity or desire for separateness. The puzzle which puzzles every atom is the same which

puzzles ourselves—a conflict of duties—our duty towards ourselves, and our duty as members of a body politic. It is swayed by its sense of being a separate thing—of having a life to itself which nothing can share; it is also swayed by the feeling that in spite of this it is only part of an individuality which is greater than itself which absorbs it" (Butler, *Selections*, ed. Geoffrey Keynes and Brian Hill [New York: Dutton, 1951], 211, 142).

28. *CE* 4, 73, 75.

29. Woolf also uses Butler's "alps and sanctuaries" as male and female images, here as well as throughout her work.

30. The "younger generation knocking at the door" theme is from *The Master Builder*, as well as the lamps with green shades of Ralph's and Mary's rooms, those essential props in Ibsen plays that most distressed Henry James. Woolf recommended that E. M. Forster read Ibsen to understand his method of combining realism and symbolism, for his achievement of "complete reality of the suburb and complete reality of the soul," like the combination of Pope and Dostoevsky that Rodney recommends to Cassandra (*CE* 1, 346).

31. Sally Seale is the self-professed "father's daughter" in *Night and Day*. Her muddle-headedness, her religious fanaticism, and her unswerving devotion to "the cause" are seen as directly deriving from being the uneducated but passionate "daughter of an educated man," as Woolf describes herself in *Three Guineas* and as Ibsen described his nineteenth-century heroines. She also reminds one of Caroline Emelia Stephen.

32. "On Not Knowing Greek," *CE* 1, 3.

33. "Jane Austen," *CE* 1, 154, 145, 146, 149, 144–45.

2. *The Years* as Götterdämmerung, Greek Play, and Domestic Novel

1. Virginia Woolf, "To Spain" (1923) *The Moment and Other Essays* (New York: Harcourt, 1948), 213 (hereafter cited as *The Moment*).

2. Bishop George Rust, *A Letter . . . Concerning Origen and . . . His Opinions* (anon.), 1661 (*The Phenix*, 1721, I, 42), cited in *OED* at Pargeting, *vbl. sb.*

3. A version of this essay was first given as a talk at the 1975 Virginia Woolf session at the MLA. At the request of David Erdman I edited a special issue of *The Bulletin of the New York Public Library*, Winter 1977, in which this essay and several others appeared as a revaluation of the novel. "Two Enormous Chunks" of galley proofs, cut at the last minute, were included and they also appear in Grace Radin's *The Years: The Evolution of a Novel* (Knoxville: University of Tennessee Press, 1981), the definitive work on the subject. Mitchell Leaska's essay now appears as the introduction to *The Pargiters: The Novel Essay Portion of The Years* (New York: New York Public Library and Readex Books, 1977). Aside from Radin, Leaska, and the contributors to the special issue, the reader should see Susan Squier's essays in *New Feminist Essays on Virginia Woolf*, ed. Jane Marcus (Lincoln: University of Nebraska Press, 1981), *Virginia Woolf: A Feminist Slant* (Lincoln: University of Nebraska Press, 1983) and her *Virginia Woolf and the Politics of the City* (Chapel Hill: University of North Carolina Press, 1985). See also Laura Moss Gottlieb's essay in *Virginia Woolf: Centennial Essays*, ed. Ginsberg and Gottlieb (Troy, N.Y.: The Whitston Press, 1983).

4. Leonard Woolf explains Virginia Woolf's love for Wagner in *Beginning Again: An Autobiography of the Years 1911–1918* (Hogarth; New York: Harcourt 1964) while not concealing his own distaste. She went with Saxon Sydney-Turner and her brother Adrian "almost ritualistically" to the Wagner festival at Bayreuth. She saw *The Ring* with Leonard at Covent Garden. "But I did not enjoy *The Ring* in my box with Virginia by my side, in 1911." He also said, "she would leave a boring party in despair as if it were the last scene of Wagner's Götterdämmerung with Hogarth House and the universe falling in

flames and ruins about her ears." In an uncollected piece ("Impressions at Bayreuth," *The Times*, Aug. 21, 1909) Woolf wrote her own impressions of Wagner:

> One feels vaguely for a crisis that never comes, for, accustomed as one is to find the explanation of a drama in the love of a man or woman, or in battle, one is bewildered by a music that continues with the utmost calm and intensity independently of them. . . . Puzzled we may be, but it is primarily because the music has reached a place not yet visited by sound. —Ecclesiastical music is too rigidly serene and too final in its spirit to penetrate as the music of Parsifal penetrates. Somehow Wagner has conveyed the desire of the Knights for the Grail in such a way that the intense emotion of human beings is combined with the unearthly nature of the thing they seek. It tears us, as we hear it, as though its wings were sharply edged—the music is intimate in a sense that none other is; one is fired with emotion and yet possessed with tranquility at the same time, for the words are continued by the music so that we hardly notice the transition.
>
> It may be that these exalted emotions, which belong to the essence of our being, and are rarely expressed, are those that are best translated by music; so that a satisfaction, or whatever one may call the sense of answer which the finest art supplies to its own question, is constantly conveyed here. Like Shakespeare, Wagner seems to have attained in the end to such a mastery of technique that he could float and soar in regions where in the beginning he could scarcely breathe; the stubborn matter of his art dissolves in his fingers, and he shapes it as he chooses.
>
> Apart from the difficulty of changing a musical impression into a literary one, and the tendency to appeal to the literary sense because of the associations of words, there is the further difficulty in the case of music that its scope is much less clearly defined than the scope of the other arts. The more beautiful a phrase of music is the richer its burden of suggestion, and if we understand the form but slightly, we are little restrained in our interpretation. We are led on to connect the beautiful sound with some experience of our own, or to make it symbolize some conception of a general nature. Perhaps music owes something of its astonishing power over us to this lack of definite articulation; its statements have all the majesty of a generalization, and yet contain our private emotions. Something of the same effect is given by Shakespeare, when he makes an old nurse the type of all the old nurses in the world, while she keeps her identity as a particular old woman.—

    5. Virginia Woolf's source for this idea was the work of the great classical scholar, Jane Ellen Harrison: *Prolegomena to the Study of Greek Religion* (Cambridge: Cambridge University Press, 1908), *Themis: A Study of the Social Origins of Greek Religion* (Cambridge, 1912), and *Reminiscences of a Student's Life* published by Leonard and Virginia Woolf at the Hogarth Press (1925). Her work was an attempt to lay bare the matriarchal origins of preclassical Greek thought. See particularly the chapter on "The Maiden Trinities" in *Prolegomena* for a source of the "triple ply" which sounds throughout Woolf's work, both to the ear and to the eye. Jane Harrison was a feminist with a sense of humor: "Zeus the Father will have no great Earth-goddess, Mother and Maid in one, in his man-fashioned Olympus, but her figure *is* the beginning, so he re-makes it; woman, who was the inspirer, becomes the temptress; she who made all things, gods and mortals alike, is become their plaything, their slave, dowered only with physical beauty, and with a slave's tricks and blandishments. To Zeus, the archpatriarchal *bourgeois*, the birth of the first woman is but a huge Olympian jest: 'He spake and the Sire of men and of gods immortal laughed.' Such myths are a necessary outcome of the shift from matriarchy to patriarchy, and the shift itself, spite of a seeming retrogression, is a necessary

stage in a real advance. Matriarchy gave to women a false because a magical prestige."
Jane Harrison appears as a fleeting beauty in *The Years*, like a beautiful green beetle,
recalling her own description of an Eton boy who didn't like her lecture but liked her
dress (130). In *Reminiscences* she expresses one of the themes of *The Years*: "Family life
never attracted me. At its best it seems to me rather narrow and selfish; at its worst a private hell. . . . On the other hand, I have a natural gift for community life. . . . If I had
been rich I should have founded a learned community for women. . . . I think, as civilization advances, family life will become, if not extinct, at least much modified and cur-
tailed." She also tells of meeting Samuel Butler in Athens: ". . . Alas! he wanted me only
as a safety valve for his theory on the woman-authorship of the Odyssey, and the buzzing
of that crazy bee drowned all rational conversation." The line from Catullus that consoles
Eleanor in her Bergsonian beliefs, "Nox est perpetua una dormienda," was Harrison's
life principle (*Reminiscences*, 87). Woolf's library contained a copy of Harrison's *Ancient
Art and Ritual* (1918) inscribed to her on Christmas 1923 from the author. The book is now
in Washington State University Library's Special Collections (Woolf Collection), along
with Woolf's copies of her *Epilegomena* (1921) and *Aspects, Aorists and the Classical
Tripos* (1919).

    6. Sir James George Frazer, *The Golden Bough* (London and New York: Macmillan,
1890); Jessie Weston, *From Ritual to Romance* (Cambridge: Cambridge University Press,
1920). Many modernist women writers rewrote the classics from the female point of view.
See H. D.'s *Helen in Egypt* (New York: New Directions, 1961) and Laura Riding's *A
Trojan Ending* (1937). Djuna Barnes's *Nightwood* recreated Artemis in the Paris underworld, and Natalie Barney and Renée Vivien sought for Sappho as Woolf does. Gilbert
and Gubar argue in their forthcoming book that the anxieties of male modernists were
due to women's success as writers.

    7. The upstairs/downstairs alternations are so insistent in the early chapters that one
feels the BBC television series should have given Woolf credit for the idea.

    8. There are elements in my reading to support Joanna Lipking's view of *The Years* as
an essentially Christian novel of spiritual renewal (*Bulletin of the New York Public
Library*, Winter 1977). But Woolf's transcendent vision is finally Bergsonian as was Jane
Harrison's. The lines from Catullus, "Nox est perpetua una dormienda," Harrison
claimed, in the book that Leonard and Virginia Woolf published, expressed Bergson's
and her own life's *credo*. For Woolf's use of Egyptian female themes, see Evelyn Haller
in *Virginia Woolf: A Feminist Slant* and *Virginia Woolf: Centennial Essays*.

    9. Margaret Comstock in her essay (*BNYPL*, Winter 1977) brilliantly analyzes, in
another context, this political force behind the novel as the working out of an anti-fascist
aesthetic. While I would state this in more positive terms as an aesthetic for the inarticulate, an opera of the oppressed, the idea is essentially the same.

    10. *TG*, 177, n. 13. The note is an attack on poets of the thirties who adopted the cause of
the workers without sacrificing their capital but refused the harder job of left intellectuals, the converting of their own class. In the "Present Day" chapter of *The Years* the
passage (360–61) on the egoism of a modern poet betrays a personal animus; once before
Woolf had lost narrative objectivity, in her attack on the psychiatric establishment in
Mrs. Dalloway.

    Woolf praised Elizabeth Mary Wright's *Life of Joseph Wright* (London: Oxford
University Press, 1932) for its lack of pretense and view of life not biased by "pro-
proletarian spectacles." An extraordinary document, it records the rise of a poor York-
shire mill-boy to become a world-renowned Oxford professor.

    11. Born in 1855 in Thackley, Township of Idle, Bradford, Yorkshire, Joseph Wright,
"worker by name and nature," used to say, "I've been an idle man all of my life, and shall
remain an idle man until I die." His philosophy of life, he said, consisted of conscien-
tiously attempting to please himself, a process that usually pleased others as well.

    12. "The Leaning Tower," *The Moment*, 136.

13. "Craftsmanship," *The Death of the Moth and Other Essays*, 204–7.

14. Eugénie's foreign beauty haunts the novel as the real Princess Eugénie haunts the life and memoirs of her friend Ethel Smyth, which Woolf admiringly reviewed. Grace Radin points out that Renny is drawn from Koteliansky, with whom Woolf translated several Russian works.

15. *AWD*.

16. "The artist must say what he or someone means and here he has hesitated between saying what Nurse Cavell meant and what people who disagree with her mean when they profess to honour her" (A. Clutton-Brock in *New Statesman* [April 10, 1920] 15). For a discussion of the role of nurse and fascism, see "Liberty, Sorority, Misogyny."

17. The word "conspiracy" has both positive and negative suggestions. In an early letter (Dec. 1910) to Violet Dickinson, Woolf says she has seen her friend Margaret Llewelyn-Davies surrounded by a band of "conspirators." But Woolf herself joined this conspiracy, the Cooperative Working Women, and spoke, organized, and held meetings.

18. The first volume (1888–1912) of Woolf's *Letters* (ed. Nigel Nicolson and Joanne Trautmann [New York and London: Harcourt, 1975]) contains many references to "Portuguese Jews," always associated with dirt, poverty, and good causes; later the "Portuguese" becomes "penniless" as she describes her forthcoming marriage to Leonard Woolf. "How I hated marrying a Jew," she wrote to Ethel Smyth on Aug. 20, 1930; "how I hated their nasal voices & their oriental jewellry and their noses and their wattles—what a snob I was: for they have immense vitality and I think I like that quality best of all."

19. Erich Neumann, *The Great Mother* (Princeton: Princeton University Press, 1955, 1974), 282–83.

20. This foreshadows the lonely scene in the country when Eleanor returns from Athens, Olympia, and Delphi to visit Morris and Celia, like Athena searching for the symbolic white owl of women's wisdom. "She felt no affection for her native land—none whatever" (199), and is more attuned to the Greece of 2,000 years before. She thinks of Edward "lecturing troops of devout school mistresses on the Acropolis" (200). The stress on the happiness of the individual being increased by the happiness of the many in the lines from Dante is contrasted with the family's dislike of a nouveau-riche neighbor. Eleanor seems larger than life listening to the "liquid call" of the owl, who nests, naturally, in the steeple, like herself a wise virgin surviving in the patriarchy.

21. See my "Salomé: The Jewish Princess Was a New Woman," *BNYPL* 78, no. 1 (Autumn 1974): 95–113.

22. Mary Augusta Arnold Ward, *A Writer's Recollections* (London: W. Collins, 1918). For details of Woolf's drawing upon Ward, see the next chapter.

23. "Two Women," *The Moment*, 197–99.

24. "Margaret Llewelyn-Davies, *Death or Life: A Call to Cooperative Women* (nd: late thirties). For Caroline Emelia Stephen as a model for Eleanor, see "The Niece of a Nun."

25. *Times Literary Supplement* (1918), 494; identified in the Kirkpatrick *Bibliography*.

26. See *Letters* 171, 219, 320. Mrs. Green, the novelist, is mentioned in *AWD* when Woolf met Forster and was insulted on the steps of the London Library. Women were still not to be on the board because of Leslie Stephen's dislike of Mrs. Green, said Forster. Woolf was furious, especially since her father spent his evenings with Widow Green. Col. Pargiter crosses Green Park to visit his mistress when his wife is dying.

27. *The New Republic*, Jan. 9, 1924, 180–81.

28. Woolf's use of color in *The Years*, especially red and gold, is explored in the next chapter.

29. Caroline Emelia Stephen, London, 1908. Aunt Caroline is "the Quaker" and "the Nun" in Woolf's *Letters*, vol. 1. She was the aunt who left Virginia Stephen a legacy of £ 500 and was memorialized in *A Room of One's Own*. Virginia wrote to Violet Dickenson

(1,331), "It is a gloomy work, I know, all gray abstractions and tremulous ecstasies and shows a beautiful Spirit." See "The Niece of a Nun."

30. See *"Night and Day* as a Comic Opera."

31. Ethel Smyth wrote *The Prison* at the beginning of their friendship (first performance, Queen's Hall, Feb. 24, 1931, Bach Choir and Sir Adrian Boult). It was a symphony for soprano and bass-baritone solos, chorus, and orchestra and is considered one of her major works along with her *Mass* and her opera *The Wreckers. The Prison* was based on a poem by H. Brewster (1891) and the title page expresses the theme in the last words of Plotinus: "I am striving to release that which is divine in us, and to merge it in the universally divine." *The Years* makes the same attempt. Whether other readers "hear" the novel as an opera is another question. (The inscribed copy of *The Prison* is in the Woolf Collection of the Washington State University Library, Pullman, Washington.)

32. "Ethel Smyth," *New Statesman*, April 23, 1921, 80, 82.

33. She also thought Virginia "arrogant" and "ungenerous" (see Christopher St. John, *Ethel Smyth* (London: Longmans, Green, 1959). Woolf objected to the egotism in Smyth's autobiographical writing, what she called "the eldritch shriek," but said of *As Time Went On* in May 1936, "if I go half way down the road to immortality, it will be because my name is on your title page." She said that the first volumes "brought me to your spiritual feet long before I set eyes on your four-cornered hat," and "I'm obsessed with the desire that you should paint me: not a thing I often feel—but what a revelation it would be; painful no doubt but like seeing one's true soul, picked out from its defacing shell, its compressing and twisting convolutions by the silver sharp pen, or sword, of Ethel's genius. . ." (*Ethel Smyth*, 230–31). In July 1940 Woolf wrote that Ethel was "thank God, not a finished precious vase, but a porous receptacle that sags slightly swells slightly, but goes on soaking up the dew, the rain, and whatever else falls upon the earth. Isn't that the point of being Ethel Smyth?" (235). I am presently editing Dame Ethel's letters to Virginia Woolf.

34. Clive Bell, *French Painting* (New York: Harcourt, 1932), 183–85.

35. "On Re-reading Novels," *The Moment*, 165–66.

36. *The Strange Death of Liberal England* (New York: Harrison Smith and Robert Haas, 1935).

37. Leonard Woolf, *Beginning Again*, 126.

38. "Royalty" (1939), *The Moment*, 233–34.

3. Pargetting *The Pargiters*

1. "Impressions at Bayreuth," *The Times*, Aug. 21, 1909.

2. See G. Lowes Dickinson, *Justice and Liberty: A Political Dialogue* (New York: Doubleday, 1908) in which one of the speakers is a professor named Martin.

3. See *Lord Byron's Cain: Twelve Essays and a Text with Variants and Annotations* by Truman Guy Steffan (Austin and London: University of Texas Press, 1968) and Carol Ochs "Nomad and Settler in Patriarchal Religion," *Feminist Studies* 3, nos. 3 & 4 (Spring/Summer 1976), 56–62.

4. See Edward W. Said, *Beginnings: Intention and Method* (New York: Basic Books, 1975).

5. George B. Cutten, *Speaking in Tongues* (New Haven and London: Yale University Press, 1927). Catherine Smith and Madeline Moore are preparing a study of Woolf in relation to the English women's mystical tradition.

6. Passages of *The Years* that were cancelled at the galley proof stage, designated "two enormous chunks" by Leonard Woolf. See the reproduction of these proofs and commentary by Grace Radin in *Bulletin of the New York Public Library* 80, no. 2 (221–51) and Radin's *Virginia Woolf's The Years* (Knoxville: University of Tennessee Press, 1981). For a description like the restaurant passage of the decor of a railway tearoom, garish because

of the split between art and craft, see Roger Fry, "The Artist in the Great State," in *The Great State* (London and New York: Harper, 1912).

7. In *Three Guineas* Woolf says it's unfortunate that there are "no lives of maids in the *Dictionary of National Biography*."

8. "Rigby" was also the name of Leslie Stephen's doctor in his last illness. For the relationship of this passage to Caroline Stephen, see "The Niece of a Nun."

9. I am grateful to the University of Sussex Library for permission to quote from the letters of Margaret Llewelyn-Davies to Virginia Woolf, as well as to Lord Llewelyn-Davies and Theodora Calvert for the estate. I am also grateful to Mrs. Calvert for providing me with materials relating to Margaret Llewelyn-Davies and the Women's Cooperative Guild, including a personal memoir by Dr. Katharine Davies. Regarding the question of Margaret's brother discouraging her from collecting the family papers, Theodora Calvert writes that her father (Maurice) used to visit Margaret every day when she and Lilian lived next door in Surrey and that he "was distressed to find her emotionally upset by continual re-reading of old family letters. He thought she was making herself ill over it and in those circumstances urged her not to go on re-living the past in this way" (Letter to the author, Aug. 2, 1977). For a different view of the friendship, see Quentin Bell, "A Radiant Friendship," *Critical Inquiry*, Spring 1984 and my reply, "Quentin's Bogey," in the Spring 1985 *Critical Inquiry*. For a detailed discussion of the two versions of Virginia Woolf's essay for *Life As We Have Known It*, see my "No More Horses: Virginia Woolf on Art and Propaganda," in the *Women's Studies* Woolf issue edited by Madeline Moore, 1976.

4. Liberty, Sorority, Misogyny

This paper was written in honor of David Erdman, given at the English Institute in 1981 and first published in *The Representation of Women in Fiction*, ed. Carolyn G. Heilbrun and Margaret R. Higonnet (Baltimore: The Johns Hopkins University Press, 1983). Members of the English Institute are aware of his encouragement of scholars in his own field. Less well known is the role he has played as mentor to feminist critics and publisher of their work on Virginia Woolf. See *Bulletin of the New York Public Library* 80, no. 2 (Winter 1977), a revaluation of *The Years*; *Bulletin of Research in the Humanities* 82, no. 3 (Autumn 1979), on *The Voyage Out*; Virginia Woolf's *The Pargiters*, ed. Mitchell Leaska (New York: New York Public Library and Readex Books, 1977); and *Melymbrosia*, ed. Louise A. De Salvo (New York: New York Public Library and Readex Books, 1982).

The title of this paper is a play on James Fitzjames Stephen's *Liberty, Equality, Fraternity* (1873), ed. R. J. White, 2d ed. (1874; reprint ed., Cambridge: At the University Press, 1967), a monument to misogyny written as a reply to John Stuart Mill.

1. *AROO*, 98.

2. *MB*, 72.

3. In *Moments of Being* Woolf wrote, "All our male relations were adepts at the game. They knew the rules and attached immense importance to them. Father laid enormous stress upon schoolmasters' reports, upon scholarships, triposes and fellowships. . . . What would have been his shape had he not been stamped and moulded by the patriarchal machinery? Every one of our male relations was shot into that machine and came out at the other end, at the age of sixty or so, a Headmaster, an Admiral, a Cabinet Minister, a Judge" (132).

4. Reviewing *A Room of One's Own*, Rebecca West, the "arrant feminist" mentioned in the text (*Room*, 53). differentiated between two types of homosexuals: "The men who despised us for our specifically female organs chastised us with whips; but those to whom they are a matter for envy chastise us with scorpions" (*Ending in Earnest* [New York: Doubleday, 1931], 208–13). She praised Woolf for braving this "invisible literary wind" of homosexual anti-feminism in her own circles. This is discussed in "Taking the Bull by the Udders."

5. Algernon Swinburne, "Itylus," *Collected Poetical Works* (New York: Harper's, 1924), 54–56. See H. D.'s *HERmione* (New York: Dial Press, 1981) for a contemporary and uncritical feminist use of Swinburne's poem: "Were all the poems no use? Some poems are useful one way, some another . . ." (158–60).

6. *Y*, 380.

7. Woolf's valorization of chastity is discussed in "Virginia Woolf and her Violin" and "'The Niece of a Nun.'"

8. Cicely Hamilton's *Marriage as a Trade* was first published in 1909 and has now been reprinted (London: The Women's Press, 1980) with an introduction by Jane Lewis. Hamilton, like Woolf, celebrates celibacy and the single life. This attitude should be compared with that of other left-wing feminists of the time, Rebecca West, for example, or Emma Goldman, who advocated free love.

9. Alice Fox's "Literary Allusion as Feminist Criticism in *A Room of One's Own*" (Paper delivered at the 1981 MLA Virginia Woolf Society Meeting, New York, December 1981) discusses the ballad, and Patricia Meyer Spacks treated it in *The Female Imagination* (New York: Alfred A. Knopf, 1975). I compare the rhetorical strategies of *A Room of One's Own* and *Three Guineas* in "No More Horses: Virginia Woolf on Art and Propaganda," in the Woolf issue of *Women's Studies*, 4, nos. 2 and 3 (1977): 265–90.

10. For other references to the influence of Jane Harrison on Virginia Woolf, see the chapters on *The Years*.

11. Queenie Leavis's attack on Woolf is discussed in my "No More Horses."

12. Macciocchi, "Female Sexuality in Fascist Ideology," in *Feminist Review*, no. 1 (London: 1979): 75. Compare *A Room of One's Own*, 54, 154–55.

13. "Female Sexuality in Fascist Ideology," 62.

14. Evelyn Haller, "Isis Unveiled," in *Virginia Woolf: A Feminist Slant*, ed. Jane Marcus (Lincoln: University of Nebraska Press, 1983). See also Haller's "The Anti-Madonna in the Work of Virginia Woolf," in *Virginia Woolf: Centennial Essays*, ed. Elaine Ginsberg and Laura Moss Gottlieb (Troy, N.Y.: Whitston Press, 1983).

15. See "The Niece of a Nun."

16. Martine Stemerick, in Ginsberg, *Virginia Woolf: Centennial Essays* and her forthcoming book for Harvester Press.

17. On nursing, see "Virginia Woolf and Her Violin."

18. Caroline Emelia Stephen, *The Service of the Poor: Being an inquiry into the reasons for and against the establishment of religious sisterhoods for charitable purposes* (London and New York: Macmillan, 1871).

19. Letters of Sir James Stephen (with biographical notes by his daughter Caroline Emelia Stephen) (Gloucester: John Bellows, 1906, private circulation). For a discussion of Fitzjames's reviews of *Little Dorrit*, see Edith Skom, "Fitzjames Stephen and Charles Dickens: A Case Study in Anonymous Reviewing" (Ph.D. diss., Northwestern University, 1978).

20. See "*The Years* as Greek Drama, Domestic Novel, and Götterdämmerung."

21. Macciocchi, "Female Sexuality in Fascist Ideology," 75.

22. James Stephen Fitzjames, *Liberty, Equality, Fraternity*. See also Sir Leslie Stephen, *The Life of Sir James Fitzjames Stephen* (London: Smith Elder, 1895). On the Maybrick case, see Mary S. Hartman, *Victorian Murderesses* (New York: Schocken, 1977), 215–55. The most interesting study of Fitzjames Stephen is a Selden Society lecture by Leon Radzinowicz, *Sir James Fitzjames Stephen, 1829–1894, and His Contribution to the Development of Criminal Law* (London: Quaritch, 1957). Leslie Stephen's *Life of Sir James Stephen Fitzjames* also contains a brief biography of Fitzjames's son, the poet J. K. Stephen. Michael Harrison's *Clarence* (London: W. H. Allen, 1972) discusses the son's candidacy for Jack the Ripper, as does Donald Rumbelow, *The Complete Jack the Ripper* (London and New York: W. H. Allen and New York Graphic Society, 1975). Two volumes of J. K. Stephen's verse, *Lapsus Calami* and *Quo Musa Tendis?*, were published in 1891 (Cambridge: Macmillan and Bowes).

23. See Rufus Jones, *The Later Periods of Quakerism*, vol. 2 (London: Macmillan, 1921) and Dr. T. Hodgkin's memoir in Caroline Stephen's *The Vision of Faith*, ed. Katharine Stephen (Cambridge: Heffer, 1911).

24. This and the following quotations are taken from Caroline Stephen's *Sir James Stephen* (Gloucester: John Bellows, 1906).

25. Ibid., 143.

26. See Adrienne Munich, "Katisha's Elbow," a study of the representation of Queen Victoria in Gilbert and Sullivan (paper given at the Northeast Victorian Studies meeting, Philadelphia, April 1980).

27. On mistresses and servants, see Stemerick, "The Madonna's Clay Feet," Diss. U. of Texas, 1983, forthcoming from Harvester Press.

28. De Salvo, *Melymbrosia*.

29. See Katharine Stephen's introduction to Caroline Stephen's *The Vision of Faith*.

30. Virginia Woolf's essay "The Enchanted Organ," about her aunt Anne Thackeray Ritchie, quotes from "Annie's" letter to her husband: "The sky was like a divine parrot's breast" (*Letters of Anne Thackeray Ritchie*, ed. Hester Ritchie [London: John Murray, 1924], 294). This letter also includes the remark that she was glad to join in the William Black Memorial Fund. Black's readers erected a lighthouse in his name on Duart Point in the Sound of Mull in the Hebrides. In *Silences* (New York: Delta, 1979), Tillie Olsen points out that Woolf may well have taken the idea of Shakespeare's sister from Olive Schreiner. Yvonne Kapp lists an 1897 London performance of a play by Eleanor Marx's common-law husband, Edward Aveling, called *Judith Shakespeare* (*Eleanor Marx*, 2 vols. [New York: Pantheon, 1977], 2:678). It is reasonable to suppose that Virginia Woolf or members of her family would have seen or heard of this production, since her half-brother Gerald Duckworth was treasurer of an avant-garde theater group organized by Elizabeth Robins for the performance of Ibsen, and Aveling was a member of these circles, along with Olive Schreiner, Eleanor Marx, and Shaw.

31. Louise De Salvo, "1897: Virginia Woolf at Fifteen," in Marcus, *Virginia Woolf: A Feminist Slant*.

32. These points on the Stephens' attitudes toward education are discussed by Martine Stemerick in "The Distaff Side of History" in Ginsberg and Gottlieb, *Virginia Woolf: Centennial Essays*.

33. "A Society," *Monday or Tuesday* (New York: Harcourt, Brace and Co., 1921), 20. This essay has finally been reprinted (after 65 years) in *The Complete Shorter Fiction of Virginia Woolf*, ed. Susan Dick, (New York: Harcourt Brace Jovanovich, 1986).

34. Ethel Smyth, *Streaks of Life* (London: Longmans, Green, 1921), 174.

35. "Friendships Gallery," ed. Ellen Hawkes, is now published in *Twentieth Century Literature* 25, nos. 3 and 4 (Fall/Winter 1979), a special issue edited by Lucio Ruotolo on unpublished manuscripts of Virginia Woolf.

36. See the last two chapters for a fuller discussion of this passage.

37. See Paul Levy, *G. E. Moore and the Cambridge Apostles* (New York: Holt, Rinehart and Winston, 1979); and Frances Mary Brookfield, *The Cambridge "Apostles"* (New York: Scribner's, 1906).

38. J. K. Stephen, *The Living Languages: A Defence of the Compulsory Study of Greek at Cambridge* (Cambridge: Macmillan and Bowes, 1891). This essay deserves comparison with Woolf's "On Not Knowing Greek." Stephen takes up the cudgels against the scientists with great rhetorical power. The study of Greek, he says, will guarantee the "non-survival of the unfittest." Throughout the essay he repeats the phrases "the highly educated man" and "the properly educated man." Virginia Woolf's painfully ironic repetition of the phrase "daughter of an educated man" in *Three Guineas* clearly derives from her cousin's essay. The study of Greek defines the "first flight" of English citizens. Stephen writes: "We are dealing with an *intellectual aristocracy*. Either as a reward for the industry, rapacity or good luck of an ancestor, immediate or remote, or as a reward

for their own sterling and unaided qualities, the young men who present themselves at Cambridge to take the first step toward a degree, have obtained entrance into a favoured class: their degree will be a certificate that they have availed themselves of admission to that class . . . and it is for those on whom these benefits have been conferred to show in after life that they are, what they ought to be, the intellectual flower of the nation. If they are not, it is their own fault" (47).

39. See Mary Ann Clawson, "Early Modern Fraternalism and the Patriarchal Family," *Feminist Studies* 6, no. 2 (Summer 1980): "Fraternalism is never a simple egalitarian relationship, even among men. With its patriarchal bias and its origin as a type of kin relation, it always carries with it notions of hierarchy and paternalist authority which appear, because of their roots in kin relations, as categories of 'natural' dominance and subordination." See also John Gillis, *Youth and History: Tradition and Change in European Age Relations 1770-Present* (New York and London: Academic Press, 1974). Walter J. Ong describes Latin as an alien language and secret code of the elite for an exclusive all-male society in "Latin Language Study as a Renaissance Puberty Rite," in *The Presence of the World* (New Haven: Yale University Press, 1967). Unfortunately, Richard Jenkyns's *The Victorians and Ancient Greece* (Cambridge, Mass.: Harvard University Press, 1980) avoids the serious implications of an ideology that provided a homosexual hegemony over British culture in the late nineteenth century, the issues of class, power, and the exclusion of women.

40. See Skom, "Fitzjames Stephen and Charles Dickens." Skom quotes an autobiographical fragment by Fitzjames Stephen on his hatred of the revolution of 1848, his feeling like a "scandalized policeman": "I should have liked first to fire grapeshot down every street in Paris, till the place ran with blood, & next to try Louis Philippe and those who advised him not to fight by court martial, & to have hanged them all as traitors and cowards."

41. Geoffrey Hartman, "The Voice of the Shuttle," in *Beyond Formalism* (New Haven: Yale University Press, 1970).

42. *Between the Acts*, 253.

43. See Naomi Black, "Virginia Woolf and the Women's Movement," in Marcus, *Virginia Woolf: A Feminist Slant*.

44. For a fine feminist study of *Between the Acts* see Sallie Sears, "Theater of War," in Marcus, *Virginia Woolf: A Feminist Slant*.

5. Virginia Woolf and Her Violin: Mothering, Madness, and Music

Versions of this essay have appeared in *Mothering the Mind*, ed. Ruth Perry and Martine Watson Brownley (New York: Holmes and Meier, 1984) and *Virginia Woolf: Centennial Essays*, ed. Elaine K. Ginsberg and Laura Moss Gottlieb (Troy, N. Y.: Whitston Press, 1983).

1. See *I Love Myself When I Am Laughing: A Zora Neale Hurston Reader*, ed. Mary Helen Washington, intro. by Alice Walker (New York: The Feminist Press, 1980).

2. Virginia Woolf, *The Moment and Other Essays* (New York: Harcourt, Brace, 1948), 179.

3. Louise A. De Salvo, "1897: The First Fully Lived Year of My Life," *Virginia Woolf: A Feminist Slant* (Lincoln: Nebraska University Press, 1983).

4. *Notes from Sick Rooms* has been reprinted (1980) by Constance Hunting at the Puckerbrush Press, Orono, Maine.

5. *The Moment and Other Essays*, 9.

6. See Caroline Emelia Stephen's edition of her father's letters, *Sir James Stephen, K.C.B., L.L.D., Letters with Biographical Notes by His Daughter, Caroline Emelia*

Stephen (printed for private circulation, John Bellows, Gloucester, 1906). All quotations in the next paragraph are from this source.

7. Information on J. K. Stephen may be found in Leslie Stephen's *Life of Sir James Fitzjames Stephen* (New York: Putnam's, 1895), Oscar Browning's memoir (*Bookman*, March, 1892), Desmond MacCarthy's *Portraits* (New York: Macmillan, 1932), E. F. Benson's *As We Were* (London: Longmans, Green, 1930), Michael Harrison's *Clarence* (London: W. H. Allen, 1972) and Donald Rumbelow's *The Complete Jack the Ripper*, intro. Colin Wilson (Boston: New York Graphic Society, 1975).

8. For details on Fitzjames Stephen and the Maybrick Case, see Mary S. Hartman, *Victorian Murderesses* (New York: Schocken, 1977).

9. George H. Savage, *Insanity and Allied Neuroses: Practical and Clinical* (Philadelphia: Henry C. Lea's Son & Co., 1884), 37.

Virginia explained to Ethel Smyth the exact nature of the relationship of influenza and heredity to her madness in February, 1930. ". . . this influenza has a special poison for what is called the nervous system; and mine being a second hand one; used by my father and his father to dictate dispatches and write books with—how I wish they had hunted and fished instead! . . . To think that my father's philosophy and The Dictionary of National Biography cost me this!" (Letter 2148, volume 4).

10. Ibid., 39.
11. Ibid., 84.
12. Ibid., 24.
13. Ibid., 108.

14. G. H. Savage, *The Increase of Insanity*, Lumleian Lectures, Royal College of Physicians (London: Cassell, 1907), 63. Lumley was commemorated in these lectures and it may or may not be a coincidence that it is outside Lumley's shop in *The Years* that Rose is terrified by the sight of a man exposing himself. Since this essay was written, Stephen Trombley's *All That Summer She Was Mad* has appeared. It also treats Dr. Savage. Though it received generally hostile reviews, see the review by Jane Lilienfeld in *Virginia Woolf Miscellany*, no. 19 (Fall 1982). I would also like to thank Louise De Salvo for bringing to my attention Susan M. Kenney's "Two Endings: Virginia Woolf's Suicide and *Between the Acts*," *University of Toronto Quarterly* 44 no. 4, (Summer 1975), a refreshingly commonsensical interpretation of Woolf's illness, though it has a regrettably narrow view of female sexuality. Joanna Lipking has brought to my attention an important study of Quentin Bell's treatment of Woolf's madness in his biography. See Dorothy E. Smith, "No One Commits Suicide: Textual Analysis of Ideological Practices," Dept. of Sociology in Education, Ontario Institute for Studies in Education, 1980, section VI in particular. Smith analyzes the final pages of the Bell biography as an ideological alternation of euphoria and depression that is set up so that the reader experiences manic depression and accepts Woolf's "suicide" as the result of madness. Smith's brilliant analysis is made even more effective by a reading of Octavia Wilberforce's letters to Elizabeth Robins which make clear that, contrary to Leonard Woolf's biography, Wilberforce did not know of Virginia's history of mental illness. Also, Smith leaves out the passages of Bell's narrative that deal with her left-wing politics and "The Leaning Tower." I would argue that the intertwining of the two themes, politics and suicide, by Bell, is a way of connecting both in an anti-feminist ideological picture of female mental weakness that sheds doubt on her political commitment or reduces it to a symptom of "madness."

15. G. H. Savage, *Ten Post Graduate Lectures*, Royal Society of Medicine 1919–1920 (London: William Wood, 1929), 5.
16. "An Unwritten Novel," *A Haunted House* (New York: Harcourt, Brace, 1944), 21.
17. Ibid., 19.
18. "Slater's Pins Have No Points," ibid., 110–11.
19. See Ellen Hawkes's edition of "Friendships Gallery," *Twentieth Century Litera-*

ture 25, nos. 3 & 4 (Fall/Winter 1979) and her "Woolf's Magical Garden of Women," *New Feminist Essays on Virginia Woolf*, ed. Jane Marcus (Macmillan/Nebraska, 1981). Also in this volume is my essay "Thinking Back Through Our Mothers," which discusses some of the issues raised here and reprints Woolf's obituary of Caroline Emelia Stephen.

20. See the edition of this story by Susan M. Squier and Louise A. De Salvo in the Virginia Woolf issue of *Twentieth Century Literature*, ibid., and an analysis of the story of Louise De Salvo, "Shakespeare's Other Sister" in *New Feminist Essays on Virginia Woolf*, ed. Jane Marcus, ibid.

21. See "The Niece of a Nun: Caroline Stephen, Virginia Woolf, and the Cloistered Imagination."

22. See the two chapters on *The Years*.

23. For a discussion of Margaret Llewelyn-Davies's political influence on Woolf, see my "No More Horses: Virginia Woolf on Art and Propaganda," *Women's Studies*, 4 (1977): 264–90.

24. *A Haunted House*, 148.

25. I am grateful to Louise De Salvo for discussions about Woolf and Vita Sackville-West and for reading her essay "Tinder and Flint," in *SIGNS* and her edition of Vita Sackville-West's letters to Virginia Woolf (New York: Morrow, 1984). Quotations from *All Passion Spent* are taken from the Doubleday, Doran edition (New York, 1931).

26. "On Being Ill," in *The Moment and Other Essays* (New York: Harcourt Brace, 1948), 10.

27. *A Haunted House*, 26.

28. Karin Stephen, *Psychoanalysis and Medicine: A Study of the Wish to Fall Ill* (Cambridge University Press, 1935).

29. See *Melymbrosia*, edited by Louise De Salvo (New York Public Library and Readex Books, 1981).

30. Letter from Ethel Smyth to Virginia Woolf (in possession of Lawrence Graham Middleton Lewis, London), quoted by permission of Letcher and Sons for the Smyth Estate.

31. Letter from Ethel Smyth to Virginia Woolf, The Berg Collection, The New York Public Library, Astor, Lennox and Tilden Foundation. For further discussion of Ethel Smyth and Virginia Woolf, see Marcus, "Thinking Back through Our Mothers" in *New Feminist Essays on Virginia Woolf* (Macmillan/Nebraska, 1981), 1–30.

32. This information on Dr. Octavia Wilberforce is taken from her letters to Elizabeth Robins in the Fales Collection, New York University, and Sussex University Library, with the permission of her estate. It is part of a more detailed study called "A Drop of Common Blood."

6. The Niece of a Nun: Virginia Woolf, Caroline Stephen, and the Cloistered Imagination

1. See Alice Fox's "Virginia Liked Elizabeth," in *Virginia Woolf: A Feminist Slant*, ed. J. Marcus (Lincoln: University of Nebraska Press, 1983).

2. Caroline Emelia Stephen, *The Service of the Poor: Being an Inquiry into the Reasons for and against the Establishment of Religious Sisterhoods for Charitable Purposes* (London and New York: Macmillan, 1871). The main argument of the book is against private philanthropy and for the professionalization of nursing and social work, a parallel to her brother Fitzjames's professionalization of law and Leslie Stephen's professionalization of the higher journalism. All three Stephens as middle-class intellectuals played the role of what J. K. Stephen called "the intellectual aristocracy" in solidifying the interests of their class and securing important positions as ministers of English culture.

Virginia Woolf's attacks on professional men are described by Beverly Schlack in "Fathers in General" in *Virginia Woolf: A Feminist Slant*, and Woolf's fears for women are expressed in "Professions for Women" and in *Three Guineas*.

3. For an attack on the Pankhursts, see David Mitchell, *Queen Christabel* (London: Macdonald and Jones, 1977). Marina Warner's *Joan of Arc: The Image of Female Heroism* (New York: Knopf, 1981) discusses the power of the image of female chastity.

4. "It should not be difficult to transmute the old idea of bodily chastity into the new ideal of mental chastity" (*TG*, 82). Nor is it difficult to revive physical celibacy as an ideal once it has been associated with mental power.

5. See Emily Jensen's essays in *Virginia Woolf: A Feminist Slant*, Suzette Henke's "*Mrs. Dalloway*: The Communion of Saints" in *New Feminist Essays on Virginia Woolf*, and Elizabeth Abel's "Narrative Structure(s) and Female Development: The Case of *Mrs. Dalloway*" in *The Voyage In: Fictions of Female Development*, ed. Elizabeth Abel, Marianne Hirsch, and Elizabeth Langland (Hanover, N. H.: University Press of New England, 1983).

6. *The Light Arising* was published by Heffer in Cambridge in 1908; *Quaker Strongholds* was published by Headley Brothers in 1890; *The Vision of Faith*, a collection of essays, was published by Heffer and Sons, Cambridge, in 1911, with a memoir by Katherine Stephen. There is an excellent monograph on Caroline Stephen by Robert Tod, which will be part of a new series of Quaker biographies. Tod's monograph also contains a bibliography and chronology of Caroline Stephen's life.

7. Caroline Stephen, *The First Sir James Stephen* (Gloucester: John Bellows, 1906, privately printed). James Fitzjames Stephen's memoir of his father appears in the fourth edition of James Stephen's *Essays in Ecclesiastical Biography* (London: Longmans, Green, 1860). Leslie Stephen described his father in *The Life of Sir James Fitzjames Stephen* (London: Smith Elder, 1895). In letters printed by Katherine Stephen in *The Vision of Faith*, Caroline wrote of her bafflement at editing her father's letters: "It seemed so impossible to *combine* satisfactorily with what my brothers had said, or to fill up the gap left by them, without the appearance of opposition." Sally Seale in *Night and Day* seems to be a partial portrait of Caroline. A suffragist, she is an enthusiast because her father was before her, "and on his tombstone I had that verse from the Psalms put, about the sowers and the seed" (*N&D*, 91). "Dressed in plum-colored velveteen, with short, gray hair, and a face that seemed permanently flushed with philanthropic enthusiasm" (*N&D*, 81), Sally Seale represents women philanthropists of Woolf's Aunt Caroline's age, who combined religion and social causes and were eventually replaced by the efficient Mr. Clactons.

8. See Woolf's letters, 1904, and her reversal, siding with Caroline's view of Leslie Stephen in *Moments of Being*. Robert Tod quotes a letter of Caroline's to Maitland from Cambridge University Library about his biography of Leslie Stephen: "Julia's death laid bare the chasm between Leslie and me," and he suggests that Caroline was hurt that Leslie turned to Stella Duckworth for comfort. Caroline, for her part, was always trying to leap over the chasm to include agnostics like her brother in her religious philosophy. In October 1902 she wrote, "Agnosticism with mystery at the heart of it seems another description of the 'rational mysticism' which is my favorite expression of my own ground" (*Vision of Faith*, cxi). This seems to me to be an exact description of Virginia Woolf's mystical philosophy. On truth-telling in biography, see also Caroline Stephen's *Caroline Fox and Her Family* (Philadelphia: Longstreth, 1883). Caroline Stephen accepted the Quaker practice of not mourning the dead. I suspect this is what alienated her from Leslie Stephen in his lugubrious guilty raving over the death of his wives, though the same principle probably soothed Virginia considerably on the death of her father. Woolf's experience with both Quakers, Violet Dickinson and Caroline Stephen, provided a sympathetic background for her description of Roger Fry in her biography. But, unlike her aunt, she could not tell the truth about his domestic life, hence the cramped

quality of the book. (While Bell calls Dickinson a Quaker, Robert Tod has been unable to find evidence of actual membership.)

9. James Fitzjames Stephen, *Liberty, Equality, Fraternity* (1873), new edition by R. J. White (Cambridge University Press, 1967). Fitzjames was an extraordinarily aggressive person even for his age and was called "the Giant Grim." He ferociously attacked his enemies in print and thundered as a judge in the High Court. He defended punishment as a natural desire of men against their fellowman and justified war and imperialism. In *Quaker Strongholds*, Caroline Stephen takes a brave stand against men like her brother and anticipates the pacifism of her niece Virginia. But the most important point in her discussion of Quaker pacifism (*Quaker Strongholds*, 134–43) constitutes a complete rebellion against her colonial administrator father and her brother Fitzjames, who codified the laws of India and England and justified war, violence, and punishment: "we regard the opposing of violence by violence as a suicidal and hopeless method of proceeding; we feel, as Christians, that the weapons of our warfare are not carnal . . . Would any one say that at the time of the Indian Mutiny the Governor-General of India ought not to have permitted the use of arms for the protection of the women and children? I doubt whether any Friend would be found to maintain this. But it is equally to be remembered that no true Friend could well have occupied the position of Governor-General. No nation which had from the beginning of its history been thoroughly Christian could, I suppose, have found itself in the position which we occupied in India in 1857. . . . Had we been from the first a thoroughly Christian nation, our whole history must have been different, and would (as we Friends believe) have been infinitely nobler" (*Quaker Strongholds*, 135, 136). Caroline Stephen goes on to argue that the roots of war and oppression are in material greed. It is a short step from this position to her niece's argument in *Three Guineas* that war and imperialism are derived from capitalism and patriarchy. John Bicknell points out that Leslie Stephen wrote some lives of women in the *DNB*, including Harriet Martineau, Mary Wollstonecraft, Elizabeth Elstab, and Eliza Craven. Caroline also agreed with Leslie's "What Is Materialism?" (*An Agnostic's Apology*, 1903 ed., 127–67, which also is the source of "Think of a kitchen table then when you're not there," from *To the Lighthouse*.)

10. Denise Levertov, "In Memory of Muriel Rukeyser," *In These Times* 26 March– 1 April 1980.

11. See *The Simone Weil Reader*, ed. George A. Panichas (New York: David McKay, 1977), and Walter Benjamin, *Reflections*, ed. Peter Demetz (New York: Harcourt Brace Jovanovich, 1978).

12. "I don't quite know how to convey to the perverse public that it is the house itself, not the entrance, which is the true Porch. What I like about the name is that it sounds plausible to the multitude and may be called 'academic,' while a smaller inner circle know what it means to me as shelter under which to sit beside the closed door, the opening of which, I trust, is to let me in to Home, a shelter I am so thankful to have reached" (*Vision of Faith*). Aside from the fact that she would have been a fascinating novelist, Caroline makes reference to George Herbert's poem—though, given her more persistent imagery of light, she reminds one of Vaughan. The Porch as a woman's nunnery, with its glass doors opening onto an enclosed garden with a pear tree, and her fierce guarding of her privacy suggest Woolf's concept of "a room of one's own." Katherine Stephen, principal of Newnham, boasted that she converted her conservative aunt to the cause of women's education once she had seen the girls' rooms at Newnham. This enclosed space surrounded by nature has an erotic charm for the woman who has had to live in the family or "public" space of a household. The place where one works, if work is a forbidden pleasure, is both erotic and chaste. This "room of one's own" recurs as a figure in women's novels.

13. The obituary is reprinted in the notes to my "Thinking Back through Our Mothers," in *New Feminist Essays on Virginia Woolf*.

14. Virginia Woolf, *L* 1,144. Virginia was also irritated with her aunt, "perpetually flowing with rather trivial talk, which nevertheless she takes great, and painful, care to express well and pronounce exquisitely. Also I disagree entirely with her whole system of tolerance and resignation."

15. Leslie Stephen, *The Mausoleum Book*, ed. Alan Bell (London: Oxford, 1977), 55. John Bicknell points out Leslie's loving concern for Milly in his letters to Julia.

16. See Rufus M. Jones, *The Later Periods of Quakerism*, vol. 2 (London: Macmillan, 1921), and Dr. T. Hodgkin's memoir in *The Vision of Faith*. Caroline Stephen's influence, while important, was not the dominant force among Victorian Quakers. Her mysticism was less influential than Rowntree's social philosophy.

17. Quoted in Jones, *Later Periods of Quakerism*, 968.

18. See Robert Tod's monograph.

19. For a discussion of Caroline Stephen's views on servants, see Martine Stemerick's dissertation, University of Texas, 1982.

20. "Women and Politics," *Nineteenth Century* 61, no. 360 (February 1907); rejoinder in April, 61, no. 362; "A Consultative Chamber for Women," *Nineteenth Century* 64, no. 382 (December 1908).

21. Jones, *Later Periods of Quakerism*, 969.

22. *Service of the Poor*, 249.

23. Ibid., 255.

24. Introduction to *Vision of Faith*.

25. Ibid.

26. *First Sir James Stephen*, 291.

27. See Sandra Gilbert's essays on "Milton's Bogey" in Sandra Gilbert and Susan Gubar, *The Madwoman in the Attic* (New Haven: Yale University Press, 1979).

28. For a fascinating aside on Scheherazade, see Susan Gubar's "The Blank Page' and the Issue of Female Creativity," *Critical Inquiry* (Writing and Sexual Difference, ed. Elizabeth Abel) 8, no. 2 (Winter 1981): 243–63.

29. Catherine F. Smith, "Jane Lead: The Feminist Mind and Art of a Seventeenth Century Protestant Mystic," in *Women of Spirit: Female Leadership, in The Jewish and Christian Traditions*, ed. Rosemary Ruether and Eleanor McLaughlin (New York: Simon and Schuster, 1979). See also Ruth Perry's "The Veil of Chastity: Mary Astell's Feminism," *Studies in Eighteenth Century Culture*, vol. 9 (Madison: University of Wisconsin Press, 1979). For an attack on Woolf's mysticism, see Quentin Bell, "A Radiant Friendship" in *Critical Inquiry* (Spring 1984) and my reply, "Quentin's Bogey," (Spring 1985). See also Madeline Moore's *The Short Season Between Two Silences: The Mystical and the Political in the Novels of Virginia Woolf* (Boston: Allen and Unwin, 1984).

30. "The Rhetoric of the Inward Light: An Examination of Extant Sermons Delivered by Early Quakers, 1671–1700," Ph.D. diss., University of Southern California, 1972.

31. "Seventeenth Century Quaker Style," *PMLA* 71 (September 1956): 725–54.

32. Simone Weil's concept of the void is much the same. See Gilbert and Gubar, *Madwoman in the Attic*.

33. "'Inward' and 'Outward': A Study in Early Quaker Language," Friends Historical Society Pamphlet (London, 1962).

34. It may be argued that late-nineteenth-century rhetoric (in religious controversy and legal discourse, which most affected Caroline Stephen) was as convoluted and elaborate as that of the seventeenth century, and women were under great restraint. Early Quaker doctrine, "Let your words be few," was "an indescribable relief." Richard Bauman, in several essays, in *For the Reputation of Truth: Politics, Religion and Conflict among the Pennsylvania Quakers, 1750–1800* (Baltimore: Johns Hopkins University Press, 1971), and his *Let Your Words Be Few: The Symbolism of Speaking and Silence among the Seventeenth Century Quakers*, (Cambridge: Cambridge University Press, 1984) has analyzed the tension between speaking and silence among the early Quakers. A similar

tension appears in Caroline Stephen's writing and in Woolf's novels, from the novel about silence of *A Voyage Out* to the gaps and "scraps, orts and fragments" of speech that make up *Between the Acts* and the unfinished sentences of the conversations in *The Years*. Bauman identifies the Quaker distinction between charismatic authority and traditional authority. Excluded from the ranks of educated men, Virginia Woolf, I believe, used these concepts of her aunt's religion as an artist. She listened to her own inner voices. Many feminists, including Adrienne Rich and Tillie Olsen, have remarked on women's connection and concern with silence and with being silenced and the feelings women writers have about breaking silence.

In "Speaking in the Light: The Role of the Quaker Minister," Bauman raises some interesting questions about the tension between speech and silence among the Quakers that seem to me to be applicable to women writers and especially to Virginia Woolf. The minister is on the edge of difficulty at all times under these conditions, for he must speak only from inspiration and a real experience of inner light; otherwise he is like any other preacher. The writer is also constrained to be original and plain—the only reason to break silence is to reveal truth. Paradoxically, then, speech is all the more valuable because it is limited—words and the Word are taken very seriously.

7. Taking the Bull by the Udders: Sexual Difference in Virginia Woolf—A Conspiracy Theory

Versions of this chapter were given at the 1982 Brown University Virginia Woolf Centenary Conference, organized by Elizabeth Weed and Roger Henkle and at the 1984 Berkshire Women's History Conference. A shorter version appears in my *Virginia Woolf and Bloomsbury: A Centenary Celebration* (Macmillan/Indiana, 1987). I would like to thank Elizabeth Abel, Louise De Salvo, Angela Ingram, and Nancy Harrison for their helpful comments on the drafts of this paper.

1. Rebecca West, "Autumn and Virginia Woolf" in *Ending in Earnest* (New York: Doubleday, 1931), 208–13.

2. For a discussion of this point, see "Liberty, Sorority, Misogyny."

3. I discuss the Oscar Browning passage in the following chapter.

4. *New Statesman*, Oct. 2, 1920, 704. Woolf's reply is reprinted in *Diary II*, Appendix III. See also *New Statesman*, Oct. 16. I discuss the *New Statesman* exchange in "Tintinnabulations," *Marxist Perspectives*, 1978. Alice Fox also discusses the *New Statesman* controversy. For a fine analysis of how Woolf's anger is used in *A Room of One's Own*, see Alice Fox, "Literary Allusion as Feminist Criticism in *A Room of One's Own*," *Philological Quarterly* (Spring 1984): 145–61. Fox takes issue with Sandra Gilbert's treatment of Milton in *A Room* in her "Patriarchal Poetry and Women Readers: Reflections on Milton's Bogey," *PMLA* 93 (1978). My argument with Gilbert is to be found in my reply to Quentin Bell called "Quentin's Bogey," *Critical Inquiry* (Spring 1985).

5. I coined this word in "Liberty, Sorority, Misogyny" (1981), and Susan Gubar has taken it up and used it in a slightly different way in the lesbian issue of *Signs*, 1984.

6. For Woolf's concern with celibacy, see "The Niece of a Nun: Virginia Woolf, Caroline Stephen, and the Cloistered Imagination."

7. See Evelyn Haller's essay in *Virginia Woolf: A Feminist Slant*, ed. Jane Marcus (Lincoln: University of Nebraska Press. 1983). Regarding "Her Sister's Voice," see my "Still Practice, A/Wrested Alphabet: Toward a Feminist Aesthetic," in *Tulsa Studies in Women's Literature* (Fall/Spring, 1984).

8. See Sandra Shattuck's essay on Jane Harrison in *Virginia Woolf and Bloomsbury: A Centenary Celebration* (Indiana/Macmillan, 1987). The quotation is from Diether Cartellieri, *TLS*, December 16, 1983, 1403.

9. For one example of Virginia's ventriloquism regarding Vanessa, see *Letters* 3, 375. For a complete revision of the idea of Vanessa as the mother goddess of Bloomsbury, see

Angelica Bell's *Deceived With Kindness* (New York: Harcourt Brace Jovanovich, 1985) and Louise De Salvo's brilliant review in *The Women's Review of Books* 2 (August 1985).

10. For a fuller discussion of the Procne and Philomel myth in *Between the Acts*, see "Liberty, Sorority, Misogyny" in this book. In "Still Practice," note 7 above, I use the myth for a theory of socialist feminist critical practice. Christine Froula does a brilliant reading of the myth as father/daughter incest in her forthcoming "The Daughter's Seduction" in *Daughters and Fathers*, ed. Lynda Boose and B. Flowers (Baltimore: Johns Hopkins University Press). She also called my attention to an essay by Patricia Joplin in *Stanford Review* 1 (1984), called "The Voice of the Shuttle is Ours," a reading different from my contention that this is a myth about the power of sisterhood. Regarding the "cut snake" as Apollo's silencing of women's power at Delphi, see my reading of the Daphne myth in "A Wilderness of One's Own" in Susan Squier's *Women Writers and the City* (Knoxville: University of Tennessee Press, 1984).

11. Richard Bauman has pointed out to me that Erving Goffman does a deconstruction of the lecture similar to my analysis here, though it is done in strictly patriarchal terms in *Forms of Talk* (Philadelphia: University of Pennsylvania Press, 1982).

12. I discuss the ballad and other aspects of the lecture form in the next chapter.

13. The typescript of D. H. Lawrence's essay is in the Harry Ransom Humanities Research Center, University of Texas at Austin.

14. In May, 1927 Vita had gone with Virginia to lecture at Oxford. She wrote to Vanessa (*Letters* 3, 380) of her admiration for her aristocratic friend's ability to take her stockings down at dinner and rub her legs with ointment, because of the midges, with no embarrassment. Her dramatization here is of the naked muse forced to put her stockings on for fear of telling the truth about women's bodies. For the relations of Virginia Woolf and Vita Sackville-West, see Louise De Salvo, "Lighting the Cave," *Signs* 8, no. 2 (Winter 1982).

15. One could make a similar point about the blank shelves in the British Museum indicating the absence of women's books.

16. "Erotics of chastity" in Woolf is a concept I discuss in "The Niece of a Nun."

17. For a brilliant study of women's education in England, see Martha Vicinus's *Independent Women: Work and Community for Single Women 1850 to 1920* (Chicago: University of Chicago Press, 1985).

18. Geoffrey Hartman, "Virginia's Web" in *Beyond Formalism* (New Haven: Yale University Press, 1970), and J. Hillis Miller in *Fiction and Repetition* (New Haven: Yale University Press, 1982). The taxi passage (100–102) is her way of relieving the "strain" of feminist thinking. It leads directly to the "big fish" of "a woman writing thinks back through her mothers" and the trial of "the androgynous mind of the artist" as a solution. The couple in the taxi is a relief, a fiction of cooperation between the sexes which she forces herself to imagine because the pain of exclusion and male contempt for women that her reading and experience have taught her are too much to bear. The preceding chapters have been a feminist reading lesson. The fiction of the taxi is not the source of Woolf's creativity but a fictional device of imagined male/female natural union, to keep her, and her readers/listeners from despair. Nelly Furman reads the passage "as a spatial metaphor for the library shelves," a vision of balance in the representation of the two sexes in culture." See "A Room of One's Own: Reading Absence," in *Women's Language and Style*, ed. Butturf and Epstein (*University of Akron Studies in Contemporary Language*, 1978). See also Woolf's short story "The Introduction" in *Mrs. Dalloway's Party*, where Lily Everit, the would-be critic, is despised and rejected as a woman but refuses to back off, realizing that "this civilization depends on me," and my discussion in "A Rose for Him to Rifle," the introduction to this book.

19. Elizabeth Abel, "Cam the Wicked: Woolf's Portrait of the Artist as Her Father's Daughter," in *Virginia Woolf and Bloomsbury: A Centenary Celebration*, ed. Jane Marcus (Indiana/Macmillan, 1986). I am indebted to Elizabeth Abel's analysis here for

the working out of the connections between *To the Lighthouse* and *A Room of One's Own*.

20. The Warboys journal of 1899 was glued page by page into Isaac Watts's *Logick or the Right Use of Reason*; see Quentin Bell, vol. 1, 65. This is interleaving the male text with a vengeance.

8. Sapphistry: Narration as Lesbian Seduction in *A Room of One's Own*

Versions of this paper were given at the June 1983 National Women's Studies Association meeting at Ohio State University in a session chaired by Beth Daugherty and at the national meeting of the Conference on British Studies in October 1983 in Washington, D. C. My thanks to my co-panelists, Martha Vicinus and Judith Walkowitz, for their helpful comments and suggestions. Angela Ingram's help and support were crucial in the writing of this chapter.

1. See Lovat Dickson, *Radclyffe Hall at the Well of Loneliness: A Sapphic Chronicle* (New York: Scribners, 1975) 132, and 71. An analysis of the tone of this book would yield interesting results. Dickson creates sado-masochistic love scenes without supporting evidence to titillate an audience, one assumes, of male readers. He insinuates that lesbianism was somehow responsible for England's naval problems in World War I, when searching for a reason for Admiral Troubridge's failure to pursue the German fleet. Had his sex life been in order, the admiral, we are asked to believe, would have followed orders. Dickson says that he cannot believe Lady Troubridge's story that her aversion to her husband coincided with his syphilis. See also Rebecca West's review of Dickson's book (London *Telegraph*, July 27, 1975):

> Fifty years ago London frequently witnessed the passage of a two-person demo. One would often see them striding down Wigmore Street . . . two ladies stepping out in designed conspicuousness, the elder, Marguerite Radclyffe Hall, was elegant in a flowing cape recalling the Italian Army and a Spanish broad-brimmed hat, which covered a beautifully cropped head of ash-blonde hair. Beside her tripped Una, Lady Troubridge, occasionally wrinkling her delicious nose and brows to keep in place her monocle, but always, however she was dressed, looking like the nicest boy in one of the best public schools. She offered, to use the words of Gray, a distant prospect of Eton College.

See also *L* 3, 487 (April 27, 1928) where Woolf wrote to Vita Sackville-West "I rang you up just now, to find you were gone nutting in the woods with Mary Campbell, or Mary Carmichael or Mary Seton, but not me . . . ."

2. Jefferson Humphries, "Haunted Words, or Deconstruction Echoed," *diacritics* (Summer 1983); 29–38. Humphries' reading does not see Echo outside of her relation to Narcissus. For a feminist reading of the myth, see Caren Greenberg, "Reading Reading: Echo's Abduction of Language in *Women and Language in Literature and Society*, ed. McConnell-Ginet, Borker, and Furman (New York: Praeger, 1980). Greenberg uses the myth to explain a non-Oedipal female textuality where the relationship of the reader to the text is seen as important. My own study of Woolf's relation to her readers can be seen in the same terms. "If the text can come to be seen as a locus of processes, as speaking itself, then it can cease being represented by and occupying the political position of dead women. It will no longer be open to critical or creative dominance. . . . Instead, domination or mastery of the text must disappear as a political necessity of criticism."

3. See Alice Fox, "Literary Allusion as Feminist Criticism in *A Room of One's Own*," *Philological Quarterly* (Spring 1984): 145–61.

4. Kathleen Raine's memoir (from *The Land Unknown*) is reprinted in *Virginia Woolf*

Miscellany, no. 10 (Spring and Summer 1978). I am indebted to Catherine Smith for pointing this out. Woolf's lecture at Newnham was perceived quite differently according to
the memoirs published in *A Newnham Anthology*, ed. Ann Phillips (Cambridge: University Press, 1979). E. E. Duncan-Jones, the first woman to write for *Granta*, recalled that
I. A. Richards told her that the Master of Magdalene vowed to vote for the most
"masculine" poem submitted anonymously for the Chancellor's Prize. Since women
were not allowed to wear academic dress because they weren't members of the university, she was going to appear in Senate House in a flounced summer dress until her tutor
talked her out of it. She claims that the notorious dinner was ruined because Virginia
Woolf was late *and* she had unexpectedly brought her husband. She found Woolf
"formidable" and only remembered from her talk high praise of Stella Gibbon's poem
"The Hippogriff." When *A Room* appeared she found the exposé of the poverty of the
women's colleges "disquieting." U. K. M. Stevenson recalled the joy of having a room of
her own, where she served biscuits and coffee to Virginia Woolf and the students after
her talk. Her room was where

> Virginia Woolf stood and sat, and looked and spoke . . . fixing me with that won-
> derful gaze, at once luminous and penetrating, what she actually said was, 'I'd no
> idea the young ladies of Newnham were so beautifully dressed.' The prig in me
> was chagrined, even if my vanity sat up and purred; but over the years what has
> persisted has been the quality of her look, which seemed to say so much more
> than the words that came with it. The look held a hint of a smile, a hint of com-
> passion, but it was above all an absolutely ruthless look; my pretty frock was no
> proof against it.

My thanks to Martha Vicinus for pointing out these passages.

5. See *Diary* 3, 206, also 193 for her letter to *The Nation* re the trial. Woolf thought *The
Well of Loneliness* was a "meretorious dull book" but joined vigorously in the protest at
its suppression. Possibly she felt guilty that she had escaped the censors with her own
comic treatment of sexuality in *Orlando*. E. M. Forster joined the protest but confessed
to Woolf that "he thought Sapphism disgusting: partly from convention, partly because
he disliked that women should be independent of men." Note that Victoria Glendinning
in *Vita* (London: Weidenfeld and Nicolson, 1983) minimizes Sackville-West's role in the
defense of Radclyffe Hall.

6. Her diary (3,200) describes Girton's "starved but valiant young women," and she
regrets that all "the splendour, all the luxury of life" is lavished on the male students, not
the women. "I felt elderly & mature. And nobody respected me. They were very eager,
egotistical, or rather not much impressed by age & repute" (201). She worried that her
strong desire "to write a history, say of Newnham or the women's movement" in the
sparkling vein of *Orlando* might have been "stimulated by applause" (203). But Desmond
Macarthy annoyed her:

> And the egotism of men surprises & shocks me even now. Is there a woman of my
> acquaintance who could sit in my arm chair from 3 to 6:30 without the semblance of
> a suspicion that I may be busy, or tired, or bored; and so sitting could talk,
> grumbling & grudging, of her difficulties, worries; then eat chocolates, then read
> a book, & go at last, apparently self-complacent & wrapped in a kind of blubber
> of misty self satisfaction? Not the girls at Newnham or Girton. They are far too
> spry; far too disciplined. None of that self-confidence is their lot. [204]

She recalls how relieved her student hostesses were when she and Vita paid for their
dinner "and they showed us the chocolate coloured corridors of Girton, like convent
cells."

7. Virginia Woolf attended the trial on November 9 and described Sir Chartres Biron (*Diary* 3, 206-7) as a "debonair and distinguished magistrate," "like a Harley St. specialist investigating a case. All black & white, tie pin, clean shaven, wax coloured & carved, in that light, like ivory." She was impressed by the law as "a very remarkable fence between us and barbarity . . . What is obscenity? What is literature?" and relieved that she did not have to testify. She met Lady Troubridge, whom she had known as a child, and "John" (Radclyffe Hall) whom she described as "lemon yellow, tough, stringy, exacerbated." It is testimony to her principles that she was there and ready to testify on behalf of a novel and a novelist whom she disliked personally but defended politically. See Angela Ingram's "Unutterable Putrefaction and Foul Stuff: Two Obscene Novels of the 1920's," delivered at South Central MLA, Tulsa, 1985, forthcoming, *International Journal of Women's Studies*.

8. Sallie Sears, "Theater of War," in *Virginia Woolf: A Feminist Slant*, ed. Jane Marcus (Lincoln: University of Nebraska Press, 1983). See Moira Ferguson, "Colonial Slavery as a White Women's Issue: British Women's Literary Involvement in the Abolition Movement, 1788," forthcoming. Ferguson argues that Christian Ignatius La Trobe's memoirs show that Lady Middleton was the first to suggest bringing anti-slavery to parliament as an issue, contrary to Wilberforce's son's insistence that he was the prime mover of the idea.

9. Sylvia Townsend Warner, *Letters*, ed. William Maxwell (New York: Viking Press, 1982), 7.

10. Alice Fox has argued that Woolf omits the fourth Mary of the ballad, Mary Hamilton, because, unlike the other victims, she was betrayed by a woman. Nelly Furman, in a provocative essay, ("*A Room of One's Own*: Reading Absence" in *Women's Language and Style*, ed. Butturf and Epstein, Studies in Contemporary Language #1, Department of English, University of Akron) points out that "the disappearance of the subject," her death, is the theme of the Scottish ballad that forms Woolf's collective voice. Mary Hamilton, who is the actual speaker of "Once there were four Marys," in the song, is indeed absent from Woolf's text. She died on the gallows for killing an unwanted child, like Judith Shakespeare who commits suicide when she is pregnant. *A Room* does point out that few great women artists had children. Perhaps Woolf is not only claiming anonymity by being Mary Whatshername, but also speaks *for* the absent Mary Hamilton as she speaks *for* Judith Shakespeare.

11. See Janice Doane, "Silence is so Windowful: The Early Novels of Gertrude Stein," Ph. D. diss., S.U.N.Y. Buffalo, 1981, and Janet Hobhouse, *Everybody Who Was Anybody: A Biography of Gertrude Stein* (New York: Putnam's). In Wendy Steiner, *Exact Resemblance to Exact Resemblance* (Yale, 1978), it is pointed out that Gertrude Stein was very much influenced by Otto Weininger's *Sex and Character* (1909). Steiner believes that Stein was too intelligent to be affected by Weininger's insane denigration of women and Jews and was interested only in his pseudo-scientific analysis of maleness and femaleness in each character. (Woolf's "androgynous mind" may owe something to Weininger's ideas as well.) In denying her Jewishness and her femaleness, Stein gave up the roles that would have helped her rebellion against the patriarchy. Woolf even appropriated her husband's Jewishness and the alienation of the working class to forge a collective identity as an Outsider. The feminist reader remains frustrated by Stein's apparent racism and sexism and finds her insidership a threat, particularly in the stereotypical rendering of black female sexuality in "Melanctha" and German servant-girl self-limitation and sexual repression in "The Good Anna" and "The Gentle Lena." I look forward to Catherine Stimpson's forthcoming book on Stein to confront some of these problems. See also Shari Benstock's *Women of the Left Bank* (University of Texas Press, 1986) and Sonia Saldívar-Hull's 1986 MLA paper.

12. Huxley's *Limbo* was published by Chatto and Windus in 1920. Susan Gubar and Sandra Gilbert use this story as exemplary of the division between the sexes and litera-

ture in their forthcoming sequel to *The Madwoman in the Attic* according to a lecture given jointly at the University of Texas, Spring, 1984. In *Virginia Woolf Miscellany*, no. 21, (Fall 1983), Patricia Joplin reads the Manx cat as "the virginal woman whose tail (by association voice, sexuality, life) is violently cut off." I do not believe that this reading of the Manx cat as a castrated female is supported by the text.

13. Leonard Woolf, *The Wise Virgins*, 1914 (rpt. New York: Harcourt Brace Jovanovich, 1979), 17–21.

14. In 1926 Marie Stopes published *Vectia: A Banned Play and a Preface on the Censorship* (London: John Bale Sons and Danielsson, Ltd.) about a jealous impotent husband. While Woolf's Mary Carmichael writes a novel radical in form, her contemporary audience would have read a radical subject as well, sexual freedom for women. In our work in the Morris Ernst papers at the Humanities Research Center at the University of Texas, Angela Ingram and I have discovered that the trial papers for *The Well of Loneliness* list under the label "lesbian" many works of fiction that deal with birth control, censorship, divorce, motherhood, etc. so that all social issues relating to women are lumped under the label "lesbian." E. M. Forster's deposition makes clear how broad this issue of the censorship of Radclyffe Hall's novel was: "If, in the opinion of the Law this book is obscene the same definition must apply to other books not necessarily dealing with the same subject or with sex matters at all but with such subjects as Birth Control, Suicide and Pacifism."

15. Jeffrey Weeks, *Coming Out: Homosexual Politics in Britain From the Nineteenth Century to the Present* (London: Quartet, 1977), and *The Making of the Modern Homosexual*, ed. Kenneth Plummer (London: Hutchinson, 1981), 76–111.

16. This term is used by Noel Annan in his important studies of the period. In "Liberty, Sorority, Misogyny," I point out that the term appears to me to have been first used by J. K. Stephen in a defense of the compulsory study of Greek at Cambridge. On Forster, see Evelyn Haller's "Only Connect: Forster and Woolf on Egypt"; on Strachey, see Michael Holroyd's biography and consider the manner of Carrington's suicide; on Lowes Dickinson, see "Enchanted Organs, Magic Bells."

17. See Paul Levy, *G. E. Moore and the Cambridge Apostles* (New York: Holt Rinehart and Winston, 1979). Moore's second paper for the Apostles was "Achilles or Patroclus?", ". . . in the discussion of sexual questions it was obligatory to make the humorous assumption that all sexual relations were homosexual ones, so that even heterosexual love had to be treated as only a special case of the Higher Sodomy" (140).

18. Lady Henry Somerset, see E. F. Benson, *As We Were: A Victorian Peep Show* (London: Longmans, Green, 1930).

19. The papers of the Chaeronea Society in the Harry Ransom Humanities Research Center at the University of Texas deserve study not only for their own sake but in order to study attitudes toward women held by English homosexuals. The Radclyffe Hall papers are in the Morris Ernst Collection at the HR HRC. There are also several strange and contradictory letters from Oscar Browning in the HR HRC, including some to George Ives in the Chaeronea Collection. In letters to Frank Harris he claims that he never knew Oscar Wilde was a homosexual and he describes Swinburne as a "loathesome beast" who had boys flogged until the blood ran, and wrote with the blood.

20. Quoted with permission of Quentin Bell. Radclyffe Hall's papers are quoted by permission of Lovat Dickson. Among the papers is a review of *The Well* by Arnold Bennett (*Evening Standard*, 9 August 1928): "Uncertain in touch at first, this novel is in the main fine. Disfigured by loose writing and marred by loose construction, it nevertheless does hold you. It is honest, convincing and extremely courageous. What it amounts to is a cry for unprejudiced social recognition of the victims." There is also a clipping from the *New York Times* in 1929 datelined London, March 5, headed "Dashing Captain Revealed as Girl." Known as Captain Barker, she said that her 9-year-old son believed she was his father. She was the leader of the "London Fascisti" who led raids on Communist demonstrations. Her identity was revealed when her restaurant went bankrupt and

she was discovered acting as host in swallowtail coat and striped trousers at the Regents Palace Hotel.

21. Among the lesbian novels of the period, see Elizabeth Russell's *The Enchanted April* (1922), where two married ladies escape to a castle, *One of Love's Jansenists* (written by Jane Harrison's companion, Hope Mirrlees and reviewed by Virginia Woolf in *TLS*, Oct. 9, 1919, as a "difficult and interesting novel"), and Yvonne (Cloud) Kapp's 1932 *Nobody Asked You* (Willy Nilly Press). Kapp is the distinguished biographer of Eleanor Marx. Her novel has only one memorable sentence, "She sewed not, neither did she type," and the lesbian figure is the South American cousin of two French aristocratic girls, one of whom dies of tuberculosis, having engaged in incest with her father in order to, rather unbelievably, keep him paying the other children's school bills. The South American ends up with a working-class lover who keeps a lesbian bar and the young aristocrat returns to her indifferent parents to escape their brawling scenes. Another interesting lesbian novel is *Hungerheart* (Methuen) by Christopher St. John (she was a friend of Hall's), anonymously published in 1915, which contains as much lugubrious Catholicism as *The Well*, and some interesting studies of suffragettes. Maurice Hewlett's *The Queen's Quair* was published by Macmillan in 1904.

22. The trial papers reveal that attitudes toward lesbianism differed widely. While the *Lancet* for September 1928 claims that "The fallacy of the book lies in the failure to recognize that strong attachments between members of the same sex occur as a phase of normal development," Dr. Norman Haire testified that the invert is "anatomically distinguished from the normal person" and that "homosexuality tends to run in families." An unsigned review in the *New Statesman* (Leonard Woolf published debate on the question for a year in *The Nation*), Aug. 25, 1928, which sounds suspiciously like Rebecca West, reads:

> *The Well of Loneliness* may be a brave book to have written but let us hope it will pave the way for someone to write a better. Homosexuality is, after all, as rich in comedy as in tragedy, and it is time it was emancipated from the aura of distinguished damnation and religious martyrdom . . . Stephen Gordon is a Victorian character, an *âme damnée*; once we are reconciled to her position, we are distressed by her lack of spirit, her failure to revenge herself on her tormentors. Sappho had never heard of the mark of Cain; she was well able to look after herself but never did she possess a disciple so conscious of her inferiority, or so lacking—for 15s!—in the rudiments of charm.

23. Lillian Faderman, *Scotch Verdict* (New York: Quill, 1983), 68.

24. In 1912 Virginia Woolf wrote to Lytton Strachey anticipating the Cambridge performance of Walter Headlam's Greek play "afterwards *in the dusk, in the college garden,* with Jane Harrison to make proclamation, we have the tragedy from start to finish" (*L* 1, 498). Woolf supposedly contributed to Walter Headlam's translation of the *Agamemnon*. It would be interesting to compare her translation (in the Berg Collection, unpublished) with his.

25. The material on Oscar Browning used here is from his *Memories of Sixty Years* (London: John Lane, 1910) and *Oscar Browning* by his nephew, H. E. Wortham (London: Constable, 1927) from which Woolf quotes in *A Room*. For a further study of Browning and an analysis of his misogyny, see my review in *Victorian Studies*, Spring 1985.

26. For more information on Fitzjames Stephen and J. K. Stephen, see "The Niece of a Nun," and "Liberty, Sorority, Misogyny."

27. My thanks to Elizabeth Inglis, librarian, Sussex University Library, for help in locating manuscript draft pages of *A Room of One's Own* and the typescript. Quoted by permission of Quentin Bell.

INDEX

Abel, Elizabeth, 153, 160, 204, 207
abortion, 170
absence, 12, 13, 146, 152, 156, 157, 161, 163–64, 169, 180
Addams, Jane, 56
aesthetics, 54
Annan, Noel, 163, 212
Antaeus, 92–93
anthropology, 37
Antigone, 36, 38, 40, 41, 43–44, 57
Aristophanes, 38, 44
Auerbach, Nina, 154–55
Austen, Jane, 19, 22, 28, 30–31, 33, 34, 35

Bachhofen, 37
Barnes, Djuna, 143–44, 162
Barney, Natalie, 37, 38, 89, 143, 167
Bauman, Richard, 206–207
Bebel, August, 37
Bell, Clive, 18, 23, 54, 73
Bell, Quentin, 55, 89, 185, 198
Bell, Vanessa, 23, 26, 73, 98, 99, 140–45
Benjamin, Walter, 11, 120–21, 133
Benstock, Shari, 211
Bergman, Ingmar, 21–22
Bergsonian durée, 40, 69
Between the Acts, 3, 15, 22, 76–77, 80, 93–95, 121, 129, 167
Bicknell, John, 205, 206
birds, 28, 38, 44, 68, 69, 93, 103, 134
Biron, Sir Chartres, 166, 169
Black, Naomi, xiii, 190
Black, William, 87, 165
blank pages, 6, 8
Bodkin, Archibald, 166
Boose, Lynda, 208
Brecht, Bertolt, 79, 80
Brock, Arthur Clutton, 21
Brittain, Vera, 31, 137, 157–58, 167
Brooks, Peter, 145
Brophy, Brigid, 23, 190
brotherhood, 21
Browning, Oscar, xiv, 137, 164, 172, 177, 181–86
Butler, Samuel, 18, 29, 30, 62
Byron, George Gordon, Lord, 32, 64

Cambridge Apostles, xiii, 20–21, 75, 78–80, 91–92, 137, 177–78
Carpenter, Edward, 178
Case, Janet, 47–48, 57, 71, 73, 85, 104, 112

Cassandra, 27–28
Caudwell, Christopher, 54, 121
Cavell, Nurse, 81
Cave of Harmony, The, 167–69
Celine and Julie Go Boating, 172
charwomen, xv, 7, 10–17, 56, 66–67, 81, 84, 88, 110, 124, 138, 158–59, 174–75, 187
chastity, 67, 75–76, 77, 79, 85, 88, 104, 110–11, 115–35, 138, 156–57, 172
Chicago, Judy, 113
child molestation, 53, 63
chorus, 37, 44, 65
Cixous, Hélène, 13, 170
Clarence, Duke of, 184
Clarissan nuns, 118
class, xv, 11, 13, 38, 41, 45, 49, 54, 56, 58, 75, 78–79, 81, 138–39, 159, 160, 177
cleanliness, 44, 62, 64, 67–68, 156
"collective sublime," xii, 134
Colette, xv, 1, 3, 5–10
colonization, 77, 83–85, 90, 205
color, 58–60
comedy, 22, 64
Comstock, Margaret, 192, 195
conspiracy, 64, 72, 138, 147, 152, 156, 166, 167
Cope, Jackson I., 134
Cornford, Francis, 147
Cowper, William, 99

Dangerfield, George, 54–55
Dante, 38, 49, 57
deformity, 44, 58
Demeter/Persephone myth, 3, 38
De Salvo, Louise, xvii, 52, 84, 87, 97, 179, 198, 200, 201, 203, 207, 208
Dickens, Charles, 81, 93
Dickinson, Goldsworthy Lowes, 19–20, 164
Dickinson, Violet, 98, 104–105, 122
Dickson, Lovat, 163, 209
dictionary, 39, 40
difference, 136–62
Doane, Janice, 211
Don Giovanni, 26, 27, 30, 33
Douglas, Mary, 144
Duckworth, Stella, 97, 98, 99
Du Plessis, Rachel, 14

Eagleton, Terry, 11–12, 189
Echo, 53–54, 163–65
Edwards, Lee, 158
elegy, 9–10, 78, 86, 119, 130

JANE MARCUS is Professor of English at C.U.N.Y. and the City College of New York. She was formerly in the English Department and Director of Women's Studies at the University of Texas, Austin. She is editor of *Virginia Woolf and Bloomsbury: A Centenary Celebration* and author of *Art and Anger: Reading Like a Woman* and numerous other books and articles.